ASCENT
CENTER FOR TECHNICAL KNOWLEDGE

I0036695

Creo Simulate 3.0
Structural and Thermal Analysis

Student Guide
1st Edition

ASCENT - Center for Technical Knowledge®
Creo Simulate 3.0
Structural and Thermal Analysis
1st Edition

Prepared and produced by:

ASCENT Center for Technical Knowledge
630 Peter Jefferson Parkway, Suite 175
Charlottesville, VA 22911

866-527-2368
www.ASCENTed.com

Lead Contributor: Scott Hendren

ASCENT - Center for Technical Knowledge is a division of Rand Worldwide, Inc., providing custom developed knowledge products and services for leading engineering software applications. ASCENT is focused on specializing in the creation of education programs that incorporate the best of classroom learning and technology-based training offerings.

We welcome any comments you may have regarding this training guide, or any of our products. To contact us please email: feedback@ASCENTed.com.

© ASCENT - Center for Technical Knowledge, 2017

All rights reserved. No part of this guide may be reproduced in any form by any photographic, electronic, mechanical or other means or used in any information storage and retrieval system without the written permission of ASCENT, a division of Rand Worldwide, Inc.

Creo Parametric 3.0 is a registered trademark of Parametric Technology Corporation.

All other brand names, product names, or trademarks belong to their respective holders.

General Disclaimer:

Notwithstanding any language to the contrary, nothing contained herein constitutes nor is intended to constitute an offer, inducement, promise, or contract of any kind. The data contained herein is for informational purposes only and is not represented to be error free. ASCENT, its agents and employees, expressly disclaim any liability for any damages, losses or other expenses arising in connection with the use of its materials or in connection with any failure of performance, error, omission even if ASCENT, or its representatives, are advised of the possibility of such damages, losses or other expenses. No consequential damages can be sought against ASCENT or Rand Worldwide, Inc. for the use of these materials by any third parties or for any direct or indirect result of that use.

The information contained herein is intended to be of general interest to you and is provided "as is", and it does not address the circumstances of any particular individual or entity. Nothing herein constitutes professional advice, nor does it constitute a comprehensive or complete statement of the issues discussed thereto. ASCENT does not warrant that the document or information will be error free or will meet any particular criteria of performance or quality. In particular (but without limitation) information may be rendered inaccurate by changes made to the subject of the materials (i.e. applicable software). Rand Worldwide, Inc. specifically disclaims any warranty, either expressed or implied, including the warranty of fitness for a particular purpose.

AS-CRS3-STA1-SG // RS-CRS3-STA1-SG

Contents

© 2017, ASCENT - Center for Technical Knowledge®

© 2017, ASCENT - Center for Technical Knowledge®

© 2017, ASCENT - Center for Technical Knowledge®

Preface

This student guide covers the fundamentals of Creo Simulate: Structural and Thermal Analysis. It provides you with the knowledge to effectively use Creo Simulate for finite element analysis, thereby reducing design time. Many concepts apply to both Structure and Thermal analysis; a portion of this guide is specifically dedicated to Thermal analysis. This is an extensive hands-on training guide, in which you have the opportunity to apply your knowledge through real-world scenarios and examples.

Topics Covered

- FEA Fundamentals: P-elements and analysis convergence methods

- Basic Modeling and Analysis

- Types of Loads and Constraints

- Idealizations: Shells and Beams

- Sensitivity and Optimization Studies

- Assembly Interfaces and Contact Analysis

- Thermal Analysis

- Modal Analysis

- Welds, Springs, and Masses

- Fasteners and Rigid Links

- Buckling Analysis

Note on Software Setup

This student guide assumes a standard installation of the software using the default preferences during installation. Lectures and practices use the standard software templates and default options for the Content Libraries.

© 2017, ASCENT - Center for Technical Knowledge®

In this Guide

The following images highlight some of the features that can be found in this Student Guide.

Practice Files

To download the practice files for this student guide, use the following steps:

1. Type the URL shown below into the address bar of your Internet browser. The URL must be typed **exactly as shown**. If you are using an ASCENT ebook you can click on the link to download the file.

2. Press <Enter> to download the .ZIP file that contains the Practice Files.

3. Once the download is complete, unzip the file to a local folder. The unzipped file contains an .EXE file.

4. Double-click on the .EXE file and follow the instructions to automatically install the Practice Files on the C:\ drive of your computer.

   Do not change the location in which the Practice Files folder is installed. Doing so can cause errors when completing the practices in this student guide.

http://www.ASCENTed.com/getfile?id=xxxxxxxx

Stay Informed!
Interested in receiving information about upcoming promotional offers, educational events, invitations to complimentary webcasts, and discounts? If so, please visit:
www.ASCENTed.com/updates/

Help us improve our product by completing the following survey:
www.ASCENTed.com/feedback
You can also contact us at: feedback@ASCENTed.com

Link for practice files

Practice Files

The Practice Files page tells you how to download and install the practice files that are provided with this student guide.

Chapter 1

Getting Started

In this chapter you learn how to start the AutoCAD® software, become familiar with the basic layout of the AutoCAD screen, how to access commands, use your pointing device, and understand the AutoCAD Cartesian workspace. You also learn how to open an existing drawing, view a drawing by zooming and panning, and save your work in the AutoCAD software.

Learning Objectives in this Chapter

- Launch the AutoCAD software and complete a basic initial setup of the drawing environment.
- Identify the basic layout and features of AutoCAD interface including the Ribbon, Drawing Window, and Application Menu.
- Locate commands and launch them using the Ribbon, shortcut menus, Application Menu, and Quick Access Toolbar.
- Locate points in the AutoCAD Cartesian workspace.
- Open and close existing drawings and navigate to file locations.
- Move around a drawing using the mouse, the **Zoom** and **Pan** commands, and the Navigation Bar.
- Save drawings in various formats and set the automatic save options using the **Save** commands.

Learning Objectives for the chapter

Chapters

Each chapter begins with a brief introduction and a list of the chapter's Learning Objectives.

Side notes

Side notes are hints or additional information for the current topic.

Practice Objectives

Instructional Content

Each chapter is split into a series of sections of instructional content on specific topics. These lectures include the descriptions, step-by-step procedures, figures, hints, and information you need to achieve the chapter's Learning Objectives.

Practices

Practices enable you to use the software to perform a hands-on review of a topic.

Some practices require you to use prepared practice files, which can be downloaded from the link found on the Practice Files page.

© 2017, ASCENT - Center for Technical Knowledge®

Practice Files

To download the practice files for this student guide, use the following steps:

1. Type the URL shown below into the address bar of your Internet browser. The URL must be typed **exactly as shown**. If you are using an ASCENT ebook, you can click on the link to download the file.

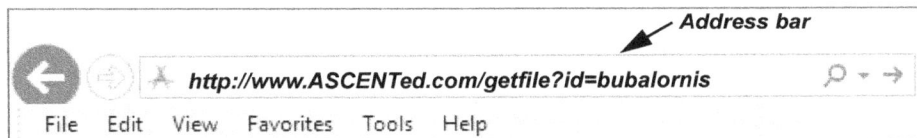

Address bar

http://www.ASCENTed.com/getfile?id=bubalornis

File   Edit   View   Favorites   Tools   Help

2. Press <Enter> to download the .ZIP file that contains the Practice Files.

3. Once the download is complete, unzip the file to a local folder. The unzipped file contains an .EXE file.

4. Double-click on the .EXE file and follow the instructions to automatically install the Practice Files on the C:\ drive of your computer.

   Do not change the location in which the Practice Files folder is installed. Doing so can cause errors when completing the practices in this student guide.

http://www.ASCENTed.com/getfile?id=bubalornis

Stay Informed!

Interested in receiving information about upcoming promotional offers, educational events, invitations to complimentary webcasts, and discounts? If so, please visit:

www.ASCENTed.com/updates/

Help us improve our product by completing the following survey:

www.ASCENTed.com/feedback

You can also contact us at: *feedback@ASCENTed.com*

© 2017, ASCENT - Center for Technical Knowledge®

Introduction to Creo Simulate

Creo Simulate is a powerful software tool that enables you to simulate structural and thermal behavior of your design to understand and improve the design's performance.

Learning Objectives in this Chapter

- Understand the concept of FEA.
- Understand the concepts of H-refinement and P-refinement.
- Understand the advantages of P-elements.
- Understand solution convergence methods in Creo Simulate.
- Understand the analysis abilities of Creo Simulate.
- Understand the steps involved in a Creo Simulate analysis.
- Understand the recommendations for CAD model preparation.
- Understand the Creo Simulate modes of operation.

1.1 Finite Element Analysis (FEA)

Finite Element Analysis is a numerical mathematical method based on the following process:

*Creo Simulate contains the **AutoGEM** tool, which automatically meshes a model.*

- Discretize (i.e., divide) the model into smaller and more simplified volumes (tetrahedra, bricks, wedges, etc.) called *finite elements*. The collection of finite elements approximates the shape of the model, and is called *finite element mesh*, or just *mesh*. An example of a meshed model is shown in Figure 1–1.

In 2D models, finite elements are triangles or quadrilaterals. In 3D models, finite elements are 4-node tetra, 6 node wedge or 8-node bricks.

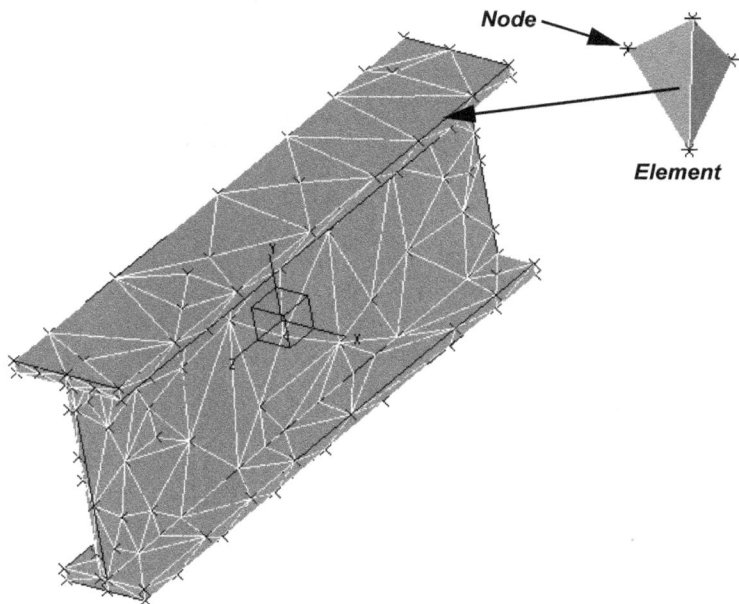

Figure 1–1

- Approximate the variation of the principal quantity of interest (such as displacement, stress, etc.), within each finite element with polynomials. These polynomials are typically called *local approximation functions* or *shape functions*.

- Connect the finite elements across the inter-element boundaries, thus effectively *sewing* elemental polynomials together. The *sewn* local polynomials now approximate a variation of the quantity of interest over the entire model, and therefore comprise the global approximation function in the form of a piece-wise polynomial.

© 2017, ASCENT - Center for Technical Knowledge®

- Solve the governing equations and boundary conditions for the global approximation function, and find the best fitting solution. In structural mechanics, the principle of minimum total potential energy is typically used to find the best fitting solution, which results in solving a large number (sometimes hundreds of thousands), of simultaneous linear equations.

- Present the results for this approximate solution.

Therefore, the key FEA concept is the use of piece-wise polynomials to approximate the sought field quantity in the model, which effectively replaces a continuum problem with an infinite number of degrees of freedom (DOF) by a discrete problem with a finite number of DOF (i.e., *finite elements* and *discretization*).

For example, consider how the FEA method works when applied to calculate deflections in a simple beam as shown in Figure 1–2. The beam is clamped at the left end, has a couple of supports in the middle, and is loaded by a couple of transversal forces and a moment. The bottom graph shown in Figure 1–2 represents the unknown true deflection of the beam, which you are trying to determine using the FEA method.

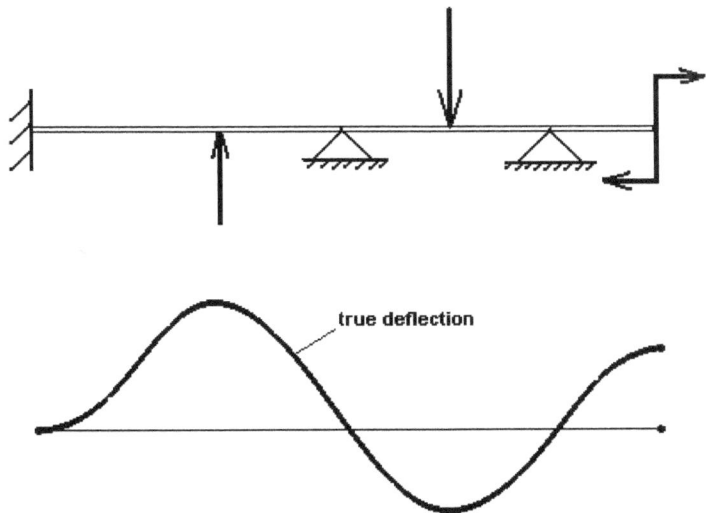

true deflection

Figure 1–2

The first step in the process (shown in the example in Figure 1–3) is to mesh the beam by breaking it into a collection of shorter pieces (i.e., finite elements) connected at their ends (i.e., the nodes).

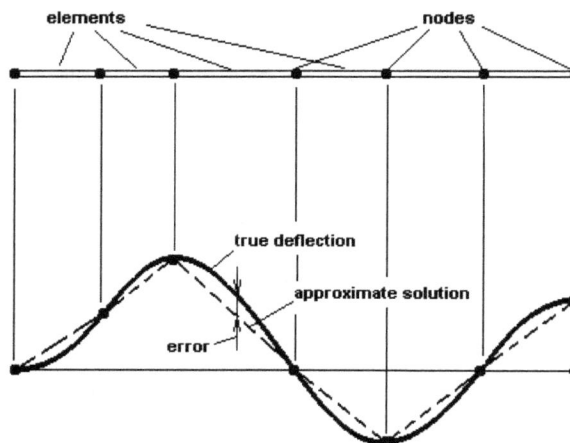

Figure 1–3

Next, the deflection **Y** within each finite element is approximated by a polynomial. In this example, you use linear polynomial **Y = $a_0 + a_1X$**, which means that deflection within each element is approximated by essentially a straight line.

Note that sewing local polynomials at the nodes ensures continuity of the global approximation function, and therefore of the FEA solution for the deflection over the entire beam

Next, the local linear polynomials are sewn together at the nodes, creating a global approximation function in the form of a piece-wise linear polynomial, which is a polyline.

Finally, the global approximation function is best-fit to satisfy both the bending differential equations and beam boundary conditions (loads and constraints). The resulting function (the dashed line shown in Figure 1–3) now represents the FEA solution for the true deflection (the solid line shown in Figure 1–3) in the beam.

It is important to note that your FEA result contains a certain amount of error, which is the deviation between the true deflection (the solid line shown in Figure 1–3) and the FEA solution (the dashed line shown in Figure 1–3), and which is called a *discretization error*.

Any FEA solution is just an approximation, which means it always contains a discretization error. Therefore, in the FEA process, it is critical to know how to estimate, how to control, and how to reduce this unavoidable approximation error to acceptable levels.

© 2017, ASCENT - Center for Technical Knowledge®

1.2 FEA Solution Refinement

The process of bringing the FEA approximation error to acceptable levels is typically called *solution refinement*. There are two alternative ways in which an FEA solution can be refined.

The first option involves making the finite elements in the mesh progressively smaller while maintaining the order of polynomials within each element.

For example, consider the beam shown in Figure 1–3. If you make the finite elements smaller without changing anything else, the approximation error becomes smaller as well, as shown in Figure 1–4.

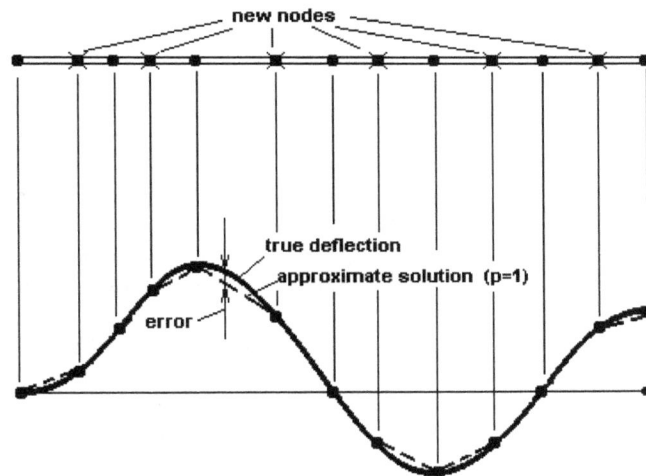

Figure 1–4

This approach is called *h-refinement* because the letter *h* in FEA literature typically refers to the size of the finite elements in the mesh. It is also worth noting that h-refinement requires re-meshing the model every time you need a more accurate solution.

The h-refinement approach is used by most FEA software systems that are commercially available today. However, this is not the only available option.

An alternative strategy involves increasing the order of polynomials within the finite elements, without changing the elements' sizes.

Again, consider the example of the beam shown in Figure 1–3. If you use second-degree polynomials $Y = a_0 + a_1X + a_2X^2$ to approximate the deflection within each element, this results in a more accurate solution, without needing to make the finite elements smaller, as shown in Figure 1–5.

Figure 1–5

This approach is called *p-refinement*, because the letter *p* in FEA literature typically refers to the order of polynomials, and the process of progressively increasing the polynomial order is called *polynomial escalation*.

The p-refinement mathematical apparatus has been historically developed much later than the h-refinement. Today, the p-refinement approach is only used by a few commercial FEA software systems, one of which is Creo Simulate.

© 2017, ASCENT - Center for Technical Knowledge®

1.3 P-Elements

Creo Simulate exclusively uses p-elements and p-refinement technology to ensure the accuracy of the solution. The maximum polynomial order in Creo Simulate can be as high as 9. (The maximum polynomial order in the h-version of FEA is typically 2.)

The advantages of p-technology over h-technology are as follows:

- Solution accuracy can be improved without having to re-mesh the model.

- P-elements use hierarchical polynomials, which permits the use of different polynomial orders in different areas of the model for better efficiency.

- The rate of convergence to the true solution is greater than that of the h-technology.

- High stress gradients, such as in stress concentrators, are simulated extremely well.

- The restrictions on the shape of elements (aspect ratio, skewness, etc.) are less stringent. Therefore a p-mesh always contains fewer elements that an h-mesh.

- P-elements have curvilinear boundaries and tend to approximate CAD geometry very well.

The rate of convergence refers to how quickly the refinement process converges to the true solution.

1.4 Convergence Methods

Convergence in FEA (also called *adaptivity*) is a process of automatic solution refinement to achieve the required accuracy. In other words, the FEA software automatically *adapts* the solution parameters to better fit the true solution.

One of the key advantages of p-refinement over h-refinement is that p-elements permit an adaptive solution improvement without re-meshing the model. Instead, the maximum orders of polynomials used to approximate the solution are increased as needed. The solution process can then be repeated on the same mesh, with the new increased polynomial orders. Such an adaptive step (called *pass* in Creo Simulate) can be repeated until the required accuracy is achieved.

In p-elements, the polynomial orders (called *P-levels* in Creo Simulate) can be assigned independently to each edge, face, or solid in the mesh. Using the convergence algorithm, Creo Simulate can pick P-levels independently for each mesh edge in the model, the goal being to select just the correct P-levels to achieve the required solution accuracy at minimum computational expense.

Multi-Pass Adaptivity (MPA) is the most commonly used convergence method in Creo Simulate. To identify the edges that warrant a P-level increase, the MPA algorithm compares displacements and element strain energies on the current solution pass with the corresponding values on the previous pass. Where the difference is larger than the user-specified percentage (i.e., convergence percentage), the P-level is increased and otherwise left unchanged. This process is repeated until the user-specified convergence percentage for the solution is met. The convergence criteria might include percentages on the default local and global quantities, such as displacement, strain energy, and RMS stress, but could also involve user-defined solution parameters.

The MPA convergence graphs can be visualized once the analysis has finished, as shown in Figure 1–6.

© 2017, ASCENT - Center for Technical Knowledge®

strain energy
convergence graph

max stress
convergence graph

Figure 1–6

Since convergence percentage(s) are selected by the user, the MPA algorithm provides the user with maximum control, and is best used if the accuracy of the solution is critical.

The second convergence algorithm in Creo Simulate, called *Single-Pass Adaptivity* (SPA), uses a different theoretical foundation to reach an accurate solution.

The SPA algorithm is based on the fact that, although displacements in an FEA solution are continuous between elements, stresses are not, and the magnitude of stress jump at the discontinuity is a good indicator of the solution accuracy (i.e., the greater the stress jump, the less accurate the solution).

In the SPA algorithm, Creo Simulate first calculates the solution for P-level 3, assigned uniformly to all edges, and average stress discontinuities around each element (i.e. element error indicators) are computed. The P-levels of edges belonging to elements with large stress jumps are increased. Edges of elements with larger errors receive a higher P-level increase than edges of elements with lower errors. The solution is then repeated, and the result obtained at this point is taken as the final answer. The element error indicators are recomputed to indicate the overall stress accuracy.

Since only two convergence passes are performed in SPA, the computation time is typically much shorter than in MPA.

No convergence graphs are available in the SPA algorithm. Instead, the RMS stress error estimate is printed out to the Creo Simulate report file, as shown in Figure 1–7.

```
RMS Stress Error Estimates:

Load Set          Stress Error   % of Max Prin Str
----------------  ------------   -----------------
LoadSet1          1.26e+01        10.3% of  1.22e+02
```

Figure 1–7

The SPA algorithm has been optimized by PTC with the goal of obtaining as good or better result as using the MPA convergence with the default (10%) convergence percentage.

The SPA convergence method provides limited control over the accuracy of the solution. Therefore, it should be reserved for quick design-analysis iterations when solution accuracy is not critical.

The third convergence method in Creo Simulate is called *Quick Check*, and does not perform a convergence process. The model is only run once, with all of the P-levels fixed at 3. The results of a Quick Check should not be trusted. The intention of a Quick Check analysis is to quickly run the model through the solver to detect any potential modeling errors (such as in constraints), before committing to a more lengthy analysis run (such as when using MPA).

© 2017, ASCENT - Center for Technical Knowledge®

1.5 Types of Analysis in Creo Simulate

Creo Simulate analysis capabilities straddle two physics domains:

- **Structural:** Determines deformations, stresses, and strains in solid bodies caused by external forces, moments, and other types of loading.

- **Thermal:** Determines temperatures and heat fluxes in solid bodies due to heat sources and/or sinks.

The Structural part of Creo Simulate can perform the following types of analysis:

- Static (including nonlinear material models, large displacements, and contact)

- Pre-stress Static

- Buckling

- Fatigue

- Modal (Natural Vibrations)

- Pre-stress Modal

- Dynamic Time Response

- Dynamic Frequency Response

- Dynamic Random Response

- Dynamic Shock Response

The two options for the Thermal analysis are as follows:

- Steady State Thermal analysis

- Transient Thermal analysis

The models in Creo Simulate can be analyzed in 3D formulations (purely solids, or combinations of solids, shells, and beams) or 2D formulations (plane stress, plane strain, or axisymmetric).

1.6 FEA Process

A typical FEA analysis process in Creo Simulate consists of three principle steps, as shown in Figure 1–8:

*   **Pre-processing:** All input data for the analysis is prepared, such as material properties, loads, and constraints.

*   **Solution:** The convergence type and criteria are specified and the analysis computation is performed.

*   **Post-processing:** The analysis results are reviewed and verified. A report is prepared.

Figure 1–8

The CAD model simplification step is optional. It might not be needed, depending on the complexity of the model.

© 2017, ASCENT - Center for Technical Knowledge®

1.7 CAD Model Preparation

A CAD model is developed to provide detailed information for manufacturing. All of the required information related to fillets, rounds, holes, and threads must be included. Processing steps and surface finishes are indicated and dimensions are fully specified.

An FEA model is developed to determine model behavior under a specific set of loading and boundary conditions. To analyze a model effectively, an FEA model is often different from a model developed for manufacturing. The symmetry of a model can often be used. Minor features, such as rounds, fillets, chamfers, and holes, can often be ignored unless they have a large effect on the result. Therefore, the general recommendation is to use the simplest model possible that is going to yield reliable results at the lowest computational time and cost.

In the example shown in Figure 1–9, the area of interest is the stress in the weld between two pipes due to high pressure. The FEA model within the component is shown on the right. In this case, the symmetry of the component (1/2 of the component) is used for the FEA model. The minor rounds, fillets, chamfers, and holes are ignored. The CAD model prepared for FEA would be different if the area of interest was the stress at the intersection of lips and pipes.

Lips

Area of interest (blend)

Figure 1–9

1.8 Creo Simulate Modes of Operation

Creo Simulate can operate in the following modes:

- **Integrated:** The simulation is fully integrated within the Creo Parametric design process (i.e., the models can be analyzed without ever leaving the Creo Parametric user interface). This is the most common way to use Creo Simulate.

- **Standalone:** Enables the loading of CAD models directly into Creo Simulate, without first loading Creo Parametric. This is useful if models originating from different software than Creo Parametric need to be analyzed.

- **FEM:** Provides pre- and post-processing capabilities only. The model has to be exported to a neutral file format and then solved by a 3rd party FEA solver (ANSYS, NASTRAN, etc.). H-elements meshing is used.

- **Simulate Lite:** Limited model size of up to 200 surfaces and also has a limited user interface. Does not require a Simulate license.

This training guide focuses on the Integrated mode, which provides the most streamlined approach to part or assembly simulation and optimization within the Creo environment.

© 2017, ASCENT - Center for Technical Knowledge®

Basic Creo Simulate Modeling

Learning Objectives in this Chapter

- Understand the Creo Simulate analysis steps and options.
- Launch Creo Simulate from Creo Parametric.
- Use the Creo Simulate user interface.
- Define the model type.
- Create idealizations.
- Apply material.
- Apply constraints.
- Apply loads.
- Mesh the model.
- Create a design study.
- Create a structural analysis.
- Select a convergence method.
- Understand the files and directories created by Creo Simulate.
- Understand the concepts of result verification.
- Visualize analysis results.

2.1 Launching Creo Simulate

The Finite element analysis process contains three different components: pre-processing, analysis, and post-processing. Each component contains a number of steps, as shown in Figure 2–1.

Figure 2–1

Each step in the structural analysis process requires a selection of the following options.

Model Analysis Steps	Creo Simulate Structure Options	
Model Type	3D Plane Stress Axisymmetric	Plane Strain 2D
Element Type	Shell Beams Solid	Springs Mass
Analysis Methods	Static Modal Buckling Prestress modal Prestress static	Dynamic Time Dynamic Frequency Dynamic Random Dynamic Shock Fatigue
Convergence Methods	Multi-Pass Adaptive Single-Pass Adaptive	Quick Check

© 2017, ASCENT - Center for Technical Knowledge®

Design Studies	Standard Optimization	Sensitivity

To launch Creo Simulate in Integrated mode, open the model in Creo Parametric, select the *Applications* tab, and click

 (Simulate). The Creo Simulate environment opens, the Ribbon appearance changes as shown in Figure 2–2, and a coordinate system labeled **WCS** is automatically added to the model.

Figure 2–2

By default, Creo Simulate opens in Structure mode. To switch to Thermal mode if needed, click (Thermal Mode).

Structure Ribbon

The Structure mode ribbon contains five tabs: *Home*, *Refine Model*, *Inspect*, *Tools*, and *View*.

The *Home* tab (shown in Figure 2–2) contains all of the most frequently used analysis tools, such as model setup, loads, constraints, analysis setup, and access to the analysis results.

The *Refine Model* tab contains tools, such as idealizations, connections, regions, and meshing as shown in Figure 2–3.

Figure 2–3

The *Inspect*, *Tools*, and *View* tabs contain common Creo tools, such as measurements, layers, views, appearances, etc.

2.2 Modeling Steps

Defining Model Type

By default, Creo Simulate assumes that the model you want to analyze is 3D. To change the analysis model type to 2D, click

📄 (Model Setup) and click **Advanced** to open the Model Setup dialog box as shown in Figure 2–4.

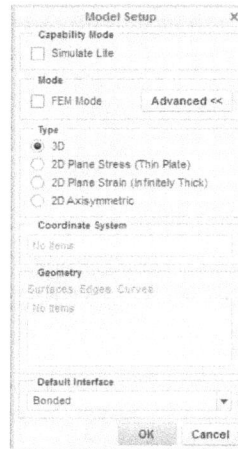

Figure 2–4

Creating Idealizations

Idealizations are tools that simplify your FEA model, resulting in a faster analysis. Idealizations are optional. If your model is not overly complex and solves in a reasonable time, Idealizations might not be needed.

The following types of Idealizations are available in Creo Simulate, as shown in Figure 2–5:

- Beams

- Springs

- Masses

- Shells

Figure 2–5

© 2017, ASCENT - Center for Technical Knowledge®

Applying Material

In Creo Simulate, applying a material to your analysis model must be done in two steps:

- Import material definition into the model.

- Assign the imported material to your part.

If a material has already been applied to your part in Creo Parametric, it is automatically imported into the Creo Simulate model as well, but not assigned.

*The **Material Orientation** option only applies to non-isotropic materials, such as laminates, etc.*

To assign the imported material, click ⬚ (Material Assignment) to open the Material Assignment dialog box as shown in Figure 2–6. Select **References**, select a material, and click **OK** to close the dialog box.

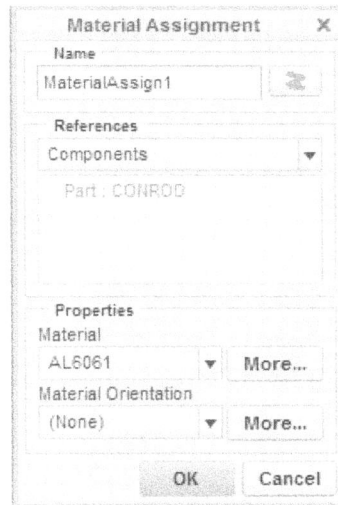

Figure 2–6

If a material has not been applied in the Creo Parametric environment, you must import a material definition into your model from within the Creo Simulate environment.

To import a material definition, click ⌐ (Materials) to open the Materials dialog box as shown in Figure 2–7. Select a material in the library (on the left in the dialog box) and click ▶▶▶ (Add Material) to import it into the model. If needed, the material properties can be viewed and/or edited in the Materials dialog box.

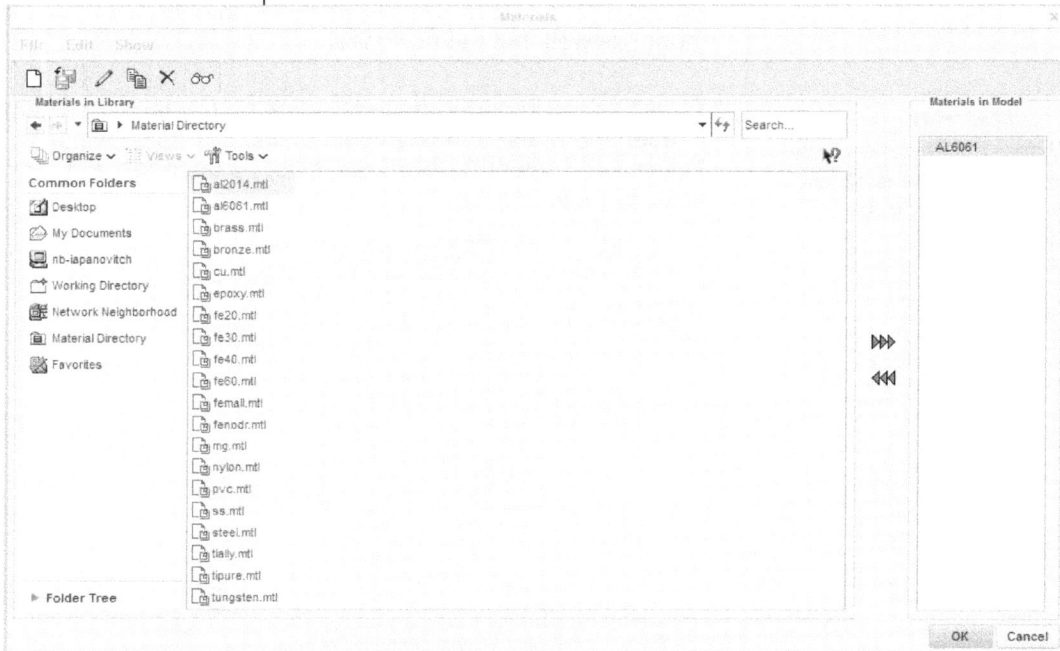

Figure 2–7

Applying Constraints

Constraints simulate supports and other boundary conditions in your model. Constraints can be applied to the part's surfaces, edges/curves, or points.

The following types of Constraints are available in Creo Simulate, as shown in Figure 2–8:

- Displacement

- Planar

- Pin

- Ball

- Symmetry

© 2017, ASCENT - Center for Technical Knowledge®

Figure 2–8

Applying Loads

Loads in your analysis are intended to simulate the actual loading conditions in your model.

The following types of Loads are available in Creo Simulate, as shown in Figure 2–9:

- Force/Moment

- Pressure

- Bearing

- Temperature

- Gravity

- Centrifugal

- Preload

Figure 2–9

The type of geometry you can apply a Load to depends on the type of load selected. For example, Force/Moment loads can be applied to surfaces, edges/curves, or points, while Pressure or Bearing loads can only be applied to surfaces.

Meshing the Model

Meshing the model before running the analysis is optional in Creo Simulate. If not pre-meshed, the model is automatically meshed during the analysis computation.

However, pre-meshing the model helps to indicate whether Creo Simulate can mesh your model successfully, and to roughly estimate the analysis runtime based on the number of elements in the mesh.

To mesh the model before the analysis, click ▦ (AutoGEM) in the *Refine Model* tab to open the AutoGEM dialog box, as shown in Figure 2–10.

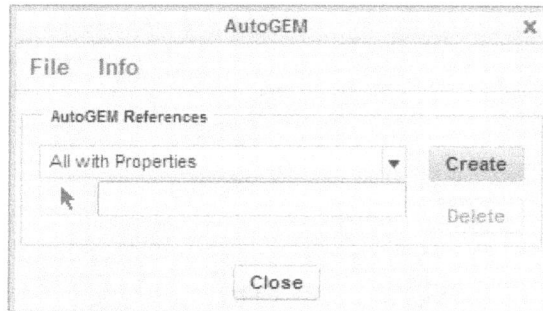

Figure 2–10

The options in the References drop-down list are as follows:

*   **Volume:** Creates Solid mesh for selected volumes.

*   **Surface:** Creates Shell mesh for selected surfaces.

*   **Curves:** Creates Beam mesh for selected curves.

*   **All with Properties:** An all-in-one option, which automatically meshes all volumes with materials assigned, all surfaces with shell properties assigned, and all curves with beam properties assigned. This option is used if mesh is created during the analysis run.

In the AutoGEM dialog box, you can review, save, and highlight areas in which the mesh fails.

© 2017, ASCENT - Center for Technical Knowledge®

2.3 Analysis

Analysis Types

Creo Simulate can perform several types of structural analysis on a model. You select an analysis type based on the type of simulation that you want to perform. Click ⛉ (Analyses and Studies) and select the appropriate option in the **File** menu, as shown in Figure 2–11.

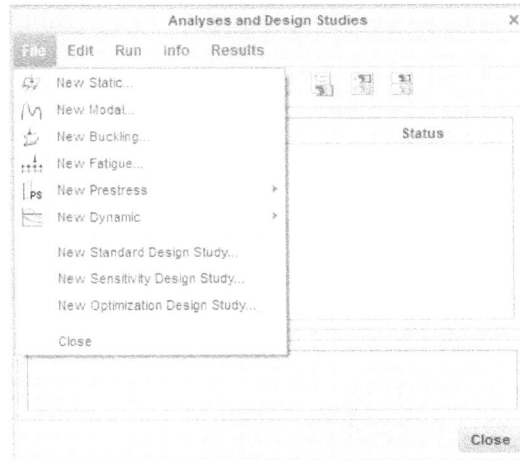

Figure 2–11

The types of structural analysis available in the Analyses and Design Studies dialog box are as follows:

Analysis Type	Description
New Static	Static analyses calculate the stresses and deformations in the model, that are caused by static loads.
New Modal	Modal analyses calculate the mode shapes (i.e., characteristic deformed shapes of natural frequencies) and natural frequencies of a model.
New Buckling	Buckling analyses calculate the Buckling Load Factor (BLF), a magnification factor of the applied load that causes buckling to occur. When applying a load of 1 unit to the model, the BLF equals the critical buckling load.
New Fatigue	Fatigue analyses calculate the effect of repeating or varying loads on a model.

New Prestress	• **Static:** Prestress Static analyses calculate the effect of a prestressed structure on a model's stresses, strains, and deformations. • **Modal:** Prestress Modal analyses calculate the effect of static loads on natural frequencies and modes.
New Dynamic	• **Time:** Dynamic Time analyses calculate displacements, velocities, accelerations, and stresses in response to a load that varies with time. • **Frequency:** Dynamic Frequency analyses determine the response of a system that is subjected to cyclical excitation (a frequency-dependent input). • **Random:** Dynamic Random analyses calculate the power spectral density (PSD) and the root mean square (RMS) values of displacements, velocities, accelerations, and stresses in a model subjected to a random loading. • **Shock:** Dynamic Shock analyses calculate the peak values of displacement and stresses in a model in response to a base excitation defined by a response spectrum curve. This type of analysis subjects a model to an earthquake-like motion.

Convergence Methods

The three analysis convergence options in Creo Simulate are as follows:

Option	Description	Uses
Quick Check	Runs a model through the solver to detect errors (e.g., in the constraints). The model is only run once for a single fixed low polynomial order. If an error occurs, Creo Simulate displays an error message prompting you with: *Run completed with a fatal error.*	• Use to determine whether an analysis has been set up correctly. • Use to generate proper elements. • Use to check problem areas in the model.
Single Pass Adaptive	Runs a model through the solver at a low polynomial order (default 3), evaluates the accuracy of the solution, and modifies the p-element values accordingly. The model is run through the solver a second time with the new p-element values. This provides reasonable results in a short computation time.	• Use for preliminary calculations. • Use when system resources are low.

© 2017, ASCENT - Center for Technical Knowledge®

Multi-Pass Adaptive	Runs a model through the solver in iterations (or *passes*), with the polynomial order of unconverged elements being increased with each pass. The passes continue until either the solution converges or the maximum order is reached (default 6 and maximum 9). Base your final decisions on the results obtained using this method.	• Use for accurate analysis. • Use when you have enough time and system resources.

Design Studies

Design studies enable you to find better design alternatives using simulation and analysis tools. Creo Simulate can run the following three types of design studies.

Study	Description
Standard	This study calculates the results for a standard analysis (e.g., Static analysis) for an alternative set of dimensions. Analogous to running a single *what if* scenario.
Sensitivity	This study calculates the results for several alternative sets of dimensions within a user-specified range. Analogous to running multiple *what if* scenarios.
Optimization	This study adjusts a model's parameters to meet a specified goal or to test the feasibility of a design. For this study, you assign a goal (e.g., minimum mass of the model) and one or more Creo Parametric dimensions (design variables), which can vary over assigned ranges.

2.4 Results

Files and Directories

Creo Simulate generates many output files that are written to an automatically created directory. The name of the result directory is the same as that of the analysis study. By default, the result directory is placed in the Creo working directory, which can be changed when you set up an analysis.

Create Simulate solver also creates many temporary files, which are only needed when the solver is running, and which are automatically deleted on completion of the analysis run. The default location for the temporary files is in the Creo working directory, which can also be changed when you set up an analysis.

The typical files created by Creo Simulate in the result directory are as follows. The names *model*, *study*, and *filename* represent your specified names.

File Type	File/Directory Name	Description
Model Files	*model.mdb*	The .MDB file contains the last-saved model database.
Solver File	*/study/study.mdb*	The engine file contains the entire model database from the time a design study is started.
Solver Output Files	*/study/study.cnv* */study/study.hst* */study/study.res* */study/study.rpt* */study/study.ro1*	The .CNV file contains convergence information. The .HST file is a backup file that updates the model during optimization. The .RES file is a measure at each pass. The .RPT file is an output report that contains information about a run including measure values and warning messages. The .RO1 file contains information about the resultant reaction of loads applied to the model.
Exchange Files	*filename.dxf* *filename.igs*	The exchange files are in formats that are used for the import or export of geometry information.
Temporary Files	*/study.tmp/*.tmp* */study.tmp/*.bas*	Temporary files contain the data that is needed to solve analyses. They are deleted automatically on completion of the design.
Results Files	*filename.rwd*	The .RWD files store your Result Window plot window for later use.

© 2017, ASCENT - Center for Technical Knowledge®

AutoGEM Files	*model.agm*	The .AGM files store information about the most recent AutoGEM operation.
AutoMesh Files	*modelname.mmp* *modelname.mma*	This file stores a mesh database. The system allocates an .MMP extension to a part model mesh file and an .MMA extension to an assembly model.

Result Verification

Creo Simulate can produce several types of results to help determine the validity and soundness of your model. Take the following considerations into account when interpreting your results.

Result	Description
Reaction Verification	The resultant reaction of loads applied to the model is automatically generated in the .RO1 file. To satisfy the equilibrium criteria, the resultant reaction must equal the resultant loads applied to the model.
Model Integrity	Model integrity determines the integrity of your model by checking the model entities (i.e., material properties, constraints, loads, and unit systems), geometry, and part accuracy before starting the run. You can also use the **Check Model** option to check for errors in the model. If the model fails the check, the model entities were probably incorrectly defined.
Displacement Animation	Displacement animation verifies whether your model is deflecting correctly and that your constraints are correct. The animation simulates the effect of real-world conditions on the model and enables you to compare them to the applied boundary conditions.
Shape Animation	Shape animation (performed after a sensitivity or optimization study) takes the geometry through the entire range of relevant parameters. This ensures that no unexpected regeneration failures occur and that the design intent is sound.
Computational Solution Quality	Computational solution quality is the percentage of error that the system calculates on the maximum principle stress. A low percentage indicates that the model is sound. This error estimate can be found in the .RPT file in the analysis directory.
Convergence Criteria	Provides an idea of the accuracy of your results. Convergence results with specific limits set by the user can be found in the .RPT file. You can create graphs based on predefined measures for strain energy and displacement.

Result Visualization

Creo Simulate enables you to visualize many different types of results:

- Displacements
- Stresses
- Strains

- Reactions
- Strain Energy
- P-Levels

The results can be displayed as a fringe plot or as a graph along an edge or curve. Fringe plots can be animated for better understanding of the model deformation.

The results are visualized and manipulated in the Creo Simulate Results environment. An overview of the icons and options available in the Creo Simulate Environment is shown in Figure 2–12.

Click to exit the Results environment

Click to create a new result window

Click to edit a specific result window

Click to delete a result window

Click to copy a result window

Figure 2–12

You can enter the Creo Simulate Results environment using one of the following options:

- Click (Review Results) in the Analyses and Design Studies dialog box.

- Click (Results) in the Creo Simulate interface, in the Home tab.

- Click (Simulate Results) in the Creo Parametric interface, in the *Applications* tab. This options enables you to open the Creo Simulate results without having to open a corresponding Creo Simulate model first.

© 2017, ASCENT - Center for Technical Knowledge®

Practice 2a

Static Stress Analysis of a Bracket

Practice Objectives

- Specify a 3D model type.
- Mesh the model.
- Set the loads, constraints, and material properties.
- Check the validity of the model.
- Set up and run a Quick Check analysis.
- Set up and run a Multi-Pass Adaptive analysis.
- Display the results.
- Animate and create sections through the part.

In this practice, you will mesh, set up, and run a static stress analysis on a simple solid bracket model. The model is shown in Figure 2–13.

Figure 2–13

Modeling Tasks

In the following tasks, you will create the simulation entities needed to analyze your model.

Task 1 - Open the solid_bracket_1 part in Creo Parametric.

1. Open **solid_bracket_1.prt**. The part displays as shown in Figure 2–14.

The model has been defeatured. The rounds on the middle hole and bolt holes have been removed.

Figure 2–14

2. Select **File>Prepare>Model Properties** to check your unit system. The unit system for this practice is **mmNs**.

Task 2 - Launch Creo Simulate.

1. Select **Applications>Simulate** to launch the Creo Simulate environment.

WCS represents the World Cartesian System (the origin is at 0,0,0).

2. Verify that ▦ (Structure Mode) is active. The model displays as shown in Figure 2–15. Verify that the datum coordinate system visibility is toggled on. Note that the WCS coordinate system displays in the model window.

Figure 2–15

Task 3 - Define the model type.

1. In the *Home* tab, select ▤ (Model Setup) and click **Advanced** to expand the Model Setup dialog box.

2. In the Model Setup dialog box, verify that the **3D** option is selected and click **OK**.

Task 4 - Mesh the bracket part.

In this task, you will mesh the bracket, which enables you to check whether Creo Simulate can mesh your model before analysis. Using this option before applying simulation entities (e.g., loads or constraints) highlights the areas (geometry) where the mesh has failed in your model. This option speeds up the analysis run time.

© 2017, ASCENT - Center for Technical Knowledge®

1. Select the *Refine Model* tab and expand the (AutoGEM) flyout and select **Settings**, as shown in Figure 2–16.

Figure 2–16

2. The AutoGEM Settings dialog box opens as shown in Figure 2–17.

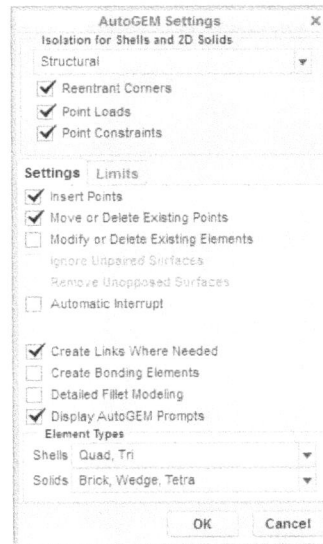

Figure 2–17

3. Expand the Solids drop-down list and verify that **Brick, Wedge, Tetra** is selected.

4. Select the *Limits* tab, as shown in Figure 2–18.

AutoGEM Settings dialog box:

Isolation for Shells and 2D Solids
Structural

- ✔ Reentrant Corners
- ✔ Point Loads
- ✔ Point Constraints

Settings | **Limits**

Limits for Creating

Allowable Angles (Degrees)

Edge Max 175.00   Edge Min 5.00

Face Max 175.00   Face Min 5.00

Max Aspect Ratio   30.00

Max Edge Turn (Degrees)   95.00

Default

OK   Cancel

Figure 2–18

5. In the AutoGEM Settings dialog box, four types of settings display in *Limits* tab: **Edge Angles**, **Face Angles**, **Edge Turn**, and **Aspect Ratio**.

    •   The allowable edge angles (**Edge Max** and **Edge Min**) between the edges of an element are shown in Figure 2–19.

Edge Angles
Default: minimum 5°
maximum 175°

Figure 2–19

© 2017, ASCENT - Center for Technical Knowledge®

- The allowable face angles (**Face Max** and **Face Min**) between the faces of an element are shown in Figure 2–20.

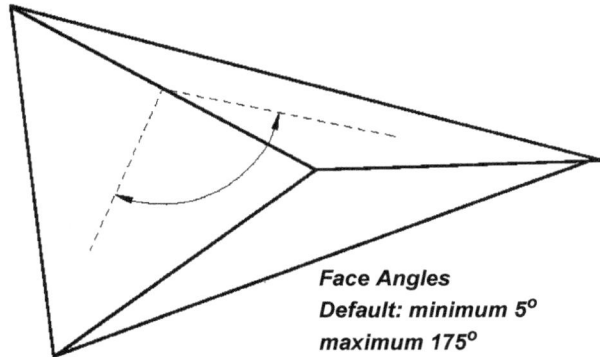

Face Angles
Default: minimum 5°
maximum 175°

Figure 2–20

The maximum allowable Edge Turn enables you to create elements that better conform to the shape of the geometry on circles and cylinders.

- The maximum allowable edge turns (**Max Edge Turn**) between 45° and 95° are shown in Figure 2–21. This limit has a valid range from 1° to 100°.

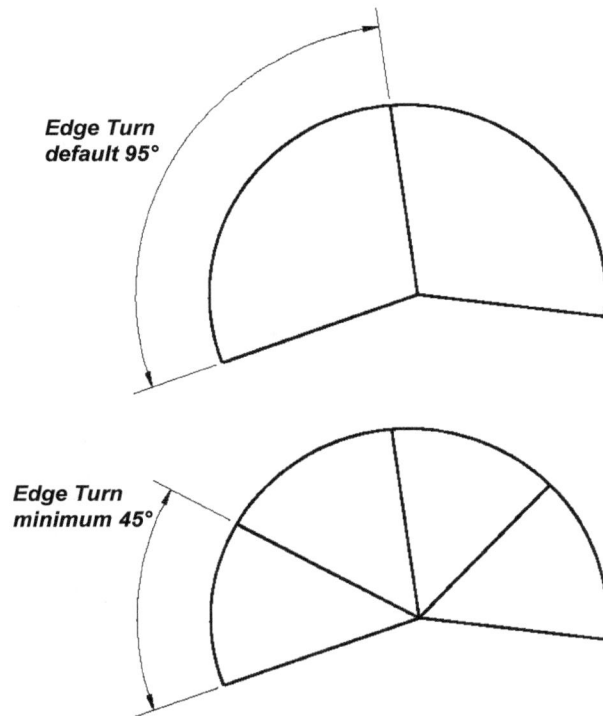

Edge Turn default 95°

Edge Turn minimum 45°

Figure 2–21

- The maximum allowable aspect ratio (**Max Aspect Ratio**), which is the ratio of length to width of an element, is shown in Figure 2–22.

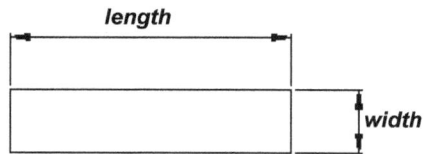

Figure 2–22

6. Click **OK** to close the AutoGEM Settings dialog box.

7. Click ▦ (AutoGEM). The AutoGEM dialog box opens as shown in Figure 2–23.

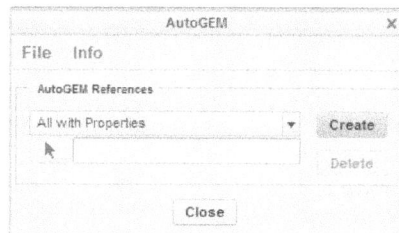

Figure 2–23

8. Expand the AutoGEM References drop-down list and select **Volume**.

9. Click ▸ and select any surface on the model.

10. In the Surface Selection box, click **OK** or click the middle mouse button.

11. Click **Create**.

AutoGEM starts to pre-process the model and display these functions in the Creo message window. When initial processing is finished, AutoGEM creates and optimizes elements. The AutoGEM optimization process reduces the number of elements by 50% on average. If any of these functions (e.g., pre-processing or creating elements) takes more than 30 seconds, the system displays a message indicating their progress. The message window for **solid_bracket_1** is shown in Figure 2–24.

© 2017, ASCENT - Center for Technical Knowledge®

- Working on 1 volume(s) ...
- Pre-processing features for surface 1 of 28 ...
- Pre-processing boundary features ...
- Optimizing boundary point locations ...
- Detecting thin features on the volume ...
- Pre-processing volume features ...
- Searching for existing solid elements inside the volume ...
- Found 0 existing solid element(s) inside the volume.
- Creating solid elements ...
- Optimizing elements ...
- Adding 96 solid elements to model ...
- Displaying Elements ...
- A total of 96 elements and 63 nodes were created.

Figure 2–24

After a short time, the AutoGEM Summary and the Diagnostics dialog boxes open as shown in Figure 2–25.

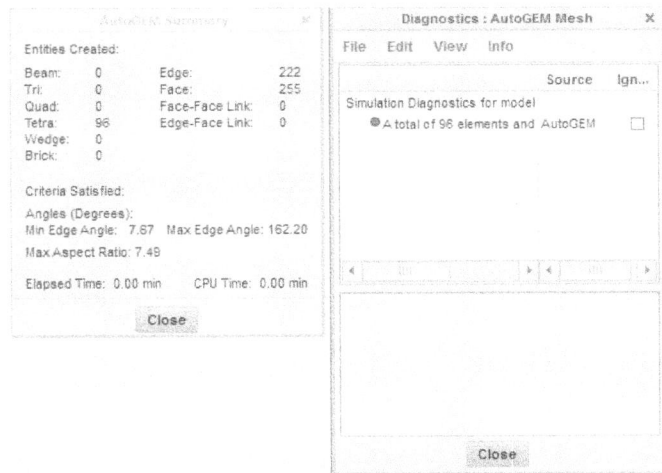

Figure 2–25

Examine the information in the boxes. For example, note that the system has discretized the volume into approximately 96 tetrahedron solid elements.

12. Close both the AutoGEM Summary and Diagnostics boxes, but do not close the AutoGEM dialog box yet. The model displays as shown in Figure 2–26.

Figure 2–26

13. Click ⚄ (Simulation Display) in the floating toolbar. The Simulation Display dialog box opens.

*The **Shrink Elements** option does not affect the analysis. It is a visualization tool that helps you display the mesh clearly.*

14. Select the *Mesh* tab. In the *Mesh Display* area, select the **Shrink Elements** option and increase the shrinkage value to 20% as shown in Figure 2–27.

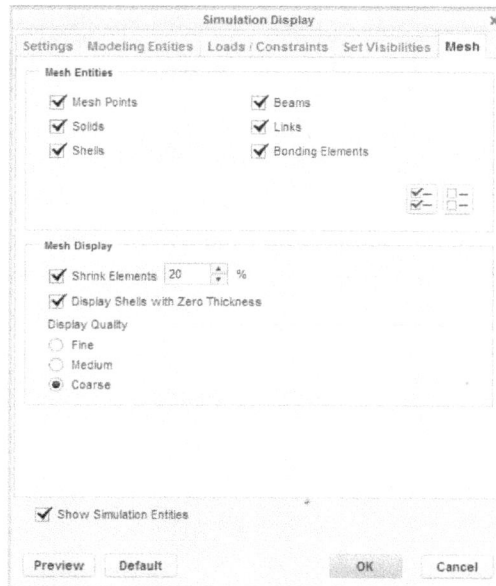

Figure 2–27

© 2017, ASCENT - Center for Technical Knowledge®

15. Click **OK** to close the Simulation Display dialog box. The model displays as shown in Figure 2–28. Spin the model and review the elements in various areas of the model.

Figure 2–28

16. Click **Close** to close the AutoGEM dialog box and the warning shown in Figure 2–29 will display.

Figure 2–29

17. Click **Yes** to save the mesh.

The following three types of solid elements are commonly used:

Element	Description	Example
Hexahedron (brick)	Brick has 12 edges, 8 nodes, and 6 quad faces.	

Pentahedron (wedge)	Wedge has 9 edges, 6 nodes, 2 triangular faces, and 3 quad faces.	
Tetrahedron (Tetra)	Tetra has 6 edges, 4 nodes, and 4 triangular faces.	

Task 5 - Apply loads to the surface of the model.

In this task, you will apply loads to the surface of the model shown in Figure 2–30 to simulate the bracket loading. This task assumes that the bracket carries a load of 140kg (approx.) at 45° to vertical.

Figure 2–30

1. In the Home tab, click ⊢ (Force/Moment). The Force/Moment Load dialog box opens as shown in Figure 2–31.

© 2017, ASCENT - Center for Technical Knowledge®

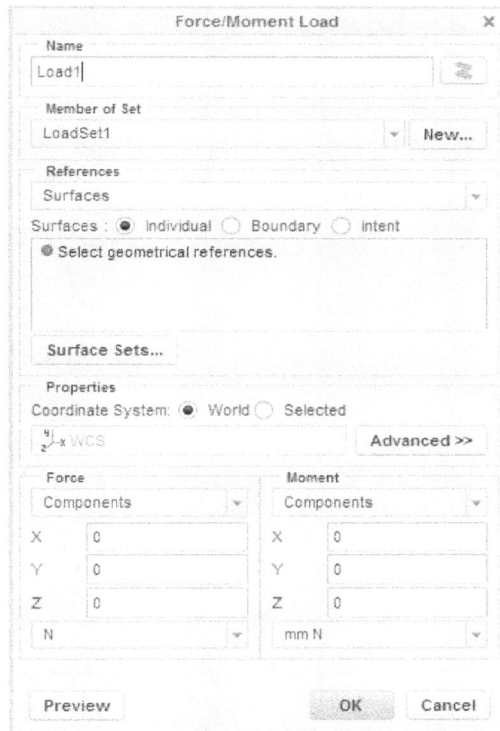

Figure 2–31

2. In the *Name* field, enter **surf_load**. For *Member of Set* accept the default **LoadSet1** option.

3. Select the region of the surface between the two lines, as shown in Figure 2–32 .

4. In the Force/Moment Load dialog box, note that the loads are defined relative to the WCS coordinate system, as indicated in the *Properties* area.

5. Click **Advanced** to display the distribution and spatial variation options. Expand and examine the drop-down lists and accept the default options.

6. Expand the Force drop-down list and accept the default **Components** option.

7. In the *Force* area, in the *Y* field, enter **1000**.

8. In the *Force* area, in the *Z* field, enter **1000**.

9. Click **Preview** to display the applied load in the model.

10. Click **OK** to finish applying the load to the solid model. The load displays as shown in Figure 2–32.

Figure 2–32

Explore the different options in the Simulation Display dialog box.

11. Click ⬚ (Simulation Display) to open the Simulation Display dialog box.

12. In the *Settings* tab, in the Load and Constraint Display area, select the **Values** option.

13. Click **OK** to close the Simulation Display dialog box. The model displays as shown in Figure 2–33.

Figure 2–33

© 2017, ASCENT - Center for Technical Knowledge®

Task 6 - Apply constraints to the surfaces of the model.

In this task, you will apply constraints to the entire end surfaces of the solid model, as shown in Figure 2–34, assuming that the load on the bracket is supported at the bracket flanges.

Constrain these surfaces

Figure 2–34

1. In the *Home* tab, click 🖎 (Displacement). The Constraint dialog box opens as shown in Figure 2–35.

Figure 2–35

Solid element nodes only have three translational degrees of freedom. The rotation of a node cannot be specified or calculated.

Depending on the orientation of your model, the load vectors might vary.

2. In the *Name* field, enter **fixed_faces**. For *Member of Set*, select the **ConstraintSet1** option.

3. Select the surfaces shown in Figure 2–34 (hold down <Ctrl> to select both surfaces).

4. The default coordinate system is WCS, as indicated in the *Coordinate System* area in the Constraint dialog box. Keep WCS as the coordinate system to be used.

5. Six possible constraints are available at the bottom of the Constraint dialog box: three translations and three rotations. The icons for these constraints are as follows. Accept the default options for all of the translation and rotation directions.

Translation Icons	Rotation Icons	Description
		Enables the constrained feature to move or rotate freely in the related direction.
		Fixes the constrained feature so that it cannot move or rotate in the related direction.
		Forces the constrained feature to move or rotate in the related direction by a specified amount.

6. Click **OK** to finish applying the constraints. The model displays as shown in Figure 2–36.

Figure 2–36

© 2017, ASCENT - Center for Technical Knowledge®

Task 7 - Apply the material.

In this task, you will select the material for the solid bracket.

1. In the *Home* tab, click ⌐ (Materials). The Materials dialog box opens as shown in Figure 2–37.

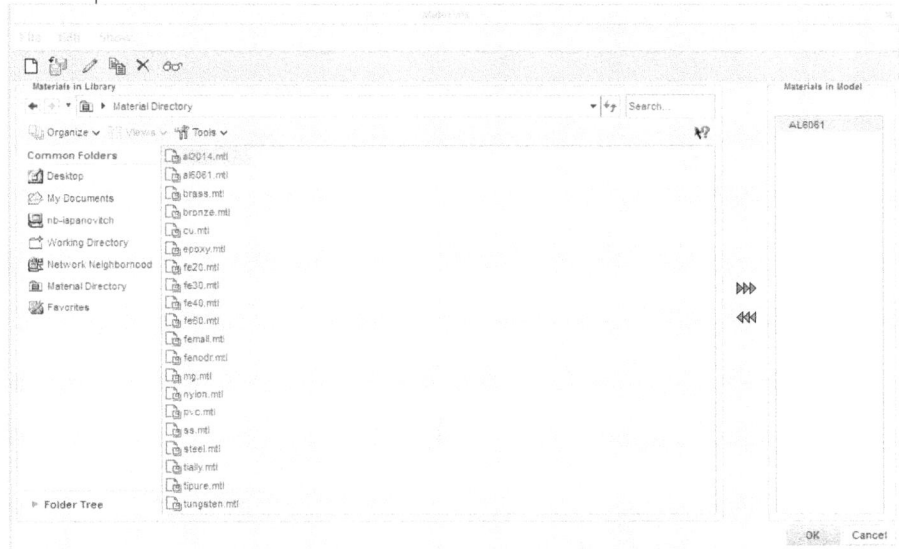

Figure 2–37

2. In the *Materials in Library* area, select **STEEL**.

The model's material should be as stated.

3. Click ▶▶▶ (Add Material) to transfer **STEEL** to the *Materials in Model* area.

4. Select ✎ (Edit) to check the material properties. The HS-low-alloy steel (STEEL) has the following default material properties:

   - Poisson's ratio = 0.27
   - Young's modulus = 199948 MPa
   - Coefficient of thermal expansion = 1.17e-5 /C
   - Density = 7.82708e-9 tonne/mm^3

5. Click **OK** to close the Materials dialog box.

6. In the *Home* tab, click 🖑 (Material Assignment). The Material Assignment dialog box opens as shown in Figure 2–38.

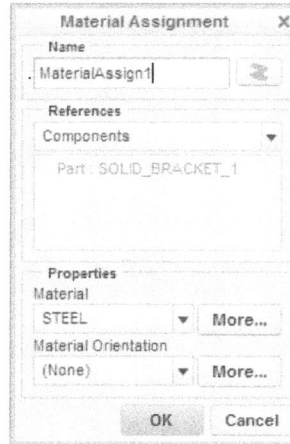

Figure 2–38

7. Note that the material **STEEL** has been automatically selected for the part.

8. Click **OK** to confirm the material assignment and to close the Material Assignment dialog box.

Analysis Tasks

In the following tasks, you will set the analysis type and convergence method, and then run the analysis.

Task 8 - Set up and run the analysis.

In this task, you will specify the analysis type. First, the solid bracket is analyzed using the **Quick Check** convergence option to check for errors. The option gives you a general feel for the results and it indicates whether the model will behave as intended with the applied boundary conditions. The importance of this option increases with the size of your model.

1. In the *Home* tab, click 🖎 (Analyses and Studies). The Analyses and Design Studies dialog box opens as shown in Figure 2–39.

© 2017, ASCENT - Center for Technical Knowledge®

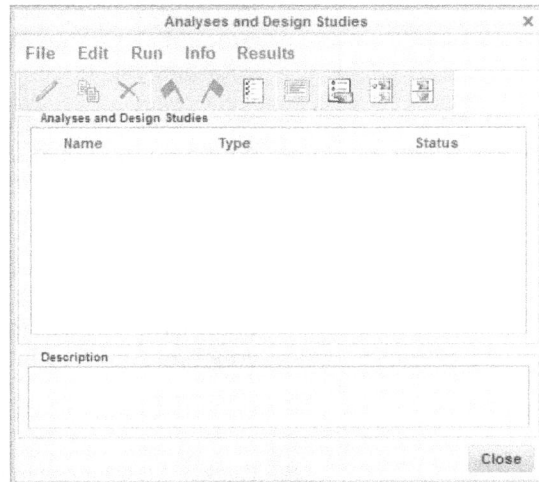

Figure 2–39

2. Select **File>New Static**. The Static Analysis Definition dialog box opens as shown in Figure 2–40.

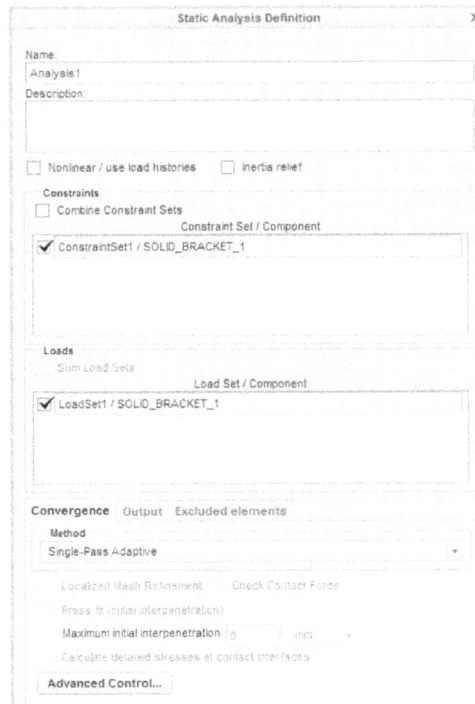

Figure 2–40

3. In the *Name* field, enter **solid_bracket** (this will be the name of a subdirectory containing all of your results files).

Each study can be set up with one constraint set and a single or multiple load sets.

By default, Creo Simulate files and directories are created in the Creo working directory. The recommended setting for the memory allocation is half the RAM in your computer.

4. In the *Description* field, enter **Static analysis of a solid bracket**. This step is optional, but is helpful for identifying your analysis later.

5. For a static stress analysis, you need to specify or select the constraint and load sets. These are the ones you created in the previous steps. In this case, they are **ConstraintSet1** and **LoadSet1**. Ensure that they are highlighted.

6. For the type of convergence, expand the Method drop-down list and select **Quick Check**. This option enables you to determine whether the analysis has been set up correctly in your first run.

7. Click **OK** in the Static Analysis Definition dialog box.

8. Click ⬚ (Settings) in the Analyses and Design Studies box to set the locations for the temporary and output files, output files format, and RAM allocation. The Run Settings dialog box opens as shown in Figure 2–41.

Figure 2–41

© 2017, ASCENT - Center for Technical Knowledge®

Note the format for the output files in the *Output File Format* area. The **ASCII** option needs a much larger disk space. The advantage of ASCII output files is that they are portable between Unix and Windows operating systems.

9. Accept the remaining default values, including the **Use Element from Existing Mesh File** option.

10. Click **OK** to close the Run Settings dialog box.

*The **Check Model** option highlights any modeling errors (e.g., load-constraint conflicts or unassigned material properties) and errors from modeling edits.*

11. Expand the **Info** menu and select **Check Model**. This command checks the validity of the simulation model. The Information dialog box opens (as shown in Figure 2–42), indicating that there are no errors.

Figure 2–42

12. Click **OK** to confirm.

13. Click ◣ (Start) in the Analyses and Design Studies dialog box to start your analysis. The Question dialog box opens as shown in Figure 2–43.

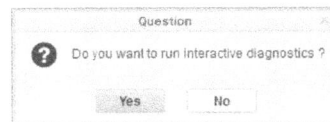

Figure 2–43

14. Click **Yes** in the Question dialog box. Creo Simulate solves the analysis. The Diagnostics dialog box opens as shown in Figure 2–44, stating that the analysis run has been completed.

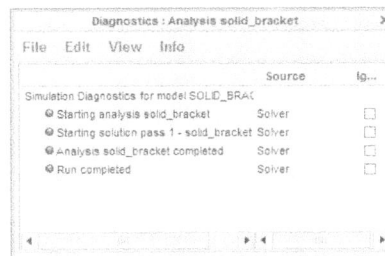

Figure 2–44

15. Click **Close** to close the Diagnostics dialog box.

16. Click 🖩 (Status) in the Analyses and Design Studies dialog box. The Run Status dialog box opens, displaying information regarding the analysis, such as the error estimates, mass moments of inertia, resultant loads, and so on, as shown in Figure 2–45. The very bottom of the window should indicate that the run has completed.

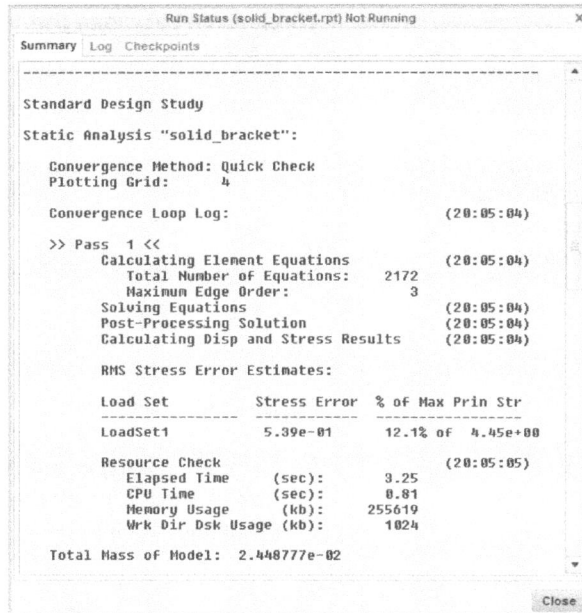

```
                    Run Status (solid_bracket.rpt) Not Running                      ×

 Summary  Log  Checkpoints

 ----------------------------------------------------------------

 Standard Design Study

 Static Analysis "solid_bracket":

      Convergence Method: Quick Check
      Plotting Grid:      4

      Convergence Loop Log:                          (20:05:04)

      >> Pass  1 <<
           Calculating Element Equations             (20:05:04)
             Total Number of Equations:    2172
             Maximum Edge Order:              3
           Solving Equations                         (20:05:04)
           Post-Processing Solution                  (20:05:04)
           Calculating Disp and Stress Results       (20:05:04)

      RMS Stress Error Estimates:

      Load Set              Stress Error  % of Max Prin Str
      ----------            ------------  -----------------
      LoadSet1              5.39e-01      12.1% of  4.45e+00

      Resource Check                                 (20:05:05)
           Elapsed Time   (sec):       3.25
           CPU Time       (sec):       0.81
           Memory Usage    (kb):     255619
           Wrk Dir Dsk Usage (kb):     1024

 Total Mass of Model:  2.448777e-02

                                                         Close
```

Figure 2–45

17. Click **Close** to close the Run Status dialog box.

18. Click **Close** in the Analyses and Design Studies dialog box. The **Quick Check** analysis is complete.

Task 9 - Solve the solid bracket using the Multi-Pass Adaptive convergence option.

In this task, the model is run through the solver in multiple passes, with the element P-levels being increased with each pass. The passes continue until either the solution converges or the maximum polynomial order (default 6, maximum 9) is reached.

1. In the *Home* tab, click 🏛 (Analyses and Studies). The Analyses and Design Studies dialog box opens as shown in Figure 2–46.

© 2017, ASCENT - Center for Technical Knowledge®

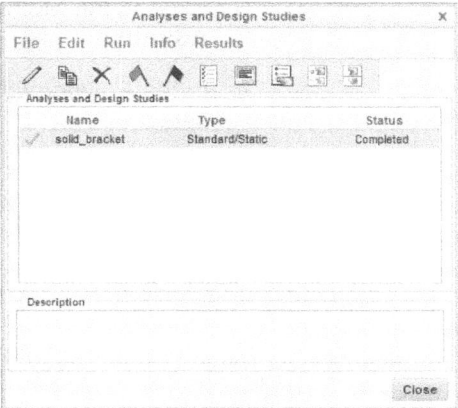

Figure 2–46

2. Highlight the **solid_bracket** analysis and click ✎ (Edit). The Static Analysis Definition dialog box opens as shown in Figure 2–47.

Figure 2–47

3. Expand the Method drop-down list and select **Multi-Pass Adaptive**.

4. In the *Polynomial Order* area, for the *Maximum value*, select **9**.

5. In the *Limits* area, in the *Percent Convergence* field, enter **5**. The Static Analysis Definition dialog box opens as shown in Figure 2–48.

Figure 2–48

6. Click **OK** in the Static Analysis Definition dialog box.

© 2017, ASCENT - Center for Technical Knowledge®

7. Click ✎ (Start) in the Analyses and Design Studies dialog box to start the analysis. The Question dialog box opens as shown in Figure 2–49.

Figure 2–49

8. Click **Yes** in the Question dialog box.

9. Another Question dialog box opens as shown in Figure 2–50.

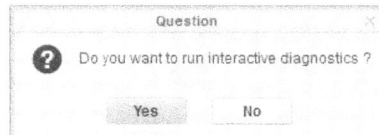

Figure 2–50

10. Click **Yes** in the Question dialog box. The message *The design study has started* displays in the Creo message window. Creo Simulate solves the problem. The Diagnostics dialog box opens as shown in Figure 2–51, stating that the analysis run has been completed.

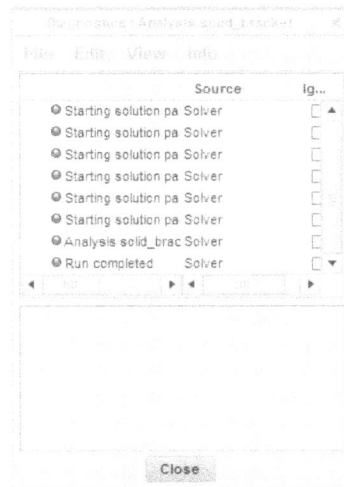

Figure 2–51

11. Click **Close** to close the Diagnostics dialog box.

12. Click ▤ (Status) in the Analyses and Design Studies dialog box. The Run Status window displays, displaying information regarding the analysis convergence. Examine the information in the window. Note that the analysis took six solution passes, up to the maximum edge order 6, to converge within the requested 5%.

13. Click **Close** to close the Run Status dialog box.

14. Do not close the Analyses and Design Studies dialog box.

Results Tasks

In the following tasks, you will display and interpret the results of this analysis.

Task 10 - Display the results.

In this task, you will create and show a Von Mises stress plot.

If Von Mises stress exceeds the yield strength, the material in that area is predicted to yield.

1. Click ▤ (Review Results) in the Analyses and Design Studies dialog box. The Result Window Definition dialog box opens as shown in Figure 2–52.

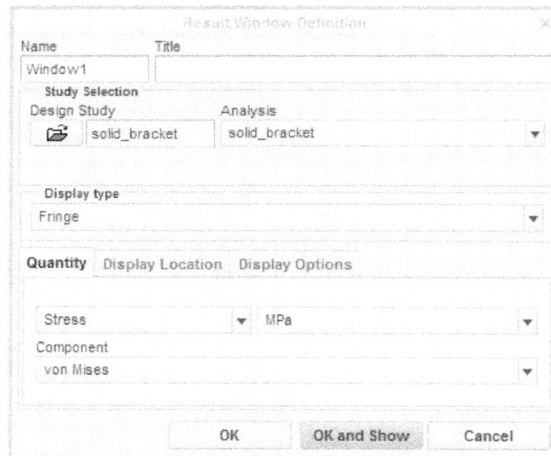

Figure 2–52

2. In the *Name* field, accept the default **Window1** option.

3. In the *Title* field, enter **VM_Plot**.

4. Select the *Display Options* tab and select **Show Element Edges**.

5. Click **OK and Show**. The Creo Simulate Results environment opens, with the Von Mises Stress fringe plot displayed.

© 2017, ASCENT - Center for Technical Knowledge®

6. In the **View** tab, expand the Appearance drop-down list and select **Visibilities**. The Visibilities window displays, as shown in Figure 2–53.

Figure 2–53

7. Select the **Loads** and **Constraints options and click Close**.

8. The results window displays as shown in Figure 2–54.

Figure 2–54

The stress values that you obtain when you run the analysis might be slightly different than those shown in Figure 2–54. This is because each new build of Creo Simulate produces slight variations in the creation of the mesh.

9. In the *Home* tab, click ✏ (Edit). The Result Window Definition dialog box opens. The *Display Options* tab is active, as shown in Figure 2–55.

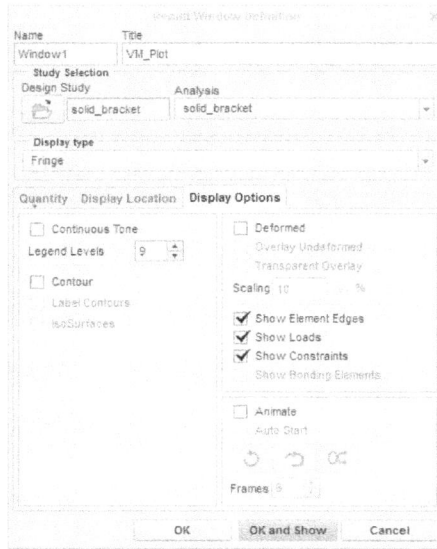

Figure 2–55

10. Select the **Continuous Tone** option and click **OK and Show**. Window1 displays as shown in Figure 2–56.

Figure 2–56

© 2017, ASCENT - Center for Technical Knowledge®

Task 11 - Use predefined measures to study the convergence.

1. Click 📇 (New) in the *Home* tab to create a new results window. The Design Study for Result Window Definition dialog box opens.

2. Select the **solid_bracket** study and click **Open**. The Result Window Definition dialog box opens.

3. In the *Name* field, enter **Convm**, and in the *Title* field, enter **Convm**.

4. Expand the Display Type drop-down list and select **Graph**.

5. Expand the first Graph Ordinate (Vertical) Axis drop-down list and select **Measure**.

6. Click 📏 (Measure). The Measures dialog box opens as shown in Figure 2–57.

A measure is a "virtual gauge" attached to your model. For example, you can set a measure to obtain the stress at a specific point on a model.

Figure 2–57

7. In the list of predefined measures, highlight **max_stress_vm** and click **OK**.

8. Click **OK** in the Result Window Definition box to confirm the creation of the graph without actually displaying it.

9. Repeat the previous eight steps to create graph measures for **max_disp_mag** and **strain_energy**. Enter **max_disp_mag** and **strain_energy**, respectively, for the names of the result window definitions.

10. In the *View* tab, click 🔲 (Show). The Display Result Window dialog box opens as shown in Figure 2–58.

Figure 2–58

11. In the Display Result Window dialog box, highlight **Convm** only (disable any highlighting on others if necessary) and click **OK** to display **max_stress_vm**. The convergence plot displays as shown in Figure 2–59.

Figure 2–59

12. In the *Format* tab, select 🔲 (Edit). The Graph Window Options dialog box opens as shown in Figure 2–60.

© 2017, ASCENT - Center for Technical Knowledge®

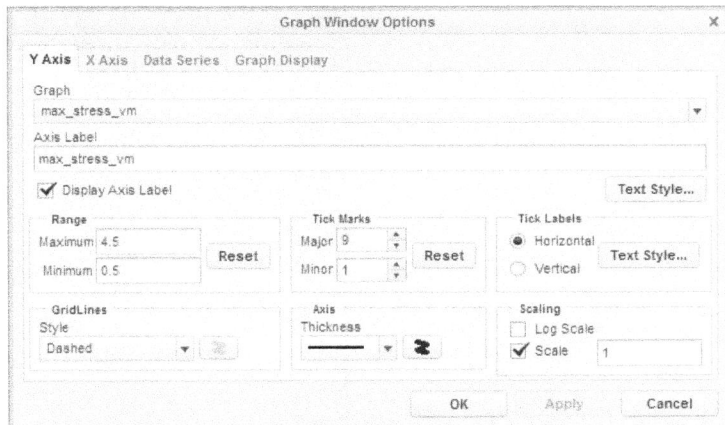

Figure 2–60

13. Explore the options in the Graph Window Options dialog box by making changes to the graph shown in Figure 2–59. Click **OK** when finished.

14. In the *View* tab, click (Show). The Display Result Window dialog box opens.

15. Highlight only **max_disp_mag** in the dialog box and click **OK** to display the next graph. The convergence plot displays as shown in Figure 2–61.

Figure 2–61

16. Repeat the previous two steps to display the **strain_energy** convergence plot, as shown in Figure 2–62.

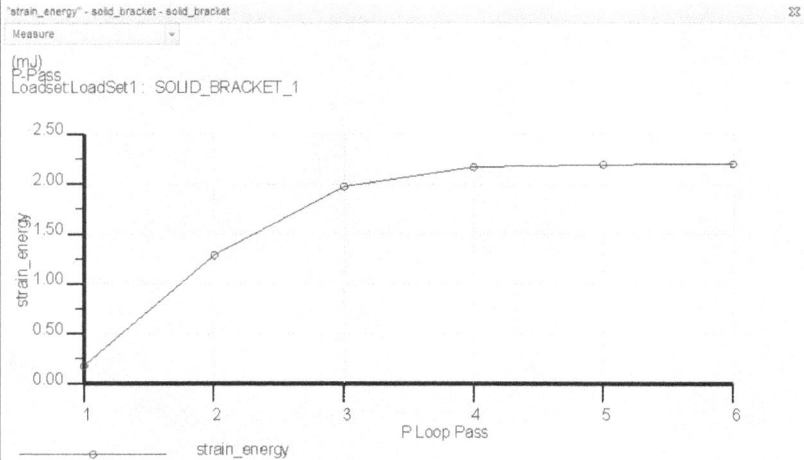

"strain_energy" - solid_bracket - solid_bracket

Measure

(mJ)
P-Pass
Loadset:LoadSet1 : SOLID_BRACKET_1

strain_energy

P Loop Pass

strain_energy

Figure 2–62

These plots indicate that the solution converges after six passes. The solution is practically unchanged after four passes.

Task 12 - Study the P-Level plot.

1. In the *Home* tab, click (New) to create a new results window. The Design Study for Result Window Definition dialog box opens.

2. Select the **solid_bracket** study and click **Open**. The Result Window Definition dialog box opens.

3. In the *Name* field, type **PLevel**.

4. Expand the Quantity drop-down list and select **P-Level**.

5. Click **OK and Show**. Both strain energy convergence and P-Level plots are displayed as shown in Figure 2–63.

© 2017, ASCENT - Center for Technical Knowledge®

Figure 2–63

6. Examine the P-Level plot. Note that the maximum P-Level needed to achieve convergence is **6**.

Task 13 - Animate the Von Mises stress plot.

*Ensure that only **Window1** is selected in the Display Result Window dialog box.*

1. In the *View* tab, click 🔲 (Show), highlight only **Window1** in the Display Result Window dialog box, and click **OK**. The Von Mises Stress fringe plot displays.

2. In the *Home* tab, click ✏ (Edit). The Result Window Definition dialog box opens.

3. Select the *Display Options* tab and clear the **Continuous Tone** option. Select the **Deformed** option and accept the default Scaling value (10%).

4. Select the **Animate** option. Clear the **Auto Start** option and accept the default Frames value (8).

5. Click **OK and Show**.

6. Click ▶ in the *View* tab to start the animation. Click ▶| or |◀ to step through the animation frames. Click ■ to stop the animation.

Task 14 - Determine the location of maximum stress

In this task, you will locate the location and value of the maximum stress.

1. In the *Home* tab, click ✏ (Edit). The Result Window Definition dialog box opens. Clear the **Deformed** and **Animate** options. Click **OK and Show**. The Von Mises stress plot displays.

2. In the *Home* tab, select ⬚ (Model Max) . The location and value of maximum Von Mises stress displays, as shown in Figure 2–64. You can spin the model to display the location of the maximum Von Mises stress.

Location of Maximum Stress

Figure 2–64

3. Investigate the other options in the **Query** group of the *Home* tab. For example, the **Dynamic Query** option displays the stress values at the cursor location. Mark a specific location with its stress level by selecting the location while the Dynamic Query is running. Select **Clear All Tags** when you are finished.

© 2017, ASCENT - Center for Technical Knowledge®

Task 15 - Create sections through the solid bracket.

1. Select the *View* tab.

*Select **View>Shaded** to remove any shading on the model.*

2. In the In-graphics toolbar, expand ⬚ (Saved Orientations) and select FRONT.

3. Select ⬚ (Shaded) to add or remove the shade. The model displays as shown in Figure 2–65.

VM_Plot

Stress   von Mises   (WCS)

(MPa)
Loadset:LoadSet1 : SOLID_BRACKET_1

4.11644
3.70502
3.29359
2.88217
2.47074
2.05932
1.64789
1.23647
0.82504
0.41362
0.00219

Figure 2–65

4. Select ⬚ (New) in the **Capping & Cutting Surfs** section of the *View* tab. The Results Surface Definition dialog box opens, as shown in Figure 2–66.

Results Surface Definition   X

Type
Cutting Surface

Define by
WCS

Plane
◯ XY   ◯ XZ   ⦿ YZ

Depth
50   ✔ %
Dynamic

OK   Apply   Cancel

Figure 2–66

5. Select the options in the Results Surface Definition dialog box as shown in Figure 2–66. Click **Apply** and reorient the model to display the section shown in Figure 2–67.

Figure 2–67

6. In the *Depth* field, enter **60** and click **Apply**. Note that the section moves along the part.

7. Click **Dynamic** . By holding the left mouse button and dragging the mouse up and down, you can move the section up and down in the model.

8. Click the middle mouse button to cancel the dynamic query.

9. Expand the Type drop-down list and select the **Capping Surface**.

10. Select the **Below** option.

11. In the *Depth* field, enter **50** and click **Apply**. The capped section displays as shown in Figure 2–68.

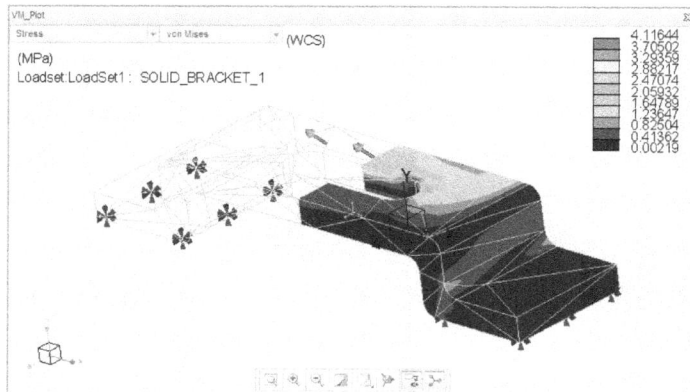

Figure 2–68

© 2017, ASCENT - Center for Technical Knowledge®

12. Click **OK** to close the Results Surface Definition dialog box.

13. . In the *View* tab, click ✕ (Delete) to delete the capping surface.

14. Select **File>Close** or click ⌛ (Close) to exit the Creo Simulate results environment. Click **Don't Save** in the Confirm Exit window.

15. Close the Analyses and Design Studies dialog box.

16. Save the model and close the window.

Practice 2b

Static Stress Analysis of a Bike Crank

Practice Objectives

- Apply loads, constraints, and material properties.
- Mesh the model.
- Check the validity of the model.
- Set up and run a Single-Pass Adaptive analysis.
- Display the results.
- Prepare the report.

In this practice, you will set up and run a static stress analysis on a bicycle crank assembly. The model is shown in Figure 2–69.

Figure 2–69

Modeling Tasks

In the following tasks, you will create the simulation entities needed to analyze your model.

Task 1 - Open the bike_crank assembly in Creo Parametric.

1. Open **bike_crank.asm**. The model displays as shown in Figure 2–70.

Figure 2–70

© 2017, ASCENT - Center for Technical Knowledge®

Task 2 - Launch Creo Simulate.

1. Select **Applications>Simulate** to launch the Creo Simulate environment. Ensure that ⊞ (Structure Mode) is active.

Task 3 - Apply materials.

In this task, you will select materials for the parts in the assembly.

1. In the *Home* tab, click 👆 (Materials). The Materials dialog box opens as shown in Figure 2–71.

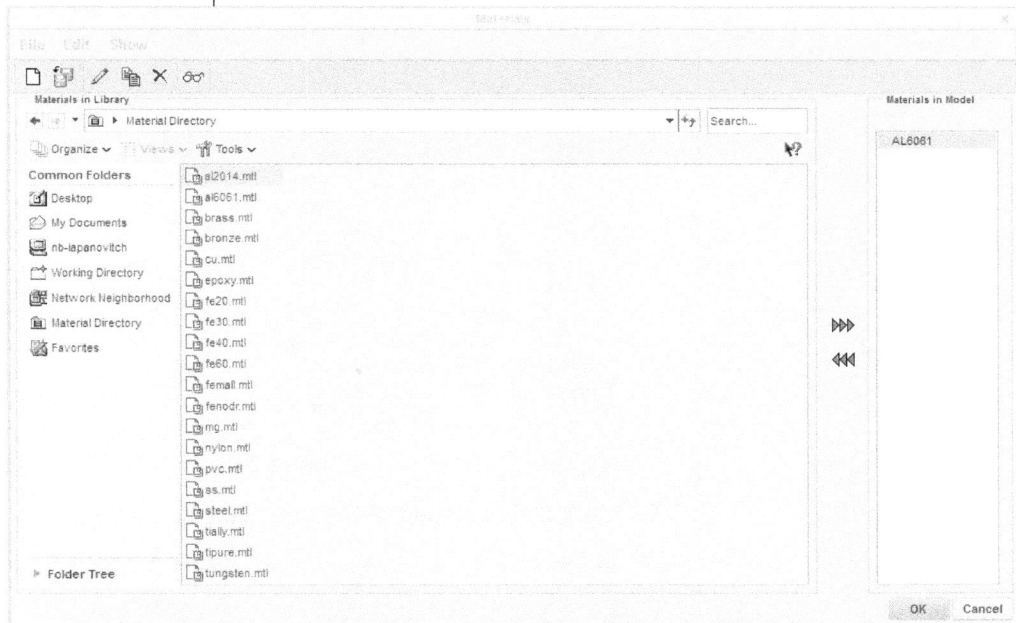

Figure 2–71

2. In the *Materials in Library* area, select **STEEL**.

3. Click ▶▶▶ (Add Material) to transfer **STEEL** to the *Materials in Model* area.

4. In the *Materials in Model* area, highlight **STEEL** and click 🖉 (Edit) to edit the material.

5. In the Material Definition dialog box, make the changes shown in Figure 2–72:
   - **Name:** STEEL AISI 304
   - **Tensile Yield Stress:** 215 MPa
   - **Failure Criterion:** Distortion Energy (von Mises)

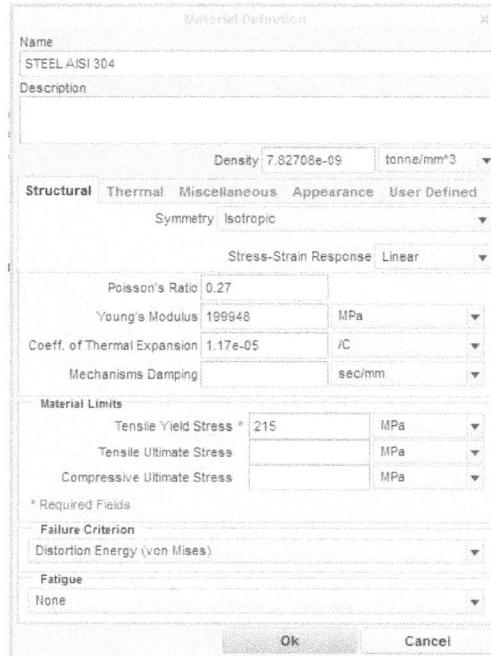

Figure 2–72

6. Click **OK** to close the Material Definition box.

7. In the *Materials in Library* area, select **AL6061**.

8. Click ▶▶▶ (Add Material) to transfer **AL6061** to the *Materials in Model* area.

9. In the *Materials in Model* area, highlight **AL6061** and click ✎ (Edit) to edit the material.

10. In the Material Definition dialog box, make the changes shown in Figure 2–73:
    - **Name:** AL6061 T4
    - **Tensile Yield Stress:** 145 MPa
    - **Failure Criterion:** Distortion Energy (von Mises)

© 2017, ASCENT - Center for Technical Knowledge®

Figure 2–73

11. Click **OK** to close the Material Definition box.

12. Click **OK** to close the Materials dialog box.

13. In the *Home* tab, click (Material Assignment). The Material Assignment dialog box opens as shown in Figure 2–74.

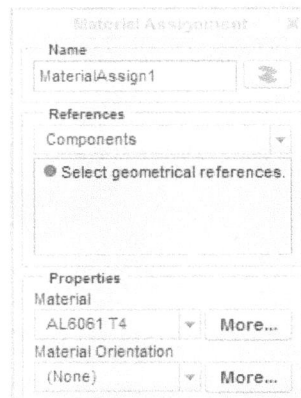

Figure 2–74

14. Select both **PEDAL** and **LHS CRANK** parts in the model (hold <Ctrl> for multiple selection) and click **OK** to assign **AL6061 T4** to both parts and close the Material Assignment dialog box.

15. In the *Home* tab, click 🖐 (Material Assignment) again. In the model, select the **BOTTOM_BRACKET** part and in the *Properties* area, select **STEEL AISI 304**, as shown in Figure 2–75.

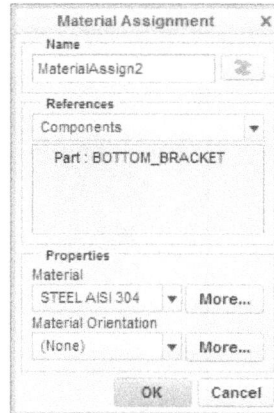

Figure 2–75

16. Click **OK** to close the Material Assignment dialog box.

Task 4 - Apply constraints.

In this task, you will constrain the entire cylindrical surface of the **BOTTOM_BRACKET** part shown in Figure 2–76.

Figure 2–76

1. In the *Home* tab, click 🖊 (Displacement).

2. In the Constraint dialog box, rename the constraint as **fixed**, select the surface shown in Figure 2–76, and accept the defaults for all of the other values. The dialog box should display as shown in Figure 2–77.

© 2017, ASCENT - Center for Technical Knowledge®

Figure 2–77

3. Click **OK** to close the Constraint dialog box. The model displays as shown in Figure 2–78.

Figure 2–78

Task 5 - Apply loads.

In this task, you will apply a 200N downward force to the top surface of the **PEDAL** part shown in Figure 2–79. The force simulates the average force a recreational bike rider applies to one pedal.

Load this surface

Figure 2–79

1. In the *Home* tab, click ⊢ (Force/Moment).

2. In the Force/Moment dialog box, enter the following values (as shown in Figure 2–80):

    *   **Name:** downward_force
    *   **References:** Select the surface shown in Figure 2–79
    *   **Force Y:** -200 N

© 2017, ASCENT - Center for Technical Knowledge®

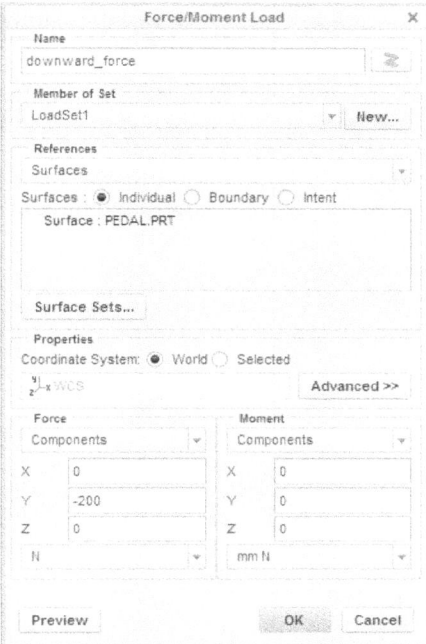

Figure 2–80

3. Click **OK** to close the Force/Moment dialog box. The model displays as shown in Figure 2–81.

Figure 2–81

Task 6 - Customize the simulation display.

1. Click 🖳 (Simulation Display) in the floating toolbar. The Simulation Display dialog box opens.

*The **Distribution Density** option adjusts the number of force arrows displayed on the loaded surface. It does not affect the analysis results.*

2. In the *Settings* tab, select **Values**. In the Load/Constraint Display area, set the *Distribution Density* to **3**, as shown in Figure 2–82.

Figure 2–82

3. In the *Modeling Entities* tab, clear the **Material Assignments** option, as shown in Figure 2–83.

© 2017, ASCENT - Center for Technical Knowledge®

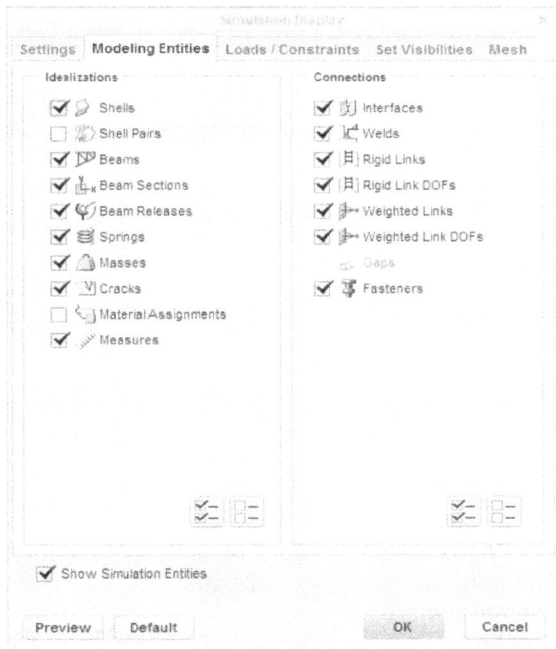

Figure 2–83

4. Click **OK** to close the Simulation Display dialog box. The model displays as shown in Figure 2–84. Note that the load magnitude (200N) is now shown and **Material Assignment** icons are now hidden.

Figure 2–84

Task 7 - Mesh the model.

1. In the *Refine Model* tab, click ▓ (AutoGEM). The AutoGEM dialog box opens as shown in Figure 2–85.

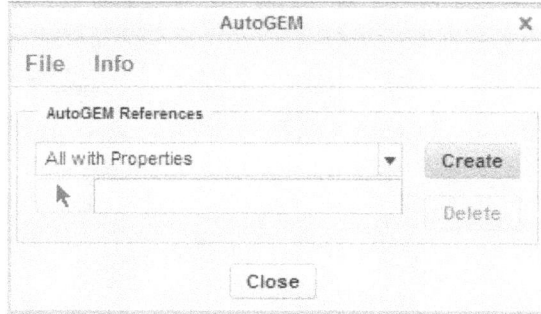

Figure 2–85

*The **All with Properties** option only meshes parts to which materials have already been assigned.*

2. Ensure that the **All with Properties** option is active and click **Create**.

3. The AutoGEM Summary and the Diagnostics dialog boxes open as shown in Figure 2–86. For this model, AutoGEM creates approximately 999 tetrahedral elements.

The number of elements might vary slightly, depending on the specific Creo build.

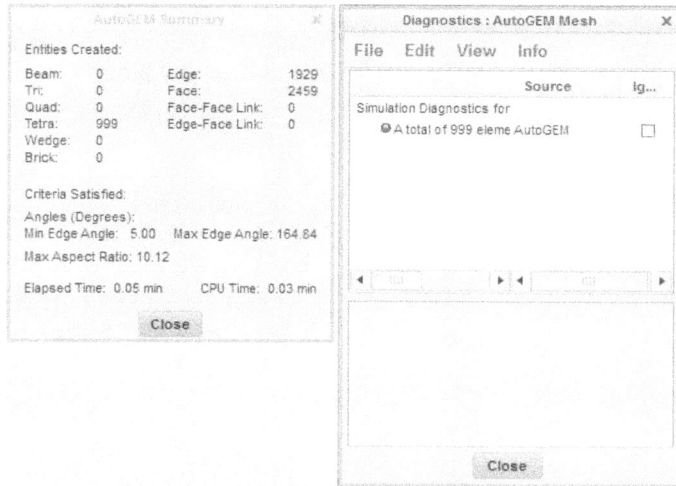

Figure 2–86

© 2017, ASCENT - Center for Technical Knowledge®

4. Close the AutoGEM Summary and Diagnostics boxes, but do not close the AutoGEM dialog box. The model displays as shown in Figure 2–87.

Figure 2–87

5. Click **Close** in the AutoGEM dialog box. The warning shown in Figure 2–88 displays.

Figure 2–88

6. Click **No** to exit without saving the mesh.

The model will be meshed during the analysis run. Since meshing this model is fast, this will not impede the analysis runtime.

Analysis Tasks

In the following tasks, you will set the analysis type and convergence method, and then run the analysis.

Task 8 - Set up the analysis.

1. In the *Home* tab, click (Analyses and Studies). The Analyses and Design Studies dialog box opens as shown in Figure 2–89.

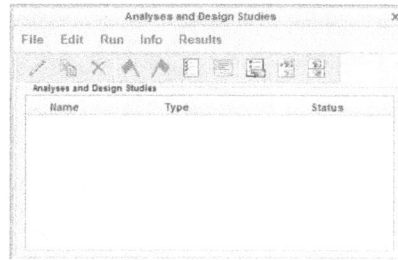

Figure 2–89

2. Select **File>New Static**. The Static Analysis Definition dialog box opens as shown in Figure 2–90.

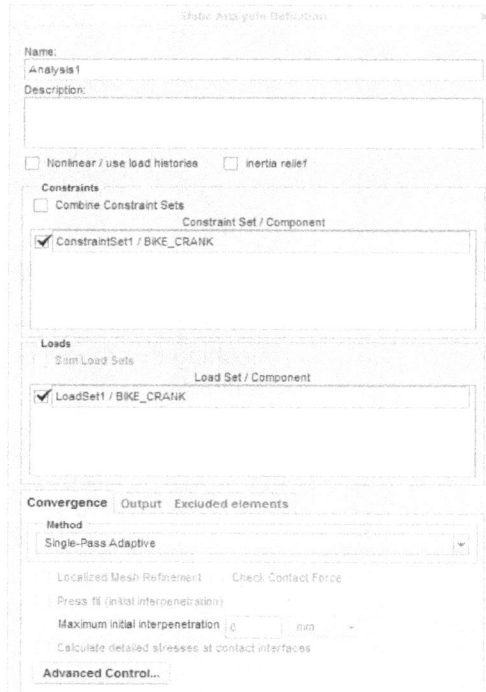

Figure 2–90

© 2017, ASCENT - Center for Technical Knowledge®

3. In the *Name* field, enter **bike_crank** (this will be the name of a subdirectory containing all of your results files).

4. For this analysis, you will use the Single-Pass Adaptive convergence method. Ensure that it is selected.

5. Click **OK** to close the Static Analysis Definition dialog box.

6. Click [icon] (Settings) in the Analyses and Design Studies dialog box. The Run Settings dialog box opens as shown in Figure 2–91.

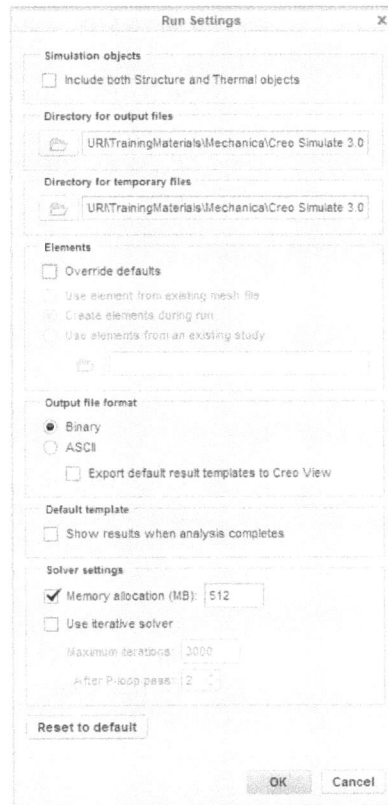

Figure 2–91

7. Note that, since you did not save the mesh file, the **Create Elements during Run** option is automatically selected in the *Elements* area.

The recommended setting for the memory allocation is half the RAM in your computer.

8. Set *Memory Allocation* to **512Mb**.

9. Click **OK** to close the Run Settings dialog box.

10. Expand the **Info** menu and select **Check Model**. This command checks the validity of the simulation model. The Information dialog box opens, as shown in Figure 2–92, stating that there are no errors.

Figure 2–92

11. Click **OK** to confirm.

Task 9 - Run the analysis.

1. Click ⚑ (Start) in the Analyses and Design Studies dialog box to start your analysis. The Question dialog box opens as shown in Figure 2–93.

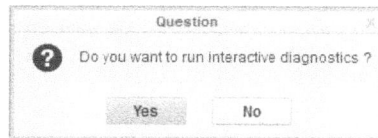

Figure 2–93

2. Click **Yes** in the Question dialog box. Creo Simulate solves the analysis. The Diagnostics dialog box opens as shown in Figure 2–94, stating that the analysis run has been completed.

   Note that a warning message was issued during the analysis run, related to the yield condition being exceeded in AL6061 T4 material.

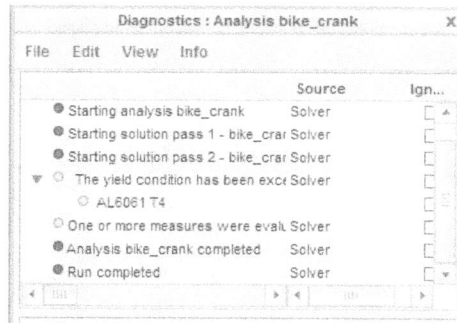

Figure 2–94

© 2017, ASCENT - Center for Technical Knowledge®

3. Click **Close** to close the Diagnostics dialog box.

4. Click 🔳 (Status) in the Analyses and Design Studies dialog box. The Run Status dialog box opens, displaying various information regarding the analysis as shown in Figure 2–95. Scroll up or down to the area that prints the RMS Stress Error Estimates and note that the estimated RMS stress error in this analysis is approximately 15.5MPa, which is 8.3% of the maximum principal stress in the model.

Since this is a preliminary analysis, which is only intended to check for gross design errors, you will accept this amount of analysis error. For a design validation analysis run, a more accurate Multi-Pass Adaptive convergence method would be recommended, with a target RMS stress error under 5%.

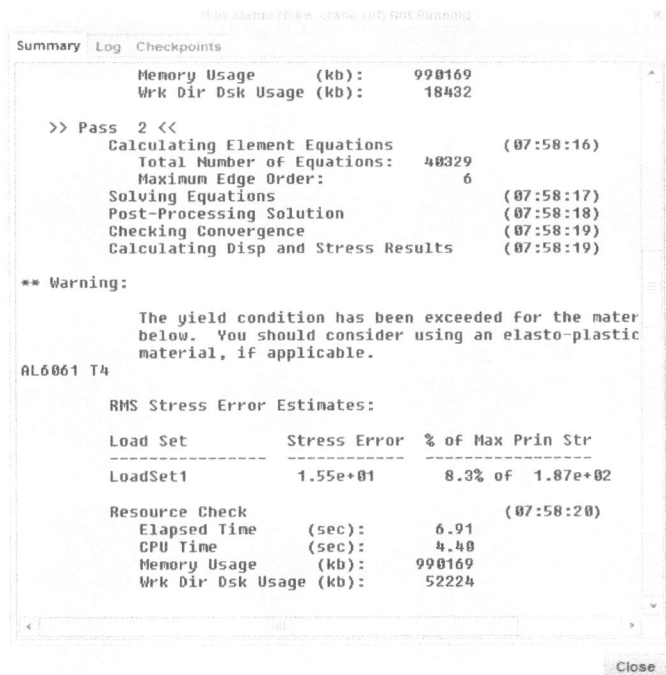

Figure 2–95

5. Click **Close** to close the Run Status dialog box, but do not close the Analyses and Design Studies dialog box yet.

Results Tasks

In the following tasks, you will display and interpret the results of this analysis.

Task 10 - Display the results using the Default Template.

In this task, you will display the analysis results using the Default Template.

1. Click ![icon] in the Analyses and Design Studies dialog box (the tooltip on the icon should say *Review Results of a Design Study from Default Template*). Creo Simulate takes a minute to prepare the visualization and then displays three result windows at once, as shown in Figure 2–96.

   The displayed result windows are as follows:

   • von Mises Stress Animation
   • Displacement Magnitude Fringe
   • Principal Stress Vectors

Figure 2–96

© 2017, ASCENT - Center for Technical Knowledge®

Task 11 - Examine the Principal Stress results.

1. In the View tab, click 🔍 (Show). The Display Result Window dialog box opens as shown in Figure 2–97.

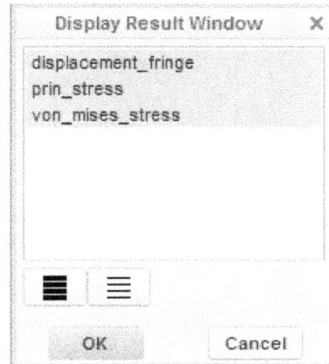

Figure 2–97

2. Clear the **displacement_fringe** and **von_mises_stress** options and click **OK**. Only the principal stress vector plot is displayed as shown in Figure 2–98.

Figure 2–98

3. In the second drop-down list at the top left corner of the window, select **Max Principal**, as shown in Figure 2–99.

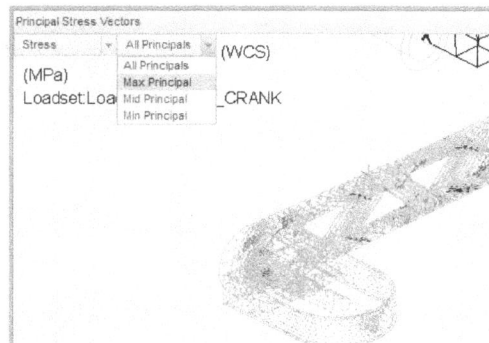

Figure 2–99

4. The result window now displays as shown in Figure 2–100.

   The maximum principal stress component is typically the tensile stress in the model, and is critical for predicting fatigue and brittle failures of the material. Use the **Rotate** and **Zoom** tools to examine the tensile stresses in the model.

Figure 2–100

5. In the View tab, click to open the Display Result Window dialog box again. Clear the **prin_stress** option and click **OK** to hide all of the result windows for now.

© 2017, ASCENT - Center for Technical Knowledge®

Task 12 - Display the Failure Index results.

*The Failure Index requires you to define a failure criterion. In Task 3, you defined **von Mises** as the failure criterion, which means the material is predicted to fail in the areas in which the **von Mises** stress exceeds the material's **Yield Stress**.*

In this task, you will display and examine the Failure Index result plot. The Failure Index is used to determine whether or not the material is predicted to fail under the given loading conditions:

- If the Failure Index is less than 1, the material is not predicted to fail.

- If the Failure Index is equal to or greater than 1, the material is predicted to fail.

1. Click in the *Home* tab to create a new results window. The Design Study for Result Window Definition dialog box opens.

2. Select the **bike_crank** study and click **Open**. The Result Window Definition dialog box opens.

3. In the *Name* field, enter **fail_index_pedal**.

4. Expand the Quantity drop-down list and select **Failure Index**. The Result Window Definition dialog box should display as shown in Figure 2–101.

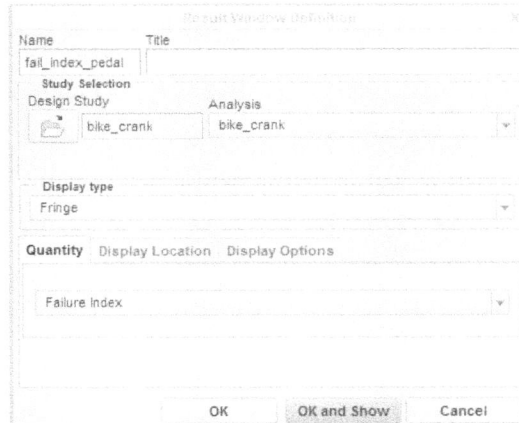

Figure 2–101

5. Click **OK and Show**. The result displays as shown in Figure 2–102.

Figure 2–102

Note that the maximum failure index in the model is about 1.2, which is greater than 1, and means that in some areas in the model the material will fail under the given loading.

In the following steps, you will examine which areas in the model are predicted to fail.

6. In the *Home* tab, click ✏ (Edit). The Result Window Definition dialog box opens. Select the *Display Location* tab as shown in Figure 2–103.

Figure 2–103

© 2017, ASCENT - Center for Technical Knowledge®

7. Expand the Display Location drop-down list and select **Components/Layers**. The Component and Layer Visibility dialog box opens as shown in Figure 2–104.

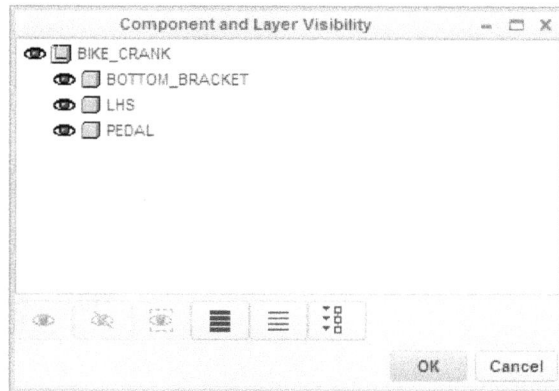

Figure 2–104

8. Set the visibility of **BOTTOM_BRACKET** and **LHS** to **Blanked**, as shown in Figure 2–105.

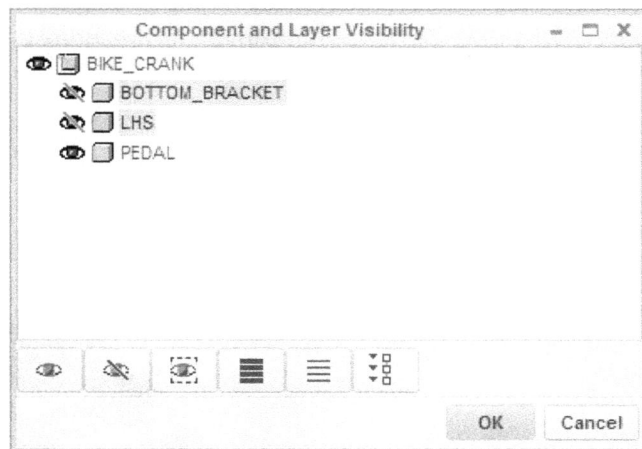

Figure 2–105

9. Click **OK** to close the Component and Layer Visibility dialog box and then click **OK and Show** to close the Result Window Definition dialog box. The result window displays as shown in Figure 2–106.

Figure 2–106

10. In the Home tab, select ▯ (Model Max) to locate the maximum failure index in the pedal, as shown in Figure 2–107.

The failure index in the fillet near the pedal's main thread is approximately 0.955. Therefore, the material in the pedal is not predicted to yield.

Figure 2–107

© 2017, ASCENT - Center for Technical Knowledge®

11. Click ⬛ (Copy) in the *Home* tab to create a copy of the current result window. The Result Window Definition dialog box opens as shown in Figure 2–108.

Figure 2–108

12. Rename the window as **fail_index_crank**.

13. Click ▸ to open the Component and Layer Visibility dialog box. Set the visibility of the **LHS** component to **Shown** and of the **BOTTOM_BRACKET** and **PEDAL** parts to **Blanked**, as shown in Figure 2–109.

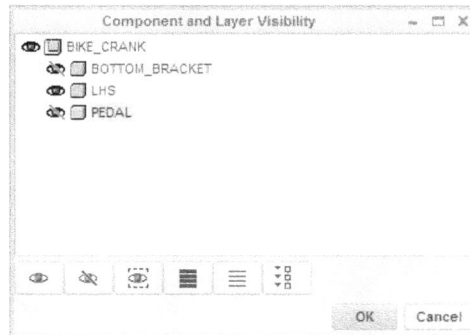

Figure 2–109

14. Click **OK** to close the Component and Layer Visibility dialog box and then click **OK** again to close the Result Window Definition dialog box and save the result definition without displaying.

15. Repeat Steps 11 to 14 to create a window named **fail_index_shaft** to display the failure index in the **BOTTOM_BRACKET** part.

16. In the *View* tab, click 🖼 (Show) to open the Display Result Window dialog box. Highlight the **fail_index_crank** line, and clear all of the others, as shown in Figure 2–110.

Display Result Window	✕
displacement_fringe	
fail_index_crank	
fail_index_pedal	
fail_index_shaft	
prin_stress	
von_mises_stress	

OK   Cancel

Figure 2–110

17. Click **OK**. The failure index result for the crank part displays as shown in Figure 2–111.

"fail_index_pedal" - bike_crank - bike_crank

Failure Index   (WCS)

Location: Components and Layers
Loadset:LoadSet1 : BIKE_CRANK

1.20252
1.08255
0.96258
0.84261
0.72264
0.60267
0.48271
0.36274
0.24277
0.12280
0.00283

Figure 2–111

© 2017, ASCENT - Center for Technical Knowledge®

18. In the Home tab, select ▯⁺ (Model Max) to locate the maximum failure index in the crank, as shown in Figure 2–112.

Note that the failure index in one of the fillets in the middle pocket is approximately 1.203. The stress in this area is 20% over the material's yield stress, which means the material in the fillet is predicted to substantially yield.

Figure 2–112

19. Click 📷 (Show) in the *View* tab again. Highlight the **fail_index_shaft** line, and clear all of the others, as shown in Figure 2–113.

Figure 2–113

20. Click **OK**. The failure index result for the shaft part displays as shown in Figure 2–114.

Note that the maximum failure index in the shaft is approximately 0.712. Therefore, this part is safe under the given loading.

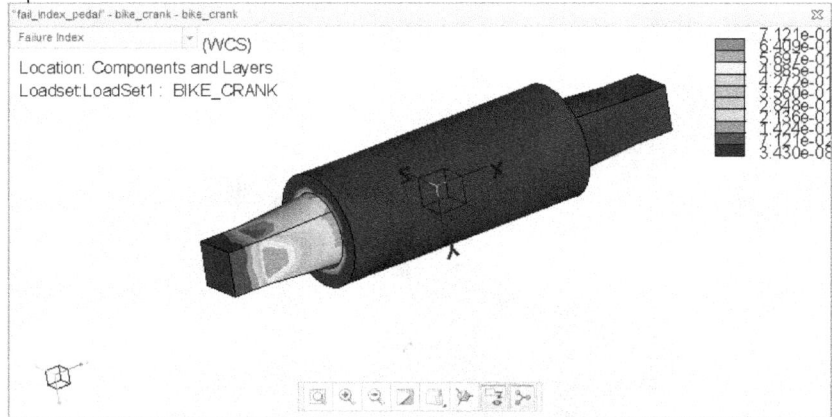

Figure 2–114

Report Tasks

In the following tasks, you will annotate the analysis results and prepare and export a report.

Task 13 - Annotate the results.

1. In the Home tab, Click ✐ (Edit). The Result Window Definition dialog box opens as shown in Figure 2–115.

Figure 2–115

© 2017, ASCENT - Center for Technical Knowledge®

2. Expand the Display Location drop-down list, select **All**, and click **OK and Show**. The result window displays as shown in Figure 2–116.

Figure 2–116

3. In the Annotation section of the *Format* tab, click ▽ (New). The Note dialog box opens as shown in Figure 2–117.

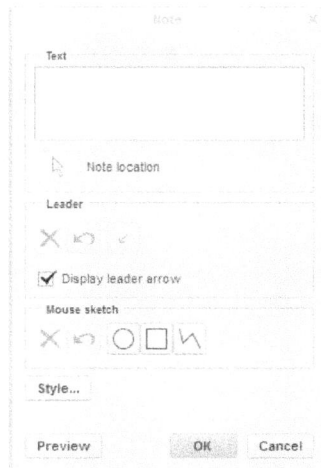

Figure 2–117

4. In the *Text* field, enter **Unsafe area. Consider increasing the fillet radius and/or using stronger material**, as shown in Figure 2–118.

Figure 2–118

5. Click [cursor] and select a location in the result window where you want to locate the top left corner of the annotation, as shown in Figure 2–119.

Figure 2–119

© 2017, ASCENT - Center for Technical Knowledge®

6. Click ↖ in the Note dialog box, and select the corner of the pocket with the maximum stress. The leader displays as shown in Figure 2–120.

Figure 2–120

7. Repeat Step 6 to add another leader as shown in Figure 2–121.

Figure 2–121

8. Click **OK** to finish creating the annotation.

Task 14 - Create a report.

1. In the top-level menu, select **File>Save As**. In the dialog box that opens, select **Web Page (*.html)** in the Type drop-down list, and enter **Bike_Crank_Preliminary_Analysis** as the file name, as shown in Figure 2–122.

Figure 2–122

2. Click **Save**. The HTML Report dialog box opens as shown in Figure 2–123.

Figure 2–123

© 2017, ASCENT - Center for Technical Knowledge®

3. Rename the report as **Bike_Crank_Preliminary_Analysis**.

4. In the Item list, highlight **fail_index_shaft** and select the **Include modeling info** option, as shown in Figure 2–124.

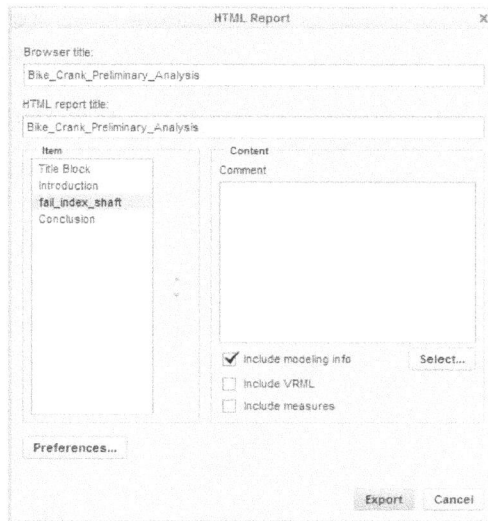

Figure 2–124

5. In the Item list, highlight **Conclusion** and enter **Bike crank predicted to fail at given loading conditions. Design modification is required**, as shown in Figure 2–125.

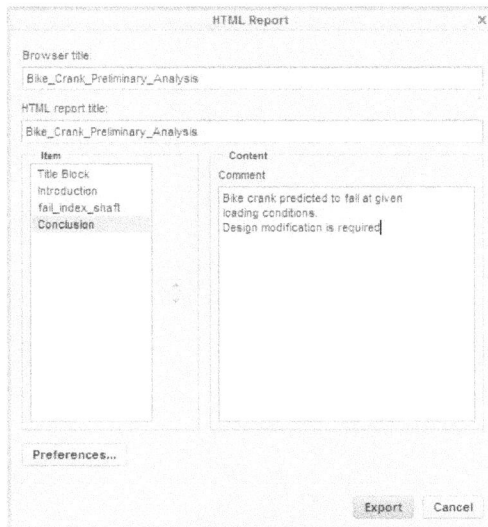

Figure 2–125

6. Click **Export**. The report is exported to the Creo working directory.

7. Open the *Bike_Crank_Preliminary_Analysis* directory in the Creo working directory and open **Bike_Crank_Preliminary_Analysis.html** in a Web browser (such as Internet Explorer), for review. The report displays as shown in Figure 2–126.

Bike_Crank_Preliminary_Analysis

fail_index_shaft

Figure 1. fail_index_shaft

Links

- Show Analysis Report File

BIKE_CRANK.ASM

Material Assignments

Material Assignment "MaterialAssign1"	
References	Model (PEDAL.PRT) Model (LHS.PRT)
Material	AL6061 T4

Figure 2–126

8. Close the report.

9. Exit Creo Simulate Results. Save and close the model.

© 2017, ASCENT - Center for Technical Knowledge®

Practice 2c

Static Stress Analysis of a Cast Part

Practice Objectives

- Apply loads, constraints, and material properties.
- Mesh the model.
- Set up and run a Multi-Pass Adaptive analysis.
- Display the results.
- Determine the failure index and the safety factor for the part.
- Create the report

In this practice, you will perform a static stress analysis on the cast part shown in Figure 2–127, with minimum instruction.

Figure 2–127

Task 1 - Prepare the model for analysis

1. Open **guide.prt** and launch Creo Simulate.

2. Apply the material:
   - **Material:** Aluminum casting alloy AA208-T4
   - **Poisson's ratio:** 0.33
   - **Young's modulus:** 71000 MPa
   - **Coefficient of thermal expansion:** 2.23e-5 /C
   - **Density:** 2.8e-9 tonne/mm^3
   - **Tensile Yield Stress:** 103 MPa
   - **Failure Criterion:** Distortion Energy (von Mises)

To create a new material that is not in the library, copy an existing material from the library into the model, then change the material's name and properties.

3. Fully constrain the five holes on the bottom flange of the part, as shown in Figure 2–128.

Figure 2–128

4. Apply 100N load in +Y direction to the bore surface, as shown in Figure 2–129.

Figure 2–129

5. Mesh the model using the **All with Properties** option. Examine and save the mesh.

Task 2 - Set up and run the analysis.

1. Create a new static analysis with the following parameters:
   - **Analysis name:** guide
   - **Convergence method:** Multi-Pass Adaptive
   - **Maximum Polynomial Order:** 9
   - **Percent Convergence:** 6

2. Run the analysis and wait until it completes.

3. Display the Status window. Check whether the analysis has converged, and note the RMS Stress Error value.

© 2017, ASCENT - Center for Technical Knowledge®

Task 3 - Visualize and examine the analysis results.

1. Visualize and examine the **strain_energy** and **max_stress_vm** convergence graphs.

2. Visualize the **P-Level** fringe plot. Determine the value and the locations of the maximum P-Level.

3. Visualize and animate the **Displacement Magnitude** fringe plot. Does the part deform according to the applied loads?

4. Display the **von Mises Stress** fringe plot. Find the location of the maximum stress.

5. Display the **Failure Index** fringe plot. Is the part predicted to fail?

Factor of Safety value is the inverse of the Failure Index value.

6. Calculate the value of the factor of safety for the part. Can you think of design changes that would lead to improving the factor of safety in this part?

7. Annotate the **von Mises Stress** plot, showing the location of the maximum stress.

8. Create and export the analysis report to HTML.

9. Save and close the model.

© 2017, ASCENT - Center for Technical Knowledge®

Loads and Constraints

Loads and constraints are the boundary conditions that the model experiences in its working environment. Selecting the correct boundary conditions for your FEA model is a critical aspect of developing an accurate simulation. Therefore, when you are analyzing a model, the loads and constraints placed on it must realistically represent the operating conditions of your product.

Learning Objectives in this Chapter

- Understand the use of constraints, rigid body motions, and constraint sets
- Create a displacement constraint.
- Create planar, pin, or ball constraints.
- Create symmetry constraints.
- Understand types of loads and load sets.
- Create a force or moment load.
- Create pressure, bearing, gravity, centrifugal and temperature loads.
- Create a preload.
- Create surface regions.
- Understand how to handle models with stress singularities.

3.1 Constraints

In Creo Simulate, a constraint is a form of boundary condition in which a *prescribed displacement* is assigned to one or more geometrical entities in the model. Prescribed displacement means that the displacement of the geometrical entity to which it is applied is enforced throughout the simulation. A prescribed displacement (i.e., constraint) can be of a zero value, which is typically used to simulate all kinds of supports in the analysis model, or of a non-zero value, which is typically used to enforce a specific motion in the model.

Constraints are commonly used to model a true support, such as where a structure is fixed to a rigid foundation or adjoining structure. Another common use is to simulate various symmetry conditions, such as mirror symmetry, cyclic symmetry, or anti-symmetry.

Although constraints are essential for structural analyses, it is usually preferable to limit the use of constraints as much as possible. Since the essence of structural FEA is to calculate displacements (along with the corresponding strains and stresses), the prescribed displacements effectively force an assumed solution onto some of the geometrical entities in the model. Therefore, too many constraints might unnaturally stiffen the model, and, consequently, the stresses might typically err on the low side.

Rigid Body Motions

In static analysis, it is necessary to provide sufficient supports to prevent rigid body motions (RBM), which are the movements of parts of the structure that do not produce strain. An example of a simply supported beam is shown in Figure 3–1.

Figure 3–1

© 2017, ASCENT - Center for Technical Knowledge®

When using handbook formulas to calculate stresses, the only supports needed are those in the Y-direction. Since no loads are applied in the X-direction, a support in that direction is not necessary. However, in FEA the lack of support in X-direction results in a fatal error or inaccurate results. This is because a small load in the X-direction occurs during the FEA solution process, because of rounding errors.

If possible RBMs are detected, Creo Simulate displays the error message: **The model is insufficiently constrained for the analysis**.

The number of possible RBMs varies from one model to another. For a single part in 3D, there are six possible RBMs: three translations and three rotations. For an assembly, the number could be much greater, since each part now has six possible RBMs that have to be eliminated by applying constraints and connections between the parts.

Constraint Sets

Every constraint in Creo Simulate belongs to a constraint set. A constraint set is a collection of constraints that act together on your model.

Constraint sets provide the means of organizing your modeling entities in a logical way, to have the additional flexibility of treating your constraints separately when setting up various analysis scenarios and load cases. A carefully considered approach to constraint sets simplifies the analyses definition.

To manage your constraint sets, select **Constraints>Constraint Sets** drop-down list in the *Home* tab to open the Constraint Sets dialog box as shown in Figure 3–2.

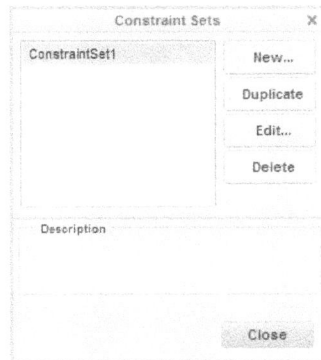

Figure 3–2

Constraint sets can be created, duplicated, edited, or deleted.

Displacement Constraint

The displacement constraint is the most commonly used tool in Creo Simulate that is used to apply constraints. To apply a displacement constraint, click 🔖 (Displacement) in the *Home* tab. The Constraint dialog box opens as shown in Figure 3–3.

Figure 3–3

The options in the Constraint dialog box are as follows:

Section	Option	Description
Name	N/A	Assigns a name to the constraint.
Member of Set	Constraint sets in the model	Selects a constraint set.
References	Surfaces	Assigns the constraint to surfaces.
	Edges/Curves	Assigns the constraint to edges or curves.
	Points	Assigns the constraint to vertices or points.
Coordinate System	World	The constraint directions are defined in WCS.
	Selected	Enables you to select another coordinate system to define constraint directions. The coordinate system can be cartesian, cylindrical, or spherical.

© 2017, ASCENT - Center for Technical Knowledge®

Translation	○		Enables mesh nodes on the selected geometry to move in a direction.
	🔧		Constrains mesh nodes on the selected geometry in a direction.
	🔧→○		Forces mesh nodes on the selected geometry to move along a direction by a non-zero prescribed displacement value.
Rotation	○⸺		Enables mesh nodes on the selected geometry to rotate about a direction. Not applicable to solid elements, which do not carry rotational degrees of freedom at their nodal points.
	○⁊⁊⁊		Constrains mesh nodes on the selected geometry against rotations about a direction. Not applicable to solid elements, which do not carry rotational degrees of freedom at their nodal points.
	△		Forces the nodes on the selected geometry into rotation about a direction by a non-zero prescribed angle. Not applicable to solid elements, which do not carry rotational degrees of freedom at their nodal points.

Planar, Pin, and Ball Constraints

The Planar constraint enables you to create a constraint that permits full planar movement, but constrains the off-plane displacement. Only planar surfaces can be selected.

To apply a planar constraint, click 🔳 (Planar) in the *Home* tab. The Constraint dialog box opens as shown in Figure 3–4.

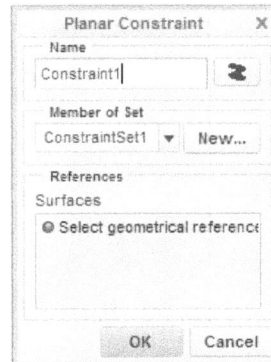

Figure 3–4

The Pin constraint enables you to control the translation or rotation about the axis of a cylindrical surface. Only cylindrical surfaces can be selected.

To apply a pin constraint, click ✧ (Pin) in the *Home* tab. Use the options to control rotation about the cylinder's axis and translation along its axis, as shown in Figure 3–5.

Figure 3–5

A Ball constraint simulates a ball support in which all of the translations are fixed while all of the rotations are free. Only spherical surfaces can be selected for this type of constraint.

To apply a ball constraint, click ✧ (Ball) in the *Home* tab. The Constraint dialog box opens as shown in Figure 3–6.

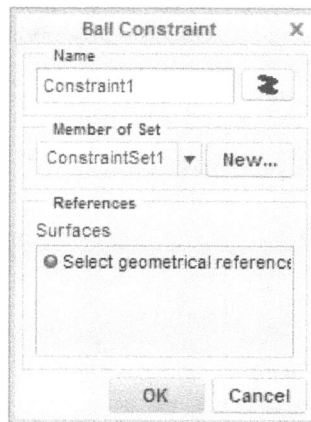

Figure 3–6

© 2017, ASCENT - Center for Technical Knowledge®

Symmetry Constraints

There are two types of symmetry constraints in Creo Simulate:

- Mirror Symmetry

- Cyclic Symmetry

Using symmetry constraints, you can take advantage of the model's symmetry to reduce meshing and analysis time. In essence, symmetry constraints enable you to analyze a segment of the model and project the result onto the entire model.

Mirror Symmetry

The mirror symmetry constraint requires that the model exhibits a *reflective* symmetry about a plane. The geometry and modeling entities on one side of the plane must mirror the geometry and modeling entities on the other side of the plane.

Use the following steps to apply a mirror symmetry constraint:

1. Cut your model in half along the plane of symmetry. The result is 1/2 of the geometry (it could be 1/4 or even 1/8 of the geometry if your analysis model exhibits more than one plane of symmetry).
2. In the *Home* tab, select **Constraints>Symmetry**. The Symmetry Constraint dialog box opens.
3. Expand the Type drop-down list and select **Mirror**. The Symmetry Constraint dialog box opens as shown in Figure 3–7.

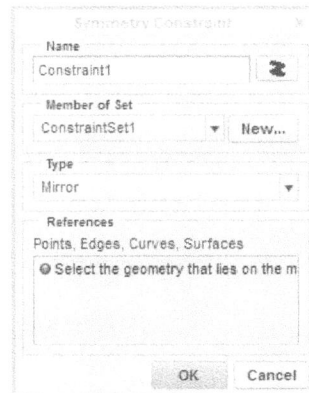

Figure 3–7

4. Select the surfaces, edges, curves, or points located on the symmetry plane.
5. Click **OK** to finish.

Cyclic Symmetry

In a model with cyclic symmetry, a 3D geometric shape is repeated a number of times around the axis of rotation. The geometry is not continuous, but rather cyclic. For example, the fan shown in Figure 3–8 is an example of a cyclically symmetric geometry.

Figure 3–8

If loads, constraints, materials, etc., are cyclic as well, you can analyze a single blade, as shown in Figure 3–9, by properly isolating it and applying constraints that capture the cyclic symmetry.

Figure 3–9

Use the following steps to apply a cyclic symmetry constraint:

1. Isolate the cyclic geometry by cutting it out of your model. The cutout surfaces do not have to be planar. The only requirement is that the cross-sections on the cutout surfaces must be identical.
2. In the *Home* tab, select **Constraints>Symmetry**. The Symmetry Constraint dialog box opens.

© 2017, ASCENT - Center for Technical Knowledge®

3. Expand the Type drop-down list and select **Cyclic**. The Symmetry Constraint dialog box opens as shown in Figure 3–10.

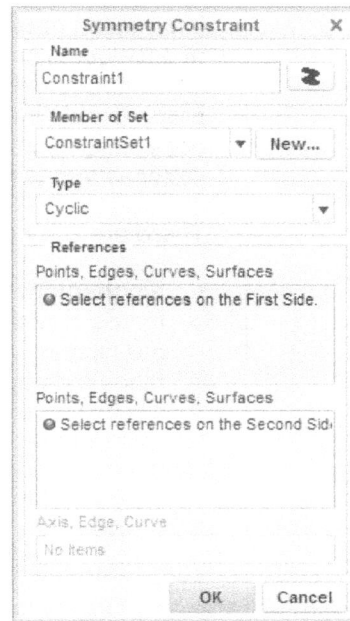

Figure 3–10

4. Select the geometry on the first cutout boundary.
5. Select the geometry on the second cutout boundary.
6. Depending on the selected geometry, Creo Simulate might or might not be able to automatically determine the axis of symmetry. If not, you need to select the axis of symmetry.
7. Click **OK** to finish.

Note that both the geometry and boundary conditions must meet the criteria of cyclic symmetry. If the constraints or loading is not repeated about the axis of rotation by the same number of repetitions as the geometry, the results are invalid.

3.2 Loads

Unsatisfactory representation of the loading is a common cause of inaccurate analysis results. Therefore, gathering adequate information about the magnitude of the loads is a critical aspect of developing an accurate simulation. It should be noted that in a linear analysis the stresses and deformations are directly proportional to the magnitude of the loading. For example, a possible error in loading of 20% leads to a minimum 20% error in stresses and deflections.

There are two main types of loading in structural FEA:

*   **Mechanical loads:** Consisting of concentrated or distributed forces or moments and body forces. The mechanical loads are typically related to a coordinate system, and consist of magnitude and orientation. The spatial distribution and time dependence of the load can also be defined. The following types of mechanical loads are available in Creo Simulate:

    *   Force/Moment load
    *   Pressure load
    *   Bearing load
    *   Gravity load
    *   Centrifugal load

*   **Initial strains:** Caused by thermal expansion, press-fit, or pre-stress. The following types of initial strain loads are available in Creo Simulate:

    *   Temperature load
    *   Preload

Load Sets

Every load in Creo Simulate belongs to a load set. A load set is a collection of loads that act together on your model.

Load sets provide a means of organizing your modeling entities in a logical way, to have the additional flexibility of treating your loads separately when setting up various analysis scenarios and load cases. A carefully considered approach to load sets simplifies the analyses definition.

To manage your load sets, select **Loads>Load Sets** in the *Home* tab to open the Load Sets dialog box as shown in Figure 3–11.

© 2017, ASCENT - Center for Technical Knowledge®

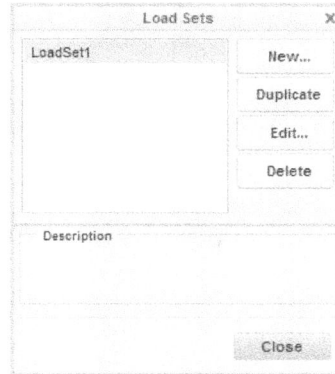

Figure 3–11

Load sets can be created, duplicated, edited, or deleted.

Force/Moment Load

To apply a Force/Moment load, click ⊢ (Force/Moment) in the *Home* tab. The Force/Moment Load dialog box opens as shown in Figure 3–12.

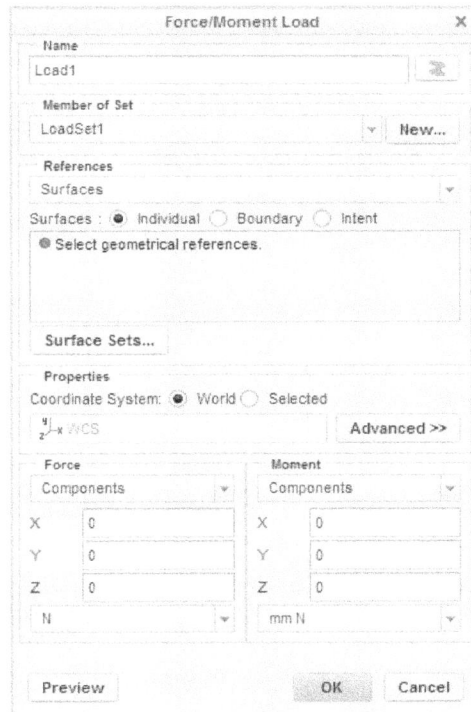

Figure 3–12

The options available in the Force/Moment Load dialog box are as follows.

Section	Option	Description
Name	N/A	Assigns a name to the load.
Member of Set	Load sets in the model	Selects a load set.
References	Surfaces	Applies the load to surfaces.
	Edges/Curves	Applies the load to edges or curves.
	Points	Applies the load to vertices or points.
Coordinate System	World	The load is related to the WCS.
	Selected	Enables you to select another coordinate system to define the load directions. The coordinate system can be cartesian, cylindrical, or spherical.
Distribution	Total Load	Applies a distributed load along the length or area of the entity, so that the sum of the distributed load equals the entered load value.
	Force Per Unit Area / Force Per Unit Length	The entered load value is interpreted as the load density (i.e., force per unit area or length) over the entity.
	Total Load At Point	Applies a distributed load (over the entity) that is statically equivalent to a load applied to a single point.
	Total Bearing Load At Point	Applies a distributed load (on a cylindrical surface) that represents the force and moment that one cylindrically shaped part exerts on another (e.g., a pin and a hole). The distributed load is made statically equivalent to the load applied at a point.
Spatial Variation	Uniform	Applies a uniform load over the entity. The load does not have a spatial variation.
	Function of Coordinates	The load's spatial variation is defined as a function of a coordinate system. Cartesian, Cylindrical, or Spherical coordinate systems can be used.
	Interpolated Over Entity	Applies a spatial variation that is either linear, quadratic, or cubic along the entity.

© 2017, ASCENT - Center for Technical Knowledge®

Pressure Load

A pressure load is a distributed load that acts in normal to the part surface direction, even if the surface is curved. The positive direction is toward the part body.

To apply a Pressure load, click ⊫ (Pressure) in the *Home* tab. The Pressure Load dialog box opens as shown in Figure 3–13.

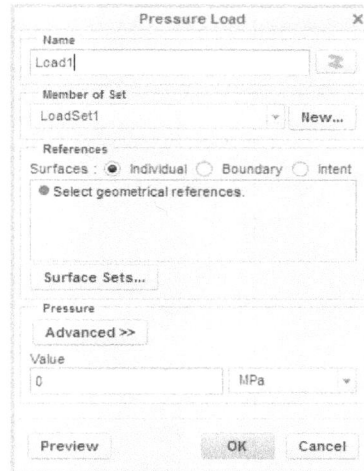

Figure 3–13

The options available in the Pressure Load dialog box are as follows:

Section	Option	Description
Name	**N/A**	Assigns a name to the load.
Member of Set	**Load sets in the model**	Selects a load set.
Spatial Variation	**Uniform**	Applies a uniform load over the entity. The load does not have a spatial variation.
	Function of Coordinates	The load's spatial variation is defined as a function of a coordinate system. Cartesian, Cylindrical, or Spherical coordinate systems can be used.
	Interpolated Over Entity	Applies a spatial variation that is either linear, quadratic, or cubic along the entity.
	External Coefficients Field	Imports a file containing the coefficients that specify the spatial variation of the load. The coefficients are automatically mapped onto the model surfaces.

Bearing Load

Bearing loads approximate the pressure applied on a cylindrical hole by a rigid pin or shaft passing through that hole.

To apply a Bearing load, click ⬚ (Bearing) in the *Home* tab. The Bearing Load dialog box opens as shown in Figure 3–14.

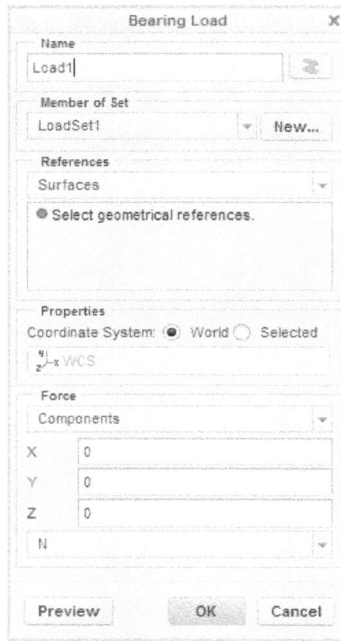

Figure 3–14

The options available in the Bearing Load dialog box are as follows:

Section	Option	Description
Name	**N/A**	Assigns a name to the load.
Member of Set	**Load sets in the model**	Selects a load set.
References	**Surfaces**	Applies the load to surfaces. Only cylindrical surfaces are permitted.
	Edges/Curves	Applies the load to edges or curves in 2D models.
Coordinate System	**World**	The load is related to the WCS.
	Selected	Enables you to select another coordinate system to define the load direction. The coordinate system can be only Cartesian.

© 2017, ASCENT - Center for Technical Knowledge®

Force	**Components**	Load direction and magnitude is determined by the entered force components.
	Dir Vector & Mag	Load direction is defined by a 3D vector.
	Dir Points & Mag	Load direction is defined by selecting two points.

Gravity Load

A gravity load simulates the body force created by the acceleration or deceleration of your model.

To apply a Gravity load, click ⬚ (Gravity) in the *Home* tab. The Gravity Load dialog box opens as shown in Figure 3–15.

Figure 3–15

The options available in the Gravity Load dialog box are as follows:

Section	Option	Description
Name	**N/A**	Assigns a name to the load.
Member of Set	**Load sets in the model**	Selects a load set.
Coordinate System	**World**	The load is related to the WCS.
	Selected	Enables you to select another coordinate system to define the load direction. The coordinate system can be only Cartesian.

Force	Components	Load direction and magnitude is determined by the entered acceleration components.
	Dir Vector & Mag	Load direction is defined by a 3D vector.
	Dir Points & Mag	Load direction is defined by selecting two points.

Centrifugal Load

A centrifugal load applies a body force that is created by the rotation of your model. Both angular velocity and acceleration can be applied.

To apply a Centrifugal load, click ⊢θ (Centrifugal) in the *Home* tab. The Centrifugal Load dialog box opens as shown in Figure 3–16.

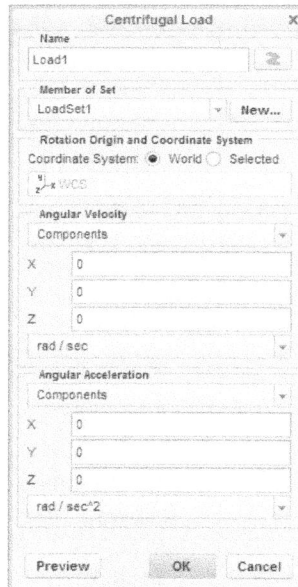

Figure 3–16

The options available in the Centrifugal Load dialog box are as follows:

Section	Option	Description
Name	**N/A**	Assigns a name to the load.
Member of Set	**Load sets in the model**	Selects a load set.

© 2017, ASCENT - Center for Technical Knowledge®

Coordinate System	World	The load is related to the WCS.
	Selected	Enables you to select another coordinate system to define the load direction. The coordinate system can be only Cartesian.
Angular Velocity	Components	Axis of rotation and velocity magnitude are determined by the entered components.
	Dir Vector & Mag	Axis of rotation is defined by a 3D vector.
	Dir Points & Mag	Axis of rotation is defined by selecting two points.
Angular Acceleration	Components	Axis of rotation and acceleration magnitude are determined by the entered components.
	Dir Vector & Mag	Axis of rotation is defined by a 3D vector.
	Dir Points & Mag	Axis of rotation is defined by selecting two points.

Temperature Load

The temperature load applies an initial strain to your model exerted by a change in the temperature of the selected geometric entities.

To apply a Temperature load, click ⬚ (Temperature) in the *Home* tab. The Structural Temperature Load dialog box opens as shown in Figure 3–17.

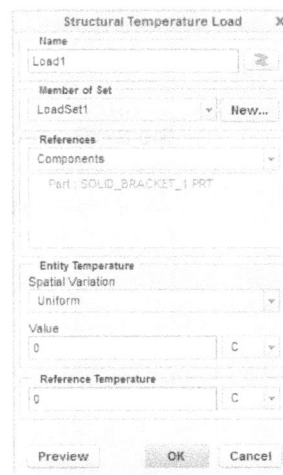

Figure 3–17

The options available in the Structural Temperature Load dialog box are as follows:

Section	Option	Description
Name	N/A	Assigns a name to the load.
Member of Set	Load sets in the model	Selects a load set.
References	Components	Applies the temperature change to assembly components.
	Volumes	Applies the temperature change to solid volumes.
	Surfaces	Applies the temperature change to surfaces.
	Edges/Curves	Applies the temperature change to edges or curves in a 2D model.
Entity Temperature> Spatial Variation	Uniform	The temperature change is distributed uniformly over the entity.
	Function of Coordinates	The temperature change is defined as a function of a coordinate system.
	External Field	Imports the temperature field from a file.
Reference Temperature	N/A	Defines the zero strain temperature.

Preload

The Preload load simulates a bolt preload on a volume or components. The preload shortens the volume or component in the axial direction.

To apply a Preload, click ⊤ (Preload) in the *Home* tab. The Preload dialog box opens as shown in Figure 3–18.

© 2017, ASCENT - Center for Technical Knowledge®

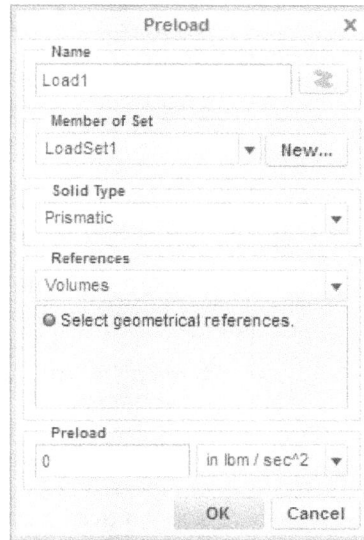

Figure 3–18

The options available in the Preload dialog box are as follows:

Section	Option	Description
Name	**N/A**	Assigns a name to the load.
Member of Set	**Load sets in the model**	Selects a load set.
Solid Type	**Prismatic**	Requires the solid to be a prism. It should have two planar bases and all side edges normal to the two bases.
	General	Applies to any solid component or volume. Requires selecting the preload direction.
References	**Volumes**	Applies the preload to solid volumes.
	Components	Applies the preload to assembly components.

3.3 Surface Regions

Surface regions in Creo Simulate enable you to apply modeling entities to a portion of a surface. The creation of surface regions is useful in the following situations:

- Loads or constraints need to be applied to specific areas of the model.

- Specific contact regions between the faces or surfaces of a model must be analyzed.

- Refinement of the mesh is required in a specific area of the model.

For example, surface regions are required for the model shown in Figure 3–19 because the loads and constraints are only applied over small portions of the part's surface.

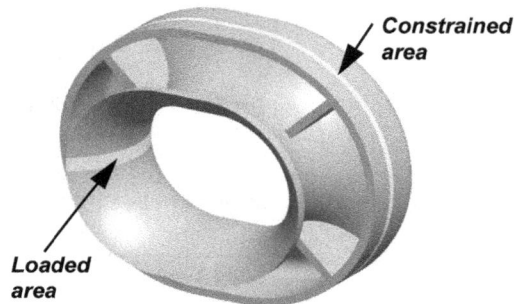

Figure 3–19

Surface region creation is a two-step process:

1. Define the boundary of the surface region. It can be created in Creo Parametric or Creo Simulate as a sketch or chain of datum curves. The datum curves must lie exactly on the part's surface, otherwise the creation of a surface region fails.
2. Define the parent surfaces for the surface region. The parent surfaces are then split by the surface region boundary, separating the surface region from the parent surface.

It is recommended that you create surface regions before you apply modeling entities, such as materials, loads, constraints, mesh controls, etc., to the model.

© 2017, ASCENT - Center for Technical Knowledge®

3.4 Singularities

A singularity is the location on a model in which theoretically infinite stress and/or displacement occurs. A simple example of a singularity is a force applied at a point. The stress as calculated by the force over area formula is infinite because the area under a point is zero.

Physically, displacement and stress cannot be infinite. Mathematically, Creo Simulate tries to solve the model exactly as defined, which results in unrealistically high stresses or displacements at the singularities. Additionally, singularities disrupt and slow down the convergence process by requiring very high p-levels, and often causing the model to not converge.

Types of Singularities

Two types of singularities occur in Creo Simulate Structural: those due to loading and constraint conditions and those due to model geometry. Combinations of loads or constraints for types of elements that result in theoretically infinite stresses or displacements for 3D models are as follows.

Load or Constraint	Beam	Shell	Solid
Points	Displacement: OK	Displacement: OK	Displacement: Infinite
	Stress: OK	Stress: Infinite	Stress: Infinite
Edges and Curves	Displacement: OK	Displacement: OK	Displacement: Infinite
	Stress: OK	Stress: OK	Stress: Infinite
Faces and Surfaces	N/A	Displacement: OK	Displacement: OK
	N/A	Stress: OK	Stress: Infinite

Along with loads and constraints, sharp reentrant corners or other abrupt changes in geometry can cause singularities. It is recommended that you smooth out the discontinuous geometry to improve convergence.

Excluded Elements

If a singularity cannot be avoided, the following technique can be used to improve convergence:

1. Mesh the close vicinity of the singularity with small elements, which can be done using the Isolate for Exclusion Auto GEM Control.
2. When setting up the analysis, request that those elements be excluded from the convergence process.

Collectively, this technique is called *excluding the elements*.

Use the following steps to exclude elements from convergence:

1. Once the loads and constraints have been set up, expand ▦ (Control) and click ▦ (Isolate for Exclusion) in the *AutoGEM* area of the *Refine Model* tab to open the Isolate for Exclusion Control dialog box, as shown in Figure 3–20.

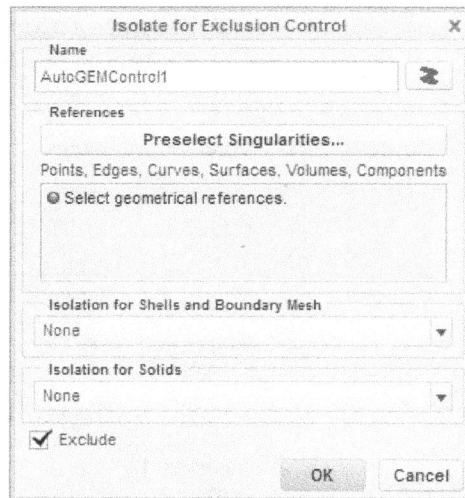

Figure 3–20

2. Manually select the singularities or click **Preselect Singularities** to have Creo Simulate detect the potential singularities automatically.
3. Based on the dimensions of your model, enter the *Maximum Element Size* for the isolation. The Isolate for Exclusion Control dialog box should display similar to the one shown in Figure 3–21. Close the dialog box.

© 2017, ASCENT - Center for Technical Knowledge®

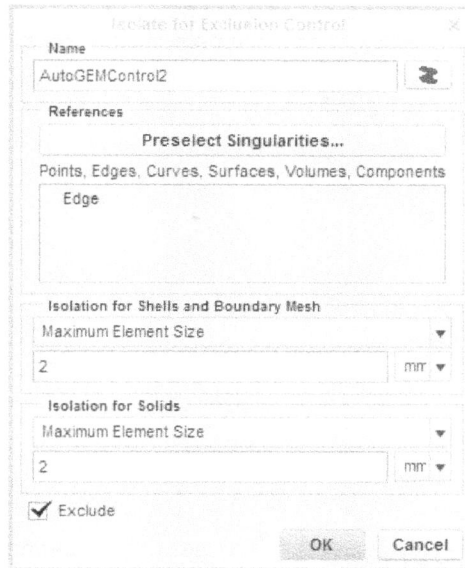

Figure 3–21

4. To highlight the isolating elements in red when meshing the model (as shown in Figure 3–22), select **Info>Isolating Elements** in the AutoGEM dialog box.

Figure 3–22

5. When setting up the analysis, in the *Excluded Elements* tab, select **Exclude Elements** as shown in Figure 3–23, and select other options as needed.

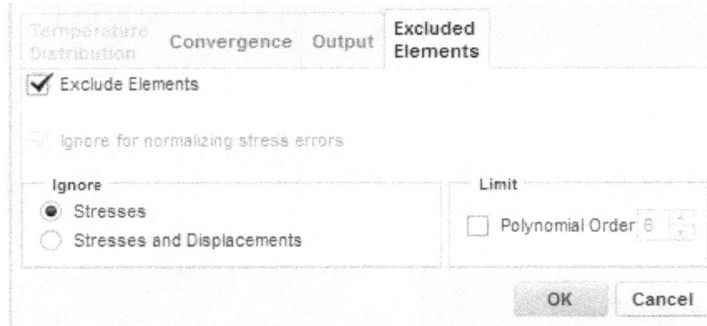

Figure 3–23

Guidelines

The general guidelines for improving convergence and obtaining more reliable analysis results are as follows:

- Spread the load or constraint over a larger area. Avoid using point or line loads and constraints in solid models.

- Prefer the use of soft and flexible supports over rigid constraints.

- If possible, alter the geometry to smooth sharp reentrant corners or other geometrical discontinuities. It is recommended that you use fillets.

- In models that still have singularities, use excluded elements in the analysis.

© 2017, ASCENT - Center for Technical Knowledge®

Practice 3a

Stress Analysis of a Crank

Practice Objectives

- Create multiple load sets.
- Apply pin constraints.
- Apply a bearing load.
- Apply a moment load using the **Total Load at Point** option.

In this practice, you will analyze the crank part shown in Figure 3–24 for two load cases:

- **Bending load case:** A force of 500N is applied to the hole in the upper boss, acting in-plane of the crank.

- **Torsional load case:** A twisting moment of 10,000 Nmm is applied to the upper boss.

The part is constrained by a pin support in the lower boss and by two bushing supports at the ends of the lower rod, as shown in Figure 3–24. This way, the lower beam of the part is not constrained against rotation at its ends, similar to a simply supported beam.

Figure 3–24

Modeling Tasks

Task 1 - Open the model.

1. Open **crank.prt** in Creo Parametric. The part displays as shown in Figure 3–25.

Figure 3–25

2. Ensure that the unit system is set to **mmNs**.

3. Switch to the Creo Simulate environment.

Task 2 - Apply the material.

In this task, you will select the material for the part.

1. In the *Home* tab, click ⬒ (Materials). The Materials dialog box opens as shown in Figure 3–26.

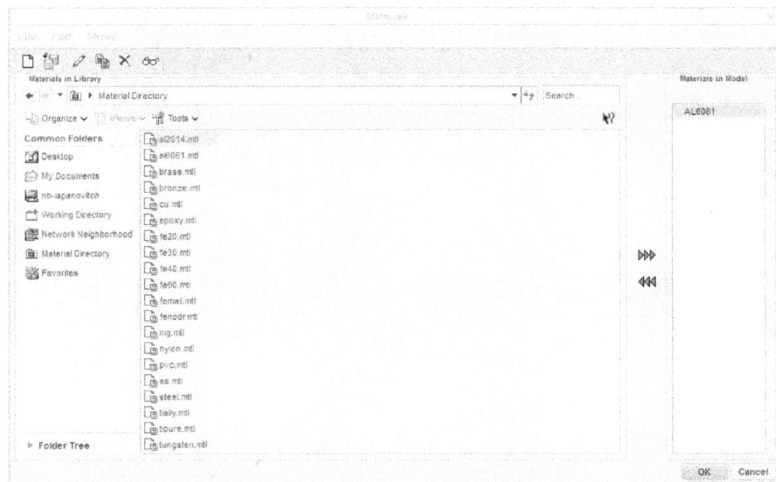

Figure 3–26

© 2017, ASCENT - Center for Technical Knowledge®

The model's material should be as stated.

2. In the *Materials in Library* area, select **STEEL**.

3. Click ▶▶▶ (Add Material) to transfer **STEEL** to the *Materials in Model* area.

4. Select **Edit>Properties** to check the material properties.

The HS-low-alloy steel (STEEL) has the following default material properties:

- Poisson's ratio = 0.27

- Young's modulus = 199948 MPa

- Coeff of thermal expansion = 1.17e-5 /C

- Density = 7.82708e-9 tonne/mm^3

5. Click **OK** to close the Materials dialog box.

6. In the *Home* tab, click 🖑 (Material Assignment). The Material Assignment dialog box opens as shown in Figure 3–27.

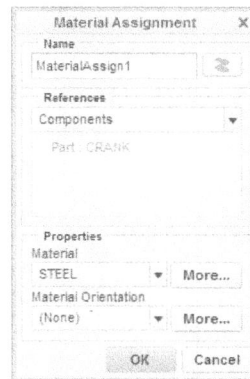

Figure 3–27

7. Note that the material **STEEL** has automatically been assigned to the part.

8. Click **OK** to close the Material Assignment dialog box.

Task 3 - Mesh the model.

1. In the Refine Model tab, click 🎛 (AutoGEM). The AutoGEM dialog box opens as shown in Figure 3–28.

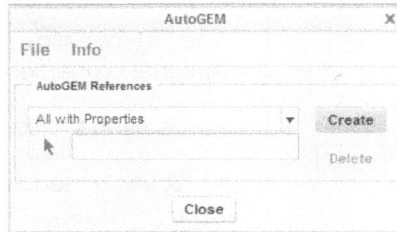

Figure 3–28

*The **All with Properties** option will automatically mesh all of the solid volumes in the model to which a material has been assigned.*

2. Expand the AutoGEM References drop-down list and select **All with Properties**.

3. Click **Create**.

4. Creo Simulate meshes the model and displays the AutoGEM Summary and Diagnostics dialog boxes. Note that AutoGEM created approximately 1030 tetra elements.

5. Close both the AutoGEM Summary and Diagnostics dialog boxes, but do not close the AutoGEM dialog box. The model displays as shown in Figure 3–29.

Figure 3–29

6. Click 🔩 (Simulation Display) in the floating toolbar. The Simulation Display dialog box opens.

7. Select the *Modeling Entities* tab and clear the **Material Assignments** option to hide the material assignment icon.

© 2017, ASCENT - Center for Technical Knowledge®

8. Select the *Mesh* tab and clear the **Mesh Points** option in the *Mesh Entities* area as shown in Figure 3–30.

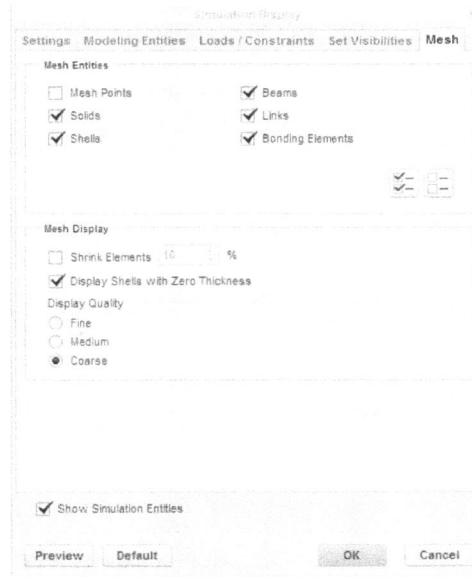

Figure 3–30

9. Click **OK** to close the Simulation Display dialog box. The model displays as shown in Figure 3–31. Rotate the model and review the elements in various areas of the model.

Figure 3–31

10. Save the mesh and close the AutoGEM dialog box.

Task 4 - Create load sets.

In this task, you will create two load sets for the two load cases in this analysis.

1. Expand the *Loads* panel in the *Home* tab, as shown in Figure 3–32.

Figure 3–32

2. Select **Load Sets**. The Load Sets dialog box opens as shown in Figure 3–33.

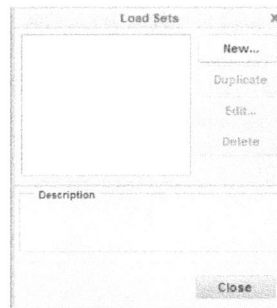

Figure 3–33

3. Click **New**. The Load Set Definition dialog box opens as shown in Figure 3–34.

© 2017, ASCENT - Center for Technical Knowledge®

Figure 3–34

4. In the *Name* field, enter **bending** and click **OK**.

5. Repeat Steps 3 and 4 and create another load set named **torsion**.

6. Click **Close** to close the Load Sets dialog box.

Task 5 - Apply a bending load.

In this task, you will apply a bearing load on the hole in the upper boss, acting in-plane of the part. The bearing load has a resultant force in a specified direction. The bearing load is applied normal to the surface in a non-uniform distribution, such as if a shaft placed in the hole would exert on the hole surface.

Ensure that the sketched points are datum points, not construction points

7. In the Refine Model tab, select ⬚ (Sketch) and sketch two datum points with datum plane FRONT as the sketching plane and datum plane RIGHT as the reference plane. Sketch the first datum point at the center of the arm hole (add the edge of the hole as a reference to enable automatic snapping to the center) and the second datum point at the dimensions shown in Figure 3–35. These points define the bearing load direction.

Figure 3–35

In the FRONT view, the model displays as shown in Figure 3–36.

Figure 3–36

8. In the *Home* tab, click ⬚ (Bearing). The Bearing Load dialog box opens as shown in Figure 3–37.

Figure 3–37

9. In the *Name* field, enter **bend_load**.

© 2017, ASCENT - Center for Technical Knowledge®

10. In the *Member of Set* field, select **bending**.

11. Select the hole shown in Figure 3–38.

Select this hole

Figure 3–38

12. Expand the Force drop-down list and select **Dir Points & Mag**. The Bearing Load dialog box opens as shown in Figure 3–39.

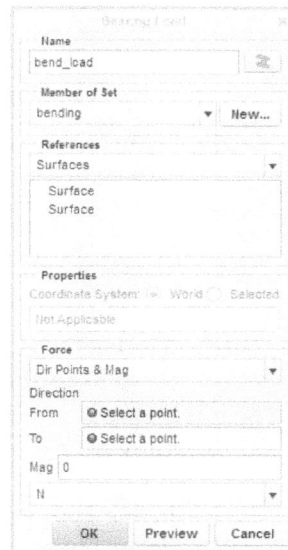

Figure 3–39

13. In the *Direction* area, for *From*, select the point at the hole's center. For *To*, select the second point to define direction for the bearing load.

14. In the *Mag* field, enter **500**.

15. Click **Preview** to display the bearing load distribution, as shown in Figure 3–40.

Figure 3–40

16. Click **OK**. The model displays as shown in Figure 3–41.

Figure 3–41

17. Use the Simulation Display dialog box to hide the bending load set.

Task 6 - Apply a torsional load.

In this task, you will apply a twisting moment on the hole in the upper boss. The moment simulates the load exerted by a shaft placed in the hole and torqued about the X-axis of the WCS.

1. In the *Home* tab, click ⊢ (Force/Moment). The Force/Moment Load dialog box opens as shown in Figure 3–42.

© 2017, ASCENT - Center for Technical Knowledge®

Figure 3–42

2. In the *Name* field, enter **twist_load**.

3. In the *Member of Set* field, select **torsion**.

4. Select the hole in the upper boss (the same hole that you selected when applying a bearing load). The Force/Moment dialog box opens as shown in Figure 3–43.

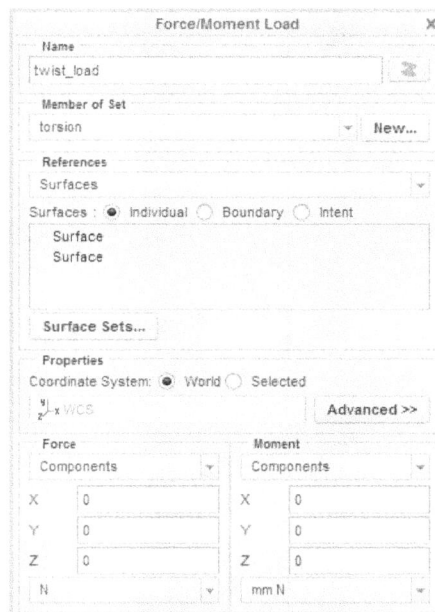

Figure 3–43

Note that a moment in a solid model must be applied as a collection of translational forces that are statically equivalent (i.e., exert the same effect) to the concentrated moment at a point. In Creo Simulate, this can be done using the **Total Load at Point** option.

5. Click **Advanced**.

6. Expand the Distribution drop-down list and select **Total Load at Point**. The Force/Moment dialog box opens as shown in Figure 3–44.

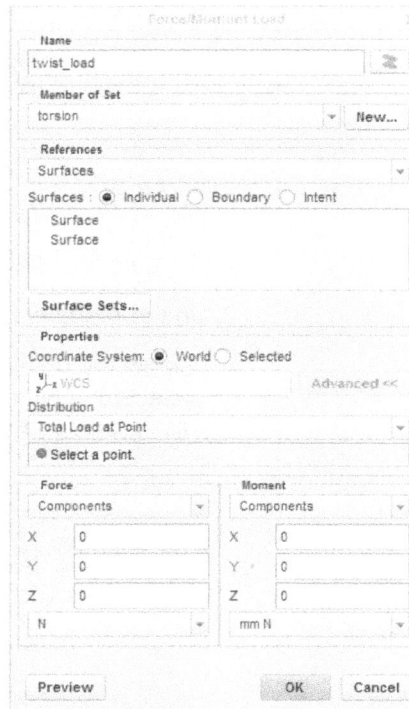

Figure 3–44

7. Select the point at the center of the hole.

8. In the *Moment* area, in the *X* field, enter **10000**.

© 2017, ASCENT - Center for Technical Knowledge®

The load distribution is statically equivalent to the 10000 mmN moment applied at the point at the center of the hole.

9. Click **Preview** to display the load distribution, as shown in Figure 3–45.

Figure 3–45

10. Click **OK**. The model displays as shown in Figure 3–46.

Figure 3–46

11. Use the Simulation Display dialog box to hide the torsion load set.

Task 7 - Apply the constraints.

In this task, you will constrain the movement of the lower boss and of the rod, as shown in Figure 3–47.

Figure 3–47

The boss is supported by a shaft and the rod is supported by two bushings. Both supports constrain translational motions, but permit rotation of the cylindrical surfaces about their respective axes. This type of support can be modeled using the Pin type of constraint.

1. Click ⚬ (Pin). The Pin Constraint dialog box opens.

2. In the *Name* field, enter **rod**.

3. Select the cylindrical surface of the rod shown in Figure 3–48, constrain the axial translation, and leave the rotation free, as shown in Figure 3–48.

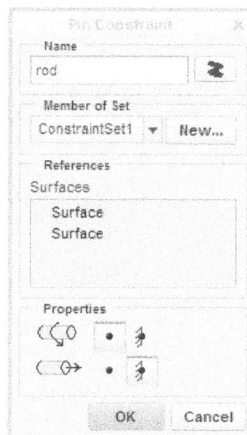

Figure 3–48

© 2017, ASCENT - Center for Technical Knowledge®

4. Click **OK**. The pin constraint displays as shown in Figure 3–49.

Figure 3–49

5. Click ⚷ (Pin) again. Select the hole surface in the lower boss shown in Figure 3–50. In the *Name* field, enter **boss**. Constrain the axial translation and leave the rotation free, as shown in Figure 3–50.

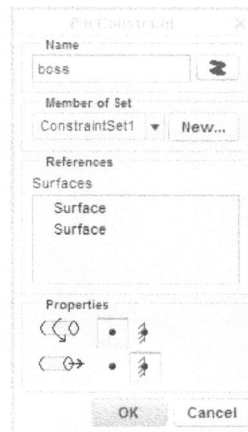

Figure 3–50

6. Click **OK**. The model displays as shown in Figure 3–51.

Figure 3–51

Analysis Tasks

Task 8 - Set up and run a Multi-Pass Adaptive analysis.

1. Create a new static analysis and name it **crank**.

2. Select both the **bending/CRANK** and **torsion/CRANK** load sets in the *Load Set / Component* area.

3. For the *Percent Convergence*, enter **10**. In the *Maximum Polynomial Order* field, enter **9**. The Static Analysis Definition dialog box opens as shown in Figure 3–52.

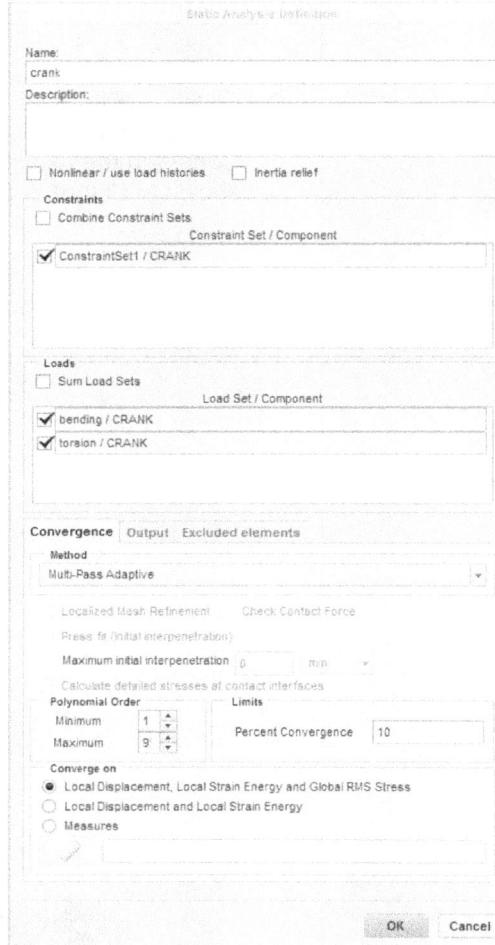

Figure 3–52

You created and saved the mesh for the part in Task 3 of Modeling Tasks.

4. Verify that the run settings are set so that the elements will be used from the existing mesh file. In the *Memory Allocation* field, enter **512**.

© 2017, ASCENT - Center for Technical Knowledge®

The recommended memory allocation is 1/2 the RAM of your computer.

5. Run the analysis. Note the warning in the Diagnostics box that states "Convergence was not obtained because the maximum polynomial order of 9 was reached". Also note the second warning in the Diagnostics box regarding the local reaction data. The warning displays because Creo Simulate uses the Cylindrical coordinate system on Pin constraints and the reaction forces could not be computed.

In the following tasks, you will explore the elements that have not converged.

Task 9 - Display the non-converged elements.

1. In the Analyses and Design Studies dialog box, click (Review Results).

2. In the Result Window Definition dialog box, check both **bending** and **torsion** load sets, then expand the Quantity drop-down list and select **P-Level**, as shown in Figure 3–53.

Figure 3–53

3. Click **OK and Show**. The P-Level plot displays as shown in Figure 3–54.

Figure 3–54

Generally, convergence is more difficult to obtain for a model with several load cases, since the optimal P-Level map for one load case might not be optimal for another load case, and vice versa.

Examine the P-Level plot, specifically elements with their edges colored red (P-Level 9) and orange (P-Level 8). These are the elements that are most likely to have not converged. Note that red and orange elements are not concentrated over one or a few small areas in the model, which would be the visual cue that non-convergence might have been due to stress singularities. Rather, the red and orange elements are spread over large areas in the upper arm of the crank, and near the rod.

Therefore, the non-convergence might be attributed to the elements being too large or too distorted. In the next task, you will refine the mesh to obtain convergence.

4. Exit the results environment and close the Analyses and Design Studies dialog box.

© 2017, ASCENT - Center for Technical Knowledge®

Mesh Refinement Tasks

Creo Simulate has a variety of tools that enable you to control the mesh in your model. These tools are the AutoGEM Controls, and are located in the AutoGEM section of the *Refine Model* tab, as shown in Figure 3-55.

Figure 3–55

The AutoGEM controls, however, are designed for fine-tuning your mesh in local areas, and might not be convenient to use if mesh needs to be changed throughout the entire model.

In this task, you will refine the mesh through the entire model, by adjusting the geometrical limits on the element size and shape.

Task 10 - Adjust the AutoGEM Settings.

1. In the *Refine Model* tab, expand the AutoGEM drop-down list and select **Settings**, as shown in Figure 3–56.

Figure 3–56

2. The AutoGEM Settings dialog box opens. Select the *Limits* tab, and change **Edge max** and **Face max** angles to **165**, and **Edge min** and **Face min** angles to **15**, as shown in Figure 3–57.

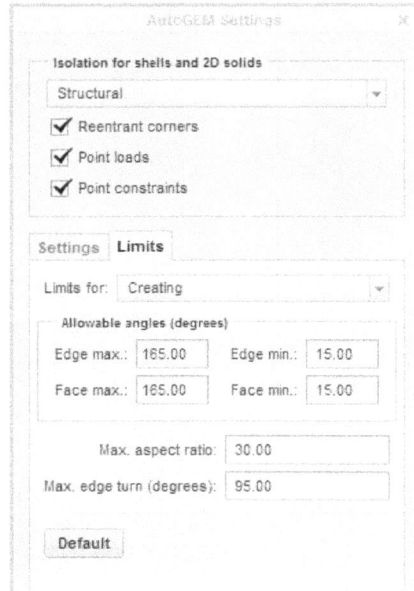

Figure 3–57

3. Click **OK** to finish.

Task 11 - Re-mesh the model.

---

1. Click ⬚ (Mesh). The Question box displays as shown in Figure 3–58.

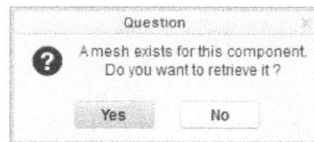

Figure 3–58

2. Click **No**. The AutoGEM dialog box opens as shown in Figure 3–59.

© 2017, ASCENT - Center for Technical Knowledge®

Figure 3–59

The mesh originally created in Task 3 contained approximately 1030 elements.

3. Click **Create**. Once meshing is finished, note that AutoGEM creates approximately 1983 tetra elements - almost twice as much as with the default meshing settings.

4. Close the AutoGEM Summary and Diagnostics dialog boxes. The model displays with loads and constraints hidden, as shown in Figure 3–60.

Figure 3–60

5. Click **Close** to close the AutoGEM dialog box and save the mesh.

Task 12 - Re-run the analysis.

1. Run the **crank** analysis again and wait until it completes.

2. Click ▤ (Status) in the Analyses and Design Studies dialog box to display the Run Status window. Scroll down and note that the analysis has converged, as shown in Figure 3–61.

```
RMS Stress Error Estimates:

Load Set              Stress Error    % of Max Prin Str
-----------------     ------------    ------------------
bending               5.76e-01         0.2% of  2.36e+02
torsion               6.19e-01         0.8% of  8.10e+01

Resource Check                          (20:39:35)
    Elapsed Time    (sec):     280.33
    CPU Time        (sec):     218.60
    Memory Usage     (kb):     990873
    Wrk Dir Dsk Usage (kb):   1856314

The analysis converged to within 10% on
edge displacement, element strain energy,
and global RMS stress.
```

Figure 3–61

3. Close the Run Status window.

Results Tasks

Task 13 - Animate the deformation for the bending load case.

1. Click ▤ (Review Results) in the Analyses and Design Studies dialog box. The Result Window Definition dialog box opens.

2. In the *Name* field, enter **deform_bending**.

3. Clear the **torsion** load set option.

4. Expand the Quantity tab drop-down list and select **Displacement**. The Result Window Definition dialog box opens as shown in Figure 3–62.

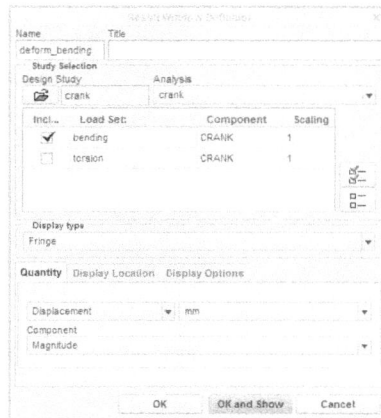

Figure 3–62

© 2017, ASCENT - Center for Technical Knowledge®

5. Select the *Display Options* tab. Select the **Deformed**, **Overlay Undeformed**, **Show Element Edges**, and **Animate** options. In the *Scaling* field, enter **20**, as shown in Figure 3–63.

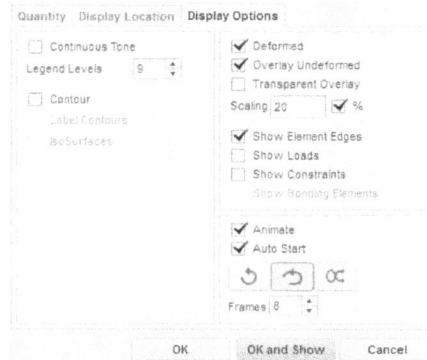

Figure 3–63

6. Click **OK and Show**. The Displacement Magnitude result plot is displayed and animated.

7. Zoom in on the rod. Note that the rod's rotation is not restricted, as if it was supported by sleeve bearings or bushings. This results from applying the Pin constraint to the rod's surface.

8. Stop the animation at Frame 5. The result plot displays as shown in Figure 3–64.

Figure 3–64

Task 14 - Animate the deformation for the torsional load case.

1. In the *Home* tab, click 📋 (Copy). The Result Window Definition dialog box opens.

2. In the *Name* field, enter **deform_torsion**.

3. Clear the **bending** load set and select the **torsion** load set. The Result Window Definition dialog box opens as shown in Figure 3–65.

Figure 3–65

4. Click **OK**.

5. In the View tab, Click 🔲 (Show). In the Display Result Window dialog box, clear **deform_bending** and select **deform_torsion** as shown in Figure 3–66.

© 2017, ASCENT - Center for Technical Knowledge®

Figure 3–66

Did the deformation display as you expected?

6. Click **OK**. The deformation plot for the torsional load case is displayed and animated.

Task 15 - Create result windows for the von Mises stress.

---

1. In the *Home* tab, click ▤ (New). Select the **crank** design study in the Design Study for Result Window dialog box that opens and click **Open**. The Result Window Definition dialog box opens as shown in Figure 3–67.

Figure 3–67

2. In the *Name* field, enter **stress_bending**.

3. Leave the **bending** load set selected and clear the **torsion** load set.

4. Select the *Display Options* tab. Select the **Deformed** and **Overlay Undeformed** options.

---

5. Click **OK**.

6. Repeat Steps 1 through 5, naming the window **stress_torsion** and selecting the **torsion** load set instead of the bending load set.

Task 16 - Display the stress results.

1. In the View tab, click ⬚ (Show). In the Display Result Window dialog box that opens, select **stress_bending** and clear all of the other windows.

2. Click **OK**. The von Mises stress plot for the bending load case is displayed as shown in Figure 3–68.

Figure 3–68

3. Locate the area of the maximum stress, as shown in Figure 3–69.

© 2017, ASCENT - Center for Technical Knowledge®

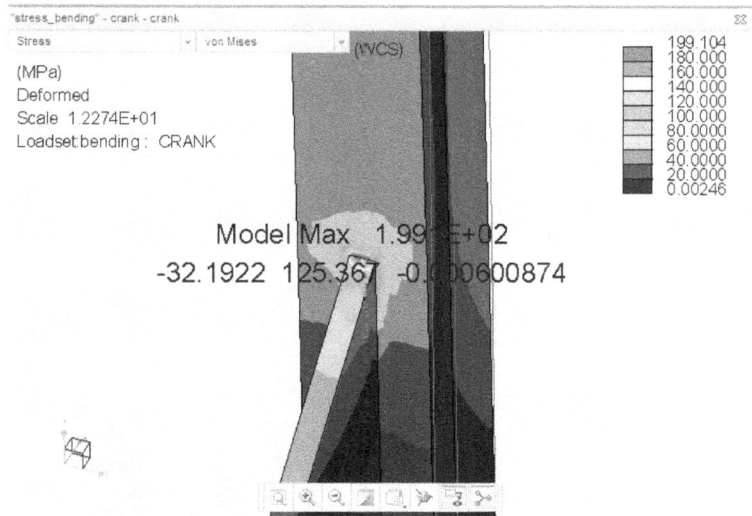

Figure 3–69

4. In the *View* tab, click 🖼 (Show). In the Display Result Window dialog box, select **stress_torsion** and clear all of the other windows.

5. Click **OK**. The von Mises stress plot for the torsional load case is displayed as shown in Figure 3–70.

Figure 3–70

6. Locate the area of the maximum stress, as shown in Figure 3–71.

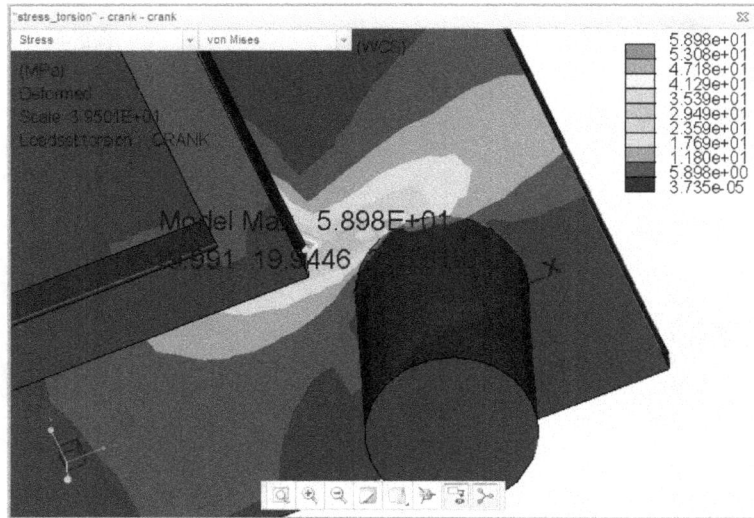

Figure 3–71

Note that the maximum stress in the torsional load case displays at a different location than in the bending load case.

Task 17 - Display the stress results for the combined load case.

In this task, you will create and display a von Mises stress result plot for the combined load case, in which both the bending and twisting loads act together.

1. In the *Home* tab, click 🗐 (Copy). The Result Window Definition dialog box opens.

2. In the *Name* field, enter **stress_combined**.

© 2017, ASCENT - Center for Technical Knowledge®

3. Select both the **bending** and **torsion** load sets. The Result Window Definition dialog box opens as shown in Figure 3–72.

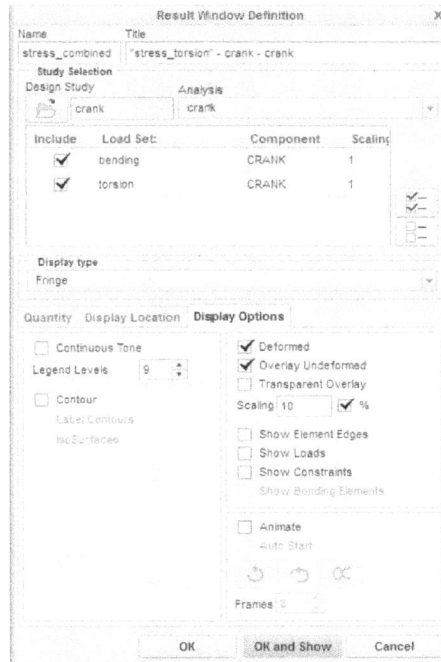

Figure 3–72

4. Click **OK**.

5. In the *View* tab, click 🖳 (Show). In the Display Result Window dialog box that opens, select **stress_combined** and clear all of the other windows.

6. Click **OK**. The von Mises stress plot for the combined load case is displayed as shown in Figure 3–73.

Figure 3–73

7. Examine the stress results. Locate the area of maximum stress.

8. Exit the Results. Save and close the model in Creo Parametric.

© 2017, ASCENT - Center for Technical Knowledge®

Practice 3b

Cyclic Symmetry Constraints

Practice Objectives

- Apply cyclic constraints to a model.
- Analyze a model using cyclic constraints.

In this practice, you will use cyclic symmetry constraints to set up, run, and analyze the fan shown in Figure 3–74. The fan is rotating at 300rpm (5 rev/sec), and the fan blades are subjected to air pressure that varies linearly along the blade length, from 0.0008psi at the tip to 0psi at the center of the fan.

You can only use cyclic symmetry constraints with solid and shell elements.

Figure 3–74

The intent of the cyclic symmetry constraint is to reduce the amount of geometry being analyzed, thus reducing the amount of time required to solve the analysis.

A model with cyclic constraints should be cyclically symmetric so that the entire model can be reproduced by rotating the symmetric section about an axis. The angle between cuts must equal $360°$ divided by the number of instances (the fan example is divided by ten). You will analyze the cyclic instance of the fan shown in Figure 3–75.

Figure 3–75

Note that both the geometry and boundary conditions must meet the criteria of cyclic symmetry. If the constraints or loading are not repeated about the axis of rotation by the same number of repetitions as the geometry, the results will be invalid.

Modeling Tasks

Task 1 - Open the model.

1. Open **fan.asm** in Creo Parametric and hide the datum planes. The model displays as shown in Figure 3–76.

Figure 3–76

2. Ensure that the unit system is set to **IPS**.

3. Switch to the Creo Simulate environment.

For this practice, the FEA model has been de-featured (e.g., various rounds have been removed).

The material properties should be as stated.

Task 2 - Apply the material.

1. Assign **AL6061** to both parts.

   The following values are the default material properties for the AL6061 aluminum alloy:

   - Poisson's ratio = 0.3
   - Young's modulus = 1e+07 psi
   - Density = 0.0002536 lbf sec^2/in^4

2. Using the Simulation Display functionality, hide the **Material Assignment** icons.

Task 3 - Apply a centrifugal load.

The fan is rotating at a high speed (5 rev/sec equals 31.4 rad/sec) about the Y-axis. In this task, you will apply a centrifugal load to the model to simulate this rotational loading.

1. In the *Loads* area, click ⊞ (Centrifugal). The Centrifugal Load dialog box opens as shown in Figure 3–77.

© 2017, ASCENT - Center for Technical Knowledge®

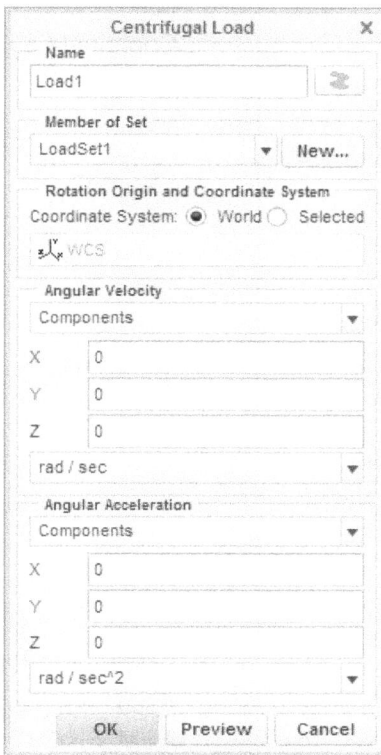

Figure 3–77

2. In the *Name* field, enter **c_force**.

3. For *Member of Set*, accept the default **LoadSet1** option.

31.4rad/sec = 5 rev/sec

4. In the *Angular Velocity* area, in the Y-field, enter **31.4**.

5. Click **OK**. The applied load in the model is represented as a vector at the origin (0,0,0), as shown in Figure 3–78.

Figure 3–78

Task 4 - Create a cylindrical coordinate system.

In this task, you will create a cylindrical coordinate system. The radial direction of this coordinate system will be used later to define the air pressure variation along the length of the fan blade.

1. In the *Refine Model* tab, click ⁴⁄₂✕ˣ (Coordinate System).

2. In the Select a Component box that opens, click **OK**. The Coordinate System dialog box opens as shown in Figure 3–79.

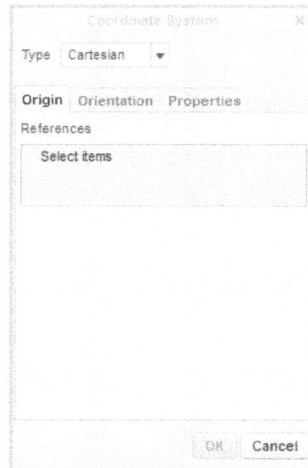

Figure 3–79

3. Expand the Type drop-down list and select **Cylindrical**.

4. Select the datum planes **ASM_RIGHT**, **ASM_TOP**, and **ASM_FRONT** (press and hold <Ctrl> to select multiples) to place the origin of the coordinate system at the intersection of the three planes. The Coordinate System dialog box opens as shown in Figure 3–80.

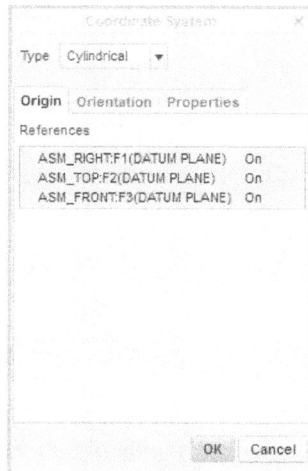

Figure 3–80

© 2017, ASCENT - Center for Technical Knowledge®

5. Select the *Orientation* tab. Use the ASM_TOP plane to orient the Z-axis of the new coordinate system and ASM_FRONT plane to orient the T = 0 axis. The Coordinate System dialog box opens as shown in Figure 3–81.

Figure 3–81

6. Click **OK** to finish. The new coordinate system ACS0 displays at the WCS origin, as shown in Figure 3–82.

Cylindrical coordinate system

Figure 3–82

Task 5 - Apply pressure load.

The fan blade is loaded with the air pressure that varies linearly along the length of the blade. In this task, you will apply a non-uniform pressure load to simulate the air pressure.

1. In the *Home* tab, click ⊨ (Pressure). The Pressure Load dialog box opens as shown in Figure 3–83.

Figure 3–83

2. In the *Name* field, enter **pressure**.

3. For *Member of Set*, accept the default **LoadSet1** option.

4. Select the blade surface that is opposite to the Y-axis side, as shown in Figure 3–84.

Figure 3–84

5. Click **Advanced**.

6. Expand the Spatial Variation drop-down list and select **Function of Coordinates**.

© 2017, ASCENT - Center for Technical Knowledge®

7. Click $f(x)$ (Function). The Functions dialog box opens as shown in Figure 3–85.

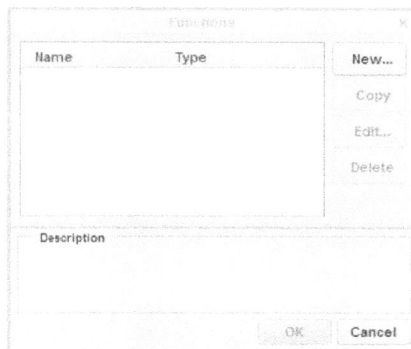

Figure 3–85

8. Click New. The Function Definition dialog box opens as shown in Figure 3–86.

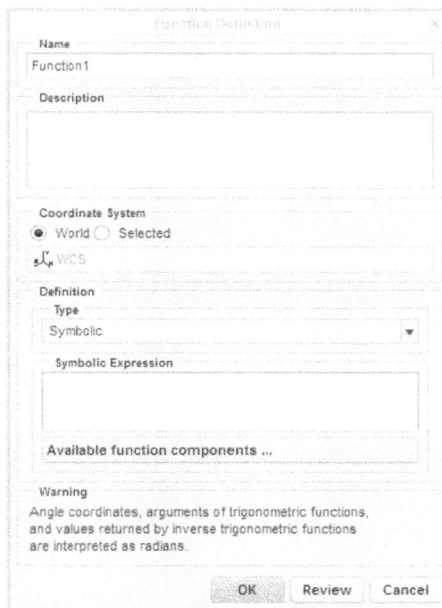

Figure 3–86

9. In the *Name* field, enter **linear**.

10. In the *Coordinate System* area, select the **Selected** option, and select the **ACS0** coordinate system.

11. Expand the Type drop-down list and select **Symbolic**.

12. Click **Available function components**. The Symbolic Options dialog box opens as shown in Figure 3–87.

Figure 3–87

13. In the *Variables* area, double-click on the R and click **Close**. The Function Definition dialog box opens as shown in Figure 3–88.

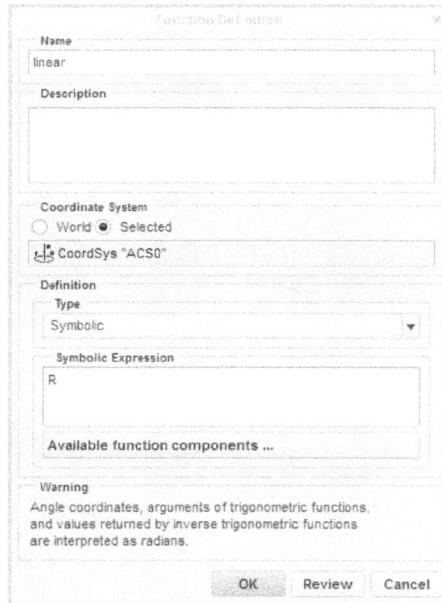

Figure 3–88

© 2017, ASCENT - Center for Technical Knowledge®

14. Click **Review**. The warning message appears as shown in Figure 3-89.

Figure 3–89

15. Click **OK** to close the message box. The Graph Function dialog box opens as shown in Figure 3–90.

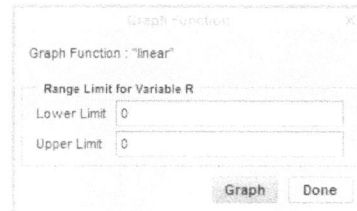

Figure 3–90

16. For the *Upper Limit*, enter **100**, and click **Graph**. The Graphtool window displays as shown in Figure 3–91.

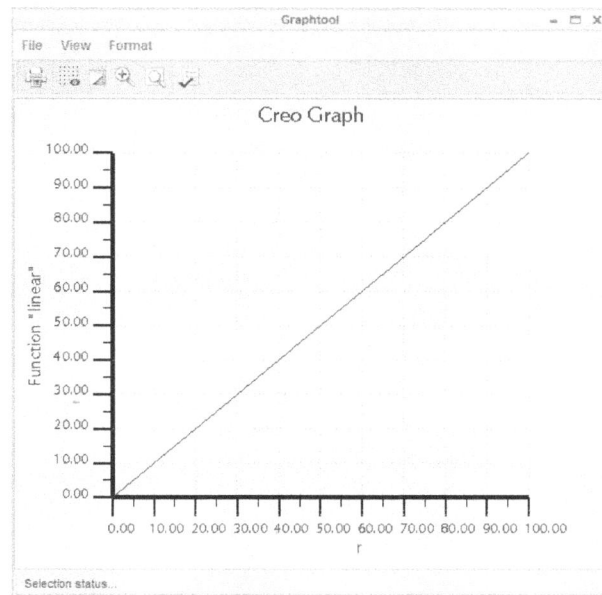

Figure 3–91

17. Verify that the function is linear and close the Graphtool window.

18. In the Graph Function dialog box, click **Done**.

19. In the Function Definition dialog box, click **OK**.

20. In the Functions dialog box, click **OK**.

*The fan radius is 20.76in and the air pressure at the tip of the blade is 0.0008psi. Given the linear R function, the value to be entered is **0.0008/20.76 = 0.00003846**.*

21. In the *Value* field, enter **0.00003846**. The Pressure Load dialog box opens as shown in Figure 3–92.

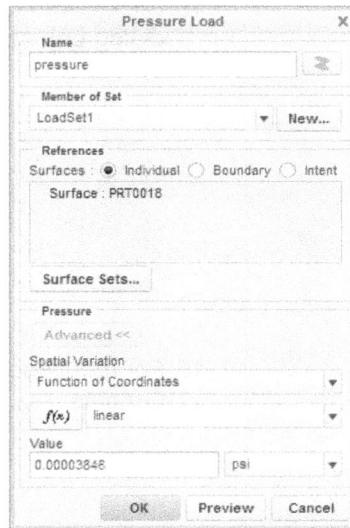

Figure 3–92

22. Click **Preview**. The model displays as shown in Figure 3–93.

Figure 3–93

Note that the pressure increases linearly with the length of the blade.

23. Click **OK**. The model displays as shown in Figure 3–94.

Figure 3–94

© 2017, ASCENT - Center for Technical Knowledge®

Task 6 - Apply the constraints.

Apply cyclic constraints to the cut faces of the fan and fully constrain the fan hole surface.

1. In the *Home* tab, expand the *Constraints* group and click

   ⫴ (Symmetry). The Symmetry Constraint dialog box opens as shown in Figure 3–95.

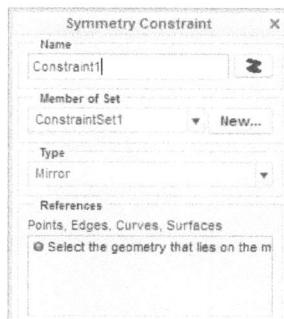

Figure 3–95

2. For the *Name*, enter **cyclic_const**.

3. Expand the Type drop-down list and select **Cyclic**.

4. Select the fan's First Side cut surface, as shown in Figure 3–96.

5. Select the fan's Second Side cut surface, as shown in Figure 3–96.

For the first or second side, you can select either side of the fan's cut surfaces.

Figure 3–96

6. Click **OK** to finish. The model displays as shown in Figure 3–97.

Figure 3–97

7. Click (Displacement) and constrain the fan's hole surface (all of the translations), as shown in Figure 3–98.

Figure 3–98

Analysis Tasks

Task 7 - Solve the model using the Single-Pass Adaptive convergence option.

1. Set up a Single-Pass Adaptive analysis. For *Name*, type **fan**.

2. Run the analysis.

3. In the Analyses and Design Studies dialog box, click (Status). The Run Status window opens. Extract the RMS Stress Error Estimates as shown in Figure 3–99.

```
RMS Stress Error Estimates:

Load Set          Stress Error    % of Max Prin Str
---------------   ------------    -----------------
LoadSet1           1.02e+01        2.1% of 4.79e+02
```

Figure 3–99

© 2017, ASCENT - Center for Technical Knowledge®

Results Tasks

Task 8 - Display the results.

In this task you will create and display color plots for von Mises stress and the deflection. Animate these plots to display the effect of the loading on the model.

1. Create and display a color plot for the von Mises stress. The von Mises fringe plot displays as shown in Figure 3–100.

Figure 3–100

Locate the maximum von Mises stress. Note that the maximum stress displays at the junction of the blade and shaft, which is a re-entrant corner. This is expected, considering the load type and the removal of the blend feature. Examine the stress in other parts of your model. Create sections of the model in high stress areas.

2. Animate the von Mises stress window and play the animation frames. Frame 5 is shown in Figure 3–101.

Figure 3–101

Task 9 - Create deflection windows.

1. Create and examine a Displacement Magnitude deflection window.

2. Create deflection windows for the X-, Y-, and Z-displacement components and animate the windows.

3. Note the value of deflection for each component.

4. Exit the Results. Save and close the model in Creo Parametric.

© 2017, ASCENT - Center for Technical Knowledge®

Practice 3c

Surface Regions

Practice Objective

- Use Surface Regions to apply loads and constraints.

In this practice, you will analyze a mooring chock that is used for fastening ships to piers, etc. The model is shown in Figure 3–102. The chock is welded into the hull of the ship over an area 1" wide going around the outside surface, and loaded by a mooring line over a 2" area, as shown in Figure 3–102.

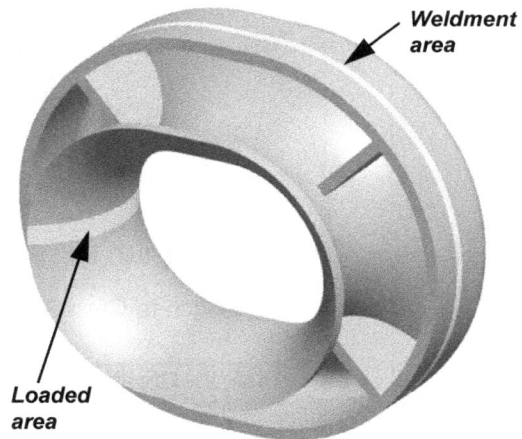

Figure 3–102

You will use surface regions to apply the loads and constraints over the areas shown in Figure 3–102.

Modeling Tasks

Task 1 - Open the model.

1. Open **chock.prt** in Creo Parametric. The part displays as shown in Figure 3–103.

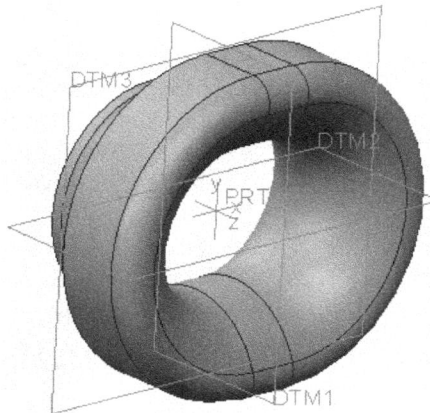

Figure 3–103

2. Ensure that the unit system is set to **IPS**.

3. Switch to Creo Simulate.

Task 2 - Create boundary curves for the weldment region.

1. In the *Refine Model* tab, Click ▱ (Plane) and create a DTM4 plane parallel to datum plane DTM3 at a distance of **3.5**, as shown in Figure 3–104.

Figure 3–104

© 2017, ASCENT - Center for Technical Knowledge®

2. Click ▱ (Plane) again and create DTM5 plane parallel to datum plane DTM4 at a distance of **1**, as shown in Figure 3–105.

Figure 3–105

3. Select the DTM4 plane and click ⤾ (Intersect) in the Editing section of the *Refine Model* tab. The Surface Intersection dashboard opens.

4. Hold down <Ctrl> and select four surfaces on the outside of the chock, as shown in Figure 3–106.

Figure 3–106

5. Click ✓ (Apply Changes) to finish. The new datum curve Intersect_1 displays in the model, as shown in Figure 3–107.

Figure 3–107

6. Repeat Steps 3 to 5, now using the DTM5 plane. The model displays as shown in Figure 3–108.

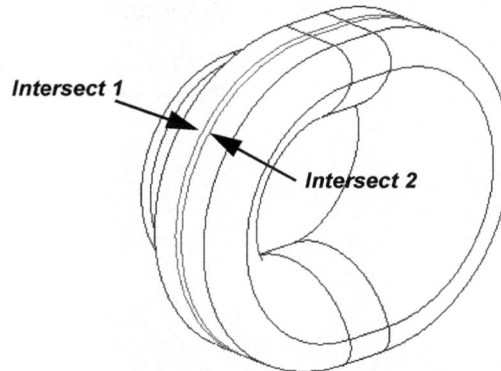

Figure 3–108

Task 3 - Create boundary curves for the loaded region.

1. In the *Refine Model* tab, click ⛫ (Sketch). Select the DTM1 plane as the Sketch Plane and DTM2 plane as the Reference Plane for the Top orientation. Ensure that the sketch viewing direction is toward the positive X-direction.

© 2017, ASCENT - Center for Technical Knowledge®

2. Sketch the profile shown in Figure 3–109.

Figure 3–109

3. Select the sketch and click ✎ (Project) in the Editing group. The Projected Curve dashboard displays.

4. Select the inside surface of the chock, toward the positive X-direction, as shown in Figure 3–110.

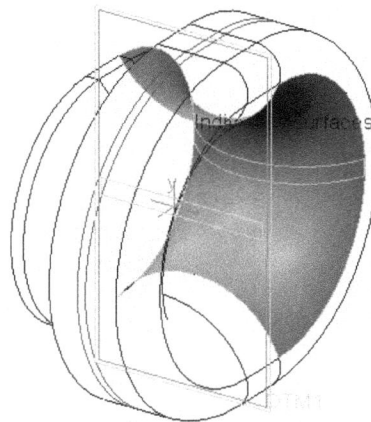

Figure 3–110

5. Click ✓ (Apply Changes) to finish. The new datum curve Project_1 displays in the model, as shown in Figure 3–111.

Figure 3–111

Task 4 - Create a surface region for the weldment constraint.

1. In the *Refine Model* tab, click ⬚ (Surface Region). The Surface Region dashboard opens as shown in Figure 3–112.

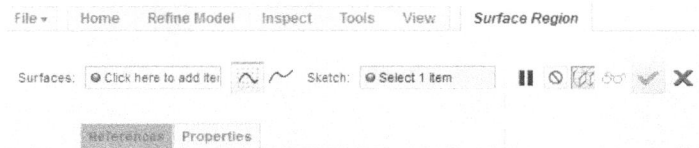

Figure 3–112

2. Select the *Surfaces* field. Hold down <Ctrl> and select four surfaces on the outside of the chock, as shown in Figure 3–113.

Figure 3–113

© 2017, ASCENT - Center for Technical Knowledge®

3. Click ◠ (Select Chain) in the dashboard.

4. Select the *Chain* field, and select the **Intersect_1** curve. The model displays as shown in Figure 3–114.

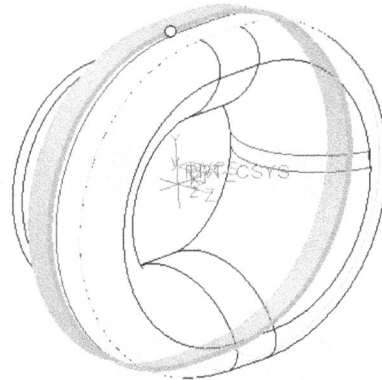

Figure 3–114

5. Click ✓ (Apply Changes) to finish. The new surface region Surface_Region_1 is created and added to the model tree.

6. Repeat Steps 2 to 6 using the curve Intersect_2. Two surface regions display in the Model Tree, as shown in Figure 3–115. Click the surface regions in the Model Tree to check how they highlight in the model.

Figure 3–115

Task 5 - Create a surface region for the load.

1. Using Task 4 as a guideline, create another surface region, now using **Project_1** and the surface shown in Figure 3–116.

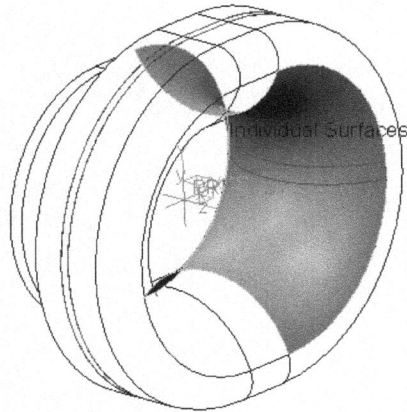

Figure 3–116

Task 6 - Apply the material.

The material properties should be as stated.

1. Assign **STEEL** to the part. The following values are the default material properties for the STEEL:
   - Poisson's ratio = **0.27**
   - Young's modulus = **2.9e+07 psi**
   - Density = **0.0007324 lbf sec^2/in^4**

2. Using the Simulation Display functionality, hide the **Material Assignment** icon.

Task 7 - Mesh the model.

1. In the *Refine Model* tab, click ▦ (AutoGEM). The AutoGEM dialog box opens as shown in Figure 3–117.

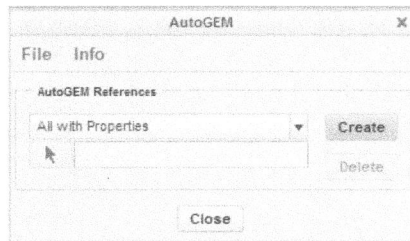

Figure 3–117

© 2017, ASCENT - Center for Technical Knowledge®

2. Expand the AutoGEM References drop-down list and select **All with Properties**.

3. Click **Create**.

4. Creo Simulate meshes the model and displays the AutoGEM Summary and Diagnostics dialog boxes.

5. Close both the AutoGEM Summary and Diagnostics dialog boxes, but do not close the AutoGEM dialog box. The model displays as shown in Figure 3–118.

Figure 3–118

6. Review the mesh. Save the mesh and close the AutoGEM dialog box.

Task 8 - Apply the constraints.

1. Fully constrain the weldment region (in all of the translations), as shown in Figure 3–119.

Figure 3–119

Task 9 - Apply the load.

The force exerted by the mooring line onto the chock is 100,000 lbs. The force is distributed accordingly to the half-sine law. The load is maximum in the middle of the loaded region, and zero at the ends of the loaded region.

1. In the Home tab, click ⊢ (Force/Moment).

2. In the *Name* field, enter **line_load**.

3. Select the surface region for the load as shown in Figure 3–120.

Figure 3–120

4. Click **Advanced**. The Force/Moment dialog box opens as shown in Figure 3–121.

© 2017, ASCENT - Center for Technical Knowledge®

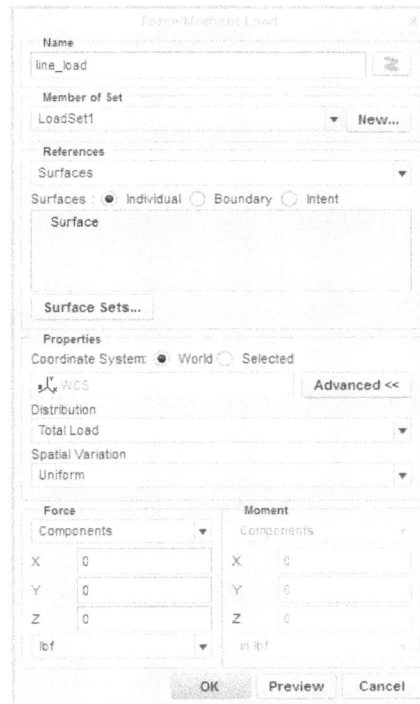

Figure 3–121

5. Expand the Spatial Variation drop-down list and select **Function of Coordinates**.

6. Click $f(x)$ (Function). The Functions dialog box opens.

7. Click **New**.

8. In the *Name* field, enter **halfsine**.

9. Expand the Type drop-down list and select **Table**.

10. In the *Row* field, select **Z**.

11. In the *Table* area, enter the tabular function as shown in Figure 3–122.

Figure 3–122

12. Click **Review** and close the warning box that opens. Click **Graph**. The Graphtool window displays as shown in Figure 3–123.

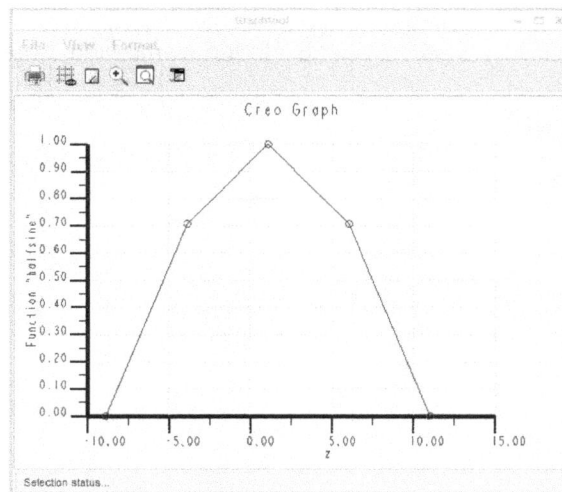

Figure 3–123

© 2017, ASCENT - Center for Technical Knowledge®

13. Verify the function and close the Graphtool window.

14. In the Graph Function dialog box, click **Done**.

15. In the Function Definition dialog box, click **OK**. .

16. In the Functions dialog box, click **OK**.

17. In the *X* field, enter **100000**. The Force/Moment Load dialog box opens as shown in Figure 3–124.

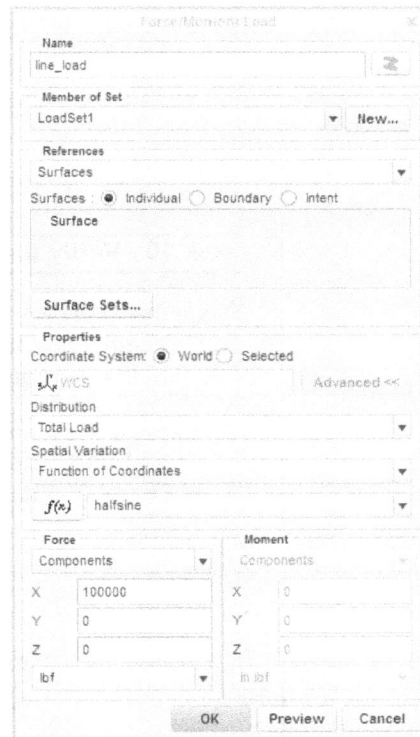

Figure 3–124

18. Click **OK**. The model displays as shown in Figure 3–125.

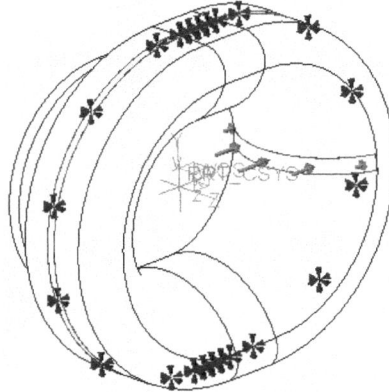

Figure 3–125

Task 10 - Verify the load.

Since the load distribution you applied is non-uniform, in this task you will verify that total amount of load applied to the model is 100,000 lbs as required.

1. Expand the Loads area in the *Home* tab and select **Review Total Load**. The Load Resultant dialog box opens as shown in Figure 3–126.

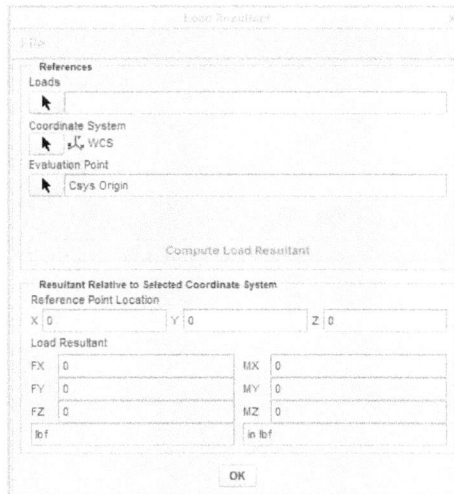

Figure 3–126

2. Click ![cursor] and select the **line_load** load in the model. Click the middle mouse button to complete the selection.

© 2017, ASCENT - Center for Technical Knowledge®

3. Click **Compute Load Resultant**. The Load Resultant dialog box opens as shown in Figure 3–127.

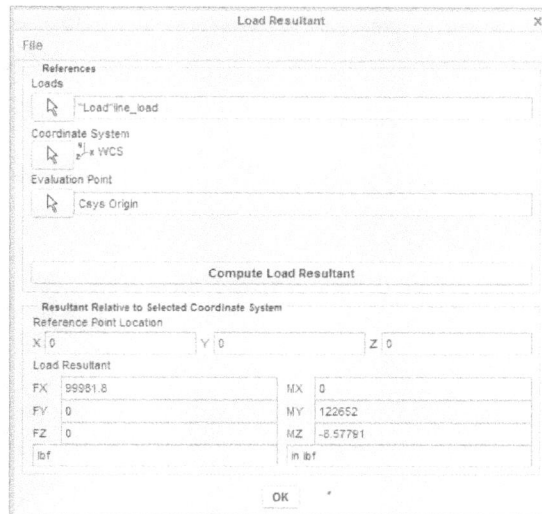

Figure 3–127

Note that the *FX* field does not read exactly **100000** as specified, but the value should be within 0.01% of that specified.

4. Click **OK** to finish.

Analysis Tasks

Task 11 - Solve the model using the Multi-Pass Adaptive convergence option.

1. Set up a Multi-Pass Adaptive analysis. For the *Name*, enter **chock**. For the *Maximum Polynomial Order*, enter **9** and in the *Percent Convergence* field, enter **10**.

2. Run the analysis.

3. In the Analyses and Design Studies dialog box, click (Status) to open the Run Status window. Extract the following information:
   - Number of solid elements in the model.
   - Number of passes to convergence.
   - Maximum P-Level on the last pass.
   - Number of equations on the last pass.
   - RMS Stress Error estimates.

Results Tasks

Task 12 - Display the deformation.

1. Create the displacement magnitude animation plot, as shown in Figure 3–128.

2. Start the animation. Check whether the applied boundary conditions behave correctly.

Figure 3–128

Task 13 - Display the von Mises stress.

1. Create the von Mises stress undeformed plot, as shown in Figure 3–129.

Figure 3–129

© 2017, ASCENT - Center for Technical Knowledge®

2. Using ▦ (Model Max), locate the area of maximum stress in the part, as shown in Figure 3–130.

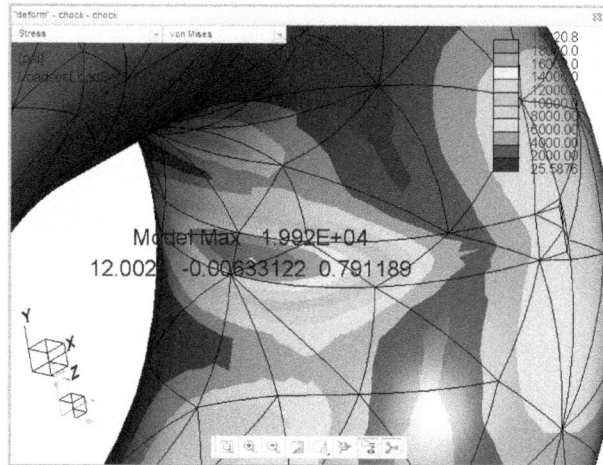

Figure 3–130

3. Select ▱ (New) in the Capping & Cutting Surfs panel in the *View* tab. In the Results Surface Definition dialog box, in the *Plane* area, select **XZ**, as shown in Figure 3–131.

Figure 3–131

4. Click **Apply**. Zoom in on the cross-section. The model displays as shown in Figure 3–132.

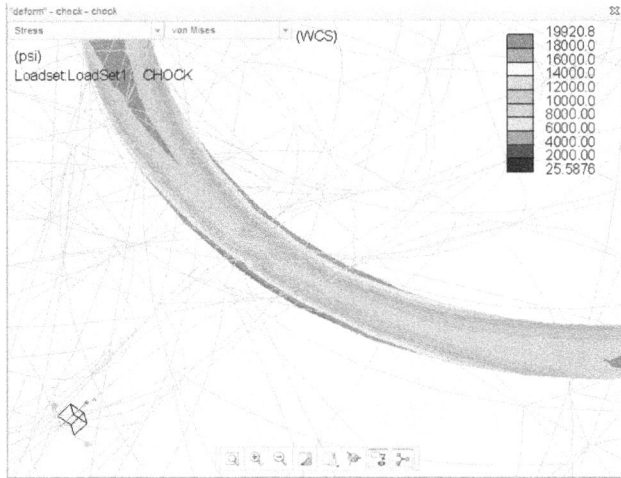

Figure 3–132

Note the characteristic bending pattern of stress through the thickness, with zero stress on the neutral fiber and maximum stress on the outermost fibers.

5. Click **Cancel** to close the Results Surface Definition dialog box.

6. Exit the Results. Save and close the model in Creo Parametric.

© 2017, ASCENT - Center for Technical Knowledge®

Practice 3d

Excluded Elements

Practice Objective

- Use excluded elements to improve convergence.

Modeling Tasks

Task 1 - Open the model.

1. Open **solid_bracket_2.prt** in Creo Parametric. The part displays as shown in Figure 3–133.

Figure 3–133

2. Switch to the Creo Simulate environment.

Task 2 - Apply the material.

1. Assign **STEEL** to the part.

   The following values are the default material properties for the STEEL material:

   - Poisson's ratio = 0.27
   - Young's modulus = 199948 MPa

Task 3 - Apply the constraints.

1. Constrain the two surfaces shown in Figure 3–134 in all translations.

Figure 3–134

Task 4 - Apply the load.

1. Apply a 500 N load in the Z-direction on the edge shown in Figure 3–135.

Figure 3–135

© 2017, ASCENT - Center for Technical Knowledge®

Analysis Tasks

Task 5 - Solve the model using the Multi-Pass Adaptive convergence option.

1. Set up a Multi-Pass Adaptive analysis. For the *Name*, enter **excluded**. For the *Maximum Polynomial Order*, enter **9** and for the *Percent Convergence* field, enter **10**.

2. Run the analysis.

3. The analysis does not converge. Note that the warning message in the Diagnostics window prompts you that *Convergence was not obtained because the maximum polynomial order of 9 was reached*.

Results Tasks

Task 6 - Display convergence graphs.

1. Display convergence graphs for the **strain_energy** and **max_stress_vm** measures, as shown in Figure 3–136.

Figure 3–136

Note that the maximum stress does not exhibit any convergence. This is due to the singularity caused by the edge load in the model.

2. Exit the Results.

Modeling Tasks

In the following tasks, you will use the excluded elements to improve convergence.

Task 7 - Isolate elements for exclusion.

1. In the *AutoGEM* group of the *Refine Model* tab, expand ⊞ (Control) and click ⊞ (Isolate for Exclusion). The Isolate for Exclusion Control dialog box opens as shown in Figure 3–137.

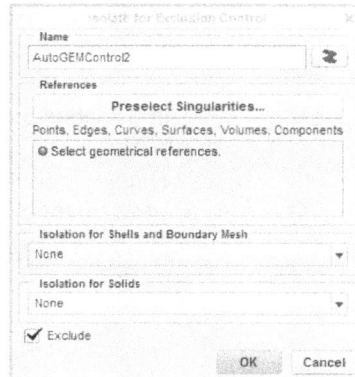

Figure 3–137

2. Click **Preselect Singularities**. In the Preselect Singularities dialog box, select the **Edge Loads** option, as shown in Figure 3–138.

Figure 3–138

3. Click **Select** and Creo Simulate automatically selects the area of singularity.

4. Expand the Isolation for Solids drop-down list and select **Maximum Element Size**. In the *Isolation for Solids* area, enter **5** as shown in Figure 3–139.

© 2017, ASCENT - Center for Technical Knowledge®

Figure 3–139

5. Click **OK**.

Task 8 - Mesh the model.

1. Use the **All with Properties** option to mesh the model.

2. Use the **Simulation Display** tool to hide the mesh points.

3. In the AutoGEM dialog box, select **Info>Isolating Elements**. Zoom in on the loaded edge. Note that AutoGEM has isolated the edge with small elements, as shown in Figure 3–140.

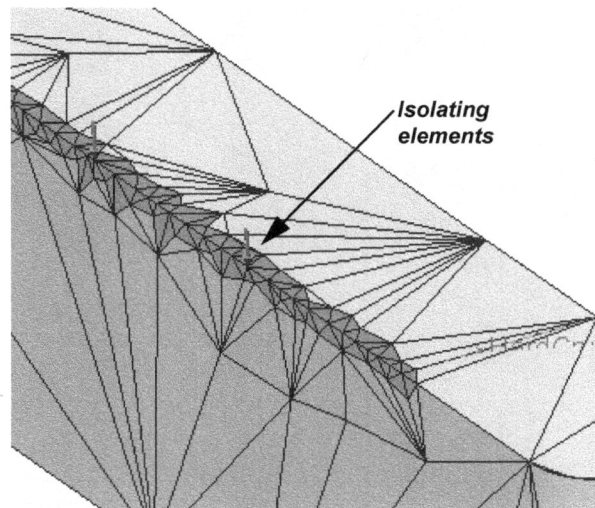

Figure 3–140

4. Close the AutoGEM without saving the mesh.

Analysis Tasks

Task 9 - Re-run the analysis.

1. Edit the **excluded** analysis study. In the *Excluded Elements* tab, select **Exclude Elements**. In the *Ignore* area, select **Stresses and Displacements**. In the *Polymonial* field, enter **3** as shown in Figure 3–141.

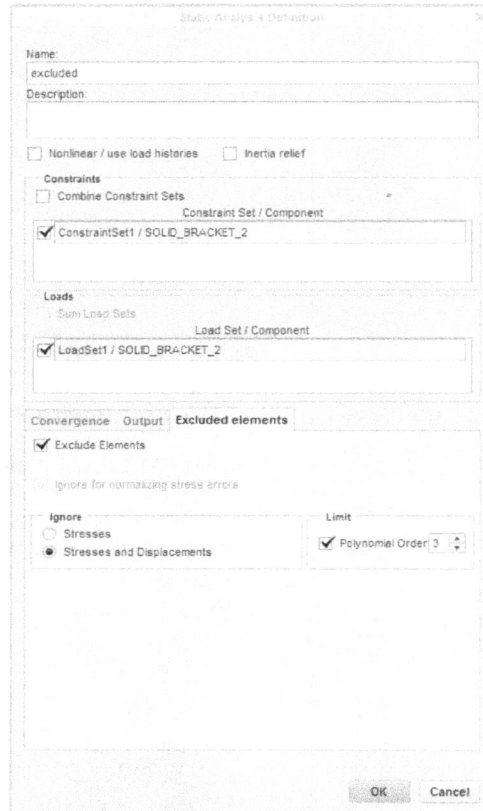

Figure 3–141

2. Re-run the analysis.

3. Click 🗒 (Status) to open the Run Status window. Verify that the analysis has now converged on pass 5, as shown in Figure 3–142.

© 2017, ASCENT - Center for Technical Knowledge®

```
>> Pass  5 <<
    Calculating Element Equations           (14:09:23)
        Total Number of Equations:   34071
        Maximum Edge Order:              5
    Solving Equations                       (14:09:24)
    Post-Processing Solution                (14:09:25)
    Calculating Disp and Stress Results     (14:09:25)
    Checking Convergence                    (14:09:26)
        Elements Not Converged:          0
        Edges Not Converged:             0
        Local Disp/Energy Index:       7.8%
        Global RMS Stress Index:       6.6%

    RMS Stress Error Estimates:

    Load Set          Stress Error  % of Max Prin Str
    ---------------   ------------  -----------------
    LoadSet1          3.76e-01       12.5% of  3.00e+00

    Resource Check                          (14:09:26)
        Elapsed Time   (sec):          9.78
        CPU Time       (sec):          4.84
        Memory Usage   (kb):        287161
        Wrk Dir Dsk Usage (kb):      47104

The analysis converged to within 10% on
edge displacement, element strain energy,
and global RMS stress.
```

Figure 3–142

Results Tasks

Task 10 - Display the convergence graphs.

1. Display convergence graphs for the **strain_energy** and **max_stress_vm** measures, as shown in Figure 3–143.

Figure 3–143

Note that the solution now displays perfect convergence on the strain energy and a reasonable convergence on stress.

Task 11 - Display the stress results.

1. Display the von Mises Stress fringe plot, as shown in Figure 3–144.

Figure 3–144

Note that the maximum stress is concentrated along the loaded edge. This is an area of singularity and the stress results are not realistic.

2. In the Format tab, select ▥ (Edit) to edit the result legend. Change the *legend minimum* to **0** and *maximum* to **0.5**. The result plot displays as shown in Figure 3–145.

Figure 3–145

The stresses away from the loaded edge are now displayed. These values are not affected by the singularity and can be trusted.

3. Exit the Results. Save and close the model in Creo Parametric.

© 2017, ASCENT - Center for Technical Knowledge®

Practice 3e

Static Stress Analysis of a Shaft

Practice Objectives

- Create surface regions.
- Apply loads, constraints, and material properties.
- Set up and run a Single-Pass Adaptive analysis.
- Display the results.

In this practice, you will perform a static stress analysis on the shaft shown in Figure 3–146, with minimum instruction.

Load applied to the hole in Z-direction

Area supported by a sleeve bearing

Fixed End

Figure 3–146

Task 1 - Create surface region for the sleeve bearing support.

1. Open **shaft.prt** and launch Creo Simulate.

Tip: Create two datum planes, then use intersections between the planes and the shaft surface to create the boundaries

2. Create the two boundaries for the surface region.
   - The 1st boundary curve is **5mm** from plane **DTM10**.
   - The 2nd boundary curve is **15mm** from plane **DTM10**.

3. Create surface region between the two boundary curves.

Task 2 - Apply material, loads, and constraints.

1. Apply the AL6061 material.

2. Fully constrain the cylindrical surface on the key end of the part, as shown in Figure 3–147.

3. Apply Pin constraint on the surface region, as shown in Figure 3–147. Leave both rotational and translational directions free.

Figure 3–147

4. Apply **150N** load in +Z direction to the hole, as shown in Figure 3–148.

Figure 3–148

© 2017, ASCENT - Center for Technical Knowledge®

Task 3 - Setup and run the analysis.

1. Create a new static analysis with the following parameters:
   - Analysis name: **shaft**
   - Convergence method: **Single-Pass Adaptive**

2. Run the analysis.

3. Display the Status window. Determine the RMS Stress Error value.

Task 4 - Visualize the analysis results.

1. Visualize and animate the **Displacement Magnitude** fringe plot. Does the part deform according to the applied loads and constraints?

2. Display the **von Mises Stress** fringe plot. Find the location of the maximum stress.

© 2017, ASCENT - Center for Technical Knowledge®

Shell Idealizations

Learning Objectives in this Chapter

- Understand shell idealization concepts.
- Create shell models from solid Creo Parametric models.
- Create shell pairs manually.
- Automatically detect shell pairs.
- Compress shell pairs to midsurface.
- Create shell models from surface Creo Parametric models.
- Apply loads and constraints to shell models.

4.1 Shell Idealizations

Idealizations are tools that simplify a finite element model, resulting in faster analysis runtime. Creo Simulate has the following idealization options: **Beams**, **Masses**, **Shells**, and **Springs**.

The most common type of idealization is shell idealization. Shell idealizations are used to simplify a thin-walled solid model. Shell models are less CPU-intensive and can be analyzed faster than solid models.

Shell elements are 3D, surface-like elements that are used to represent features that are thin in comparison to the length and width of the surface in your part. The rule of thumb is to use shell elements when the thickness dimension is less than 1/10 of the length and width of the feature. Shell elements in Creo Simulate must be placed on the midsurface of the part, which is a surface that is equidistant from the side surfaces.

An example of a solid model that could be simplified using a shell idealization is shown in Figure 4–1. Portions of the solid model are composed of thin-walled features. The number of solid elements required to represent these features could be large. Therefore, the thin-walled features could be idealized as 3D shell elements represented by pairs of parallel surfaces.

Figure 4–1

© 2017, ASCENT - Center for Technical Knowledge®

There are two types of shells in Creo Simulate:

- **Midsurface Shells:** The opposing faces of the solid model are paired and then compressed to form the midsurfaces for the shell element placement. Shell thickness is automatically imported from the solid model.

- **Standard Shells:** A solid model of the part is not required. Modeling the part geometry with datum surfaces is sufficient. You select surfaces that are assumed to be the midsurfaces for the shell element placement. You must assign shell properties, such as thickness. This option also enables you to define a shell as a laminate consisting of several layers of materials.

4.2 Midsurface Shells

For midsurface shells, Creo Simulate pairs opposing surfaces of a thin-walled feature and compresses them to a midsurface, on which shell elements are placed.

The shell thickness is read directly from the Creo model. The paired surfaces can be parallel planar or non-planar surfaces, and the shell elements can be flat or curved as long as the pairing surfaces are parallel.

Use the following steps to create shell elements in Creo Simulate:

1. Pair two parallel surfaces. Two surfaces that can be paired are shown in Figure 4–2.

Surface1 is parallel to surface2.

Figure 4–2

2. Compress the paired surfaces to a midsurface, as shown in Figure 4–3.

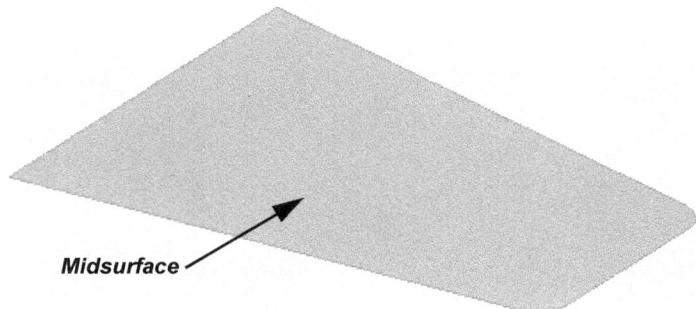

Figure 4–3

© 2017, ASCENT - Center for Technical Knowledge®

3. Create shell elements on the midsurface, as shown in Figure 4–4.

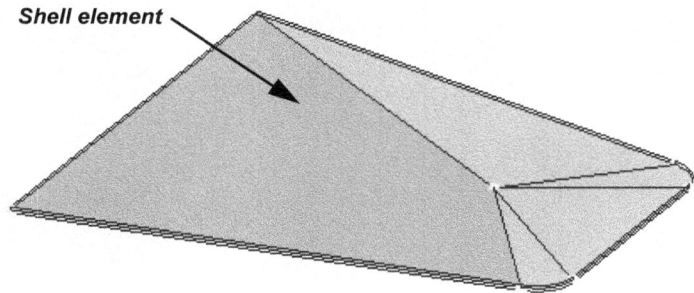

Shell element

Figure 4–4

Shell Pair Creation

Shell pair creation tools are located in the *Refine Model* tab as shown in Figure 4–5.

Shell Pair
Detect Shell Pairs
Adjust Tangent Pairs

Figure 4–5

There are two options for creating shell pairs:

*   **Manual:** You manually select opposing surfaces to be paired.

*   **Automatic:** Creo Simulate detects and pairs surfaces based on feature types or feature thicknesses.

Manual Shell Pairs

Manual shell pairing requires you to select opposing surfaces in the part. To create a manual shell pair, click 🖉 (Shell Pair) to open the Shell Pair Definition dialog box, as shown in Figure 4–6.

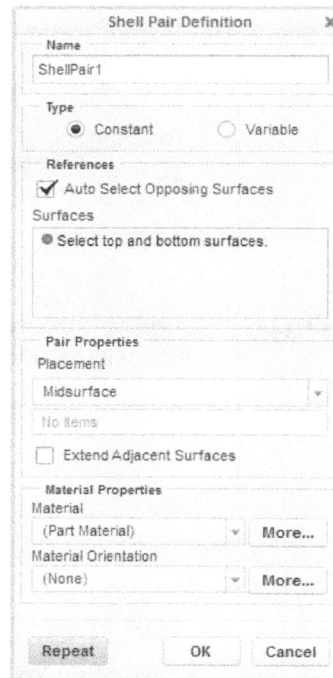

Figure 4–6

The Shell Pair Definition options are as follows.

Option	Description
Constant/Variable	Thickness type of shell pair.
Surfaces	Selection collector for surfaces to be paired.
Placement	Enables you to change shell element placement for the pair. The default is **Midsurface**. Other options are: **Top**, **Bottom**, or **Selected Surface**.
Material	Enables you to apply materials to your shell model. By default, the part material is applied.
Material Orientation	Enables you to create and assign new material orientations in your shell model. Applies to non-isotropic materials only.

© 2017, ASCENT - Center for Technical Knowledge®

Automatic Shell Pairs

Creo Simulate can automatically pair surfaces using the **Detect Shell Pairs** option. In the *Refine Model* tab, expand the **Shell Pair** group and select **Detect Shell Pairs** to open the Auto Detect Shell Pairs dialog box, as shown in Figure 4–7.

Figure 4–7

Two shell pair detection methods are available:

*   **Use Geometry Analysis is toggled ON:** Creo Simulate searches for all shell pairs with a thickness of equal to or less than the Characteristic Thickness.

*   **Use Geometry Analysis is toggled OFF:** Creo Simulate detects shell pairs based only on feature type. The following feature types are detected: Shells, Ribs, Thin protrusions, Ears, Sheet metal, and Plastic ribs.

When you click **Start**, Creo Simulate runs the detection algorithm, and displays all of the created shell pairs in the Model Tree. When you select the Shell Pairs in the Model Tree, they are highlighted in the model, one side in green and the other in cyan. These surfaces are compressed to create a midsurface.

Shell Pair Compression

After you have defined the shell pairs, you need to check the compressed to midsurface geometry. Click ⬚ (Review Geometry) in the *AutoGEM* area in the *Refine Model* tab to open the Simulation Geometry dialog box. Select the required options as shown in Figure 4–8.

Figure 4–8

Click **Apply**. The midsurfaces are shaded in green, as shown in Figure 4–9.

Figure 4–9

Alternatively, you can select **Original Geometry**, to display the original solid geometry (wireframe) over the compressed geometry (shaded), as shown in Figure 4–10.

Figure 4–10

© 2017, ASCENT - Center for Technical Knowledge®

4.3 Standard Shells

For Standard Shells, having a solid model of the part is not necessary. You select datum surfaces that are assumed to be the midsurfaces for the shell element placement. You must assign shell properties, such as thickness.

Standard Shells are useful in parts for which datum surfaces rather than solids are typically used to model part geometry, such as thin stampings, car body panels, aircraft skins, etc. An example of this type of model is shown in Figure 4–11.

Figure 4–11

Standard Shell Creation

To create a standard shell, click ✏ (Shell). The Shell Definition dialog box opens as shown in Figure 4–12.

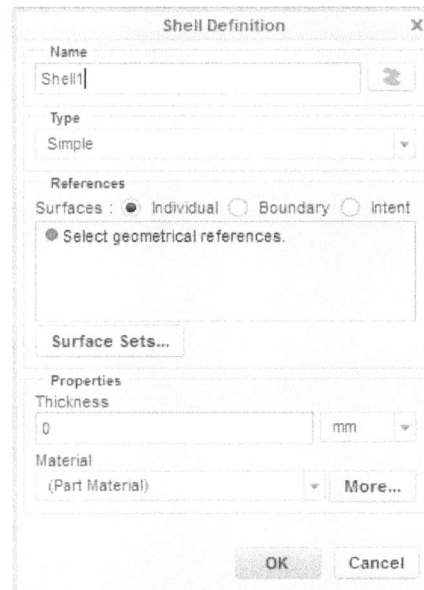

Figure 4–12

Expand the Type drop-down list and select one of the following:

- **Simple:** Only **Thickness** and **Material** are required to define the shell properties.

- **Advanced:** Can be used to define shell properties for laminates.

Select surfaces for the shell, enter the shell properties as required, and click **OK** to finish.

© 2017, ASCENT - Center for Technical Knowledge®

4.4 Applying Loads and Constraints to Shell Models

Creo Simulate supports the same loads and constraints for both solid and shell models. However, because model geometry is automatically redefined during midsurface compression, you need to use caution when placing loads and constraints in shell models.

In general, loads and constraints applied to either side of the uncompressed model are automatically transferred by Creo Simulate to the midsurface. If you apply a load on both sides of the uncompressed model, the amount of load on the midsurface doubles. However, if you apply a constraint on both sides, Creo Simulate detects a conflict and aborts the analysis, because constraints in this case are effectively applied twice on the same midsurface.

The same applies to the edges. In the example shown in Figure 4–13, a load is applied to an edge on one side of the shell pair. After the midsurface compression, the load is transferred to the corresponding edge on the midsurface.

Figure 4–13

However, in the example shown in Figure 4–14, the same load is applied to the edges on both sides of the shell pair. After the midsurface compression, two loads are transferred and summed on the midsurface edge, which doubles the load in the analysis.

Figure 4–14

Practice 4a | Automatic Shell Creation

Practice Objectives

- Understand how to create shell element models.
- Set up loads, constraints, and material properties.
- Run and analyze a part.

In this practice, you will use shell element idealizations to set up and analyze the thin-walled pressure relief tank shown in Figure 4–15. You will use the **Detect Shell Pairs** option to create shell elements. The tank is created in Creo Parametric using surface features, and then the **Thicken** option is used to create a wall thickness of 0.5 mm.

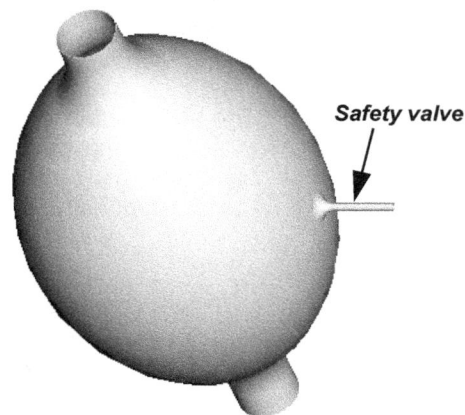

Figure 4–15

The existing symmetry is used to create a vertical cut through the tank to remove the front half of the tank. You will analyze 1/2 of the tank part shown in Figure 4–16, applying the Mirror Symmetry constraint on the cutting surface.

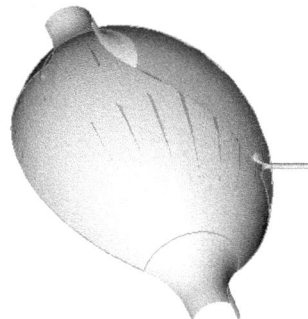

Figure 4–16

© 2017, ASCENT - Center for Technical Knowledge®

Modeling Tasks

Task 1 - Open the auto_p_t_02 part in Creo Parametric.

1. Open **auto_p_t_02.prt**. The part displays as shown in Figure 4–17.

Figure 4–17

2. Ensure that the unit system is set to **mmNs**.

Task 2 - Launch Creo Simulate.

1. Select **Applications>Simulate**.

2. Ensure that **Structure** mode is active.

3. Turn off the datum planes and datum axes.

Task 3 - Define the shell elements.

1. In the *Refine Model* tab, in the *Idealizations* area, select **Shell Pair>Detect Shell Pairs**. The Auto Detect Shell Pairs dialog box opens as shown in Figure 4–18.

Figure 4–18

Shells can be either flat or curved.

2. Clear **Use Geometry Analysis** and click **Start**. Creo Simulate creates six shell pairs that display in the Model Tree.

3. In the *Refine Model* tab, in the *AutoGEM* area, click 🔲 (Review Geometry) to open the Simulation Geometry dialog box. Select the required options as shown in Figure 4–19.

Figure 4–19

4. Click **Apply**. The model displays as shown in Figure 4–20.

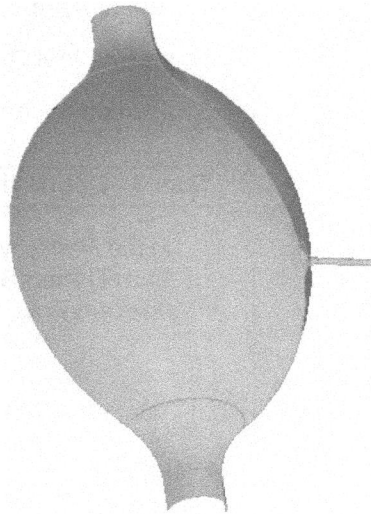

Figure 4–20

© 2017, ASCENT - Center for Technical Knowledge®

5. Select the **Original Geometry** option and click **Apply**. The midsurface is now shaded in green, while the solid edges are displayed as a black wireframe. Zoom in to display these edges more clearly, as shown in Figure 4–21.

Figure 4–21

6. Click **Close** to finish.

Task 4 - Mesh the model.

1. Expand the AutoGEM drop-down list and select **Midsurface**, as shown in Figure 4–22

Figure 4–22

2. Click ▦ (AutoGEM). The AutoGEM dialog box opens as shown in Figure 4–23.

Figure 4–23

3. Expand the AutoGEM References drop-down list and select **Surface**.

4. Click ⬉ . The Surface Selection box opens as shown in Figure 4–24.

Figure 4–24

5. Draw a box around the model to select all of the surfaces.

6. In the Surface Selection dialog box, click **OK** or click the middle mouse button.

7. Click **Create**. The AutoGEM Summary and Diagnostics dialog boxes open as shown in Figure 4–25.

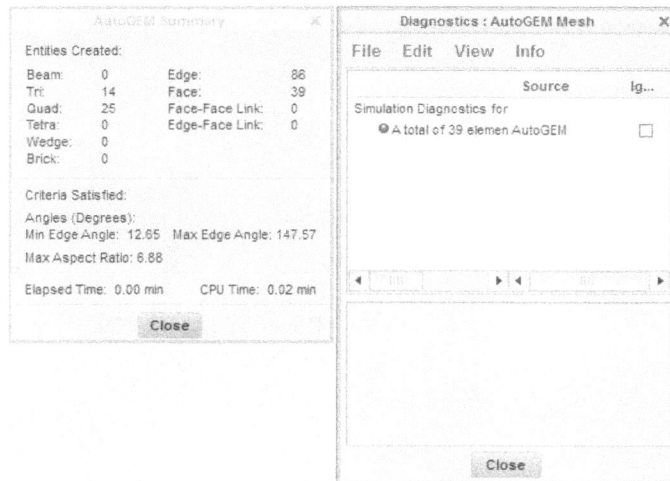

Figure 4–25

Note the information displayed in this dialog box, such as the number of Tri and Quad shell elements.

8. Close both the AutoGEM Summary and Diagnostics boxes, but do not close the AutoGEM dialog box yet. The model displays as shown in Figure 4–26.

© 2017, ASCENT - Center for Technical Knowledge®

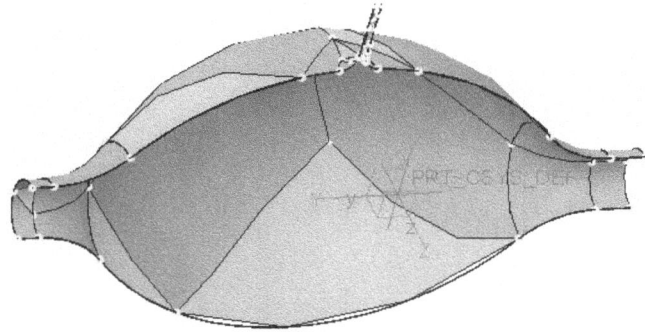

Figure 4–26

9. In the In-graphics toolbar, click 🔩 (Simulation Display). The Simulation Display dialog box opens.

*The **Shrink Elements** option does not affect the analysis. It is only a visualization tool that helps to display the mesh more clearly.*

10. Select the *Mesh* tab, in the *Mesh Display* area, select the **Shrink Elements** option and increase the shrinkage value to 20%.

11. Click **OK**. The model displays as shown in Figure 4–27.

Figure 4–27

*The mesh is saved with model name and extension .MMP (**auto_p_t.mmp**).*

12. Click **Close** to close the AutoGEM dialog box and save the mesh.

Task 5 - Apply a load to the model.

In this task, you will apply a pressure load to the interior surfaces of the model. This load represents the pressure exerted on the inside walls of the tank when the tank is pressurized.

1. In the *Loads* group of the *Home* tab, click ⊨ (Pressure). The Pressure Load dialog box opens as shown in Figure 4–28.

Figure 4–28

2. In the *Name* field, enter **preload**.

3. For *Member of Set*, accept the default **LoadSet1** option.

4. Select the **Intent** option and select any interior surface of the tank. (This effectively selects all of the interior surfaces).

5. Click **Advanced**. Expand the Spatial Variation drop-down list and select **Uniform** (the other options are **Function Of Coordinates** and **External Coefficients Field**).

6. In the *Value* field for the pressure magnitude, enter **1**.

7. Click **Preview** to review the load.

8. Click **OK** to finish applying the load. The model displays as shown in Figure 4–29.

Load and constraint sets provide a logical means of organizing your modeling entities so that you can define the analyses clearly and effectively. A load set is a set of loads that act together on the model.

© 2017, ASCENT - Center for Technical Knowledge®

Figure 4–29

Task 6 - Control load settings and visibilities.

1. In the floating toolbar, click 🕮 (Simulation Display). The Simulation Display dialog box opens as shown in Figure 4–30.

Figure 4–30

Examine the settings and visibilities in the Simulation Display dialog box. Note that in the *Settings* tab, the load arrows can be set to **Arrow Tails Touching** to help visualize your loads. Additionally, you can remove the pressure load from the display (e.g., to see other constraints or loads more clearly).

2. Select the *Set Visibilities* tab.

3. Clear the **LoadSet1** row to turn off the display of the pressure load.

4. Click **Preview** to display the model without the pressure load.

5. Click **OK** to close the Simulation Display dialog box.

Task 7 - Apply constraints to the model.

In this task, you will constrain the edges at the top of the inlet/outlet pipes and the side of the safety valve pipe.

Shell Elements have six degrees of freedom (three translations and three rotations).

1. In the *Constraints* panel, click ⬚ (Displacement).

2. In the Constraint dialog box, in the *Name* field, enter **sidepipe**. For *Member of Set*, accept the default **ConstraintSet1** option.

3. Expand the References drop-down list and select **Edge(s)/ Curve(s)**.

4. Select the outer edges of the pipes (hold down <Ctrl> to select all of the outer edges of the pipes).

5. Constrain all of the Translation and Rotation directions. The Constraint dialog box opens as shown in Figure 4–31.

© 2017, ASCENT - Center for Technical Knowledge®

Figure 4–31

6. Click **OK**. The constraints display as shown in Figure 4–32.

Figure 4–32

Task 8 - Apply symmetry constraints.

In this task you will apply a Mirror Symmetry constraint to the edges in the plane of symmetry to use the model's symmetry.

To edit and delete your constraint sets, right-click and select the required option.

1. In the *Home* tab, expand the *Constraints* panel, and click ⫴ (Symmetry). The Symmetry Constraint dialog box opens as shown in Figure 4–33.

Figure 4–33

2. In the *Name* field, enter **sym_edges**. For *Member of Set,* select **ConstraintSet1**.

3. For the *Type*, select **Mirror**.

4. Select all of the outside edges of the model that are on the symmetry plane (do not select the interior edges). (Hold <Ctrl> to select all of the edges.)

5. Click **OK**. The model displays as shown in Figure 4–34.

Figure 4–34

© 2017, ASCENT - Center for Technical Knowledge®

6. Click ⬚ (Simulation Display). The Simulation Display dialog box opens.

7. In the *Setting* tab, select **Icons** and clear **Distribution**, as shown in Figure 4–35.

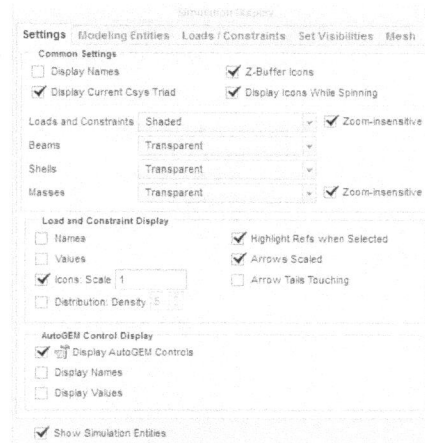

Figure 4–35

8. Click **OK** to close the Simulation Display dialog box. The constraints display as shown in Figure 4–36.

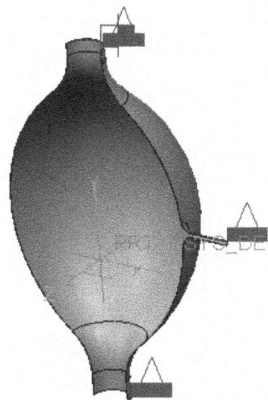

Figure 4–36

Task 9 - Apply the material for the pressure tank.

1. Click ⬚ (Materials). The Materials dialog box opens.

2. In the *Materials in Library* area, scroll through the list and select **SS** (stainless steel).

---

3. Click ▶▶▶ (Add Material) to transfer **SS** to the *Materials in Model* area.

4. Click ✎ (Edit) to check the material properties. Click **OK** when finished.

    The following values are the default material properties for stainless steel (SS):

    *   Poisson's Ratio= 0.3
    *   Young's modulus = 193053 MPa
    *   Density = 7.74372e-9 tonne/mm^3

5. Click **OK** to close the Materials dialog box.

6. Click ↘ (Material Assignment) to assign the material to the part. Click **OK** to close the Material Assignment dialog box.

7. In the Simulation Display dialog box, in *Set Visibilities* tab, toggle on the loads display.

Analysis Tasks

Task 10 - Set up and run the analysis.

1. In the Home tab, click 🗂 (Analyses and Studies). The Analyses and Design Studies dialog box opens as shown in Figure 4–37.

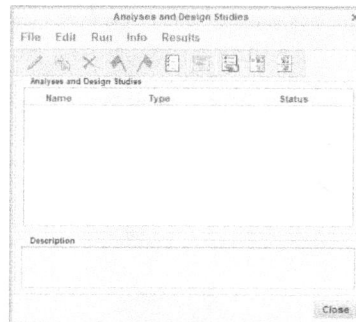

Figure 4–37

2. Select **File>New Static**. The Static Analysis Definition dialog box opens as shown in Figure 4–38.

© 2017, ASCENT - Center for Technical Knowledge®

Figure 4–38

3. In the *Name* field, enter **tank**. (Tank becomes the name of a sub-directory containing all of your results files).

4. (Optional) In the *Description* field, enter **static analysis of a relieve pressure tank**. This help to identify your analysis.

5. For a static stress analysis, you need to specify or select the constraint and load sets, which have already been created. In this case, they are **ConstraintSet1** and **LoadSet1**. Ensure that these sets are highlighted.

6. To define the type of convergence, expand the Method drop-down list and select **Multi-Pass Adaptive**.

7. In the *Limits* area, in the *Percent Convergence* field, enter **5** percent convergence.

8. In the *Polynomial Order* area, set the *Maximum polynomial order* to **9**.

The Plotting Grid is a grid of points that Creo Simulate uses to display results within the elements. A higher density plotting grid is recommended to obtain smoother looking result plots.

9. Select the *Output* tab and set the *Plotting Grid* to **9**. The Static Analysis Definition dialog box opens as shown in Figure 4–39.

Figure 4–39

10. In the Static Analysis Definition dialog box, click **OK**.

11. Expand the **Info** menu and select **Check Model**. This command checks the validity of the simulation model.

12. The Information dialog box opens, as shown in Figure 4–40, prompting you that there are no errors.

*The **Check Model** option highlights any modeling errors (e.g., load-constraint conflicts or unassigned material properties) and errors from modeling edits.*

Figure 4–40

13. Click **OK** to finish checking the validity of the model.

© 2017, ASCENT - Center for Technical Knowledge®

14. Click ✎ (Start) in the Analyses and Design Studies dialog box to start your analysis. The Question dialog box opens as shown in Figure 4–41.

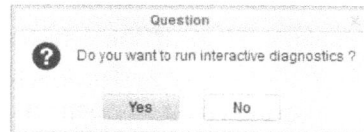

Figure 4–41

15. In the Question dialog box, click **Yes**. The prompt: *The design study has started*, displays in the message window.

16. The Diagnostics dialog box opens, displaying information about the analysis progress. Wait until the last line in the box says *Run completed*, as shown in Figure 4–42.

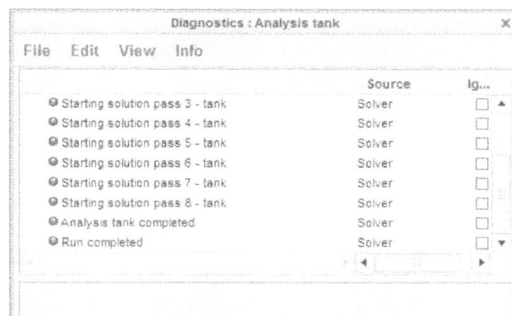

Figure 4–42

17. Click **Close** to close the Diagnostics dialog box.

Task 11 - Explore the Run Status box.

1. In the Analyses and Design Studies dialog box, click ▤ (Status). The Run Status window opens displaying a variety of information about the analysis.

2. Extract the following information from the dialog box:
   • Number of shell elements
   • Number of elements not converged at pass 4
   • Number of edges not converged at pass 7
   • RMS stress error estimates

   Did the solution converge at 5% (you set the convergence percentage in Step 7 of Task 1)?

Results Tasks

Task 12 - Display the results.

In this task, you will create and display von Mises stress and Displacement color plots.

1. In the Analyses and Design Studies dialog box, click
   (Review Results). The Result Window Definition dialog box opens as shown in Figure 4–43.

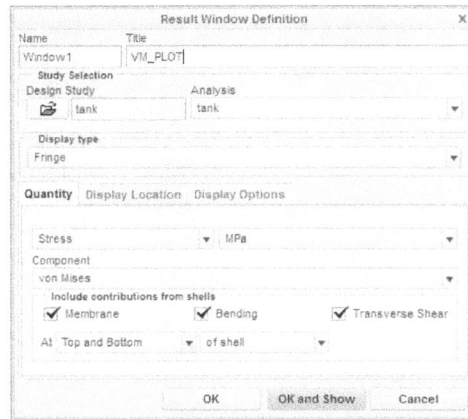

Result Window Definition	X
Name	Title
Window1	VM_PLOT

Study Selection
Design Study | Analysis
tank | tank

Display type
Fringe

Quantity | Display Location | Display Options

Stress | MPa
Component
von Mises
Include contributions from shells
✓ Membrane   ✓ Bending   ✓ Transverse Shear
At Top and Bottom   of shell

OK   OK and Show   Cancel

Figure 4–43

2. In the *Name* field, accept the default of **Window1**.

3. In the *Title* field, enter **VM_PLOT**.

4. Select the *Display Options* tab and clear the **Show Element Edges**, **Show Loads**, and **Show Constraints** options.

5. Click **OK and Show**. The Creo Simulate Results environment displays, with the Von Mises Stress fringe plot displayed, as shown in Figure 4–44.

© 2017, ASCENT - Center for Technical Knowledge®

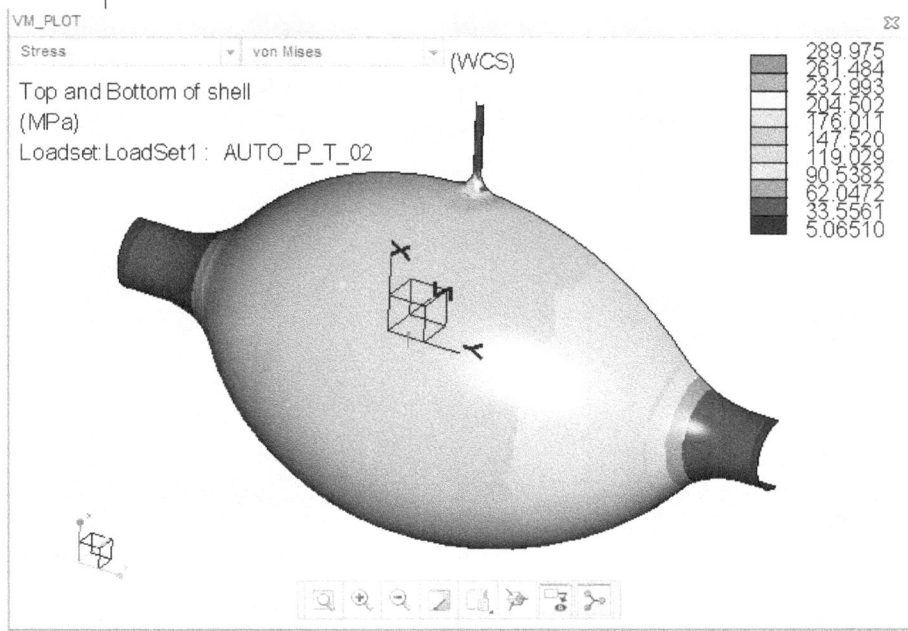

Figure 4–44

6. In the *Home* tab, click 📋 (Copy). The Result Window Definition dialog box opens.

7. In the *Name* field, enter **deformation**.

8. In the *Title* field, enter **DEF_PLOT**.

9. Expand the Quantity drop-down list and select **Displacement**.

10. In the *Display Options* tab, select the **Deformed** and **Animate** options.

11. Clear the **Auto Start** option and click **OK**.

12. In the *View* tab, click (Show). In the Display Result Window dialog box, clear **Window1** and select **deformation**, as shown in Figure 4–45.

Figure 4–45

Did the deformation display correctly?

13. Click **OK**. The deformation plot displays.

14. In the *View* tab, click ▶ to start the animation.

Use animations to check for errors and verify your results.

15. Click ◀◀ or ▶▶ to step through the animation.

16. Click ■ to stop the deformation window at Frame 5 of the animation, as shown in Figure 4–46.

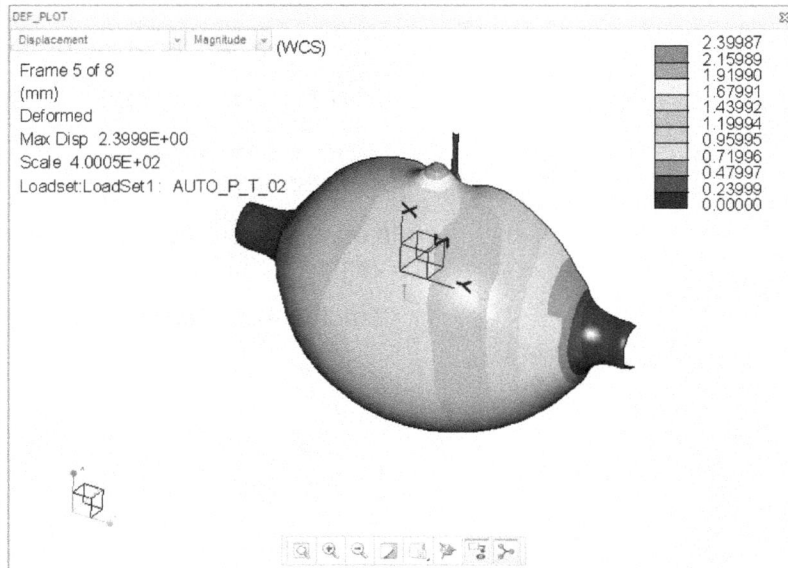

Figure 4–46

© 2017, ASCENT - Center for Technical Knowledge®

Note that the area around the small pipe seems to have excessive deformation. This is only a visual effect, due to Creo Simulate magnifying the amount of displayed deformation, for better clarity. Note the Scale value (shown in the top left corner in Figure 4–46), which is approximately 400, this is the deformation magnification factor. Therefore, the displayed deformation is 400 times the actual deformation (which is actually approximately 2.4mm).

17. In the *Home* tab, click✎ (Edit).

18. In the *Display Options* tab, select the **Overlay Undeformed** and **Transparent Overlay** options.

*If **%** is selected, the magnification factor is automatically set by Creo Simulation, based on the size of the model.*

19. Near the *Scaling* field, clear the **%** option. In the *Scaling* field, enter **50**. This is the magnification factor that is used to display deformation in the model.

20. In the *Display Options* tab, clear the **Animate** option. The Result Window Definition box opens as shown in Figure 4–47.

Figure 4–47

21. Click **OK and Show**. The DEF_PLOT displays as shown in Figure 4–48. Note that the deformation around the small pipe is not now excessive (even though it is still magnified by the factor of 50).

DEF_PLOT

Displacement   Magnitude   (WCS)

(mm)
Deformed
Max Disp 2.3999E+00
Scale 5.0000E+01
Loadset:LoadSet1: AUTO_P_T_02

2.39987
2.15989
1.91990
1.67991
1.43992
1.19994
0.95995
0.71996
0.47997
0.23999
0.00000

Figure 4–48

Task 13 - Use predefined measures to study the convergence.

1. In the *Home* tab, click (New) to create a new results window. The Design Study for Result Window Definition dialog box opens.

2. Select the **tank** study and click **Open**. The Result Window Definition dialog box opens.

3. In the *Name* field, enter **strain_energy**.

4. Expand the Display type drop-down list and select **Graph**.

5. Expand the first Graph Ordinate (Vertical) Axis drop-down list and select **Measure**.

© 2017, ASCENT - Center for Technical Knowledge®

6. Click ✐ (Measure). The Measures dialog box opens as shown in Figure 4–49.

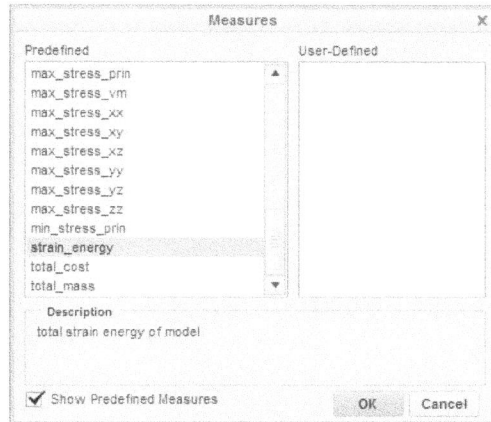

Figure 4–49

7. Highlight **strain_energy** (near the bottom of the list) and click **OK**. The Result Window Definition dialog box opens.

8. Click **OK and Show**.

9. In the *View* tab, click ⬛ (Show). The Display Result Window dialog box opens as shown in Figure 4–50.

Figure 4–50

10. In the Display Result Window dialog box, select only **strain_energy** and click **OK**. The convergence plot displays as shown in Figure 4–51.

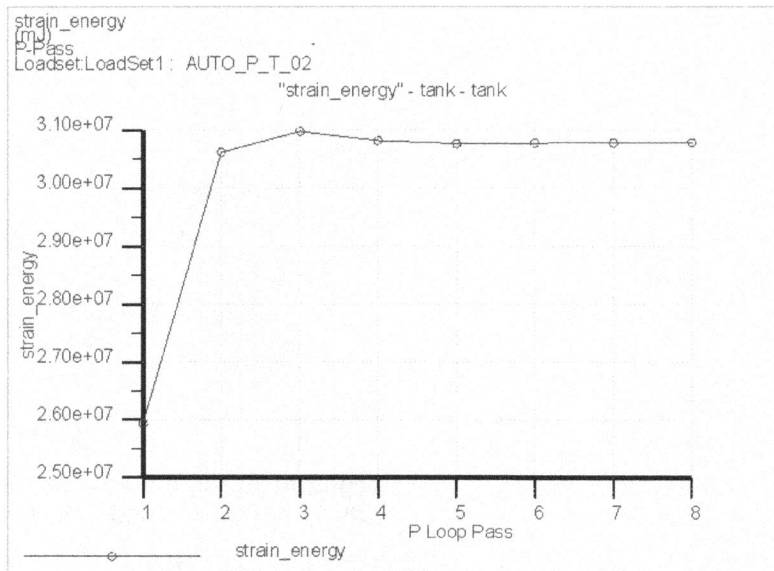

strain_energy
(mJ)
P-Pass
Loadset:LoadSet1 : AUTO_P_T_02

"strain_energy" - tank - tank

Figure 4–51

Note that the strain energy converges after pass 4.

11. Repeat the first eight steps of this task to create a convergence graph for the **max_disp_mag** measure.

12. Click (Show) in the *View* tab. The Display Result Window dialog box opens.

© 2017, ASCENT - Center for Technical Knowledge®

13. In the dialog box, highlight only **max_disp_mag** and then click **OK**. The convergence plot displays as shown in Figure 4–52.

Figure 4–52

Note that the displacement curve converges after pass 7.

Task 14 - Explore the Query options.

In this task, you will use the options in the **Query** section of the *Home* tab. You will also locate the point and value of the maximum stress.

1. Click ☐ (Show) in the *View* tab. In the Display Result window, highlight only **Window1** and then click **OK**.

2. Select (Model Max). The location and value of maximum von Mises stress displays as shown in Figure 4–53. Rotate and/or zoom in on the model to display the location more clearly.

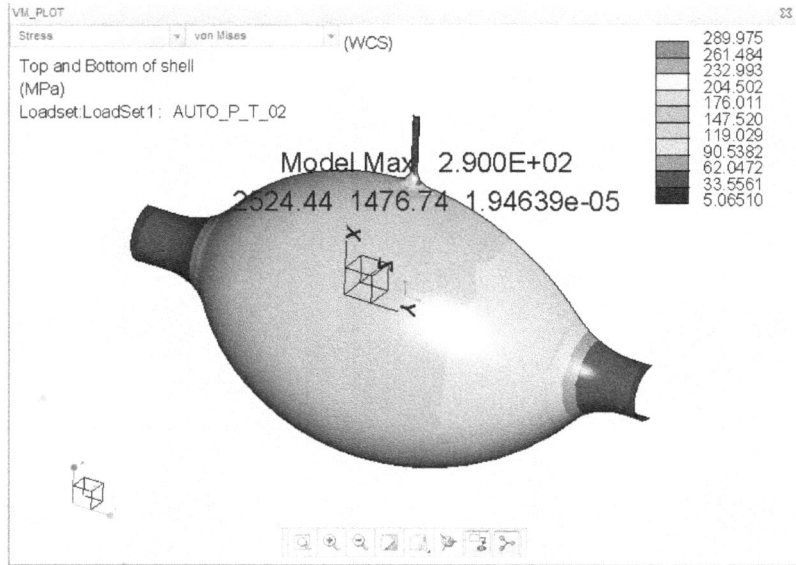

VM_PLOT

Stress   von Mises   (WCS)

Top and Bottom of shell
(MPa)
Loadset:LoadSet1 : AUTO_P_T_02

Model Max   2.900E+02
2324.44 1476.74 1.94639e-05

289.975
261.484
232.993
204.502
176.011
147.520
119.029
90.5382
62.0472
33.5561
5.06510

Figure 4–53

3. Investigate the other options in the Query section. For example, the **Dynamic Query** tool displays the result values dynamically in the Query dialog box, as you move the mouse cursor along the model. .

Task 15 - Save and close the model.

1. Select **File>Close** or click (Close) to exit Creo Simulate results environment. Click **Don't Save** in the Confirm Exit window.

2. Close the Analyses and Design Studies dialog box.

3. Exit Creo Simulate. Save and close the model in Creo Parametric.

© 2017, ASCENT - Center for Technical Knowledge®

Practice 4b

Manual Shell Creation

Practice Objective

- Set up and run an analysis on an assembly using shell element idealizations.

In this practice, you will use shell element idealizations to set up, run, and analyze a thin-walled assembly (a miniature model of a diving stand). The assembly consists of two cross members with a bend part, diving board, and supporting wedge. The assembly is shown in Figure 4–54.

In assemblies, shell pairs can be defined on component level or assembly level. In this practice, you will use both methods.

All parts in the assembly must use the same unit system.

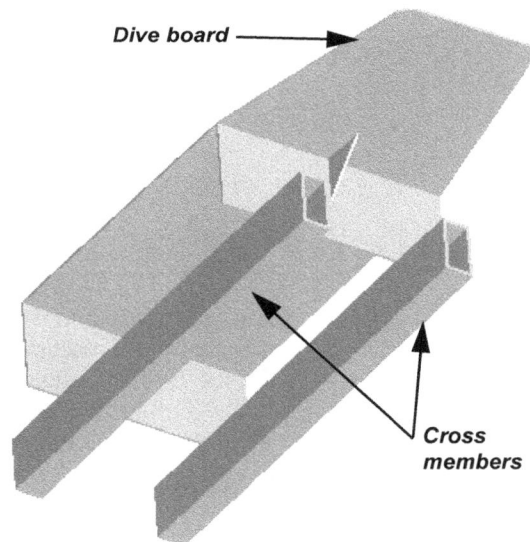

Figure 4–54

Modeling Tasks

Task 1 - Open the assembly.

1. Open **dive_board.asm** in Creo Parametric. The assembly displays as shown in Figure 4–55.

Figure 4–55

2. Turn off the datum planes and datum axes.

3. Ensure that the unit system is set to **mmNs**.

4. Select **Applications>Simulate** to enter the Creo Simulate environment.

Task 2 - Define shell pairs for the part called BOX.prt.

Examine the structure of the assembly. Note that there are two instances of the part called **BOX.prt**. Therefore, it is more efficient to create shell pairs for this part on the component level, which will automatically apply the shell pairs to all of the instances of the part in the assembly.

1. In the Model Tree, right-click on **box.prt** and select **Open**. The part opens in a new window, as shown in Figure 4–56.

Figure 4–56

2. Select **Applications>Simulate** to enter the Creo Simulate environment.

© 2017, ASCENT - Center for Technical Knowledge®

Although it would be more efficient to use the automatic shell pair detection tool in this part, in this case you will use manual shell pair creation.

3. In the *Refine Model* tab, click (Shell Pair). The Shell Pair Definition dialog box opens as shown in Figure 4–57. Ensure that the **Auto Select Opposing Surfaces** option is selected.

Figure 4–57

4. Select the outer surface of the top flange, as shown in Figure 4–58. Click **Repeat** to complete the shell pair and reopen the Shell Pair Definition dialog box.

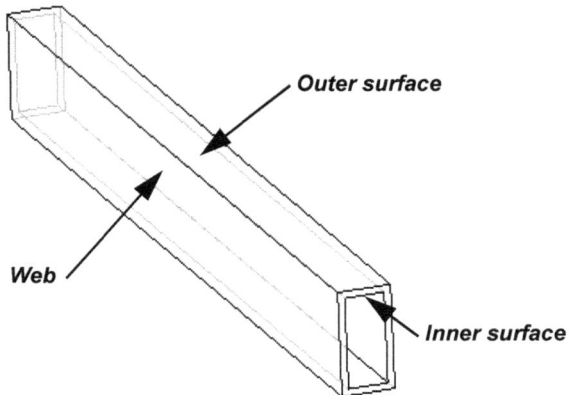

Figure 4–58

5. Repeat the previous Step for all other outer surfaces of the part. When selecting the last outer surface, click **OK** to close the Shell Pair Definition dialog box.

6. Four shell pairs should now be displayed in the Model Tree.

7. Click ▦ (Review Geometry) in the AutoGEM area and click **Apply**. The compressed model displays as shown in Figure 4–59.

Figure 4–59

8. Close the Simulation Geometry dialog box.

9. Exit Creo Simulate.

10. Save and close the part to return to the assembly window.

Task 3 - Define shell pairs for all of the other parts.

Shell pairs for all of the other parts in the assembly will be defined on the assembly level. You will use the **Detect Shell Pairs** tool to automatically create the shell pairs.

1. In the *Refine Model* tab, expand the ▦ (Shell Pair) drop-down list and select **Detect Shell Pairs**. The Auto Detect Shell Pairs dialog box opens as shown in Figure 4–60.

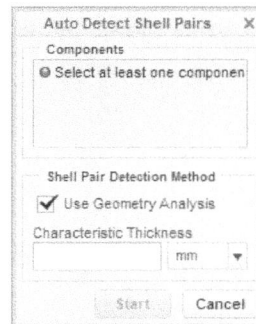

Figure 4–60

2. In the assembly, select the **TOP_SHAPE.PRT**, **PLATE.PRT**, and **WEDGE.PRT** parts (hold down <Ctrl> to multi-select).

© 2017, ASCENT - Center for Technical Knowledge®

The thickness of the parts in this assembly is 0.3mm.

3. Ensure that **Use Geometry Analysis** is selected. In the *Characteristic Thickness* field, enter **0.4**. The Auto Detect Shell Pairs dialog box opens as shown in Figure 4–61.

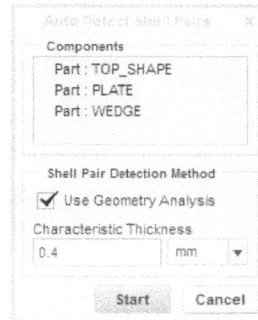

Figure 4–61

4. Click **Start**. Creo Simulate runs the automatic detection algorithm and closes the Auto Detect Shell Pairs dialog box.

5. Five shell pairs should now be displayed in the Model Tree on the assembly level.

Task 4 - Test the midsurface compression.

1. In the *Refine Model* tab, in the *AutoGEM* area, click

   (Review Geometry) to open the Simulation Geometry dialog box. Select the required options as shown in Figure 4–62.

Figure 4–62

2. Click **Apply**. The model displays as shown in Figure 4–63. Ensure that there are no unpaired surfaces (displayed in red) or unopposed surfaces (displayed in orange) in the model.

Figure 4–63

3. Zoom in on the areas where the parts join, and note that there are gaps between the midsurface, as shown in Figure 4–64. This is because the midsurfaces are obtained by offsetting the part surfaces by a half thickness. Therefore, even though the part surfaces being mated in the assembly, the midsurfaces are not mated.

Figure 4–64

© 2017, ASCENT - Center for Technical Knowledge®

4. In the Simulation Geometry dialog box, select the **Bonded Interface** option, as shown in Figure 4–65.

Figure 4–65

5. Click **Apply**. The model displays as shown in Figure 4–66.

Note that the areas of contact between the parts are now highlighted in magenta. Creo Simulate detects the mated in assembly surfaces, and assumes that the parts in those areas should be bonded during the analysis.

Figure 4–66

6. Click **Close** to finish.

Task 5 - Apply material to parts in the assembly.

---

1. In the *Home* tab, click ⌐ (Materials). The Materials dialog box opens.

2. In the *Materials in Library* area, scroll down the list and select **STEEL** (HS-low-alloy steel).

3. Click ▶▶▶ (Add Material) to transfer **STEEL** to the *Materials in Model* area.

The model's material properties should be as stated.

4. Click ✎ (Edit) to check your material properties and click **OK** when finished.

   The following values are the default material properties for HS-low-alloy steel (STEEL):

   - Poisson = 0.27
   - Young's modulus = 199948 MPa
   - Density = 7.82708e-9 tonne/mm^3

5. Click **OK** to close the Materials dialog box.

6. Click ⬚ (Material Assignment) to assign the material to the parts.

7. Select all of the parts in the assembly (hold down <Ctrl> to multi-select). The Material Assignment dialog box should be as shown in Figure 4–67.

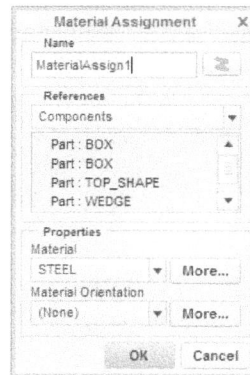

Figure 4–67

8. Click **OK** to close the Material Assignment dialog box.

9. Click ⬚ (Simulation Display) in the In-graphics toolbar. The Simulation Display dialog box opens.

10. In the *Modeling Entities* tab, clear the **Material Assignments** option.

11. Click **OK** to close the Simulation Display dialog box.

© 2017, ASCENT - Center for Technical Knowledge®

Task 6 - Mesh the model.

1. Expand the AutoGEM drop-down list and select **Midsurface**, as shown in Figure 4–68.

Figure 4–68

2. Click (AutoGEM). The AutoGEM dialog box opens as shown in Figure 4–69.

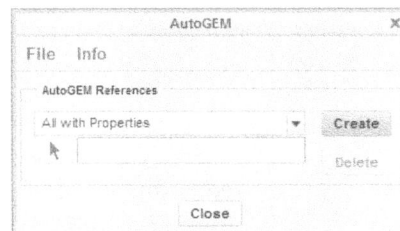

Figure 4–69

*The **All with Properties** option requires that materials be applied before meshing.*

3. Expand the AutoGEM References drop-down list, select **All with Properties**, and click **Create**. The AutoGEM Summary and Diagnostics dialog boxes open as shown in Figure 4–70.

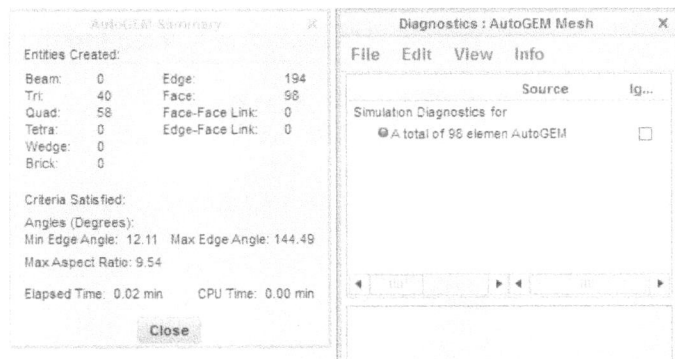

Figure 4–70

4. Close both of the AutoGEM Summary and Diagnostics boxes, but do not close the AutoGEM dialog box yet. The model displays as shown in Figure 4–71.

Figure 4–71

5. Zoom in on the model and examine the areas where the parts join, as shown in Figure 4–72.

Figure 4–72

Note that the shell elements (displayed in green) in those areas that are connected using blue elements, which are the Bonding elements. Bonding elements in Creo Simulate are specifically designed to connect compressed parts in shell assemblies.

6. Click **Close** to close the AutoGEM dialog box and save the mesh.

Task 7 - Apply a load to the model.

In this task, you will apply a load of 15N to the top surface of **plate.prt** (dive board).

1. In the Home tab, click ⊢ (Force/Moment). Select the top surface of the plate, and enter the information in the Force/Moment dialog box, as shown in Figure 4–73.

© 2017, ASCENT - Center for Technical Knowledge®

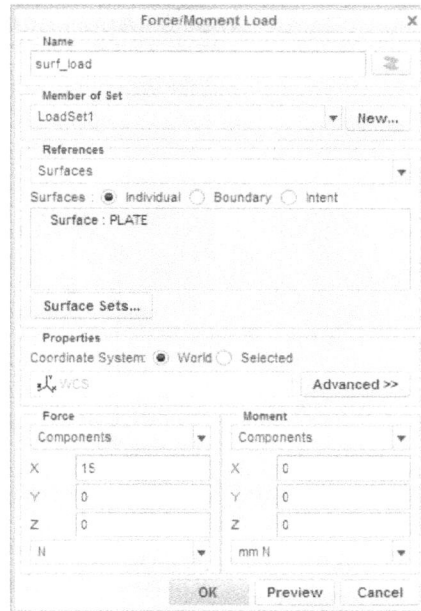

Figure 4–73

2. Click **OK** to finish. The assembly displays as shown in Figure 4–74.

Figure 4–74

Task 8 - Apply constraints to the model.

In this task, you will apply constraints to the ends of the beams shown in Figure 4–75.

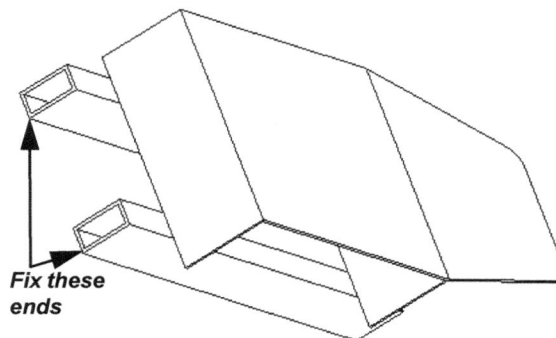

Figure 4–75

1. Click ⬚ (Displacement). The Constraint dialog box opens.

2. In the *Name* field, enter **asm_const**. For *Member of Set*, accept the default **ConstraintSet1**.

3. Expand the References drop-down list and select **Edges/Curves**.

4. Select eight outer edges on the end faces, as shown in Figure 4–76. (Hold <Ctrl> to multi-select.)

Figure 4–76

© 2017, ASCENT - Center for Technical Knowledge®

5. Fix all of the Translations and Rotations, as shown in Figure 4–77.

Figure 4–77

6. Click **OK**. The constraints display as shown in Figure 4–78.

Figure 4–78

Analysis Tasks

Task 9 - Set up the analysis.

1. Set up a Quick Check static analysis. For the name of the analysis, enter **dive_asm**.

2. In the Analyses and Design Studies dialog box, run **Info> Check Model** to check the validity of the model.

3. Run the Quick Check analysis to check for errors in loads or constraints.

Task 10 - Solve the assembly using the Multi-Pass Adaptive convergence option.

1. Change *Quick Check* to the **Multi-Pass Adaptive convergence** method.

2. In the *Polynomial Order* field, enter **9** maximum and in the *Limits* area, in the *Percent Convergence* field, enter **10** percent convergence.

3. In the *Output* tab, increase the *Plotting Grid* value to **10**.

4. Start the analysis run and wait until it completes.

5. In the Analyses and Design Studies dialog box, click ▤ (Status). The Run Status window opens displaying information about the analysis, as shown in Figure 4–79.

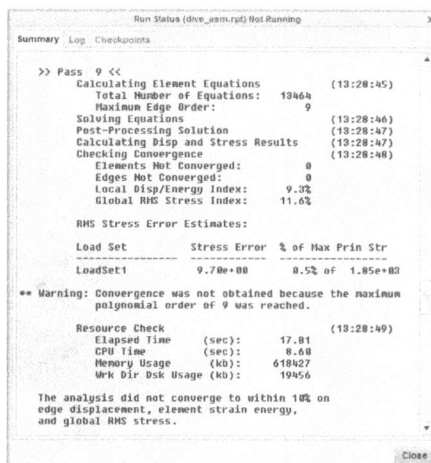

Figure 4–79

© 2017, ASCENT - Center for Technical Knowledge®

Note that the analysis did not converge on the Global RMS Stress to the required 10% because the maximum polynomial order 9 was not sufficient to obtain the convergence. In the following tasks, you will explore the elements that have not converged.

6. Close the Run Status window.

Task 11 - Display the non-converged elements.

1. In the Analyses and Design Studies dialog box, click
   . In the Result Window Definition dialog box, expand the Quantity drop-down list and select **P-Level**, as shown in Figure 4–80.

Figure 4–80

2. Click **OK and Show**. The P-Level plot displays as shown in Figure 4–81.

Figure 4–81

Examine the P-Levels and note that majority of the elements, in all but the beam parts, have their edges displayed in red, which corresponds to P-Level 9. These are the elements that are most likely to have not converged.

Note that the elements in the model are very large. Therefore, the non-convergence might be attributed to the elements being too large. In the following task, you will refine the mesh to obtain convergence.

3. Select **File>Close** and exit without saving the result window.

4. Close the Analyses and Design Studies dialog box.

Mesh Refinement Tasks

Task 12 - Set up the AutoGEM Controls.

1. In the *Refine Model* tab, in the *AutoGEM* area, expand the Control drop-down list and select **Maximum Element Size**, as shown in Figure 4–82.

Figure 4–82

2. The Maximum Element Size Control dialog box opens. Expand the References drop-down list and select **Components**. Select all of the parts in the assembly (hold down <Ctrl> to multi-select), and in the *Element Size* field, enter **8** as shown in Figure 4–83.

© 2017, ASCENT - Center for Technical Knowledge®

Figure 4–83

3. Click **OK** to finish. Note that AutoGEM Control icons display in the model and in the Model Tree.

Task 13 - Re-mesh the model.

1. Click ▦ (AutoGEM). The Question box displays as shown in Figure 4–84.

Figure 4–84

2. Click **No**. The AutoGEM dialog box opens as shown in Figure 4–85.

Figure 4–85

3. Click **Create**. Once meshing is finished, close both the AutoGEM Summary and Diagnostics dialog boxes. The model displays (with loads and constraints hidden) as shown in Figure 4–86.

Figure 4–86

Note that AutoGEM now creates a much finer mesh, according to the element size that you specified in an earlier task.

4. Click **Close** to close the AutoGEM dialog box and save the mesh.

Task 14 - Re-run the analysis.

1. Run the **dive_asm** analysis again and wait until it completes.

2. In the Analyses and Design Studies dialog box, click ▤ (Status) to open the Run Status window and check whether the analysis has converged, as shown in Figure 4–87.

© 2017, ASCENT - Center for Technical Knowledge®

Figure 4–87

Note that the analysis now converges on Pass 8, with the maximum P-level 8 (**Maximum Edge Order** in the Run Status window).

3. Click **Close** to close the Run Status window.

Results Tasks

Task 15 - Display the stress results.

1. Create and display a color plot of the von Mises stress. It should display as shown in Figure 4–88.

Figure 4–88

The stress values that you obtain once you run the analysis might be slightly different than those that have been provided. This is because each build of Creo Simulate has a slightly different solver, which will produce variations in the creation of the mesh and the solution of the analysis.

2. In the *Format* tab, click ▥ (Edit). The Edit Legend dialog box opens as shown in Figure 4–89. Explore the options in the box.

Figure 4–89

3. Clear the **Show View Min/Max** option and change the *Max* value to **500**, as shown in Figure 4–90.

Figure 4–90

4. Click **OK**. The model displays as shown in Figure 4–91. Note that the changed legend enables the stress distribution in the model to be displayed more clearly.

© 2017, ASCENT - Center for Technical Knowledge®

Figure 4–91

Task 16 - Examine areas of high stress.

1. Select ▧ (Model Max). The result plot displays as shown in Figure 4–92. Zoom in on the location of the maximum stress.

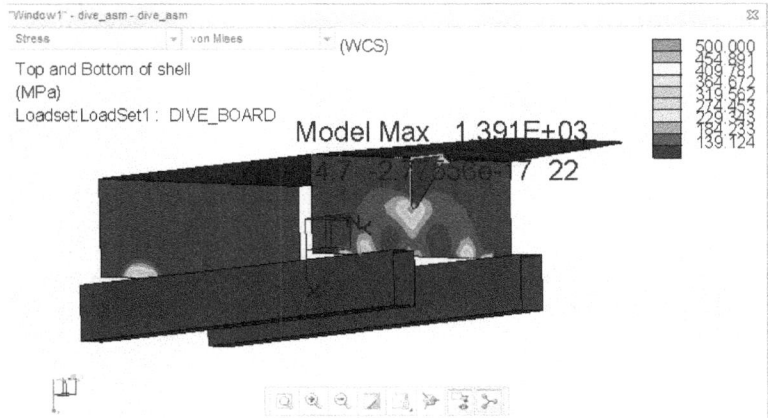

Figure 4–92

2. Zoom in on the area in which the top C-shape is attached to the left beam, and select ⊤ (View Max). Creo Simulate now only displays the location of the maximum stress within the viewing area, as shown in Figure 4–93.

Figure 4–93

3. Click (Dynamic Query) and explore the stresses in the area by moving the cursor over the model, as shown in Figure 4–94. Note that the Query box displays the coordinates of the queried point as well.

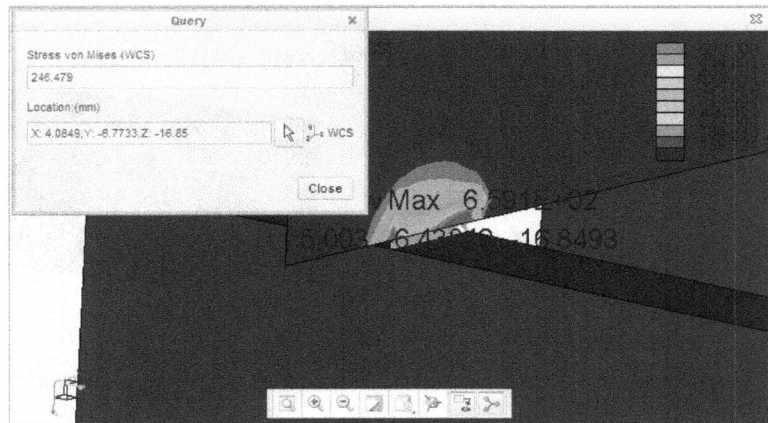

Figure 4–94

4. Click **Close** in the Query box to finish.

© 2017, ASCENT - Center for Technical Knowledge®

Task 17 - Display the displacement results.

1. In the *Home* tab, click ▢ (Copy). The Result Window Definition dialog box opens.

2. In the *Name* field, enter **deformation**.

3. In the *Title* field, enter **DEF_PLOT**.

4. Expand the Quantity drop-down list and select **Displacement**.

5. In the *Display Options* tab, select the **Deformed**, **Overlay Undeformed**, **Transparent Overlay**, and **Animate** options.

6. Clear the **Auto Start** option.

7. Click **OK**.

Ensure that only **deformation** *is highlighted in the Display Result Window.*

8. In the *View* tab, click ▢ (Show). In the Display Result Window dialog box, highlight the **deformation** as shown in Figure 4–95.

Figure 4–95

Did the deformation display correctly?

9. Click **OK**. The deformation plot displays.

10. In the *View* tab, click ▶ to start the animation.

11. Click ◀ or ▶ to step through] the animation.

Use animations to check for errors and verify your results.

12. Click ■ to stop the animation at Frame 5, as shown in Figure 4–96.

Figure 4–96

Task 18 - Use predefined measures to study the convergence.

1. Create convergence graphs (i.e., against the P-loop pass) for the following predefined measures:
   - max_stress_vm
   - max_disp_mag
   - strain_energy

   The convergence plot for the **max_vm_stress** displays as shown in Figure 4–97.

Figure 4–97

© 2017, ASCENT - Center for Technical Knowledge®

2. The convergence plot for **strain_energy** displays as shown in Figure 4–98.

Figure 4–98

3. The convergence plot for the **max_disp_mag** displays as shown in Figure 4–99.

Figure 4–99

These plots indicate that the solution converges after eight passes.

Task 19 - Use the Graph Window Options dialog box.

1. In the Format tab, click ⌖ (Edit). The Graph Window Options dialog box opens as shown in Figure 4–100.

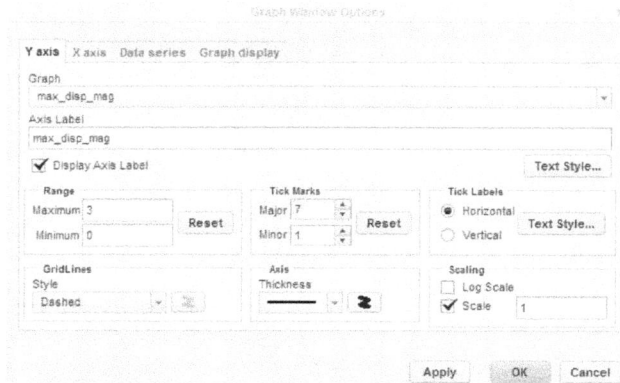

Figure 4–100

2. Select the *Data Series* tab. Change *Point Display* to **Rectangle** and *Interpolation* to **Smooth**, as shown in Figure 4–101.

Figure 4–101

3. Click **OK** to finish. The graph displays as shown in Figure 4–102.

© 2017, ASCENT - Center for Technical Knowledge®

Figure 4–102

4. Click on any square symbol in the graph at P Loop Pass to obtain the **max_disp_mag** value in that analysis pass, as shown in Figure 4–103.

Figure 4–103

Task 20 - Save and close the model.

1. Select **File>Close**. Click **Don't Save** when prompted to save the results.

2. Close the Analyses and Design Studies dialog box.

3. Exit Creo Simulate. Save and close the model in Creo Parametric.

Practice 4c

Shells from Surfaces

Practice Objectives

- Create shell elements from surface models.
- Set up loads, constraints, and material properties.
- Run and analyze a part.

In this practice, you will use shell element idealizations to set up and analyze the bent tube with flanges shown in Figure 4–104. The tube is created in Creo Parametric using surface features only (i.e., there are no solid volumes in the model). The tube is about 13in long and just over 3in in diameter. The tube wall thickness is 0.15in and flange thickness 0.4in.

Figure 4–104

Modeling Tasks

Task 1 - Open the tube_quilt part.

1. Open **tube_quilt.prt** in Creo Parametric. The part displays as shown in Figure 4–105.

© 2017, ASCENT - Center for Technical Knowledge®

Figure 4–105

2. Select **Applications>Simulate** to switch to the Creo Simulate environment. Ensure that the **Structure** mode is active.

Task 2 - Apply material.

1. Click ⬒ (Materials) and transfer **STEEL** to the *Materials in Model* area.

2. Click ✎ (Edit) to check your material properties and click **OK** when finished.

The model's material properties should be as stated.

The following values are the default material properties for HS-low-alloy steel (STEEL):

*   Poisson's ratio= 0.27
*   Young's modulus = 2.9e+7 psi
*   Density = 0.0007324 lbf sec^2/in^4

3. Click **OK** to close the Materials dialog box.

4. Click ⬒ (Material Assignment) to assign the material to the part.

5. Since there is only one material in the model, Creo Simulate automatically selects it for the part. Click **OK** to close the Material Assignment dialog box.

Task 3 - Define the shells.

Since this part is not a solid model, the compression from solid to midsurface does not apply. In this task you will use the standard **Shell** option to define the shell elements.

1. In the *Refine Model* tab, in the *Idealizations* area, click
   (Shell). The Shell Definition dialog box opens as shown in Figure 4–106.

Figure 4–106

2. Select the **Quilt** option and select any surface in the tube portion of the part. This selects all of the individual surfaces that comprise the tube surface.

Creo Simulate assumes the selected surface is the midsurface through the thickness of the part. The tube material in the analysis is extended by 0.075in to the inside and outside of the surface.

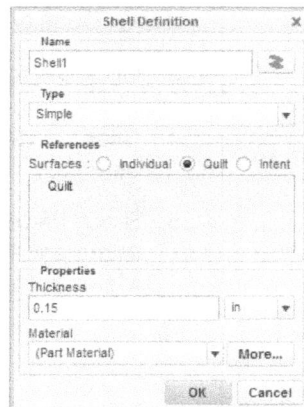

3. In the *Thickness* field, enter **0.15**. The dialog box opens as shown in Figure 4–107.

Figure 4–107

© 2017, ASCENT - Center for Technical Knowledge®

4. Click **OK** to finish.

5. Click ✎ (Shell) again.

6. Select **Individual** and then multi-select both flange surfaces.

7. In the *Thickness* field, enter **0.4**. The dialog box opens as shown in Figure 4–108.

Creo Simulate assumes the selected surfaces to be the midsurfaces of the part. The flange material is extended by 0.2in in either direction.

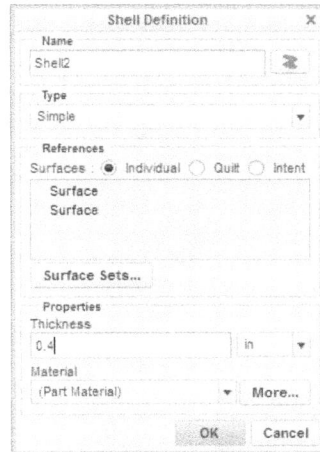

Figure 4–108

8. Click **OK** to finish.

9. The model displays as shown in Figure 4–109. Note that Creo Simulate visually thickens the created shells, according to their actual thicknesses, and shows them as transparent solids.

Figure 4–109

10. Click 🖳 (Simulation Display) in the floating toolbar. The Simulation Display dialog box opens as shown in Figure 4–110.

Figure 4–110

11. Explore the **Shells** drop-down list by selecting various options (i.e., Outline, Wireframe, Shaded, Transparent) and clicking **Preview**.

12. Select the *Modeling Entities* tab and clear the **Shells** and **Material Assignments** options, as shown in Figure 4–111.

Figure 4–111

© 2017, ASCENT - Center for Technical Knowledge®

13. Click **OK**. The model displays as shown in Figure 4–112.

Figure 4–112

14. In the *Refine Model* tab, in the *AutoGEM* area, click

    ⬚ (Review Geometry) to open the Simulation Geometry
    dialog box and then click **Apply**. The model displays as
    shown in Figure 4–113. Check whether all of the surfaces are
    highlighted in green - these are the shell surfaces.

Figure 4–113

15. Click **Close**.

Task 4 - Mesh the model.

1. In the *Refine Model* tab, in the *AutoGEM* area, expand the Control drop-down list and select **Edge Length By Curvature**, as shown in Figure 4–114.

Figure 4–114

*The **Edge Length By Curvature** option is useful for accurate meshing of curved surfaces. Ratio 1.0 means that the mesh size will be made roughly equal to the radius of curvature of the surface.*

2. In the Edge Length By Curvature Control dialog box that opens, expand the References drop-down list and select **Components**. This automatically selects the part. In the *Edge Length / Radius of Curvature ratio* field, enter **1** as shown in Figure 4–115.

Figure 4–115

3. Click **OK** to finish.

4. Click (AutoGEM). The AutoGEM dialog box opens. Click **Create**.

© 2017, ASCENT - Center for Technical Knowledge®

5. Once the meshing has finished, close both the AutoGEM Summary and Diagnostics dialog boxes. The model displays as shown in Figure 4–116.

Figure 4–116

6. Click ⬚ (Simulation Display) in the floating toolbar. The Simulation Display dialog box opens.

7. Select the *Mesh* tab and clear the **Display Shells with Zero Thickness** option, as shown in Figure 4–117.

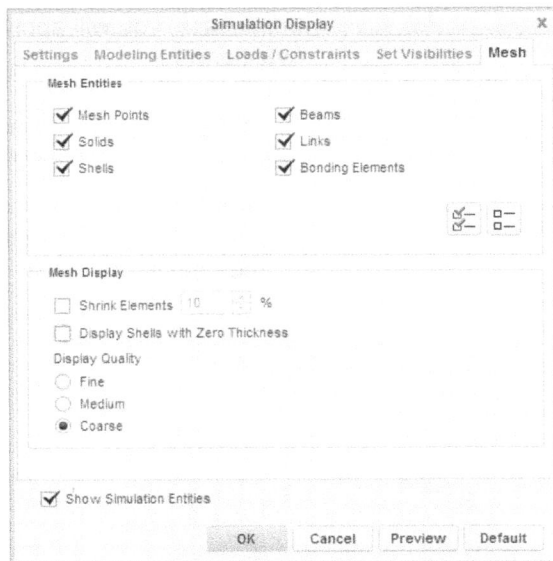

Figure 4–117

8. Click **OK**. The model displays as shown in Figure 4–118.

Figure 4–118

Note that the elements have now been thickened, using the thicknesses that you applied when creating the shells.

9. Click **Close** to close the AutoGEM dialog box and save the mesh.

Task 5 - Apply a load to the model.

In this task, you will apply a load of 1000lb to the holes in the oval flange.

1. In the *Home* tab, click ⊢ (Force/Moment). The Force/Moment dialog box opens.

2. Expand the References drop-down list, select **Edges/ Curves**, and then multi-select the edges of the two holes in the oval flange, as shown in Figure 4–119.

Figure 4–119

© 2017, ASCENT - Center for Technical Knowledge®

3. In the Force/Moment dialog box, enter the other required information as shown in Figure 4–120.

Figure 4–120

4. Click **OK**. The model displays as shown in Figure 4–121.

Figure 4–121

Task 6 - Apply constraints to the model.

In this task, you will constrain the four holes in the square flange.

1. Click (Displacement). The Constraint dialog box opens.

2. Expand the References drop-down list, select **Edges/Curves**, and then multi-select the edges of the four holes in the square flange, as shown in Figure 4–122.

Figure 4–122

3. For the constraint, for the *Name*, enter **fixed**. Fix all of the Translations and Rotations, as shown in Figure 4–123.

Figure 4–123

© 2017, ASCENT - Center for Technical Knowledge®

4. Click **OK**. The model displays as shown in Figure 4–124.

Figure 4–124

Analysis Tasks

Task 7 - Solve the model using the Multi-Pass Adaptive convergence option.

1. Create a Static Analysis named **tube_shell**.

2. Select the **Multi-Pass Adaptive** convergence method.

3. In the *Polynomial Order* field, enter **9** for *Maximum* and in the *Limits* area, in the *Percent Convergence* field, enter **5** percent convergence, as shown in Figure 4–125.

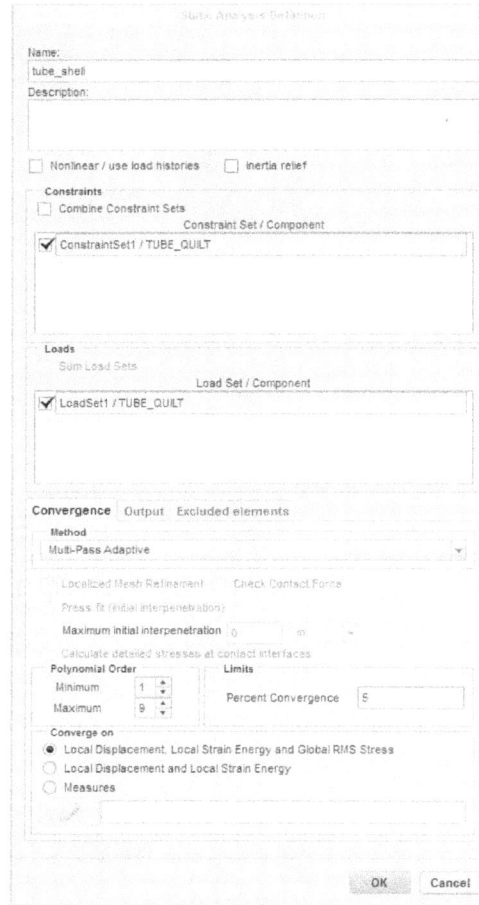

Figure 4–125

4. Start the analysis run and wait until it finishes.

5. In the Analyses and Design Studies dialog box, click (Status). In the Run Status window, verify that the analysis has converged, as shown in Figure 4–126.

© 2017, ASCENT - Center for Technical Knowledge®

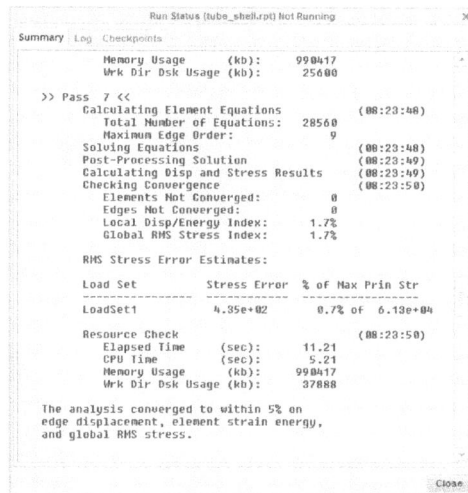

Figure 4–126

Results Tasks

Task 8 - Display the displacement results.

1. Create and display an animated fringe plot of the
   Displacement Magnitude. Use the animation controls to start,
   stop, and step through the frames of the animation. Note
   Frame 5 of the animation, it should display as shown in
   Figure 4–127.

Figure 4–127

Note that the maximum displacement in the model is
approximately 0.0447 inches.

2. Create and display an undeformed fringe plot of the von Mises Stress. It should display as shown in Figure 4–128.

Figure 4–128

Note that the maximum stress is approximately 59ksi, and that it occurs at one of the holes in the square flange. Use ◼⁺ (Model Max) to find the exact location if needed.

3. Click ✎ (Edit) to edit the von Mises Stress plot. In the Result Window Definition dialog box, in the *Quantity* tab, clear the **Bending** and **Transverse Shear** options, as shown in Figure 4–129.

Figure 4–129

© 2017, ASCENT - Center for Technical Knowledge®

The membrane component of the stress is constant through the shell thickness, and is due to loads acting in-plane of the midsurface.

4. Click **OK and Show**. Now the result plot displays only the membrane component of stress in the part, as shown in Figure 4–130.

Figure 4–130

Note that the maximum membrane stress occurs in the tube walls near the square flange.

5. Click ✎ (Edit) again. In the Result Window Definition dialog box, in the *Quantity* tab, clear the **Membrane** and **Transverse Shear** options, and select the **Bending** option, as shown in Figure 4–131.

Figure 4–131

The bending component of stress is anti-symmetric through the thickness, (i.e., it is tensile on one side and compressive on the other side). It is caused by the out-of-plane bending loads.

6. Click **OK and Show**. Now the result plot only displays the bending component of stress in the part, as shown in Figure 4–132.

Figure 4–132

Note that the bending stress (i.e., deformation) is most pronounced in the square flange of the part.

Task 9 - Save and close the model.

1. Select **File>Close**. Click **Don't Save** when prompted to save the results.

2. Close the Analyses and Design Studies dialog box.

3. Exit Creo Simulate. Save and close the model in Creo Parametric.

© 2017, ASCENT - Center for Technical Knowledge®

Practice 4d

Shell and Solid Combination

Practice Objective

* Set up and run an analysis on a part using a combination of solid and shell elements.

Shell elements can drastically reduce the number of elements in the model and computation time to obtain a solution.

In this practice, you will use the shell element idealizations to set up and analyze a crank part, as shown in Figure 4–133. The crank arms are thin-walls. The part can be analyzed using solid elements. However, it is more efficient to idealize any thin-walled features using shell elements.

Figure 4–133

Modeling Tasks

Task 1 - Open the part.

1. Open **solid_shell.prt** in Creo Parametric. The part displays as shown in Figure 4–134.

Figure 4–134

2. Turn off the datum plane and datum axis display.

3. Ensure that the unit system is set to **mmNs**.

4. Switch to Creo Simulate environment.

Task 2 - Apply the material.

1. Click ⬑ (Materials). The Materials dialog box opens.

2. In the *Materials in Library* area, scroll through the list and select **SS** (stainless steel).

3. Click ▶▶▶ (Add Material) to transfer **SS** to the *Materials in Model* area.

4. Click ✐ (Edit) to check your material properties and click **OK** when done.

   The following values are the default material properties for stainless steel (SS):

   • Poisson = 0.3
   • Young's modulus = 193053 MPa
   • Density = 7.74372e-9 tonne/mm^3

5. Click **OK** to close the Materials dialog box.

© 2017, ASCENT - Center for Technical Knowledge®

6. Click (Material Assignment) to assign the material to the part.

7. Since there is only one material in the model, Creo Simulate automatically selects it for the part. Click **OK** to close the Material Assignment dialog box.

8. Using the Simulation Display dialog box, toggle off the Material Assignment visualization.

Task 3 - Define the shell elements.

The wall and flange thickness in the arms of the crank is 5mm. You will use the **Detect Shell Pairs** tool to automatically create the shell pairs in those areas.

1. In the *Refine Model* tab, expand the Shell Pair drop-down list and select **Detect Shell Pairs**. The Auto Detect Shell Pairs dialog box opens as shown in Figure 4–135.

```
Auto Detect Shell Pairs      X
Components
  Part  SOLID_SHELL

  Shell Pair Detection Method
  ✔ Use Geometry Analysis
  Characteristic Thickness
  |              mm   ▼

            Start    Cancel
```

Figure 4–135

Creo Simulate will pair all of the parallel surfaces in the model that are closer than 6mm.

2. In the *Characteristic Thickness* field, enter **6** and click **Start**. Creo Simulate runs the automatic detection algorithm and closes the Auto Detect Shell Pairs dialog box.

3. Check the Model Tree. Six shell pairs should be displayed in the Model Tree.

4. In the *Refine Model* tab, in the *AutoGEM* area, click
   ⬚ (Review Geometry) to open the Simulation Geometry
   dialog box. Select the required options as shown in
   Figure 4–136.

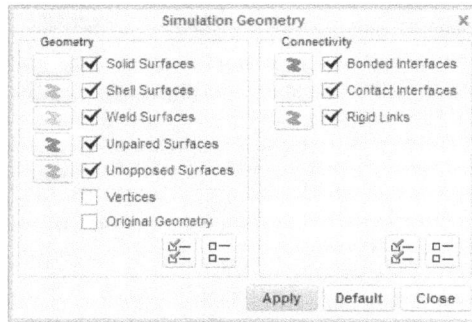

Figure 4–136

5. Click **Apply**. The model displays as shown in Figure 4–137.

Figure 4–137

Verify that the end bosses and pin are displayed in gray (these
are the uncompressed areas), and that the thin-walled arms are
displayed in green (these are the shell pairs compressed to a
midsurface).

6. In the Simulation Geometry dialog box, click **Close**.

© 2017, ASCENT - Center for Technical Knowledge®

Task 4 - Mesh the model.

1. Expand the AutoGEM drop-down list and verify that the **Solid/Midsurface** option is enabled, as shown in Figure 4–138.

Figure 4–138

2. Expand the AutoGEM drop-down list and select **Settings**. The AutoGEM Settings dialog box opens. Clear the **Create Links Where Needed** option, as shown in Figure 4–139.

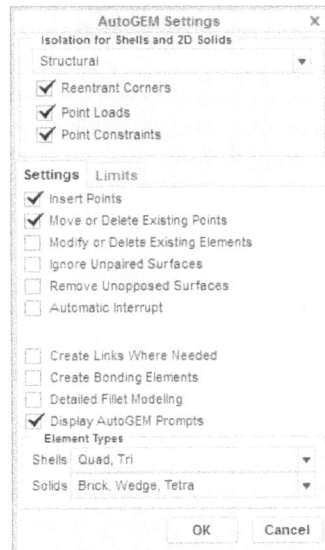

Figure 4–139

The Links in Creo Simulate are used to ensure the connectivity of the shell and solid elements along rotational degrees of freedom, so the shells attached to solids do not rotate like a hinge. The Links can significantly increase the analysis runtime.

Links are only needed if you have a shell in your model that is connected to a solid along a straight line. In the crank model, shells are connected to solids along T-shaped lines. Therefore, Links are not needed.

3. Click **OK**.

4. Click ▦ (AutoGEM). The AutoGEM dialog box opens as shown in Figure 4–140.

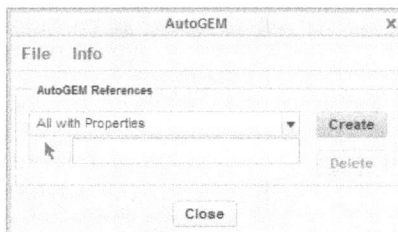

Figure 4–140

*The **All with Properties** option requires that materials be applied before meshing.*

5. Expand the AutoGEM References drop-down list, select **All with Properties**, and click **Create**.

6. The AutoGEM Summary and Diagnostics dialog boxes open as shown in Figure 4–141.

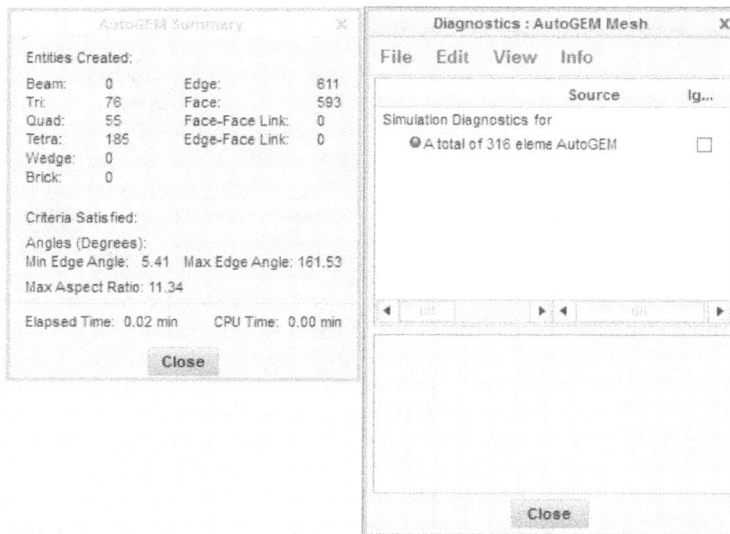

Figure 4–141

In the AutoGEM Summary box, note that the AutoGEM has now created both the solid elements (185 Tetra) and shell elements (76 Tri and 55 Quad).

© 2017, ASCENT - Center for Technical Knowledge®

7. Close both the AutoGEM Summary and Diagnostics boxes, but do not close the AutoGEM dialog box yet. The model displays as shown in Figure 4–142.

Figure 4–142

Note that two end bosses and the pin have been meshed onto solid elements (displayed in blue), while the arms have been meshed onto shell elements (displayed in green).

8. Click **Close** to close the AutoGEM dialog box and save the mesh.

Task 5 - Apply loads to the model.

In this task, you will apply a bearing load on the hole in the boss shown in Figure 4–143. The bearing load has a resultant force in a specified direction (in this case, the negative Y-direction in the WCS). The bearing load is applied normal to the bearing surface in a non-uniform distribution. The bearing load simulates a lateral load that is exerted on a hole by a shaft placed in the hole.

Figure 4–143

1. In the *Loads* area of the *Home* tab, click ⊠ (Bearing). The Bearing Load dialog box opens as shown in Figure 4–144.

Figure 4–144

2. In the *Name* field, enter **b_load**.

© 2017, ASCENT - Center for Technical Knowledge®

3. Select the arm hole shown in Figure 4–145.

Select this arm hole

Figure 4–145

4. In the *Y* field, enter **-500**.

5. Click **Preview** to display the bearing load distribution, as shown in Figure 4–146.

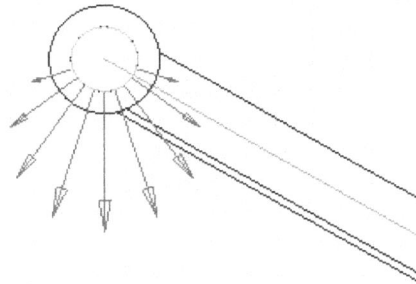

Figure 4–146

6. Click **OK**. The bearing load displays as shown in Figure 4–147.

Figure 4–147

Task 6 - Apply constraints.

In this task, you will constrain the movement of the central rod and the end boss of the crank arms, as shown in Figure 4–148.

End boss

Central rod

Figure 4–148

You will constrain each cylindrical surface against radial and axial motion, but enable rotation around their axes. This can be done using **Pin** constraint.

1. Click ⊘ (Pin). The Pin Constraint dialog box opens.

© 2017, ASCENT - Center for Technical Knowledge®

Fixing the axial direction and freeing the rotation simulates the rod being supported by a sleeve bearing or bushing.

2. Select the cylindrical surface of the central rod (shown in Figure 4–148). In the *Name* field, enter **rod**. Constrain the axial translation and leave the rotation free, as shown in Figure 4–149.

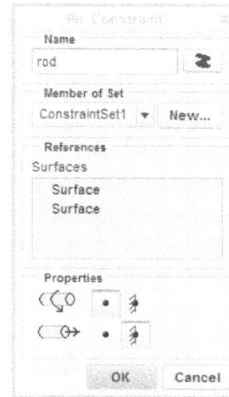

Figure 4–149

3. Click **OK**. The pin constraint displays as shown in Figure 4–150.

Figure 4–150

Fixing the axial direction and freeing the rotation simulates the end boss being supported by a pin.

4. Click (Pin) again. Select the hole surface in the end boss (shown in Figure 4–148). In the *Name* field, enter **end_boss**. Constrain the axial translation and leave the rotation free, as shown in Figure 4–151.

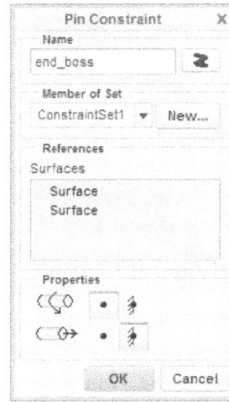

Figure 4–151

5. Click **OK**. The pin constraint displays as shown in Figure 4–152.

Figure 4–152

Analysis Tasks

Task 7 - Solve the model using the Single-Pass Adaptive convergence option.

1. Create a Static Analysis named **crank_shell**.

2. Select the **Single-Pass Adaptive** convergence method.

3. In the *Output* tab, increase the *Plotting Grid* value to **10**.

4. Start the analysis run and wait until it finishes.

5. In the Analyses and Design Studies dialog box, click (Status). Examine the Run Status window that displays. Scroll up or down to the *RMS Stress Error Estimates* area and note that the analysis converged to approximately 6.5% RMS Stress Error, as shown in Figure 4–153.

The Plotting Grid is a grid of points that Creo Simulate uses to display results within the elements. A higher density plotting grid is recommended to obtain smoother looking result plots.

© 2017, ASCENT - Center for Technical Knowledge®

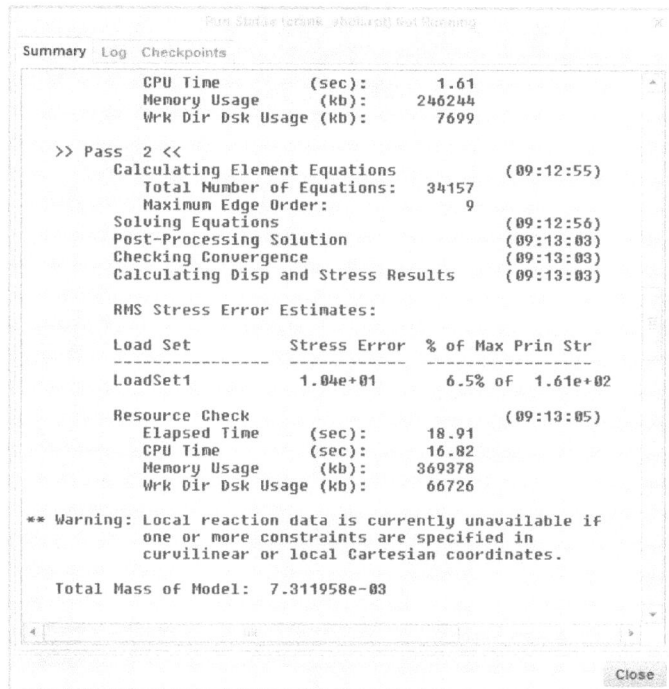

Figure 4–153

Ignore the warning prompting you about the local reaction data. This is just a notification that force reactions are not available on Pin constraints.

6. Close the Run Status window.

Results Tasks

Task 8 - Display and animate the displacement results.

1. In the Analyses and Design Studies dialog box, click (Review Results). The Result Window Definition dialog box opens.

2. In the *Name* field, enter **deformation**.

3. Expand the Quantity tab drop-down list and select **Displacement**.

4. In the *Display Options* tab, select the **Deformed**, **Overlay Undeformed**, **Show Element Edges,** and **Animate** options.

5. Click **OK and Show**. The Displacement Magnitude result plot is displayed and animated.

6. Zoom in on the rod. Note that the rod's rotation is not restricted, as if the rod was supported by sleeve bearings or bushings. This is because you applied the Pin Constraint in a previous task.

7. Stop the animation at Frame 5. The result plot displays as shown in Figure 4–154.

Figure 4–154

Note that the maximum displacement magnitude under the given loading is approximately 5.4mm.

Task 9 - Display the stress results.

---

1. In the *Home* tab, click (Copy). The Result Window Definition dialog box opens.

2. In the *Name* field, enter **von_mises**.

3. Expand the Quantity tab drop-down list and select **Stress**.

4. Clear the **Overlay Undeformed**, **Animate, Deformed**, and **Show Element Edges** options.

5. Click **OK and Show**. The Stress von Mises result plot is displayed along with the Displacement Magnitude result plot.

© 2017, ASCENT - Center for Technical Knowledge®

6. In the *View* tab, Click (Show). In the Display Result Window dialog box, clear **deformation**, as shown in Figure 4–155.

Figure 4–155

7. Click **OK**. The von Mises stress plot displays as shown in Figure 4–156.

Figure 4–156

8. In the *View* tab, expand the Appearance drop-down list and select **Visibilities**. In the Visibilities window, clear the **Labels** and **Coordinate Systems** options, as shown in Figure 4–157. Click **Close** when finished.

Figure 4–157

9. In the *Format* tab, select ▐▌ (Edit). In the Edit Legend dialog box, change the *Max value* to **80**, as shown in Figure 4–158.

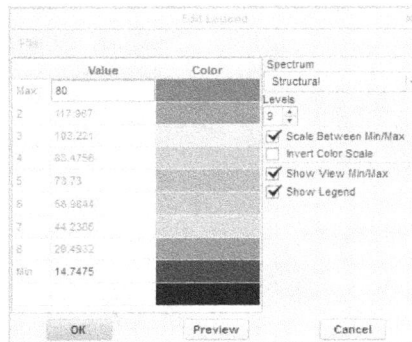

Figure 4–158

© 2017, ASCENT - Center for Technical Knowledge®

10. Click **OK**. The von Mises stress result plot displays as shown in Figure 4–159.

"deformation" - crank_shell - crank_shell

147.458
80.0000
71.8434
63.6869
55.5303
47.3738
39.2172
31.0606
22.9041
14.7475
0.00193

Figure 4–159

Note that the result window is now less cluttered and that it is easier to examine the results.

Task 10 - Save and close the model.

1. Select **File>Close**. Click **Don't Save** when prompted to save the results.

2. Close the Analyses and Design Studies dialog box.

3. Exit Creo Simulate. Save and close the model in Creo Parametric.

Practice 4e

Analysis of a Sheet Metal Bracket

Practice Objectives

- Create shell pairs.
- Apply loads, constraints, and material properties.
- Set up and run a Multi-Pass Adaptive analysis.
- Display the results.

In this practice, you will perform a static stress analysis on the sheet metal bracket shown in Figure 4–160, with minimum instruction.

Figure 4–160

Task 1 - Create shell pairs.

1. Open **sm_bracket.prt** and launch Creo Simulate.

2. Using the Detect Shell Pairs tool, create shell pairs.

Task 2 - Apply material, loads, and constraints.

*Tip: The part is sheet metal, therefore there is no need to use the **Use Geometry Analysis** option.*

1. Apply the SS material:
   - **Tensile Yield Stress:** 50 ksi
   - **Failure Criterion:** Distortion Energy (von Mises)

© 2017, ASCENT - Center for Technical Knowledge®

2. Fully constrain both tabs and the back surface of the bracket, as shown in Figure 4–161.

Full constraint

Figure 4–161

3. Apply **100lbf** load in the +Y direction to the edge shown in Figure 4–162.

100lbf load in +Y direction

Figure 4–162

Task 3 - Set up and run the analysis.

1. Create a new static analysis with the following parameters:
   - **Analysis name:** sm_bracket
   - **Convergence method:** Multi-Pass Adaptive
   - **Maximum Polynomial Order:** 9
   - **Percent Convergence:** 5
   - **Plotting Grid:** 10

2. Run the analysis.

3. Display the Status window. Note the RMS Stress Error value.

Task 4 - Visualize the analysis results.

1. Visualize and animate the **Displacement Magnitude** fringe plot.
   - Does the part deform according to the applied loads and constraints?

2. Visualize the **Displacement Y** fringe plot.
   - What is the maximum deflection of the part in the direction of the load?

3. Display the **von Mises Stress** fringe plot. Find the location of the maximum stress.
   - Does the maximum stress exceed the yield strength of the material?

© 2017, ASCENT - Center for Technical Knowledge®

Beams and Frames

Learning Objectives in this Chapter

- Understand beam idealizations.
- Create beam elements.
- Define beam sections.
- Understand beam coordinate systems.
- Define the beam action coordinate system.
- Define the beam shape coordinate system.

5.1 Beam Elements

Beam elements are one-dimensional elements, but represent 3D idealizations. An FEA model might only be composed of beam elements. Beam elements can also be mixed with shells and solids to represent a FEA model. An example of a simple beam is shown in Figure 5–1.

Figure 5–1

The idealized version of the beam shown in Figure 5–1 is shown in Figure 5–2.

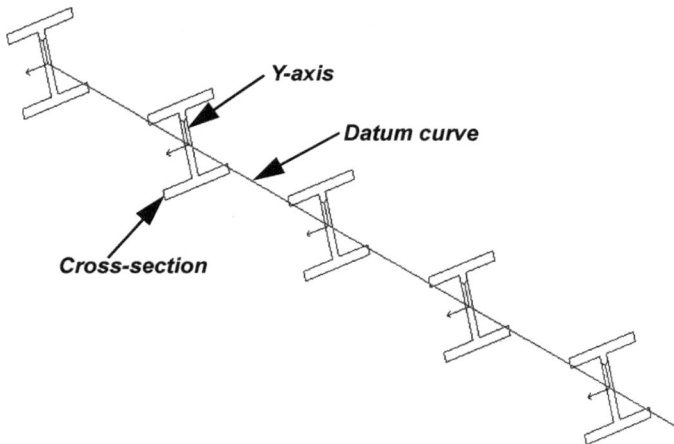

Figure 5–2

Simulation features created in Creo Simulate do not display when you return to Creo Parametric.

In Creo Simulate, a beam element is represented by a straight line or planar curve with an assigned cross-section. The line or curve can be created as a datum curve in Creo Parametric or as a simulation feature in Creo Simulate. In the example shown in Figure 5–2 an I-beam section is used and the straight line is a sketched datum curve.

© 2017, ASCENT - Center for Technical Knowledge®

Different beam section shapes can be used for different purposes. In the example shown in Figure 5–3, a hollow circle section and a sketched datum curve are used for a frame.

Figure 5–3

The idealized version of the frame is shown in Figure 5–4.

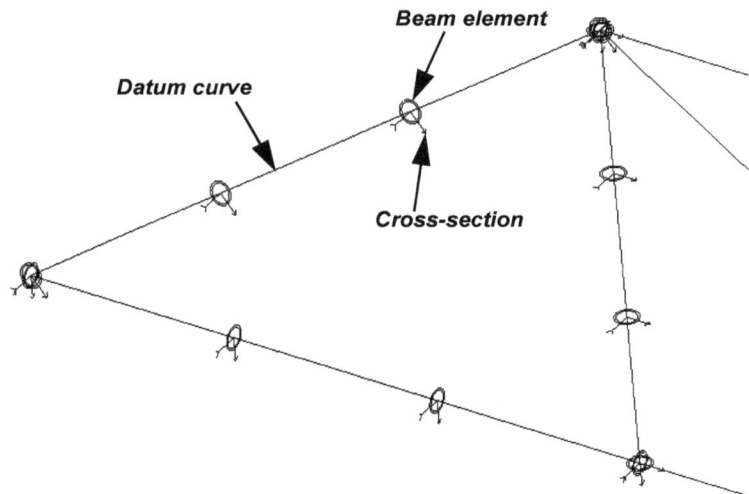

Figure 5–4

Creo Simulate automatically places beam elements on a specified datum curve or simulation feature. However, you must define the attributes of the beam element before running the analysis.

Beam Definitions

Use the following steps to define the attributes (e.g., material, beam cross-section, etc.) of the beam:

1. In the *Refine Model* tab, click (Beam). The Beam Definition dialog box opens, as shown in Figure 5–5.

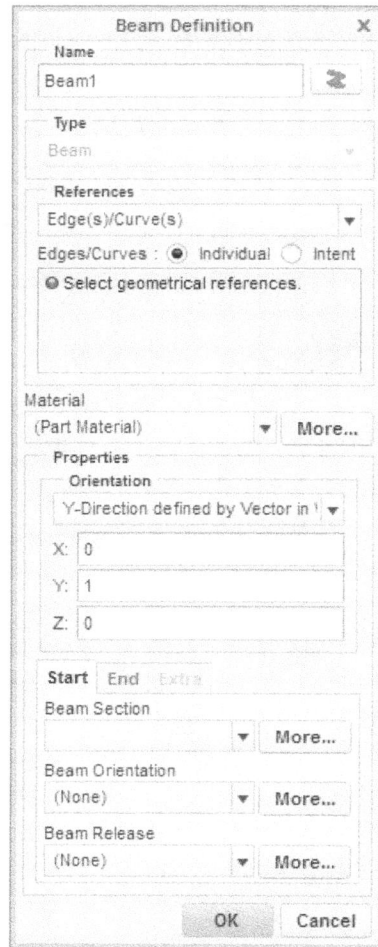

Figure 5–5

2. In the *Name* field, enter a name for the beam.
3. Define the geometry references. References define the underlying curve. The following types of geometry references are available:
   - Point-Point
   - Point-Surface (Projection)
   - Point-Edge (Projection)
   - Chain
   - Edge(s)/Curve(s)
   - Point-Point Pairs

© 2017, ASCENT - Center for Technical Knowledge®

4. Expand the Material drop-down list and select an option to define the material of the beam.
5. Define the direction of the Y-axis by selecting a point, axis, or vector in WCS. If you use a vector to define the Y-axis, you must specify the X-, Y-, and Z-coordinates. The rotation of the beam around its local X-axis, relative to the World Coordinate System (WCS), is defined by specifying the direction in which the Beam Action Coordinate System (BACS) Y-axis is pointing.
6. Define the type of beam section.
7. Define the orientation of the beam relative to BACS.
8. Define the degrees of freedom to release at the beam's ends.
9. Click **OK** to complete the beam definition.

Beam Sections

Creo Simulate has 11 standard types of beams that you can use for your analysis. These beams are shown in Figure 5–6.

Square   Rectangle   Hollow Rectangle   Channel

I-Beam   L-Section   Diamond   Solid Circle

Hollow Circle   Solid Ellipse   Hollow Ellipse

Figure 5–6

You can also use a Creo sketch (.SEC file) as a beam cross-section.

5.2 Beam Coordinate Systems

Each beam model starts with a World Coordinate System (WCS), which is Creo Simulate's default coordinate system. Creo Simulate also uses two local coordinate systems to define the beam's cross-section orientation relative to the WCS. The local coordinate systems are oriented with respect to the WCS. This is notably valid for curved beams and beams whose cross-sections are asymmetrical about their centroid in at least one lateral direction. For example, these can include channels and angles, as shown in Figure 5–7.

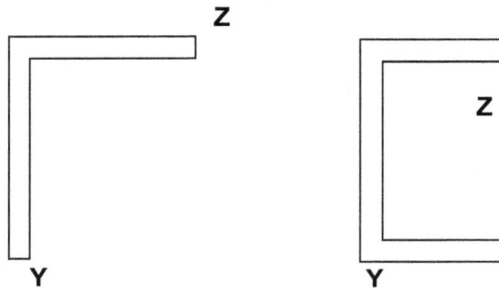

Figure 5–7

The two local coordinate systems used by Creo Simulate in beam analysis are as follows:

• Beam Action Coordinate System (BACS)

• Beam Shape Coordinate System (BSCS)

© 2017, ASCENT - Center for Technical Knowledge®

5.3 Beam Action Coordinate System (BACS)

Forces and moments applied to the beams are transmitted to the beams using the Beam Action Coordinate System (BACS). The underlying curve or points define the X-axis of the beam's BACS, as shown in Figure 5–8.

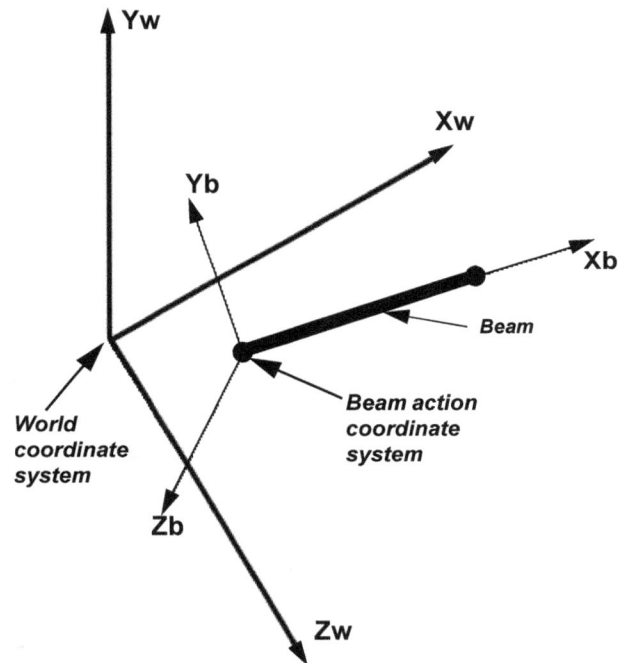

Figure 5–8

The beam's BACS Y- and Z-axes are perpendicular to the beam. The orientation of the beam relative to WCS is defined by the direction of the BACS Y-axis around the beam's BACS X-axis.

Curves and points on a beam can be created as datum curves or points in Creo Parametric or as simulation features in Creo Simulate.

Beams are associated with geometry curves or by connecting two or more points defined in the WCS. For straight beams, the underlying curve or points define the X-axis of the beam's BACS, as shown in Figure 5–8. The beam's local Y- and Z-axes are perpendicular to the beam. The rotation of the beam around its local X-axis, relative to the WCS, is defined by specifying the direction of the BACS Y-axis.

Several beams with the same properties can be created simultaneously.

This direction can be determined by specifying an axis direction, edge, or point, or providing vector components in the WCS. Some examples of the specification of the BACS Y-axis using vector components are shown in Figure 5–9.

x,y,z = Beam (BACS)
X,Y,Z = World Coordinate (WCS)

Figure 5–9

All of the properties of each beam element are set in the Beam Definition dialog box. For straight beams, the example in Figure 5–10 shows how the system assigns BACS coordinates relative to WCS using the **Vector in WCS** option.

The BACS X-axis always lies along the length of the beam. The specified orientation vector **0,-1,0** makes the BACS Y-axis aligned with the opposite to the WCS Y-axis direction. The system then uses the right-hand rule to determine the BACS Z-axis.

© 2017, ASCENT - Center for Technical Knowledge®

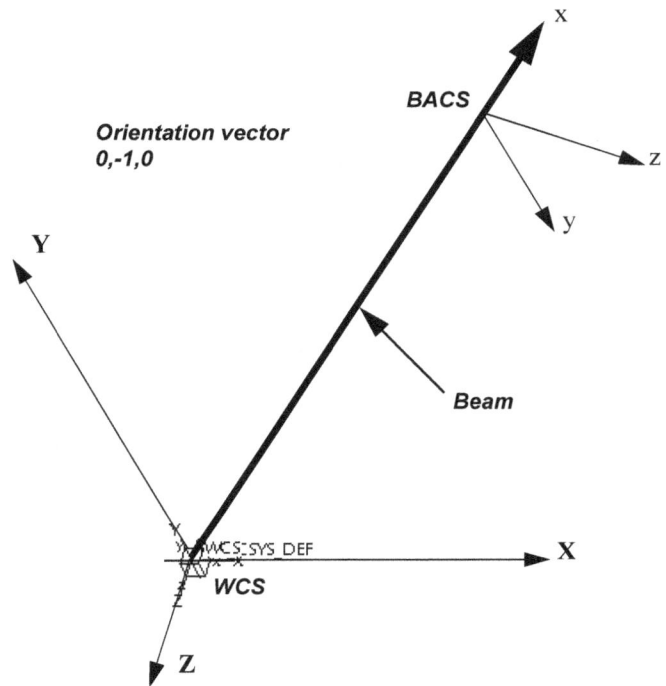

Figure 5–10

For curved beams (which must lie in a plane), the BACS X-axis
lies along the length of the beam, tangent to the beam. The
BACS Y-axis lies in the plane of the curved beam. The BACS
Z-axis is perpendicular to the plane of the curved beam. The
BACS Y-axis changes direction as the beam curves. Figure 5–11
shows an example of a curved beam.

Figure 5–11

5.4 Beam Shape Coordinate System (BSCS)

For most standard shapes, the origin of the BSCS coincides with the centroid of the section.

The beam cross-sectional shape and position are defined relative to the BSCS. The shape is defined in the BSCS YZ plane. The X-axis of the BSCS is always parallel to the BACS X-axis, as shown in Figure 5–12.

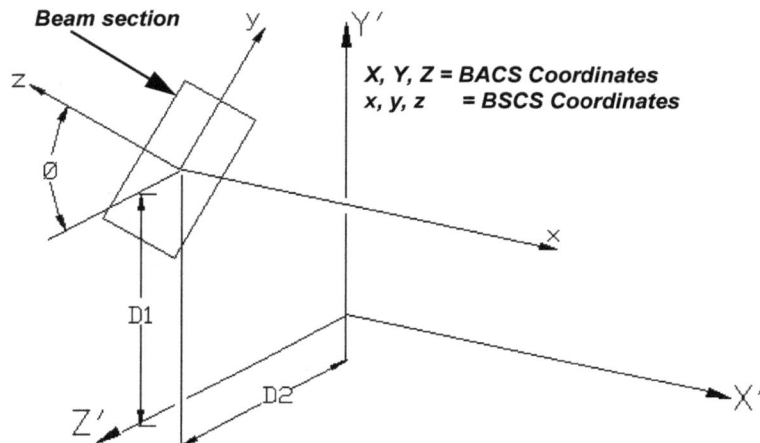

Figure 5–12

The BSCS origin (shear center) is defined by the offsets D1 and D2, measured from the origin of the BACS. The orientation of the BSCS is determined by the angle (Ø). If Ø is zero, the BSCS is parallel to the BACS. If the offsets D1 and D2 are zero, the BSCS coincides with the BACS. Examples of standard Creo Simulate beam section shapes defined in the BSCS axes are shown in Figure 5–13.

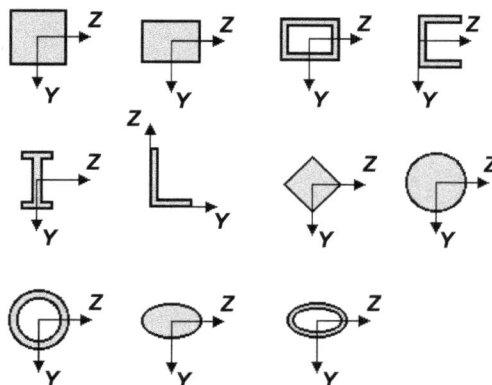

Figure 5–13

© 2017, ASCENT - Center for Technical Knowledge®

Use the following steps to position the origin of the BSCS relative to the BACS:

1. In the Beam Orientation Definition dialog box, enter the beam offset values for DY (i.e., D1) and DZ (i.e., D2). Alternatively, select the **Shear Center** option to position the beam section relative to the BACS. The Beam Orientation Definition dialog box is shown in Figure 5–14.

Figure 5–14

2. In the *Name* field, enter a name for the beam orientation.
3. Specify the angle about which you want the beam's X-axis to rotate.
4. Select the **Shape Origin** or **Shear Center** option to define the value used for the offset of the beam shape coordinate system (BSCS)
5. Define the values for each offset in the BACS X-, Y- and Z-directions.
6. Click **OK** to complete the beam orientation definition.

Shear center is the point on a beam section about which the section rotates under deflection.

Practice 5a | Beam Analysis

Practice Objectives

- Set up a beam model.
- Set up beam releases.
- Run a beam model.
- Analyze a beam model.

The aspect ratio of the beam element should be greater than 10:1(the ratio of its length to its largest section dimension).

In this practice, you will use beam element idealizations to set up, run, and analyze a beam model. The beam model is shown in Figure 5–15. The beam cross section is an I-beam. The beam's ends are fixed and the middle support is a roller.

Figure 5–15

You will apply linear distributed loads to a section of the model and a point load 3.5 m from the left side of the beam, as shown in Figure 5–16.

Figure 5–16

© 2017, ASCENT - Center for Technical Knowledge®

Modeling Tasks

Task 1 - Open 1d_beam.prt and start Creo Simulate.

1. Open **1d_beam.prt** in Creo Parametric. The part displays as shown in Figure 5–17.

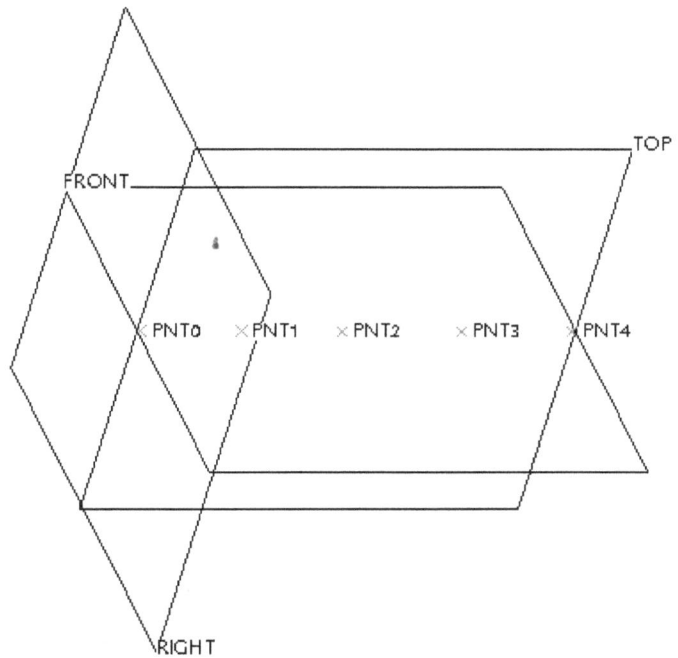

Figure 5–17

2. Ensure that the unit systems are **MKS**.

3. Switch to the Creo Simulate environment.

4. In the *View* tab, in the *Show* area, click ⣿ (Point Tag Display) to visualize the datum point tags. The model displays as shown in Figure 5–18.

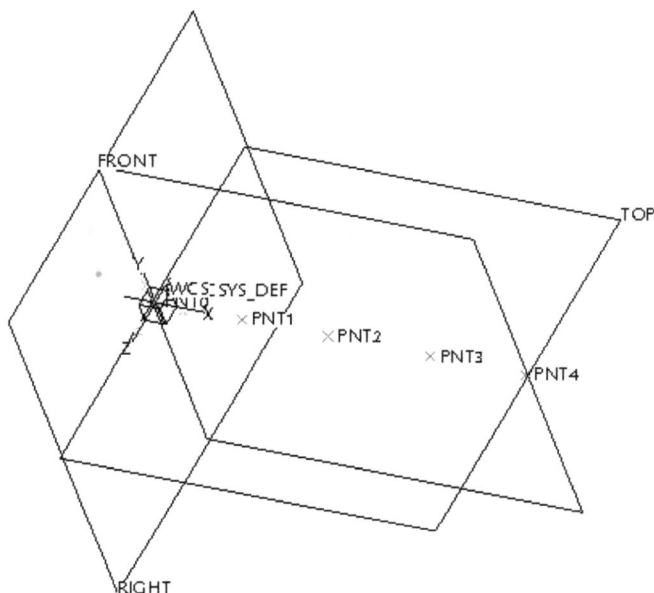

Figure 5–18

Task 2 - Create a datum curve as a simulation feature.

In beam models, distributed loads can only be defined on datum curves. The load is transferred to the beam elements created on the curve.

1. In the *Refine Model* tab, expand the *Datum* area (as shown in Figure 5–19), and click ∿ (Curve).

Figure 5–19

© 2017, ASCENT - Center for Technical Knowledge®

2. Create a datum curve between PNT1 and PNT2. The datum curve displays as shown in Figure 5–20.

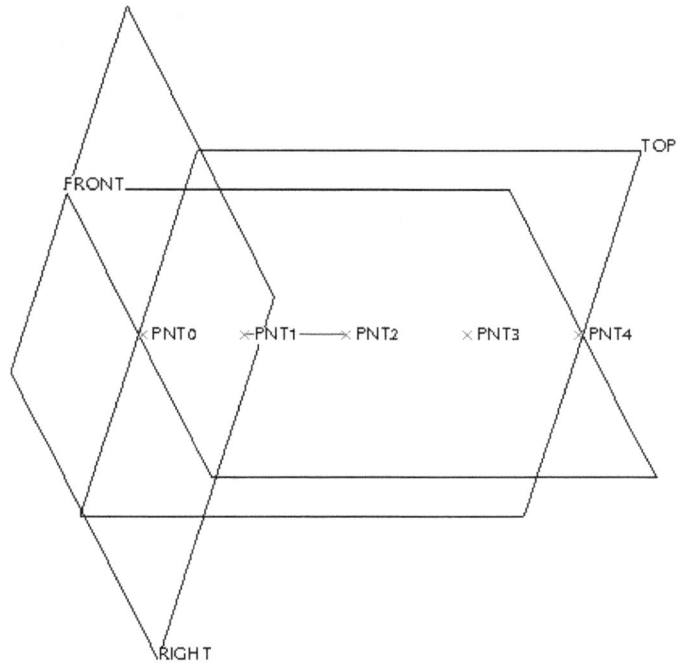

Figure 5–20

Task 3 - Create a beam element between PNT0 and PNT1.

1. In the *Refine Model* tab, click ⬚ (Beam). The Beam Definition dialog box opens as shown in Figure 5–21.

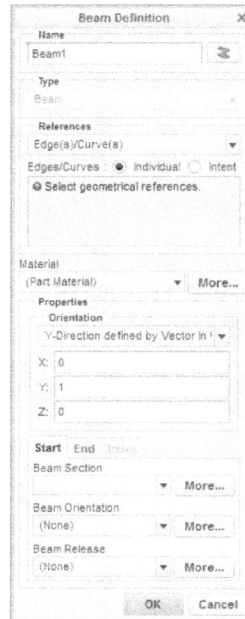

Figure 5–21

2. In the *Name* field, enter **beam_1**.

3. Expand the References drop-down list and select **Point-Point**.

4. Select **PNT0** and **PNT1**.

5. In the *Material* area, click **More**. The Materials dialog box opens.

6. In the *Materials in Library* area, select **STEEL**. Click ▶▶▶ (Add Material) to transfer STEEL to the *Materials in Model* area.

The model's material properties should be as stated.

7. Click ✎ (Edit) to check the material properties. The following values are the default material properties for HS-low-alloy steel (STEEL):
   - Poisson = 0.27
   - Young's modulus = 1.99948 e11 Pa
   - Density = 7827.08 Kg/m^3

© 2017, ASCENT - Center for Technical Knowledge®

8. Click **OK** in the Material Definition dialog box and Materials dialog box. STEEL displays in the *Material* area in the Beam Definition dialog box.

9. In the *Orientation* area, accept the default X-, Y-, and Z-values.

10. Next to the Beam Section drop-down list, click **More**. The Beam Sections dialog box opens as shown in Figure 5–22.

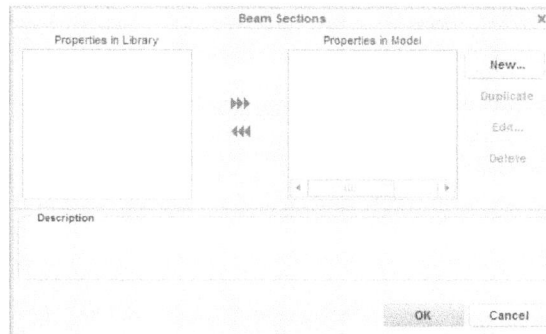

Figure 5–22

11. Click **New**. The Beam Section Definition dialog box opens as shown in Figure 5–23.

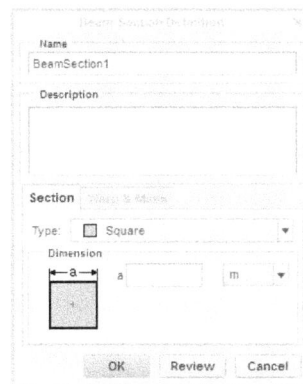

Figure 5–23

12. In the *Name* field, enter **I_beam_section**.

*If the section is not listed in the Type drop-down list, you can sketch it using the **Sketched Solid** and **Sketched Thin** sketch options in the Type drop-down list. These options open Sketcher in Creo Parametric.*

13. Expand the Type drop-down list and select **I-Beam** as shown in Figure 5–24.

Figure 5–24

14. In the *b* field, enter **0.092**.

15. In the *t* field, enter **0.009**.

16. In the *di* field, enter **0.164**.

17. In the *tw* field, enter **0.006**.

18. Click **Review**. The Simulation Information window displays. The window contains the section properties shown in Figure 5–25.

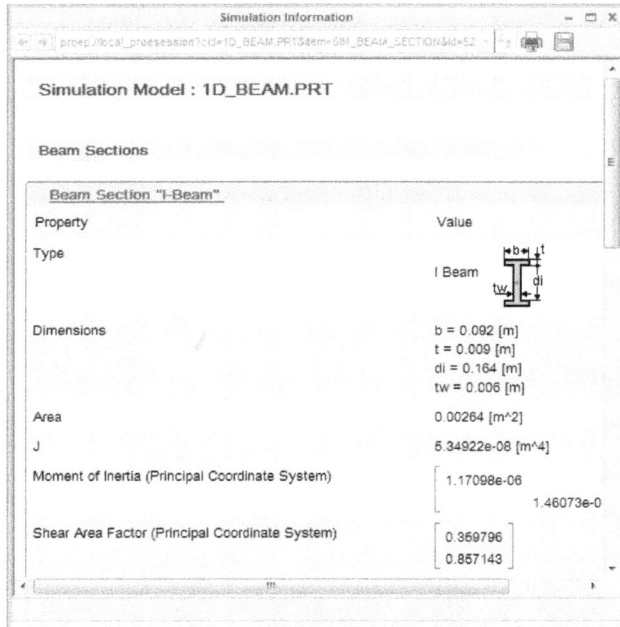

Figure 5–25

19. Close the Simulation Information window.

© 2017, ASCENT - Center for Technical Knowledge®

20. Click **OK** to close the Beam Section Definition dialog box.

21. Click **OK** to close the Beam Sections dialog box.

22. Click **OK** to close the Beam Definition dialog box. The model displays as shown in Figure 5–26.

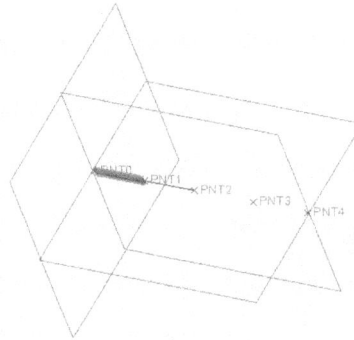

Figure 5–26

Task 4 - Create a beam element between PNT1 and PNT2.

1. Click (Beam). The Beam Definition dialog box opens.

2. In the *Name* field, enter **beam_2**.

3. Expand the References drop-down list and select **Edge/Curve**.

4. Select the curve between PNT1 and PNT2.

5. Expand the Material drop-down list and select **STEEL**.

6. In the *Orientation* area, in the *X*, *Y*, and *Z* fields, accept the default values.

The section property of the beam is the I_beam_section that you created in the previous task.

7. Click **OK** to close the Beam Definition dialog box. The model displays as shown in Figure 5–27.

Figure 5–27

Task 5 - Create a beam element between PNT2 and PNT3.

1. Click (Beam). The Beam Definition dialog box opens.

2. In the *Name* field, enter **beam_3**.

3. Expand the References drop-down list and select **Point-Point**.

4. Select **PNT2** and **PNT3**.

5. Expand the Material drop-down list and select **STEEL**.

6. In the Beam Definition dialog box, accept the other defaults.

To display the section icons, use the zoom function.

7. Click **OK** to close the Beam Definition dialog box. The model displays as shown in Figure 5–28.

Figure 5–28

© 2017, ASCENT - Center for Technical Knowledge®

Task 6 - Create a beam element between PNT3 and PNT4.

1. Click ▷ (Beam). The Beam Definition dialog box opens.

2. In the *Name* field, enter **beam_4**.

3. Expand the References drop-down list and select **Point-Point**.

4. Select **PNT3** and **PNT4**.

5. Expand the Material drop-down list and select **STEEL**.

6. In the Beam Definition dialog box, accept the other defaults.

7. Click **OK** to close the Beam Definition dialog box. The model displays as shown in Figure 5–29.

Figure 5–29

Task 7 - Explore Beam visualization options.

1. In the floating toolbar, click ⬛ (Simulation Display). The Simulation Display dialog box opens as shown in Figure 5–30.

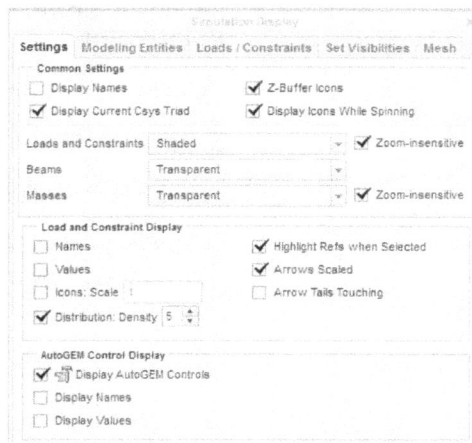

Figure 5–30

2. Select the **Wireframe** option in the **Beams** drop-down list and click **Preview**. With the datum planes turned off, the model displays as shown in Figure 5–31.

Figure 5–31

3. Select the *Modeling Entities* tab and clear the **Beam Sections** option.

4. Click **OK** to close the Simulation Display dialog box. The model displays as shown in Figure 5–32 with the default datum planes and coordinate systems turned off.

Figure 5–32

© 2017, ASCENT - Center for Technical Knowledge®

Task 8 - Apply the loads.

The loading is uniformly distributed on the section between PNT1 and PNT2 of the model, and a point load is also applied at PNT3. In this task, you will apply the distributed load to the curve between PNT1 and PNT2.

1. In the *Home* tab, click ⊢ (Force/Moment). The Force/Moment dialog box opens as shown in Figure 5–33.

Figure 5–33

2. In the *Name* field, enter **uniform_load**.

3. For *Member of Set*, accept the default **LoadSet1** option.

4. Expand the References drop-down list and select **Edges/ Curves**.

The load is related to the WCS.

5. Select the curve between PNT1 and PNT2, as shown in Figure 5–34.

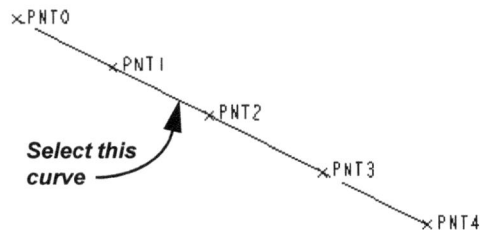

Figure 5–34

6. Click **Advanced**.

7. Expand the Distribution drop-down list and select **Force Per Unit Length**.

8. In the *Spatial Variation* area, select the **Uniform** option.

9. In the Force/Moment dialog box, in the *Force* area, in the *Y* field, enter **-2200**.

10. Click **OK**. The model displays as shown in Figure 5–35. Default datum planes are turned off.

You can toggle off the load values in the Simulation Display dialog box.

Figure 5–35

Task 9 - Apply the point load to the PNT3.

1. Click ╠ (Force/Moment). The Force/Moment Load dialog box opens.

2. In the *Name* field, enter **point_load**.

3. For *Member of Set*, accept the default **LoadSet1** option.

The load is related to the WCS.

4. Expand the References drop-down list and select **Points**.

5. Select **PNT3**.

6. In the Force/Moment dialog box, in the *Force* area, in the *Y* field, enter **-3500**.

7. Click **OK**. The model displays as shown in Figure 5–36 with the default datum planes turned off.

Figure 5–36

© 2017, ASCENT - Center for Technical Knowledge®

Task 10 - Apply the constraints.

The beam ends (PNT0 and PNT4) are constrained (fixed) and the middle support (PNT2) is a roller (free Z-rotation and free X-translation). In this task, you will constrain the beam ends.

1. Click ▨ (Displacement). The Constraint dialog box opens.

2. In the *Name* field, enter **end_constraints**.

3. For *Member of Set*, accept the default **ConstraintSet1** option.

4. Expand the References drop-down list and select **Points**.

5. Multi-select **PNT0** and **PNT4**.

6. Fix all of the Translations and Rotations.

7. Click **OK**. The model displays as shown in Figure 5–37.

Figure 5–37

Task 11 - Apply the constraints to PNT2.

1. Click ▨ (Displacement).The Constraint dialog box opens.

2. In the *Name* field, enter **roller**.

3. For Member of Set, accept the default **ConstraintSet1** option.

4. Expand the References drop-down list and select **Points**.

5. Select **PNT2**.

6. Free X-translation and Z-rotation, and fix all of the other degrees of freedom, as shown in Figure 5–38.

Figure 5–38

7. Click **OK** to close the dialog box. The model displays as shown in Figure 5–39.

Figure 5–39

© 2017, ASCENT - Center for Technical Knowledge®

Analysis Tasks

Task 12 - Set up the analysis.

1. Set up a Quick Check analysis to check for errors. For the name of the analysis, enter **beam_q_c**.

2. In the *Output* tab, increase the plotting grid to **10**.

3. In the Analyses and Design Studies dialog box, in the **Info** menu, select **Check Model** to check the validity of the model.

4. Click ▤ (Settings) and ensure that the **Create Elements during Run** option is selected in the Run Settings dialog box.

5. Click **OK** to close the Run Settings dialog box.

*The **Check Model** option highlights any modeling errors (e.g., load-constraint conflicts or unassigned material properties) and errors from modeling edits.*

Task 13 - Run the Quick Check analysis.

1. Click ✎ (Start) to start the analysis.

2. Click ▤ (Status) to display the status of the run and any errors or warnings.

3. Close the Run Status dialog box when the run is complete.

Task 14 - Solve the analysis using the Multi-Pass Adaptive convergence option.

1. Change the convergence method to Multi-Pass Adaptive. In the *Maximum Polynomial Order* field, enter **6**. In the *Limits* area, in the *Percent Convergence* field, enter **1**.

2. Re-run the analysis.

Results Tasks

Task 15 - Display the results.

Create and display the color plot for the displacement. Animate the plot to ensure that the boundary conditions are correct.

1. In the Analyses and Design Studies dialog box, click ▤ (Review Results). The Result Window Definition dialog box opens.

2. Create, animate and display a fringe color plot for the displacement.

3. Stop the animation. In the *View* tab, expand the Appearance drop-down list and select **Visibilities**. Select **Loads** and **Constraints** and close the Visibilities dialog box.

4. Click ◄ and ►| to step through the animation frames. Frame 5 is shown in Figure 5–40.

"Window1" - beam_q_c - beam_q_c

Displacement ▾ Magnitude ▾ (WCS)

Frame 5 of 8
(m)
Deformed
Max Disp 1.4087E-04
Scale 3.3365E+03
Loadset:LoadSet1 : 1D_BEAM

1.409e-04
1.268e-04
1.127e-04
9.861e-05
8.452e-05
7.043e-05
5.635e-05
4.226e-05
2.817e-05
1.409e-05
0.000e+00

Figure 5–40

Note that the deflection is zero at the beam ends and at the roller support, which is correct.

5. Animate and display the components of displacement (X, Y, and Z). Note that the deflection of the model in the X- and Z-directions is zero.

Task 16 - Create a shear and bending moment plot window for beam elements.

1. Click ⧉ (Copy) in the *Home* tab. The Result Window Definition dialog box opens.

2. In the *Name* field, enter **shear_moment_window**.

3. In the *Title* field, enter **shear_moment_graph**.

4. Expand the Display type drop-down list and select **Graph**.

5. Expand the first Graph Ordinate drop-down list and select **Shear & Moment**.

© 2017, ASCENT - Center for Technical Knowledge®

6. In the *Shear and Moment* area, clear all of the options except **Vy** and **Mz** in the *Beam* area.

7. Expand the Graph Location drop-down list and select **Beams**.

8. Click ⬚ (Select) and select all four beam elements from left to right (hold down <Ctrl> to multi-select). Click the middle mouse button. The Information dialog box opens as shown in Figure 5–41.

Figure 5–41

9. Read the information and verify that the start of the graph corresponds to the point PNT0.

10. In the Information dialog box, click **OK**. The Result Window Definition dialog box opens as shown in Figure 5–42.

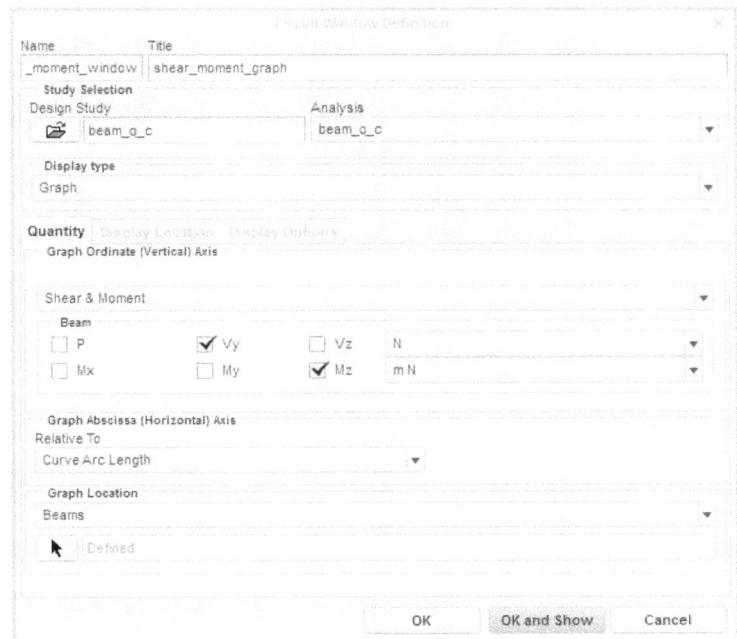

Figure 5–42

11. Click **OK**.

12. In the *View* tab, click 🔲 (Show). In the Display Result Window dialog box, clear **Window1** and select **shear_moment_window**.

13. Click **OK**. The result window displays as shown in Figure 5–43.

Figure 5–43

The plot shown in Figure 5–43 displays the shear and moment plots along the beam elements in the model. Note the bending moment continuity along the model. Note the shear force discontinuity at the roller support and at the point load.

14. Select **File>Close**. Click **Don't Save** when prompted to save the results.

15. Close the Analyses and Design Studies dialog box.

Task 17 - Set up the beam releases.

Beam release is a term that describes the type of connections (pinned or rigid) between two beam elements.

In this task, you will release the **beam_4** start point (free rotation in the Z-direction) to simulate a pinned connection between **beam_3** and **beam_4**.

© 2017, ASCENT - Center for Technical Knowledge®

Release can only be applied directly to beam elements.

1. Select **beam_4** (the curve between PNT3 and PNT4) in the model tree. The curve will highlight in green. Right-click and select **Edit Definition**. The Beam Definition dialog box opens as shown in Figure 5–44.

Figure 5–44

2. Next to the Beam Release drop-down list, click **More**. The Beam Releases dialog box opens as shown Figure 5–45.

Releases are handy when modeling trusses (because no moment is transmitted through a connection), modeling an expansion joint (because no axial load is transmitted), or when modeling dovetails (because all of the forces and moments are transmitted except shear in one direction).

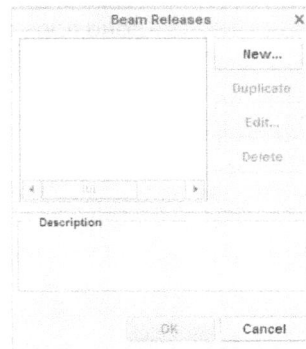

Figure 5–45

3. In the Beam Releases dialog box, click **New**. The Beam Release Definition dialog box opens as shown in Figure 5–46.

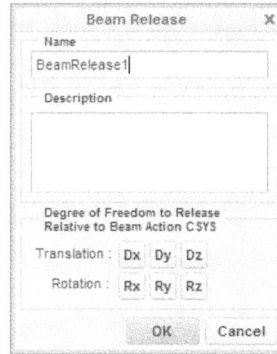

Beam Release ✕

Name

BeamRelease1

Description

Degree of Freedom to Release
Relative to Beam Action C SYS

Translation :   Dx   Dy   Dz

Rotation :   Rx   Ry   Rz

OK   Cancel

Figure 5–46

4. In the *Name* field, enter **beam_4_rz**.

5. Click **Rz** to release (free) the beam element rotation in the Z-direction at PNT3.

6. Click **OK** to close the Beam Release Definition dialog box.

7. Click **OK** to close the Beam Releases dialog box.

8. Click **OK** to close the Beam Definition dialog box.

9. Create and run a new Multi-Pass Adaptive analysis **d1_beam** for the modified model.

Task 18 - Display the results.

1. Create and display a color plot for the displacement. Additionally, animate this plot to ensure that the boundary conditions are correct. The deformed shape is shown in Figure 5–47. Note the changes in the slope at the point of the release.

 (Beam Release) indicates the degrees of freedom and the end of the beam on which the release is acting.

© 2017, ASCENT - Center for Technical Knowledge®

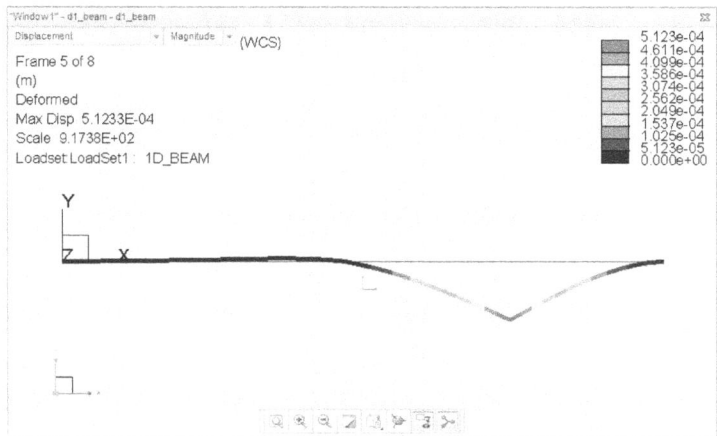

Figure 5–47

2. Create shear and bending moment plot windows for the beam elements (four beam elements), as shown in Figure 5–48. Note that the shear is non-zero and that the bending moment is zero at the release.

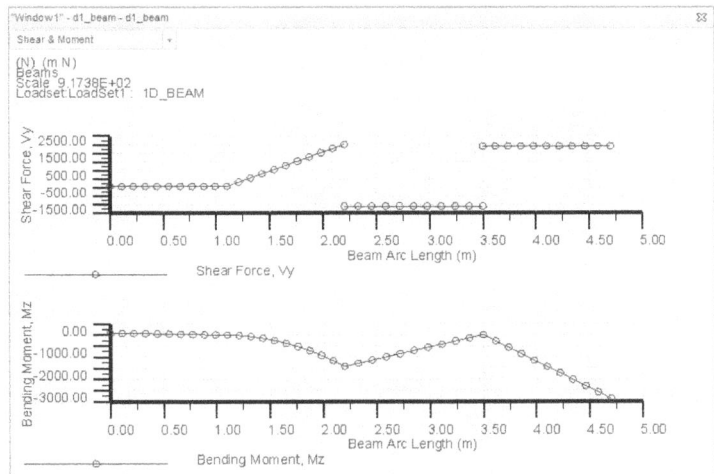

Figure 5–48

Task 19 - Save and close the model.

1. Select **File>Close**. Click **Don't Save** when prompted to save the results.

2. Close the Analyses and Design Studies dialog box.

3. Exit Creo Simulate. Save and close the model in Creo Parametric.

Practice 5b | 2D Frame Analysis

Practice Objectives

- Set up a 2D beam model.
- Run a 2D beam model.
- Analyze a 2D beam model.

The aspect ratio of the beam element should be greater than 10:1(the ratio of its length to its largest section dimension).

In this practice, you will use beam element idealizations to analyze a 2D frame. The frame part is shown in Figure 5–49. The beam section is a hollow circular pipe and the frame ends are fixed. The frame loading is a linearly distributed load in the Y-direction, a uniform total load in the Z-direction, a point load in the X-direction and a load due to gravity.

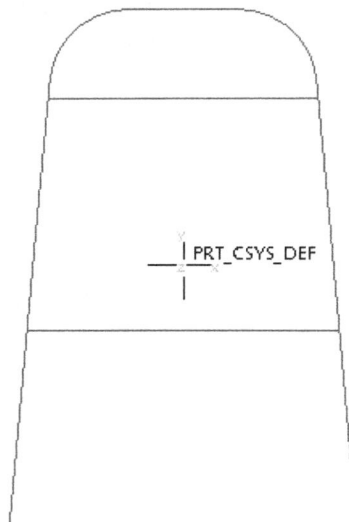

Figure 5–49

© 2017, ASCENT - Center for Technical Knowledge®

Modeling Tasks

Task 1 - Open the d2_frame.prt.

1. Open **d2_frame.prt** in Creo Parametric.

2. In the *View* tab, in the *Show* group, click ⚏ (Point Tag Display) to visualize the datum point tags. The part displays as shown in Figure 5–50.

Figure 5–50

3. Ensure that the unit system is **IPS**.

4. Switch to the Creo Simulate environment.

5. Click ⚏ (Simulation Display). In the Simulation Display dialog box, clear the **Display AutoGEM Controls** option.

Task 2 - Create a datum point as a simulation feature.

In beam models, Creo Simulate can only define distributed loads on curves. The load is transferred to the beam elements created on the curve. Concentrated loads can be defined on the curve's vertices (i.e., ends) and on datum points within the curve. In this task, you will create a datum point on curve, to which you will later apply a concentrated force.

1. In the *Refine Model* tab, click ⚏ (Point).

2. Create a datum point at the end of the curve in the location shown in Figure 5–51.

Simulation datum point feature

Figure 5–51

Task 3 - Create beam elements.

1. Click 🏳 (Beam). The Beam Definition dialog box opens.

2. In the *Name* field, enter **d2_beam_1**.

3. Expand the References drop-down list and select **Edge/ Curve**.

4. Select the curve shown in Figure 5–52. As you select the curve, a direction arrow displays on the curve (clicking the curve again changes the direction of the arrow). The direction is shown in Figure 5–52.

© 2017, ASCENT - Center for Technical Knowledge®

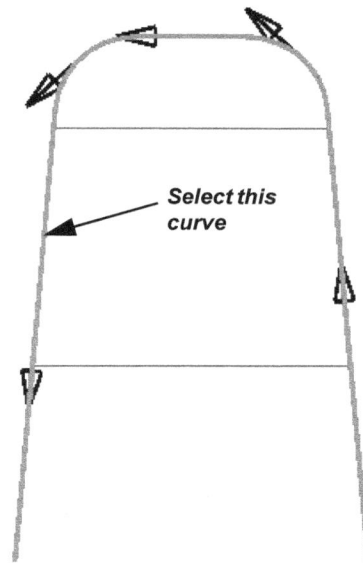

Figure 5–52

5. In the *Material* area, click **More**. The Materials dialog box opens.

6. in the *Materials in Library* area, select **AL2014**. Click
   ▶▶▶ (Add Material) to transfer **AL2014** to the *Materials in Model* area.

7. Select ✎ (Edit) to check the material properties. The following values are the default material properties for Aluminum alloy 2014-T6:
   - Poisson = 0.33
   - Young's modulus = 1.06e+07 psi
   - Density = 0.0002614 lbf sec^2/in^4

8. Click **OK** in the Material Definition dialog box and Materials dialog box. AL2014 displays in the *Material* area in the Beam Definition dialog box.

9. In the *Orientation* area, in the *X* field, accept the default, in the *Y* field, enter **0**, and in the *Z* field, enter **1**.

10. Next to the Beam Section drop-down list, click **More**. The Beam Sections dialog box opens.

Since the cross-section is round, the Y-direction of the beam's BACS can be defined as any direction, as long as it does not coincide with the beam's axis.

11. Click **New**. The Beam Section Definition dialog box opens as shown in Figure 5–53.

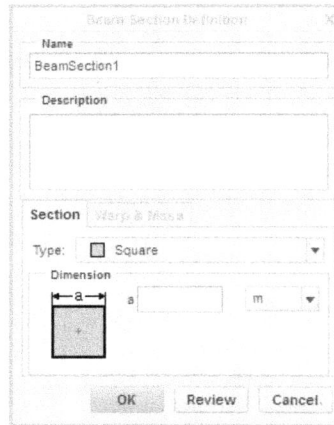

Figure 5–53

12. In the *Name* field, enter **d2_frame_section_1**.

If the section is not in the Type drop-down list, you can sketch the section using the Sketched Solid and Sketched Thin sketch options in the Type drop-down list. These options open Sketcher in Creo Parametric.

13. Expand the Type drop-down list and select **Hollow Circle**.

14. In the *R* field, enter **1.50**.

15. In the *Ri* field, enter **1.10**.

16. Click **OK** to close the Beam Section Definition dialog box.

17. Click **OK** to close the Beam Sections dialog box.

18. Click **OK** to close the Beam Definition dialog box. The model displays as shown in Figure 5–54.

Figure 5–54

© 2017, ASCENT - Center for Technical Knowledge®

19. Click 🏳 (Beam). The Beam Definition dialog box opens.

20. In the *Name* field, enter **d2_beam_2**.

21. Expand the References drop-down list and select **Edge/ Curve**.

22. Select the curves shown in Figure 5–55. As you select each curve, a direction arrow displays on the curve (selecting the curve again will change the direction of the arrow). The direction is shown in Figure 5–55.

Figure 5–55

23. In the *Material* field, select **AL2014**.

24. In the *Orientation* area, in the *X* field, accept the default, in the *Y* field, enter **0** in the *Z* field, enter **1**.

25. Next to the Beam Section drop-down list, click **More**. The Beam Sections dialog box opens.

26. Click **New**. The Beam Section Definition dialog box opens.

27. In the *Name* field, enter **d2_frame_section_2**.

28. Expand the Type drop-down list and select **Hollow Circle**.

29. In the *R* field, enter **1.20**.

30. In the *Ri* field, enter **0.80**.

31. Click **OK** to close the Beam Section Definition dialog box.

32. Click **OK** to close the Beam Sections dialog box.

33. Click **OK** to close the Beam Definition dialog box. The model displays as shown in Figure 5–56.

Figure 5–56

34. Click 🗗 (Simulation Display). The Simulation Display dialog box opens.

35. In the **Settings** tab, in the Beam drop-down list, select **Wireframe**.

36. Select the *Modeling Entities* tab and clear the **Beam Sections** option.

37. Close the Simulation Display dialog box. The model displays as shown in Figure 5–57 with the default datum planes, points, and coordinate systems turned off.

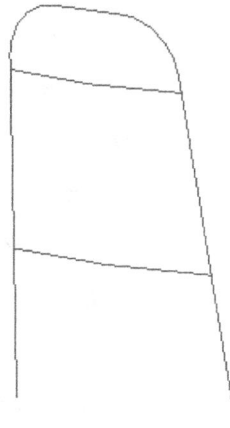

Figure 5–57

© 2017, ASCENT - Center for Technical Knowledge®

Task 4 - Apply the loads.

The loading is a linearly distributed load in the Y-direction, a uniform total load in the Z-direction, a point load in the X-direction and a load due to gravity. In this task, you will apply the linear distributed load to the curve shown in Figure 5–58.

1. In the *Home* tab, click (Force/Moment). The Force/Moment Load dialog box opens.

2. In the *Name* field, enter **distributed_load**.

3. For *Member of Set*, accept the default **LoadSet1** option.

4. Expand the References drop-down list and select **Edges/ Curves**.

*The easiest way to select this section of the curve is to hover the cursor over the curve, hold the right mouse button, and select **Pick From List** in the context menu. Toggle through the items in the Pick From List dialog box, until the required curve highlights.*

5. Select the section of the curve shown in Figure 5–58.

Select this curve

Figure 5–58

6. Click **Advanced**. Expand the Distribution drop-down list and select **ForcePerUnitLength**.

7. Expand the Spatial Variation drop-down list and select **InterpolatedOverEntity**.

8. In the 1st row of the *Value* column, enter **0.25**.

The values (0.25, 1) are scale factors that Creo Simulate applies to the load at the ends of the curve.

9. In the 2nd row of the *Value* column, enter **1.00**.

10. In the *Force* area, in the *Y* field, enter **-4350**. The Force/Moment dialog box opens as shown in Figure 5–59.

Figure 5–59

*If the load distribution is reversed, swap the **0.25** and **1** values defined in Steps 8 and 9.*

11. Click **Preview** to verify that the load distribution is linear, as shown in Figure 5–60.

Figure 5–60

© 2017, ASCENT - Center for Technical Knowledge®

12. Click **OK**. The model displays as shown in Figure 5–61. Default datum planes are turned off.

You can turn the load values off in the Simulation Display dialog box.

Figure 5–61

Name the load ***distributed_load_1***.

13. Repeat Steps 1 to 7 of this task to apply the load to the curve shown in Figure 5–62.

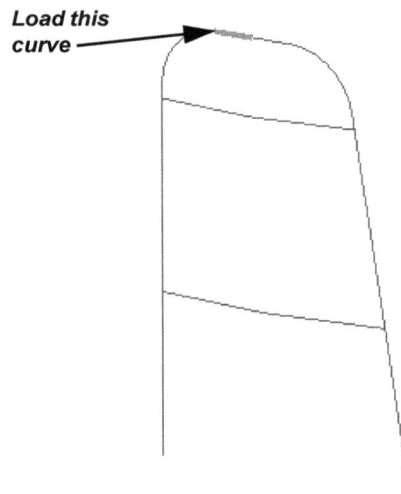

Load this curve

Figure 5–62

14. In the 1st row of the *Value* column, enter **1.00**.

15. In the 2nd row of the *Value* column, enter **0.25**.

16. Repeat Steps 10 to 12 to finish applying the loads. The model displays as shown in Figure 5–63.

Figure 5–63

Task 5 - Apply the point load.

1. Click (Force/Moment). The Force/Moment Load dialog box opens.

2. In the *Name* field, enter **point_load**.

3. For *Member of Set*, accept the default **LoadSet1** option.

The load is related to the WCS.

4. Expand the References drop-down list and select **Points**.

5. Select **PNT14**, as shown in Figure 5–64.

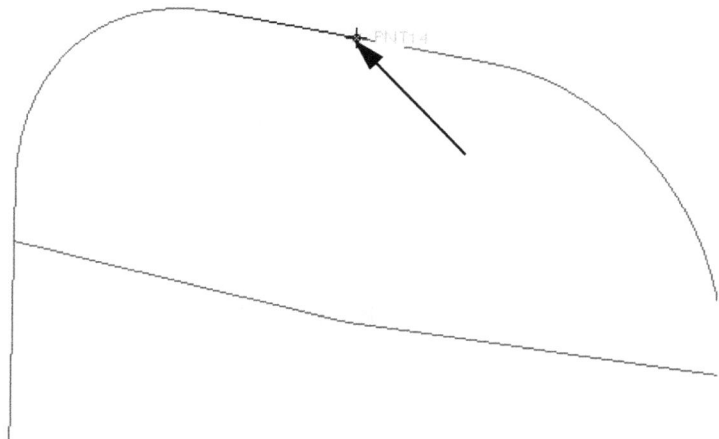

Figure 5–64

6. In the Force/Moment Load dialog box, in the *Force* area, in the *X* field, enter **-1930**.

7. Click **OK** to create the load.

© 2017, ASCENT - Center for Technical Knowledge®

Task 6 - Apply a uniform total load in the Z-direction.

1. Click ⊢ (Force/Moment). The Force/Moment Load dialog box opens.

2. In the *Name* field, enter **total_uniform_load**.

3. In *Member of Set*, accept the default **LoadSet1** option.

The load is related to the WCS.

4. Expand the References drop-down list and select **Edges/ Curves**. Select the two curves shown in Figure 5–65.

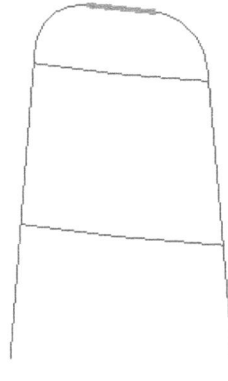

Figure 5–65

5. In the Force/Moment Load dialog box, in the *Force* area, in the *Z* field, enter **1930**.

6. Click **OK** to finish. The model displays as shown in Figure 5–66.

Figure 5–66

Task 7 - Apply the gravity load.

1. Click ▯↓ (Gravity). The Gravity Load dialog box opens as shown in Figure 5–67.

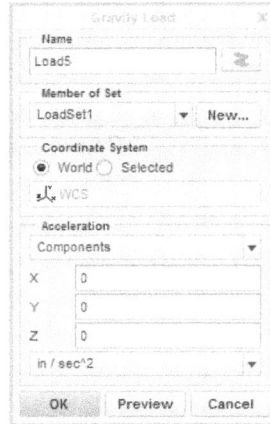

Figure 5–67

2. In the *Name* field, enter **gravity**.

3. Click **New** to define a new load set. The Load Set dialog box opens as shown in Figure 5–68.

Figure 5–68

4. Accept the default name and click **OK**.

386in/sec^2 is the 1G acceleration.

5. In the dialog box, in the *Acceleration* area, in the *Y* field, enter **-386**.

6. Click **OK** to finish defining the gravity load. The model displays as shown in Figure 5–69.

© 2017, ASCENT - Center for Technical Knowledge®

Figure 5–69

Task 8 - Apply the constraints.

In this task, you will constrain the ends of the frame model (fix in translation and rotation). To constrain the ends, create two datum points as simulation features at the ends of the frame model.

A beam end point has six degrees of freedom.

1. In Creo Simulate, create the two datum points shown in Figure 5–70.

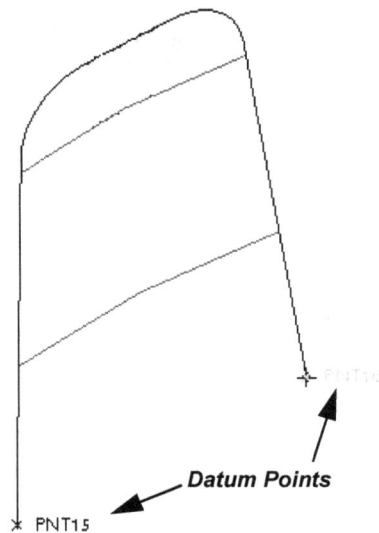

Figure 5–70

2. In the *Home* tab, click 🖉 (Displacement). The Constraint dialog box opens.

3. In the *Name* field, enter **end_constraints**.

4. Expand the References drop-down list and select **Points**.

5. Select the points created in Step 1 of this task.

6. Fix all of the Translations and Rotations.

7. Click **OK**. The model displays as shown in Figure 5–71.

Figure 5–71

Analysis Tasks

Task 9 - Set up the analysis.

In this task, you will set up and run a Multi-Pass Adaptive convergence analysis.

1. For the name of the analysis, enter **d2_frame**.

2. Select both load sets.

3. In the *Limits* area, in the *Polynomial Order* field, enter **6** and in the *Percent Convergence* field, enter **1**.

4. In the *Output* tab, increase the *Plotting Grid* to **10**.

5. Run the analysis.

Results Tasks

Task 10 - Display the results.

In this task, you will create and display four result windows.

1. In the Analyses and Design Studies dialog box, click
   ![icon] (Review Results). The Result Window Definition dialog box opens as shown in Figure 5–72.

© 2017, ASCENT - Center for Technical Knowledge®

Note that both load sets are included. You can display results for them individually or combined. The default combination factor is 1. You can change it for a different load combination ratio.
*Note the **Bending**, **Tensile**, and **Torsional** stress options.*

Figure 5–72

2. Create, display, and animate a displacement result window. Include both load sets. The display type is **Fringe** and the displacement component is **Magnitude**. The window displays as shown in Figure 5–73.

Figure 5–73

Note that the displacements at the end points of the frame are zero, according to the applied constraints.

*The **Model Max** option is not available in an animated result window.*

3. Create and display the beam bending stress plot for the combined load sets. The plot displays as shown in Figure 5–74. Select (Model Max) to display the maximum beam bending stress.

Figure 5–74

4. Create and display the deformed torsional stress plot for the combined load sets. Display the minimum and maximum torsional stress locations. The plot displays as shown in Figure 5–75.

Figure 5–75

© 2017, ASCENT - Center for Technical Knowledge®

5. Create and display the reaction force Y at the point constraints. The plot displays as shown in Figure 5–76. Enter the information in the Result Window Definition dialog box, as shown in Figure 5–76.

Figure 5–76

Task 11 - Save and close the model.

1. Select **File>Close**. Click **Don't Save** when prompted to save the results.

2. Close the Analyses and Design Studies dialog box.

3. Exit Creo Simulate. Save and close the model in Creo Parametric.

Practice 5c | 3D Frame Analysis

Practice Objectives

- Set up a 3D beam model.
- Run a 3D beam model.
- Analyze a 3D beam model.

In this practice, you will use beam element idealizations to set up, run, and analyze a 3D Aluminum walker frame. The frame part is shown in Figure 5–77. The beam section is a hollow circular pipe and the frame ends are fixed. The walker supports a 225lb person.

Figure 5–77

Modeling Tasks

Task 1 - Open the d3_frame.prt.

1. Open **d3_frame.prt** in Creo Parametric. The part displays as shown in Figure 5–78.

© 2017, ASCENT - Center for Technical Knowledge®

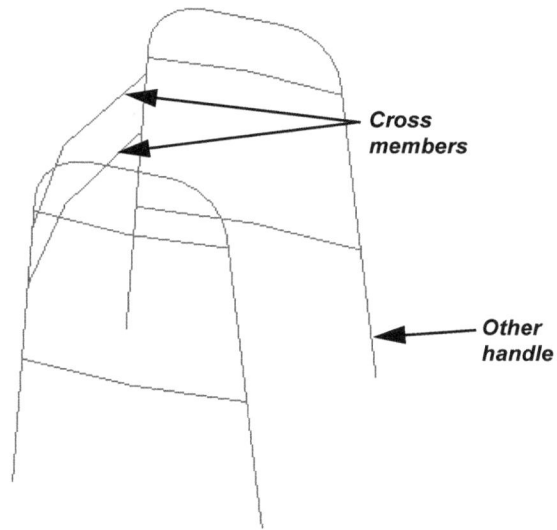

Cross members

Other handle

Figure 5–78

2. The unit systems are set to the Creo Parametric default.

3. Switch to the Creo Simulate environment.

4. Click 🖧 (Simulation Display). In the Simulation Display dialog box, select **Wireframe** in the **Beams** drop-down list, and clear the **Display AutoGEM Controls** option.

5. The frame model displays as shown in Figure 5–79.

The 2D frame (original curves) in the previous practice was used to create this 3D frame. The 2D frame sections and properties are maintained in this practice.

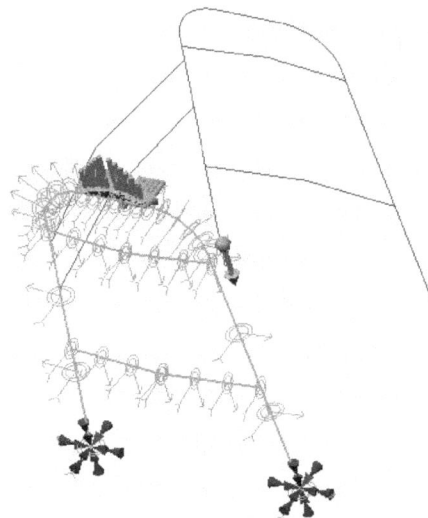

Figure 5–79

Task 2 - Create the beam elements for the other walker handle.

1. Double-click on the curve shown in Figure 5–80. The Beam Definition dialog box opens.

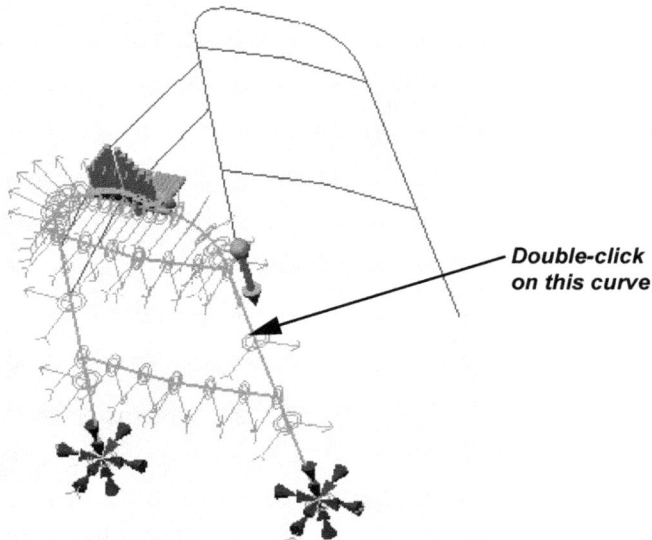

Double-click on this curve

Figure 5–80

2. Hold down <Ctrl> and select the other handle curve shown in Figure 5–81.

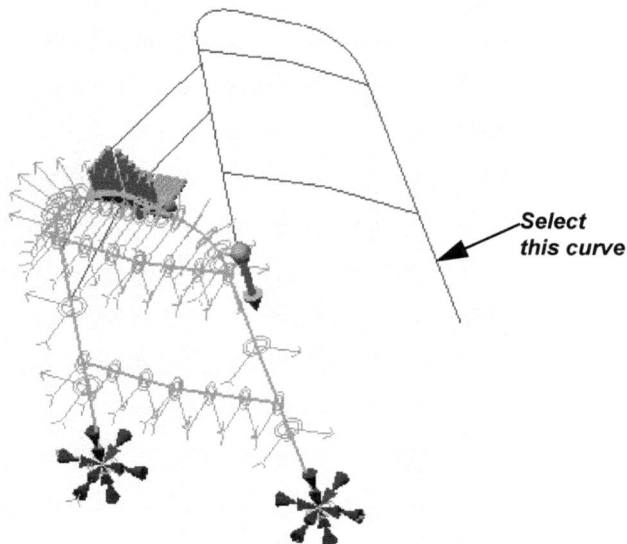

Select this curve

Figure 5–81

© 2017, ASCENT - Center for Technical Knowledge®

3. Click **OK** to close the Beam Definition dialog box. The model displays as shown in Figure 5–82.

The beam section is **d2_frame_section_1**.

Figure 5–82

4. Double-click on the curve shown in Figure 5–83. The Beam Definition dialog box opens.

Double-click on this curve

Figure 5–83

5. Hold down <Ctrl> and select two cross member curves on the other handle and two cross member curves that connect the handles.

6. Click **OK** to close the Beam Definition dialog box. The model displays as shown in Figure 5–84.

Figure 5–84

7. Click ⬡ (Simulation Display). The Simulation Display dialog box opens.

8. Select the *Modeling Entities* tab and clear the **Beam Sections** option.

Task 3 - Delete the gravity load.

1. Expand the Model Tree and locate the **gravity** load, as shown in Figure 5–85.

Figure 5–85

2. Right-click on the **gravity** load and select **Delete**. In the Question dialog box, click **Yes**.

© 2017, ASCENT - Center for Technical Knowledge®

Task 4 - Copy the vertical load to the other handle.

*Assign **LoadSet1** to all of the loads.*

1. In the Model Tree, highlight the **distributed_load** load, right-click and select **Copy**.

2. In the Model Tree, highlight **Load Set Load Set1**, right-click, and select **Paste**. The Force/Moment Load dialog box opens as shown in Figure 5–86.

Figure 5–86

3. Right-click in the selection collector and select **Remove** to clear the selection.

4. Select the curve on the other handle, as shown in Figure 5–87

Select this curve

Figure 5–87

5. In the 1st row of the *Value* column, enter **0.25** and in the 2nd row of the *Value* column, enter **1.00**. The Force/Moment Load dialog box opens as shown in Figure 5–88.

Figure 5–88

© 2017, ASCENT - Center for Technical Knowledge®

6. Click **OK**. The model displays as shown in Figure 5–89.

Figure 5–89

7. Follow Steps 1 to 6 to copy **distributed_load_1** to the other handle. The model displays as shown in Figure 5–90.

Figure 5–90

Task 5 - Copy the side load to the other handle.

Changing the sign of the force is necessary to maintain the symmetry of the loading.

1. Follow Steps 1 to 6 in the previous task to copy **total_uniform_load** to the other handle. However, change the sign of the force in the Z-direction from *1930* to **-1930**. The model displays as shown in Figure 5–91.

Figure 5–91

Task 6 - Copy the point load to the other handle.

1. Create a datum point in the middle of the other handle, as shown in Figure 5–92.

Figure 5–92

2. In the Model Tree, right-click on **point_load** load and select **Edit Definition**. The Force/Moment Load dialog box opens.

3. Hold down <Ctrl> and click the point you created in Step 1. The selection collector displays two points.

© 2017, ASCENT - Center for Technical Knowledge®

*The **Load Per Point** option applies the entered amount of load to each selected point. The other option is **Total Load**, which evenly divides the entered load among all of the points.*

4. Expand the Distribution drop-down list and verify that the **Load Per Point** option is selected. The Force/Moment Load dialog box opens as shown in Figure 5–93.

Figure 5–93

5. Click **OK**. The model displays as shown in Figure 5–94.

Figure 5–94

Task 7 - Constrain the ends of the other handle.

1. In the Model Tree, right-click on the **end_constraints** load and select **Edit Definition**. The Constraint dialog box opens.

2. Hold down <Ctrl> and click the end points on the other handle. The selection collector displays the four selected points.

3. Click **OK**. The model displays as shown in Figure 5–95

Figure 5–95

Analysis Tasks

Task 8 - Set up the analysis.

Set up and run a Multi-Pass Adaptive convergence analysis.

1. For the name of the analysis, enter **d3_frame**.

2. In the *Limits* area, in the *Polynomial Order* field, enter **6**, and in the *Percent Convergence* field, enter **1**.

3. In the *Output* tab, increase the *Plotting Grid* to **10**.

4. Run the analysis. Ignore the warning messages in the Diagnostics window.

Task 9 - Display the results.

1. Create and display a color plot of the displacement for the frame model. Animate this plot to verify that the boundary conditions are correct and the deformation is symmetrical.

© 2017, ASCENT - Center for Technical Knowledge®

2. Step through the animation. On Frame 5 the result window displays as shown in Figure 5–96.

Figure 5–96

3. Start the animation. Note that each beam displays some bending.

Task 10 - Modify the constraint on PNT15.

In this task, you will modify the constraint on PNT15 to simulate a settling foundation for the walker at this corner. This represents a forced displacement in the Y-direction for the constraint at PNT15.

1. Select **File>Close**. Click **Don't Save** when prompted to save the results. Close the Analyses and Design Studies dialog box.

2. In the Model Tree, right-click on the **end_constraints** load and select **Edit Definition**. The Constraint dialog box opens.

3. Right-click on the PNT15 in the selection collector and select **Remove**.

4. Click **OK** to close the Constraint dialog box.

5. Click (Displacement). The Constraint dialog box opens.

6. In the *Name* field, enter **forced_constraint**.

7. Expand the References drop-down list and select **Points**.

8. Select **PNT15**.

9. Fix Translations X and Z and fix all of the Rotations.

10. In the *Translation* area, for *Y*, click 🔧. In the *Y* field, enter **-0.0625**.

11. Click **OK** to close the Constraint dialog box.

12. Re-run the analysis.

The frame at this corner will be forced to move down by 0.0625in (the unit length is inch).

Task 11 - Display the results.

1. Create and display a color plot of the displacement for the frame model. Overlay the undeformed model and animate the plot to verify that the boundary conditions are correct.

2. Step through the animation. On Frame 5 the result window displays as shown in Figure 5–97.

Figure 5–97

Note that the end of the frame with the enforced displacement constraint is moving down, as required.

3. Exit the Creo Simulate results. Save and close the model in Creo Parametric.

© 2017, ASCENT - Center for Technical Knowledge®

Practice 5d

Analysis of a Grain Hopper

Practice Objectives

- Create standard shells.
- Create beams.
- Apply loads and constraints.
- Set up and run a Single-Pass Adaptive analysis.
- Display the results.

In this practice, you will perform a static stress analysis on the grain hopper shown in Figure 5–98, with minimum instruction.

The hopper consists of a steel box mounted on a tubular frame.

Figure 5–98

Task 1 - Create shells.

1. Open **hopper.prt** and launch Creo Simulate.

2. For all datum surfaces comprising the box (five surfaces altogether, as shown on Figure 5–99), create Shells with the following properties:

   - Thickness: **0.5 in**
   - Material: **STEEL**

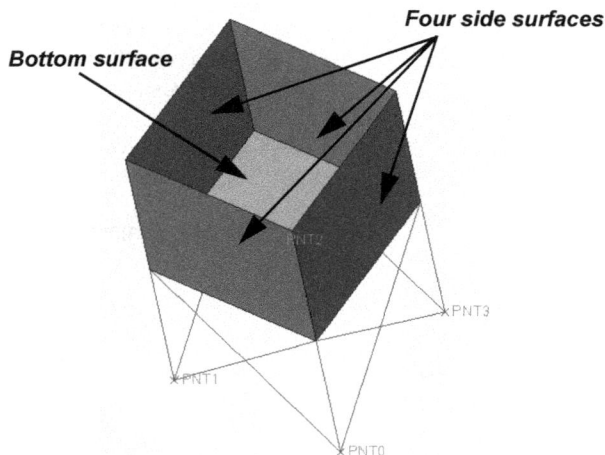

Figure 5–99

Task 2 - Create beams.

Since each beam cross-section is round, the only requirement for the orientation vector is that it doesn't coincide with any beam's axis.

1. For the twelve datum curves shown in Figure 5–100, create Beams with the following properties:

   - Cross-section: Hollow tube **2in OD** and **0.1in thick**
   - Material: **STEEL**
   - Orientation: **WCS Z-direction**

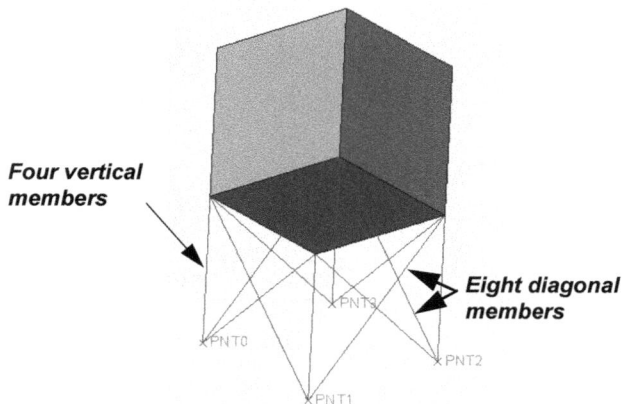

Figure 5–100

© 2017, ASCENT - Center for Technical Knowledge®

2. For the four edges at the bottom of the box shown in
   Figure 5–101, create Beams with the following properties:
   - Cross-section and material: Same as for the vertical and
     diagonal beams
   - Orientation: **WCS Y-direction**

Figure 5–101

Task 3 - Apply loads and constraints.

1. Fully constrain (translations and rotations) the four points at
   the bottom of the frame, as shown in Figure 5–102.

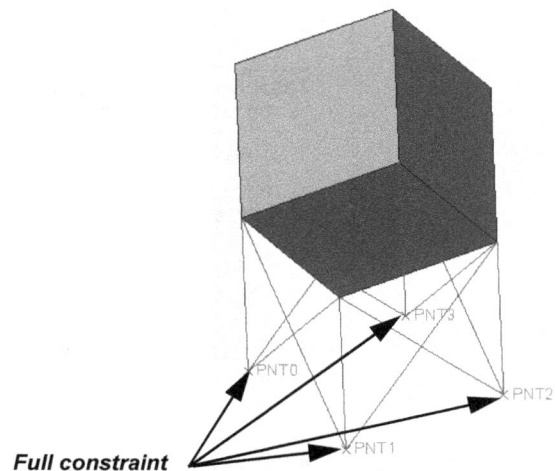

Figure 5–102

2. Apply **100psi** pressure load in the downward direction to the bottom surface of the box, as shown in Figure 5–103.

Figure 5–103

Task 4 - Set up and run the analysis.

1. Create a new static analysis with the following parameters:
   - Analysis name: **hopper**
   - Convergence method: **Multi-Pass Adaptive, P-max=9**
   - Plotting Grid: **10**

2. Run the analysis.

3. If the analysis does not converge, change the mesh size for the box's surfaces to 1/2 size of the box, and then re-run the analysis.

Task 5 - Visualize the analysis results.

1. Visualize and animate the **Displacement Magnitude** fringe plot. Does the part deform according to the applied loads and constraints?

2. Display the **von Mises Stress** fringe plot. Does the maximum stress occur in the box, or in the frame?

3. Display the **von Mises Stress** fringe plot for the box only. Do you think the bottom of the box might require additional structural support?

4. Display the **von Mises Stress** plot for the beams only. Which beams are loaded the most?

© 2017, ASCENT - Center for Technical Knowledge®

Sensitivity and Optimization Design Studies

Design studies enable you to explore design alternatives and to optimize your model. You can perform three types of design studies in Creo Simulate: standard, sensitivity, and optimization. Standard design studies calculate results for an analysis with different design variable settings. Sensitivity design studies calculate results for several different values of design variables (e.g., dimensions). Optimization design studies adjust a model's parameters to meet a specified goal or to test the feasibility of a design.

Learning Objectives in this Chapter

- Understand the design study objectives and variables.
- Understand the Standard, Sensitivity, and Optimization design studies.
- Set up the variables for a design study.

6.1 Design Considerations

Before you set up a design study, it is recommended that you define your objectives, measures, and design variables. This enables you to organize and provide the correct data to Creo Simulate for the study.

For example, the lift point shown in Figure 6–1 needs to be run through a design study in order to minimize its mass. Before the design study is set up, the objective, design limits, measures, and design variables need to be defined.

Figure 6–1

- The objective is to minimize the mass of the part.Therefore, we need to have a simulation measure that measures the mass of the part.

- The maximum stress in the part cannot exceed the yield strength of the material. This becomes the design limit, for which we need the 2nd simulation measure, the maximum von Mises stress in the part.

- The design variables are the dimensions that will be varied or adjusted during the design study. For this example, these include the diameter of the trunnion, and the diameter of the leg distance from the center of the trunnion to the center of the leg.

© 2017, ASCENT - Center for Technical Knowledge®

Objectives

Objectives are the goals that you want to achieve with a design study (e.g., minimize weight, minimize reaction forces, etc.). You set your objectives during the setup of the optimization design studies. Your objective can be user-defined or system-defined using the options in the *Predefined* area in the Measures dialog box, as shown in Figure 6–2. For example, a system-defined objective might be to minimize stress (i.e., the system-defined simulation measure **max_stress_vm**). An example of a user-defined objective would be to ensure that clearance (i.e., a user-defined parameter calculated by subtracting 2D values) is maximized.

Objectives are only required for optimization design studies.

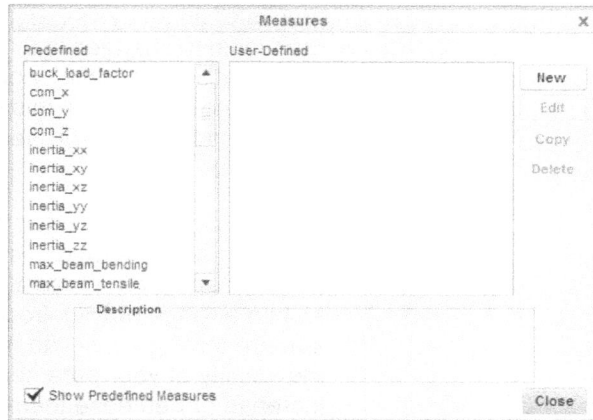

Figure 6–2

Measures

Measures are the scalar quantities of interest that Creo Simulate calculates during analysis (e.g., maximum von Mises stress, maximum principal stress, etc.).

Design Variables

Design variables are the Creo Parametric dimensions or parameters that you set to achieve your objective.

6.2 Types of Design Studies

Standard Studies

Standard design studies evaluate the model for an alternative set of design variables, similarly to running a *what if* scenario.

Sensitivity Studies

Sensitivity studies calculate how the variation in a design variable affects the results in which you are interested (i.e., the maximum stress or deflection). You might want to determine how a particular dimension or model property is going to affect the results of an analysis (i.e., you want to assess the sensitivity of the model to changes in this parameter). You could manually edit the model (i.e., geometry or properties) and perform the analysis many times. However, this method would be time-consuming and potentially error-prone. A Creo Simulate sensitivity study automates this task.

You can perform two types of sensitivity studies: local and global. Local sensitivity studies assess which parameters have the greatest effect on a measure at the current parameter values (within a range of 2%). Local sensitivity studies are useful when you are testing small variations of data. They enable you to test the validity of your parameters and provide data on whether to increase or decrease them to meet your design goal.

Global sensitivity studies vary a parameter over a user-defined range of values (the range is larger than that in a local sensitivity study). They are useful when you have done a local study and want to test a larger range of variables to get the best possible parameter values to achieve your design goal.

Optimization Studies

Optimization studies manipulate parameters and determine an optimal solution to your design goal, within the specified design limits. It is necessary to have a design goal or design limit or both. If you do not have a goal, Creo Simulate searches for the first possible design while conforming to your design limit. This is called feasibility study.

Optimization studies are set up and run using the same procedure as sensitivity studies. The report generated by an optimization study contains the following information:

- Optimized value of each parameter

- Value of the goal and of each design limit measure

© 2017, ASCENT - Center for Technical Knowledge®

Setting Up Design Studies

In Creo Simulate, design studies are set up and run in the following order:

1. Run an analysis to ensure that the model converges to a solution.
2. Set up the design parameters for the design studies.
3. Run a local sensitivity study and select the parameters that have an effect on the measures and on the goal.
4. Run a global sensitivity study on the selected parameters and find the parameter values (maximum or minimum) that have the greatest effect on the goal and on the measures.
5. Run an optimization study for the parameters that have the greatest effect on the goal. Select initial values for the parameters based on data from the global sensitivity study.

6.3 Design Variables

Design variables are Creo Parametric dimensions and/or parameters that you want to change during a design study. Design variables are selected in the Design Study Definition dialog box, which is opened from the Analyses and Design Studies dialog box.

For example, the Optimization Study Definition dialog box is shown in Figure 6–3. ⌖ (Select Dimension) enables the selection of model dimensions to vary and ⌖ (Select Parameter) enables you to select the model parameters.

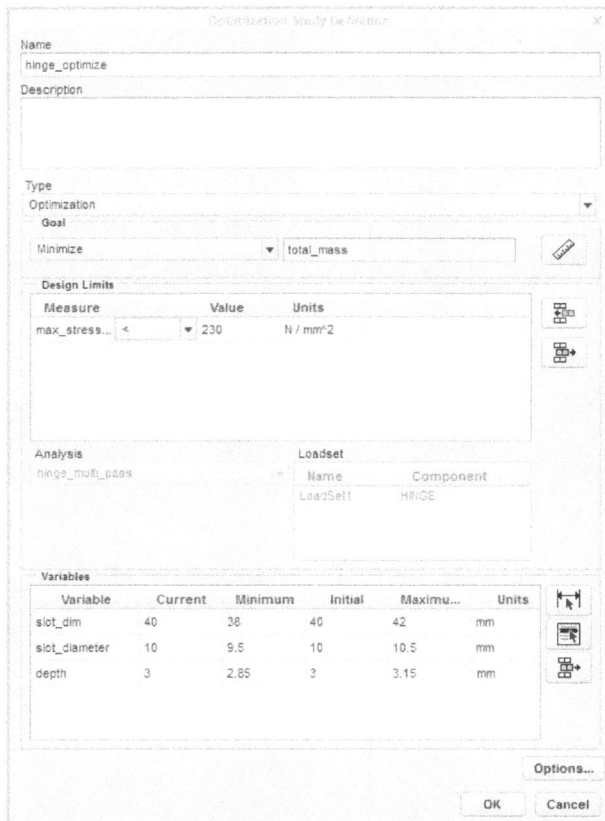

Figure 6–3

© 2017, ASCENT - Center for Technical Knowledge®

Practice 6a

Sensitivity and optimization design studies automate some of the repetitive work involved in design.

Design Study of a Hinge Plate

Practice Objectives

- Set up and run sensitivity design studies.
- Set up and run an optimization design study.

In this practice, you will use sensitivity and optimization design studies to set up, run, analyze, and optimize a hinge plate part, as shown in Figure 6–4. The part is made of steel.

Figure 6–4

When setting up design studies, you need to define the following information:

- The goal for the study.

- The measure to be used to analyze the parameter's effect on the hinge part.

- The design variables (Creo Simulate dimensions).

These requirements are summarized as follows:

Objective	Measure	Parameters
Minimize the weight of the part.	• Von Mises stress • Total mass	• Dimension from left edge to center of vertical slots (40 mm) • Holes and slots diameter (10 mm) • Hinge Plate thickness (3 mm) • Dimension from left edge to center of right hand side hole (75 mm)

Modeling Tasks

Task 1 - Open hinge.prt.

1. Open **hinge.prt** in Creo Parametric. The part displays as shown in Figure 6–5.

Figure 6–5

2. Ensure that the unit system is set to **mmNs**.

Task 2 - Rename the design variables.

In this task, you will rename the Creo Parametric dimensions to make it easier to identify the design variables in Creo Simulate.

d7 =d23

1. In the Ribbon, in the *Tools* tab, select ᵈ= (Relations). The Relations dialog box opens. Enter the relation shown in Figure 6–6. It ties the plate thickness to the slot depth.

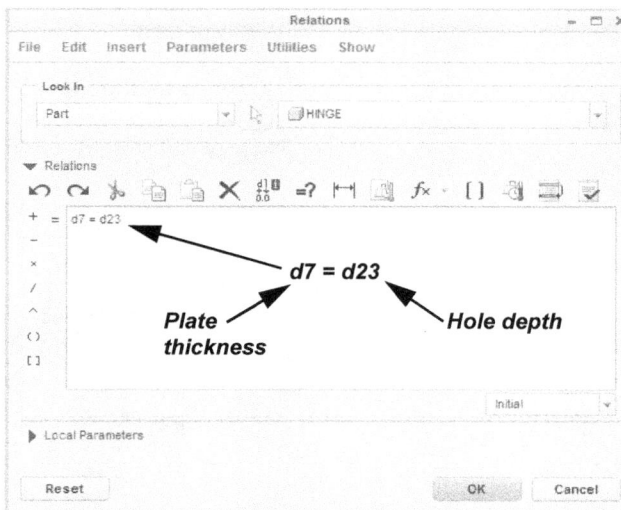

Figure 6–6

© 2017, ASCENT - Center for Technical Knowledge®

2. Click **OK** to close the Relations dialog box.

3. In the Model Tree, right-click on Cut id 226 and select
   $\overset{\longleftrightarrow}{d1}$ (Edit). The part displays. Select the 40 dimension as
   shown in Figure 6–7.

Select this dimension

Figure 6–7

4. Right-click and select **Properties**. The Dimension Properties
   dialog box opens.

5. In the *Name* field, enter **slot_dim**, as shown in Figure 6–8.

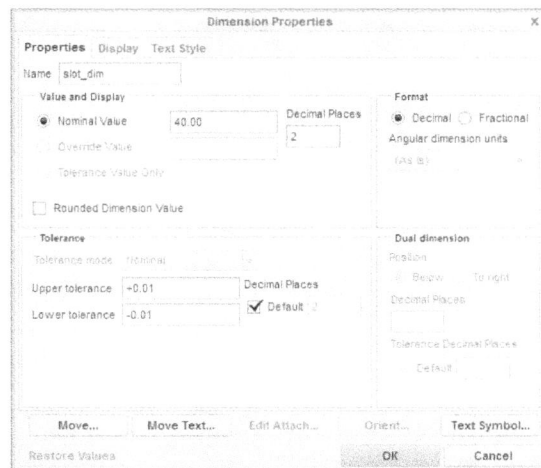

Figure 6–8

The 3 dimension is the depth of the holes in the plate, which is equal to the plate thickness.

6. Click **OK**.

7. Repeat Steps 3 to 7 for the 75, Ø10, and 3 dimensions. For the *75* dimension, enter **hole_dim**, for the Ø10 dimension, enter **slot_diameter**, and for the 3 dimension, enter **depth**.

8. In the *Tools* tab, select ⅕⅖ (Switch Dimensions). The part displays as shown in Figure 6–9.

Figure 6–9

9. Save the part.

Task 3 - Mesh the part with 3D solid elements.

1. Switch to Creo Simulate.

2. In the *Refine Model* tab, click ▦ (AutoGEM).

3. Expand the AutoGEM References drop-down list and select **Volume**.

4. Select the part and click **Create** to create the mesh.

© 2017, ASCENT - Center for Technical Knowledge®

5. The AutoGEM Summary and Diagnostics dialog boxes open with a summary of the entities created, criteria satisfied, and time elapsed. Close both dialog boxes. The meshed model displays as shown in Figure 6–10.

Figure 6–10

6. Close the AutoGEM dialog box and save the mesh. The mesh is saved with your model name and the .MMP extension (e.g., **hinge.mmp**) in your working directory.

Task 4 - Apply loads.

10° is an exaggerated measurement.

The hinge supports a door of 200Kg = 2000N at 10° to the vertical. In this task, you will apply this force in two components.

1. In the Home tab, click ⊢ (Force/Moment). The Force/Moment Load dialog box opens.

2. In the *Name* field, enter **hinge _force_1** and select the surface shown in Figure 6–11.

Figure 6–11

3. In the *Force* area, in the *Y* field, enter **-1970**.

4. Click **OK**. The model displays as shown in Figure 6–12.

*You can use the **Simulation Display** option to place the load vectors as **Tails Touching** and to toggle off the load values.*

Figure 6–12

5. Click ⊢ (Force/Moment). The Force/Moment Load dialog box opens.

© 2017, ASCENT - Center for Technical Knowledge®

Select the internal surface of the hinge hook.

6. In the *Name* field, enter **hinge _force_2** and select the inside surface of the hinge hook as shown in Figure 6–13.

Select this surface

Figure 6–13

7. In the *Force* area, in the *X* field, enter **375**.

8. Click **OK**. The model displays as shown in Figure 6–14.

You can toggle off the load values in the Simulation Display dialog box.

Horizontal load

Figure 6–14

Task 5 - Constrain the surface of the hinge plate.

1. Click 🖉 (Displacement). The Constraint dialog box opens.

2. In the *Name* field, enter **hinge_surface_const**. Select the surface shown in Figure 6–15, and fix all of the Translations.

Figure 6–15

3. Click **OK**. The model displays as shown in Figure 6–16.

Figure 6–16

Task 6 - Apply the material.

1. Assign STEEL to the model. The following values are the default material properties for HS-low-alloy steel (STEEL):

   - **Poisson:** 0.27
   - **Young's modulus:** 199948 MPa
   - **Coeff of thermal expansion:** 1.17e-5 /C
   - **Density:** 7.82708e-9 tonne/mm^3

© 2017, ASCENT - Center for Technical Knowledge®

Analysis Tasks

Task 7 - Set up and run the analysis.

1. Set up a Multi-Pass Adaptive analysis with a 5% convergence and a maximum polynomial order of 9. For the name of the analysis, enter **hinge_multi_pass**.

2. Run the analysis. It should converge after 6 passes.

Task 8 - Display the results.

1. Create and display a fringe color plot of the von Mises stress for the hinge. It displays as shown in Figure 6–17.

Figure 6–17

2. Exit the Creo Simulate Results and close the Analyses and Design Studies dialog box.

Summary

Design variables = Creo dimensions or parameters.

In the previous tasks, you ensured that no errors have occurred in the model and that convergence is achieved. In the following tasks, you will determine the changes in the measure due to small variations in each parameter. This is a local sensitivity study.

The maximum von Mises stress is approximately 166MPa. The yield strength for the hinge material is 230MPa. The difference (230 - 166 = 64MPa) leaves a good margin for weight optimization.

Task 9 - Run a local sensitivity study.

In this task, you will vary the parameters by a small amount (± 2%) and examine the effect of the small parameter's variation on your measure (von Mises stress).

1. Open the Analyses and Design Studies dialog box and select **File>New Sensitivity Design Study.** The Sensitivity Study Definition dialog box opens.

2. In the *Name* field, enter **hinge_local**.

3. Expand the Type drop-down list and select **Local Sensitivity**.

4. In the *Analyses* field, highlight **hinge_multi_pass (Static)**.

5. Click 🔣 (Select Dimension) and select **cut id 226** in the Model Tree. In the *Tools* tab, click 🔢 (Switch Dimensions). The model displays as shown in Figure 6–18.

Figure 6–18

© 2017, ASCENT - Center for Technical Knowledge®

*Select the **Cut id 226** in the Model Tree. The dimensions display. Select the dimension symbol named **slot_dim**.*

6. Select **slot_dim (40mm)**.

7. Click 🔲 (Select Dimension) and select **cut id 226**.

8. Select **hole_dim (75mm)**.

9. Click 🔲 (Select Dimension).

10. Select **depth (3mm)** and then select **cut id 226**.

11. Click 🔲 (Select Dimension) and select **cut id 226**.

12. Select **slot_diameter (10mm)**.

13. The Sensitivity Study Definition dialog box opens as shown in Figure 6–19.

Figure 6–19

14. Click **OK** to close the Sensitivity Study Definition dialog box.

15. Run the design study.

Results Tasks

Task 10 - Display the results.

1. In the Analyses and Design Studies dialog box, click 🖥 (Review Results). The Result Window Definition dialog box opens, as shown in Figure 6–20.

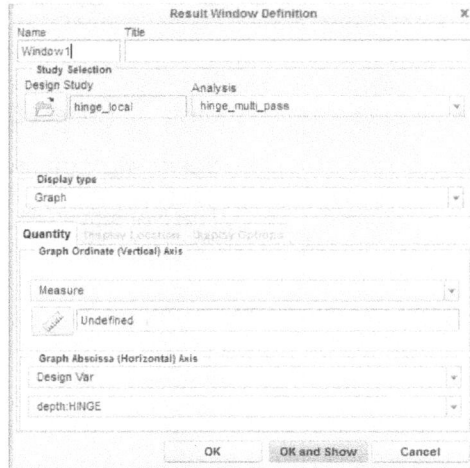

Figure 6–20

2. Click ✏ (Measure) and select **max_stress_vm** in the list of predefined measures.

3. Expand the drop-down menu at the bottom and select **slot_dim: HINGE**. The dialog box opens as shown in Figure 6–21.

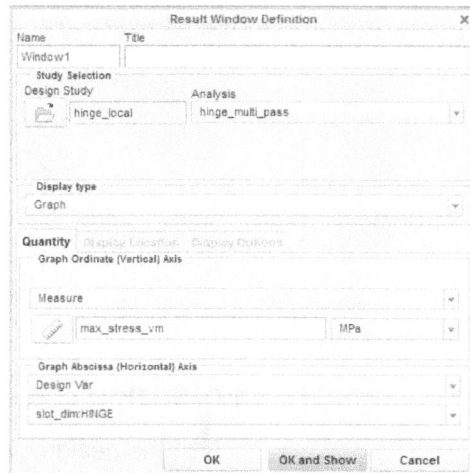

Figure 6–21

© 2017, ASCENT - Center for Technical Knowledge®

4. Click **OK and Show**. The result graph displays as shown in Figure 6–22.

Figure 6–22

Examine the graph. Note that the slot_dim dimension has been varied in the study from *39.6mm* to **40.4mm**, which is ± 2% of the nominal 40mm, while max_stress_vm changed from *166.5MPa* to **165.2MPa**, which is only ± 0.4% of the average 165.85MPa at 40mm. In other words, for every 1% change in the dimension value, there is a 0.2% change in the stress result.

5. Repeat Steps 1 through 4 to create **max_stress_vm** sensitivity graphs for the **depth**, **hole_dim**, and **slot_diameter** dimensions. The results are shown in Figure 6–23.

Figure 6–23

You will now determine which dimensions have the greatest effect on the maximum stress in the model.

Note that the largest variation of the **max_stress_vm** (which is approx. between 164 and 168MPa) is exhibited for the dimension **depth**, which is the graph at the top right corner. You will now display the other three graphs in the same scale, from 164 to 168MPa.

6. Select the graph for the **slot_dim** dimension (top left corner).

   In the *Format* tab, click 🔺 (Edit).

7. In the Graph Window Options dialog box, enter **168** in the *Range Maximum* field and **164** in the *Range Minimum* field.

8. Close the Graph Window Options dialog box. The results display as shown in Figure 6–24.

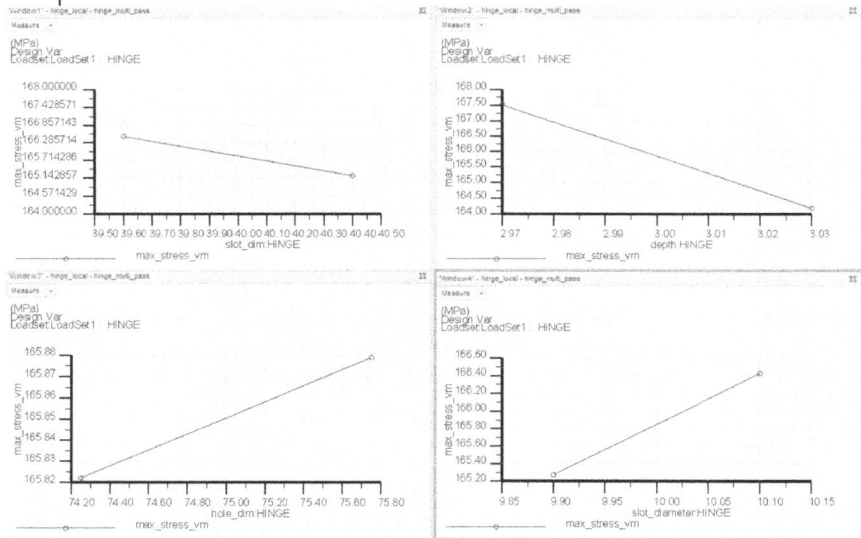

Figure 6–24

9. Repeat Steps 6 to 8 for the remaining two graphs (dimensions **hole_dim** and **slot_diameter**). The results display as shown in Figure 6-25.

© 2017, ASCENT - Center for Technical Knowledge®

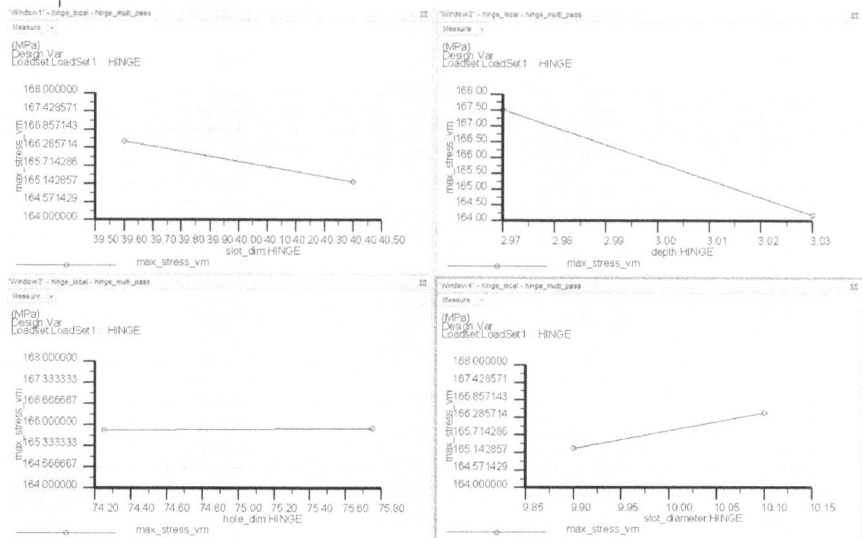

Figure 6–25

Examining the graphs in Figure 6–25 determines that the maximum stress measure is not sensitive to the **hole_dim** parameter. The slope of the sensitivity graph (bottom left corner) is rather shallow, and the difference in measure in the parameter range (4%) is only 165.88 -165.82 = 0.06MPa.

The other three dimensions (**slot_dim**, **slot_diameter**, and **depth**) exhibit sensitivity graphs with much steeper slopes, which means that the maximum stress in the model is sensitive to changes in those dimensions.

10. Close the results window.

Summary

If the von Mises stress is not sensitive to a specific parameter, the parameter should not be carried over for the next task.

At this stage, you have completed the local sensitivity studies and created the result windows. Use local sensitivity studies to determine which parameters have the greatest effect on a measure (such as the maximum von Mises stress) with a small variation in the parameter values. The result windows indicate that the measure is sensitive to the **slot_dim**, **hole_diameter**, and **depth** parameters.

Those three parameters are now selected for the next task, in which you will run a global sensitivity study and determine the variations of the stress measure over a larger range of dimensions.

Task 11 - Create global sensitivity design studies.

In this task, you will examine the variation of the selected three parameters over a range of user-defined values and examine the effect of the parameter's variation on the measure (von Mises stress).

In order to determine the effect of variation in each parameter separately, you will create and run three global sensitivity studies.

1. In the Analyses and Design Studies dialog box, select the **hinge_local** study and click 📋 (Copy).

2. Select the **Copy_of_hinge_local** study and click ✏ (Edit). The Sensitivity Study Definition dialog box opens as shown in Figure 6–26.

Figure 6–26

3. In the *Name* field, enter **hinge_global_slot_dim**.

4. Expand the Type drop-down list and select **Global Sensitivity**.

© 2017, ASCENT - Center for Technical Knowledge®

5. Select **hole_dim** from the variables and click ⬚ (Delete Row) to remove it.

6. Repeat Step 5 to remove the **depth** and **slot_diameter** parameters from the study. When you are finished, the only remaining parameter in the study is **slot_dim**.

7. In the Variables, set the **Start** value as **20** and the **End** value as **60**. Set the **Steps** value to **4**, as shown in Figure 6–27.

*Use the **Options** button to set the **Repeat P-Loop Convergence** option when the parameter's range is high and the shape of the model changes considerably.*

Figure 6–27

8. Click **Options**. The Design Study Options dialog box opens as shown in Figure 6–28.

Figure 6–28

9. Click **Shape Animate the Model** and step through the model shape animation to ensure that the model regenerates on each sensitivity study step. Restore the model to its original shape in the end.

10. Click **Close** to close the Design Study Options dialog box.

11. Click **OK** to close the Sensitivity Study Definition dialog box.

12. Run the design study.

13. Repeat steps 1 through 12 using the following settings:
    - **Name of the study:** hinge_global_depth
    - **Parameter to keep:** depth
    - **Start value:** 1
    - **End value:** 5
    - **Steps:** 4

14. Repeat steps 1 through 12 again, using the following settings:
    - **Name of the study:** hinge_global_slot_diameter
    - **Parameter to keep:** slot_diameter
    - **Start value:** 5
    - **End value:** 12
    - **Steps:** 4

15. Close the Analyses and Design Studies dialog box.

Task 12 - Display the results.

1. In the Home tab, click ▦ (Results).

2. Click ▦ (New).

© 2017, ASCENT - Center for Technical Knowledge®

3. In the dialog box that opens, select **hinge_global_slot_dim** study and click **Open**. The Result Window Definition dialog box displays, as shown in Figure 6–29.

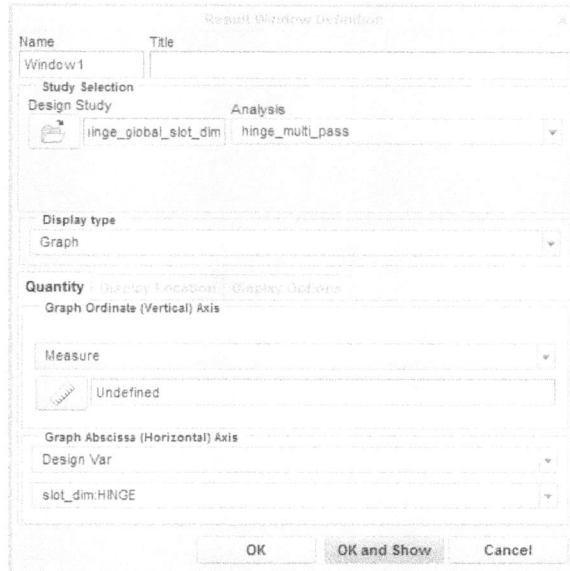

Figure 6–29

4. Click ✏ (Measure), select **max_stress_vm** from the list and then click **OK**. In the Result Window Definition dialog box, click **OK and Show**. The result window displays as shown in Figure 6–30.

Figure 6–30

5. Repeat Steps 2 to 4 using the **hinge_global_depth** study. The result window for the **depth** dimension displays as shown in Figure 6–31.

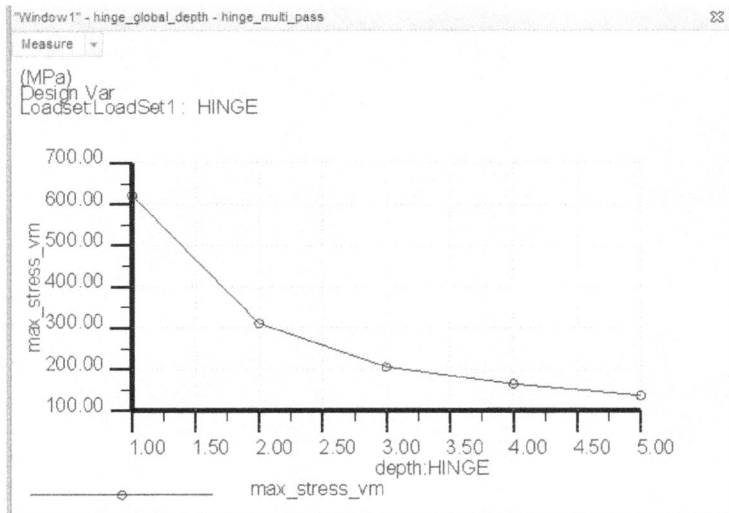

Figure 6–31

6. Repeat Steps 2 to 4 using the **hinge_global_slot_diameter** study. The result window for the **slot_diameter** dimension displays as shown in Figure 6–32.

Figure 6–32

© 2017, ASCENT - Center for Technical Knowledge®

7. Note that the greatest variation of the **max_stress_vm** is exhibited for the dimension **depth**, and is approximately between 100 and 700MPa. The other two design variables (**slot_dim** and **slot_diameter**) have a lesser, but still substantial effect on the stress. Therefore, all three design variables should be carried over into the optimization study.

8. Close the results.

Summary

You ran this study to determine the parameters that have an effect on the von Mises stress.

At this stage, you have completed your global sensitivity study and examined the sensitivity graphs. The sensitivity graphs indicate that the following dimensions could be optimized for minimum von Mises stress:

• Maximum depth (plate thickness)

• Minimum slot_diameter (holes diameter)

• Maximum slot_dim

In the next tasks, you will determine the dimension values that result in the minimum weight of the hinge model without exceeding the allowable stress for the material.

Task 13 - Create an optimization design study.

In this task, you will create a design study to optimize your model weight.

1. In the Analyses and Design Studies dialog box, select **File>New Optimization Design Study**. The Optimization Study Definition dialog box opens.

2. In the *Name* field, enter **hinge_optimize**.

3. Configure the Optimization Design Study Definition dialog box as shown in Figure 6–33.

Figure 6–33

4. Click **OK** to close the Optimization Study Definition dialog box.

5. Run the design study.

© 2017, ASCENT - Center for Technical Knowledge®

Task 14 - Display the results.

In this task, you will locate the optimum model mass and dimension values. You will also create two graphs displaying the optimization process for measures: **max_stress_vm** and **total_mass**.

1. Highlight **hinge_optimize** in the Analyses and Design Studies dialog box and then click ▦ (Status). The Run Status window displays.

*Note that the unit mass is **metric tons** and the unit length is **mm**.*

2. Locate the optimum model mass and parameter values as shown in Figure 6–34.

```
Best Design Found:
Parameters:
    depth                   2.85
    slot_diameter           10.5
    slot_dim                  40
Goal:  2.0017e-04
```

Figure 6–34

Task 15 - Create two graphs for the measures:
max_stress_vm and total_mass.

1. Create a graph for the **max_stress_vm** measure versus the **Optimization Pass**. The graph displays as shown in Figure 6–35.

Figure 6–35

2. Create a graph for the **total_mass** measure versus **Optimization Pass**. The graph displays as shown in Figure 6–36.

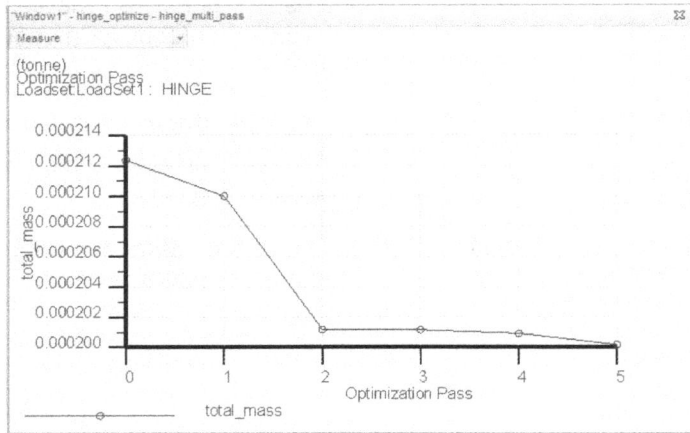

Figure 6–36

Note that the optimization algorithm reduced the weight of the hinge from **0.000212356** tonne to **0.000200172** tonne, which is approximately 5.7% less than the original design.

Task 16 - Display the stress plot.

---

1. Create and display a fringe plot for the von Mises stress in the optimized model. The result plot displays as shown in Figure 6–37.

Figure 6–37

2. Close the results and save the model in Creo Parametric.

© 2017, ASCENT - Center for Technical Knowledge®

Practice 6b

Design Study of a Hanger

Sensitivity design studies automate some of the repetitive work involved in design.

Practice Objectives

- Set up and run a sensitivity design study.
- Set up and run a standard design study.

In this practice, you will use sensitivity and standard design studies to set up, run, analyze, and redesign a hanger part shown in Figure 6–38.

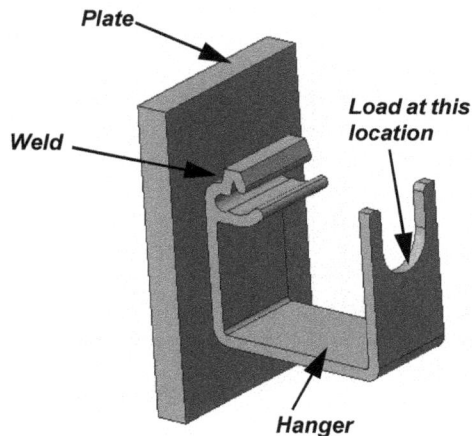

Figure 6–38

The hanger is made of aluminum alloy 6005-T6, which has the following settings:

- **Modulus of elasticity:** 10600ksi

- **Poisson's ratio:** 0.33

- **Tensile yield stress:** 36ksi

The part is welded to the support plate at the top, and is loaded by a downward force of 65lbf at the bottom of the cutout on the other end, as shown above in Figure 6–38.

The design requirement for the part is that the factor of safety against yielding under the given load should be no less than 1.2. The goal of the study is to ensure that this design requirement is met.

Check the Current Design

The goal of the following tasks is to check the current design by setting up and running a static stress analysis.

Task 1 - Open gearrack.prt.

1. Open **gearrack.prt** in Creo Parametric. The part displays as shown in Figure 6–39.

Figure 6–39

2. Ensure that the unit system is set to **IPS**.

3. Switch to Creo Simulate.

Task 2 - Apply the material.

1. In the *Home* tab, click ⬁ (Materials). Select **al2014.mtl** and move it to the Materials in Model.

2. Select ✎ (Edit) and change the following material properties, as shown in Figure 6–40:
   - **Name:** AL6005-T6
   - **Poisson's Ratio:** 0.33
   - **Young's Modulus:** 1.06e+07 psi

© 2017, ASCENT - Center for Technical Knowledge®

Figure 6–40

3. Click **OK** to close the Material Definition dialog box, and click **OK** again to close the Materials dialog box.

4. Assign the material **AL6005-T6** to the part.

Task 3 - Apply constraints.

This constraint simulates the weldment to the support plate.

1. Click ⬚ (Displacement) and fully constrain (all translations) the two surfaces shown in Figure 6–41.

Constrain these surfaces

Figure 6–41

2. Click **OK** to close the Constraint dialog box.

The second constraint models the support provided by the plate at the bottom of the hanger, when the load tries to bend the hanger downward.

3. Click ⬚ (Displacement) again and constrain the edge at the bottom of the hanger (shown in Figure 6–42) in the **X** direction only.

Constrain this edge

Figure 6–42

© 2017, ASCENT - Center for Technical Knowledge®

4. Click **OK** to close the Constraint dialog box. The model displays as shown in Figure 6–43.

Figure 6–43

Task 4 - Apply the load.

1. Click ⊢ (Force/Moment) and apply **65lbf** force in the -**Y** direction to the surface shown in Figure 6–44.

Load this
surface

Figure 6–44

2. Click **OK** to close the Force/Moment Load dialog box. The model displays as shown in Figure 6–45.

Figure 6–45

Task 5 - Set up and run an analysis and display the results.

1. Set up a Single-Pass Adaptive analysis. For the name of the analysis, enter **hanger_anls**.

2. Run the analysis.

3. Create and display a fringe plot of the von Mises stress for the part. It displays as shown in Figure 6–46.

Figure 6–46

© 2017, ASCENT - Center for Technical Knowledge®

- Note that the maximum stress is over 38000psi.
- Note that the yield strength of the material is 36ksi = 36000psi. Given the required factor of safety 1.2, this means that the maximum permitted stress for the part is 36000/1.2 = 30000psi. Therefore, in the current design of the hanger, the factor of safety requirement is not met and the part's design should be modified.
- Note that the maximum stress occurs in the inside fillet at the bottom of the hanger, which is likely due to the stress concentration effect. It is well known that stress concentration around fillets and holes is greatly affected by the fillet radius. Therefore, in the next tasks you will study how sensitive the maximum stress is to the radius of that fillet.

4. Exit the Creo Simulate Results and close the Analyses and Design Studies dialog box.

5. Exit Creo Simulate.

Run a Sensitivity Study

In the following tasks you will determine if the design requirements could be met by adjusting the fillet radius.

Task 6 - Rename the design variables.

In this task, you will rename the Creo Parametric fillet radius to make it easier to identify in the sensitivity study.

1. In the Model Tree, right-click on **Round 8** and select d1 (Edit). The part displays. Select the **R.062** dimension, as shown in Figure 6–47.

Select this dimension

R.062

Figure 6–47

2. Right-click on the dimension and select **Properties**. The Dimension Properties dialog box opens.

3. In the *Name* field, enter **round_radius**, as shown in Figure 6–48.

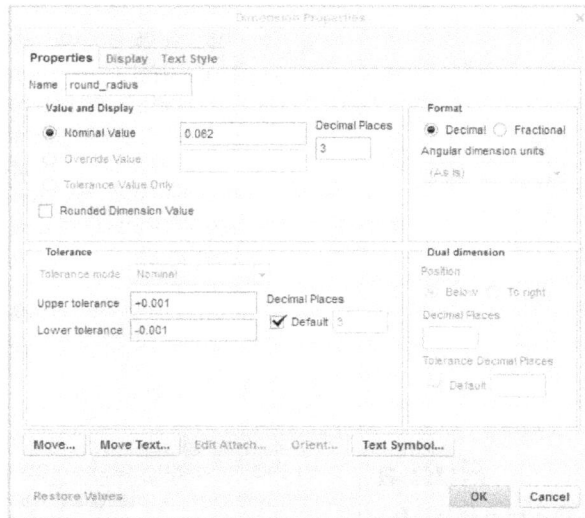

Figure 6–48

4. Click **OK**.

5. In the *Tools* tab, click ![icon] (Switch Dimensions). The part displays as shown in Figure 6–49.

Figure 6–49

6. Save the part.

© 2017, ASCENT - Center for Technical Knowledge®

Task 7 - Run a sensitivity study.

In this task, you will vary the fillet radius and examine its effect on the von Mises stress.

1. Switch to Creo Simulate.

2. Open the Analyses and Design Studies dialog box and select **File>New Sensitivity Design Study**. The Sensitivity Study Definition dialog box opens.

3. In the *Name* field, enter **hanger_sensitivity**.

4. Expand the Type drop-down list and select **Global Sensitivity**.

5. In the *Analyses* field, highlight **hanger_anls (Static)**.

6. Click ⌖ (Select Dimension) and select **Round 8** in the Model Tree. In the *Tools* tab, select ⅕ (Switch Dimensions). The model displays as shown in Figure 6–50.

Figure 6–50

7. Select **round_radius**.

8. In the Sensitivity Study Definition dialog box, set the following, as shown in Figure 6–51:

   • Enter **0.062** in the *Start* column.

   • Enter **0.162** in the *End* column.

   • Ensure that **10** is set as the number of *Steps*.

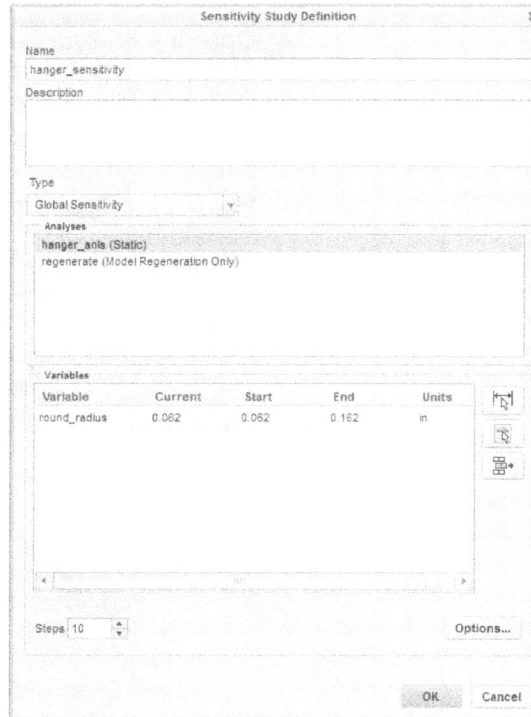

Figure 6–51

9. Click **OK** to close the Sensitivity Study Definition dialog box.

10. Run the design study.

Task 8 - Display the results.

1. In the Analyses and Design Studies dialog box, highlight **hanger_sensitivity** and then click (Review Results). The Result Window Definition dialog box opens, as shown in Figure 6–52.

© 2017, ASCENT - Center for Technical Knowledge®

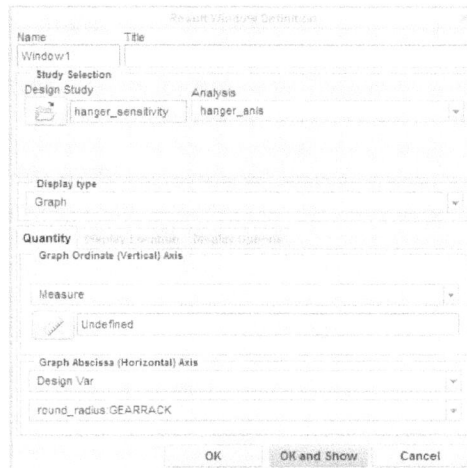

Figure 6–52

2. Click (Measure), select **max_stress_vm** from the list, and then click **OK**.

3. In the Result Window Definition dialog box, click **OK and Show**. The result window displays as shown in Figure 6–53.

Figure 6–53

The sensitivity graph clearly shows that the maximum stress in the hanger can be brought down to under the permitted stress of 30000psi by increasing the radius of the fillet at the bottom of the hanger. At the 6th step of the sensitivity study, the stress has already dropped under 30000psi, and at the last step of the study (radius 0.162in) the stress is under 26000psi.

Task 9 - Calculate the proposed fillet radius.

In this task, you will calculate the new fillet radius using the sensitivity graph.

1. Click on the point in the graph that corresponds to the 5th step in the study, shown in Figure 6–54. The bottom status bar in the window should read **round_radius: GEARRACK: 0.102,max_stress_vm: 30815.4**.

Figure 6–54

2. Click on the point in the graph that corresponds to the 6th step in the study, shown in Figure 6–55. The bottom status bar in the window should read **round_radius: GEARRACK: 0.112,max_stress_vm: 29678.1**.

© 2017, ASCENT - Center for Technical Knowledge®

"Window1" - hanger_sensitivity - hanger_anls

Measure ▾

(psi)
Design Var
Loadset:LoadSet1 : GEARRACK

Click this point

max_stress_vm

round_radius:GEARRACK

max_stress_vm

• round_radius:GEARRACK: 0.112,max_stress_vm: 29678.1

Figure 6–55

3. Using linear interpolation between the graph points, the radius that corresponds to the 30000psi stress is:

$$0.102 + (30000 - 30815.4) \times \frac{0.112 - 0.102}{29678.1 - 30815.4} = 0.1092$$

Since linear interpolation was used between the points while the sensitivity graph is in reality a curve, to account for the inaccuracy, add a10% margin to the calculated radius:

0.1092 + 10% = 0.12012

Rounded to the tenth of an inch, the proposed fillet radius that corresponds to maximum stress just under 30000psi, becomes 0.12in.

4. Exit Creo Simulate results.

Validate the Design Change

In the following tasks you will validate the proposed design change of an increase in fillet radius from 0.062in to 0.12in by using a standard design study.

Task 10 - Create and run standard design study.

1. Open the Analyses and Design Studies dialog box and select **File>New Standard Design Study.** The Standard Study Definition dialog box opens.

2. In the *Name* field, enter **hanger_new_design**.

3. In the *Analyses* field, select **hanger_anls (Static)**.

4. Click ⌖ (Select Dimension) and select **Round 8** in the Model Tree. In the *Tools* tab, select ⅊ (Switch Dimensions). The model displays as shown in Figure 6–56.

Figure 6–56

5. Select **round_radius**.

© 2017, ASCENT - Center for Technical Knowledge®

6. Enter **0.12** in the *Setting* column. The Standard Design Study dialog box opens as shown in Figure 6–57.

Standard Study Definition				✕

Name

hanger_new_design

Description

Analyses

hanger_anls (Static)
regenerate (Model Regeneration Only)

Variables

Variable	Current	Setting	Units	
round_radius	0.062	0.12	in	

OK   Cancel

Figure 6–57

7. Click **OK** to close the dialog box.

8. Run the **hanger_new_design** study.

Task 11 - Display the results.

1. In the Analyses and Design Studies dialog box, select **hanger_new_design** and click 🖼 (Review Results).

2. Create a von Mises stress plot. The plot displays as shown in Figure 6–58.

Figure 6–58

Note that the maximum stress is now 29111.3psi.

The factor of safety for the new design is 36000/29111.3 = 1.237, which is greater than the required minimum 1.2.

Therefore, the new design meets the stress requirements.

3. Exit Creo Simulate results.

4. Exit Creo Simulate and save and close the part in Creo Parametric.

© 2017, ASCENT - Center for Technical Knowledge®

Assembly Interfaces

In this chapter you learn how to model the interfaces between assembly components, and to setup a contact analysis.

Learning Objectives in this Chapter

- Understand the types of part interfaces in Creo Simulate.
- Create Bonded Interfaces.
- Create Free Interfaces.
- Understand the Contact Interface properties.
- Create Contact Interfaces manually.
- Create Contact Interfaces automatically.
- Review the interfaces in your model.
- Set up an analysis with Contact Interfaces.
- Refine the mesh in contact areas.

7.1 Types of Interfaces

Interfaces in Creo Simulate define the treatment of mated or overlapping surfaces in an assembly model.

There are three types of Interfaces in Creo Simulate Structural:

- **Bonded:** The interfacing surfaces are essentially *glued* together.

- **Free:** The interfacing surfaces are not connected in any way.

- **Contact:** The interfacing surfaces cannot interpenetrate, but can still separate and/or slide along each other under the applied loading.

Default Interface

By default, Creo Simulate treats all of the mated surfaces in the model according to the option selected in the Default Interface drop-down list in the Model Setup dialog box, as shown in Figure 7–1.

Figure 7–1

© 2017, ASCENT - Center for Technical Knowledge®

7.2 Bonded Interface

A Bonded Interface is a connection that essentially *glues* two parts together. Displacement continuity between the interfacing surfaces is ensured (i.e., the surfaces remain *attached* to each other during the analysis).

This type of interface is typically used for, but not limited to, bonded, glued, surface-welded, etc., connections between parts in an assembly. The key criterion for the correct use is either no or negligible separation or the sliding of the two surfaces under applied loading.

The applied forces are fully transmitted through the Bonded Interfaces. Creo Simulate automatically creates a simulation measure to calculate the resultant force over each Bonded Interface.

Use the following steps to create a Bonded Interface:

1. In the *Refine* tab, in the *Connections* group, click

    (Interface) to open the Interface Definition dialog box.
2. Expand the Type drop-down list and select **Bonded**. The Interface Definition dialog box opens as shown in Figure 7–2.

Figure 7–2

3. Select the geometrical references (**Surface-Surface** or **Component-Component**).
4. Click **OK** to finish.

7.3 Free Interface

A Free Interface does not connect the two surfaces in any way. The surfaces can freely separate or pass through each other under the applied loading, and no forces are transmitted through the interface. The surfaces ignore each other.

This type of interface should only be used for parts that are expected to separate and never to press against each other under the loading in the model. The analysis results should also be carefully reviewed afterward, to ensure there is no interpenetration of the surfaces in the model, which would otherwise render the analysis as incorrect.

Use the following steps to create a Free Interface:

1. In the *Refine* tab, in the *Connections* group, click
   (Interface) to open the Interface Definition dialog box.
2. Expand the Type drop-down list and select **Free**. The Interface Definition dialog box opens as shown in Figure 7–3.

Figure 7–3

3. Select the geometrical references (**Surface-Surface** or **Component-Component**).
4. Click **OK** to finish.

© 2017, ASCENT - Center for Technical Knowledge®

7.4 Contact Interface

In a Contact Interface, the two surfaces are free to move apart and/or slide along each other under the applied loading, but they cannot interpenetrate. The surfaces are initially permitted to be at a clearance, but might come into contact during the analysis. Only compressive normal stresses are transmitted through the interface (i.e., the interfacing surfaces cannot *pull* each other).

The Contact Interface is the most realistic model for simulating parts that must remain separate from each other during the analysis, yet do not interpenetrate. From the FEA standpoint, the Contact Interface represents a boundary condition that changes during the loading. For example, when a chain roller is pressed against a sprocket, the line contact changes to an area contact.

In the example shown in Figure 7–4, there is a gap between the plate and block initially (configuration 1 in Figure 7–4). Once the load has been applied, the plate bends freely, until it comes into contact with the block, as shown in configuration 2 in Figure 7–4. If the load is further increased, the area of contact shifts from the edge of the plate to the edge of the block (configuration 3 in Figure 7–4). Therefore, the contact area and location change depending on the amount of load applied.

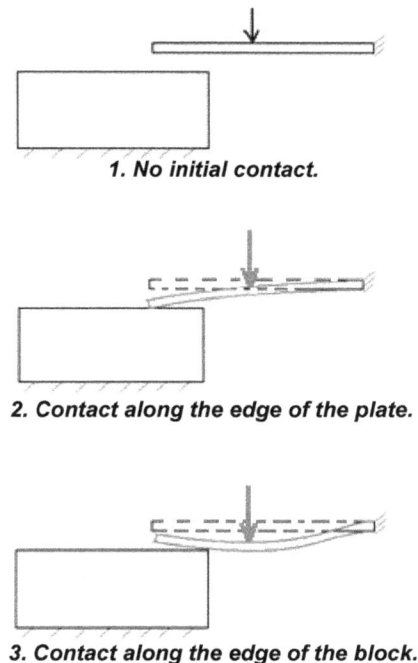

1. No initial contact.

2. Contact along the edge of the plate.

3. Contact along the edge of the block.

Figure 7–4

Contact in Creo Simulate can use or ignore friction. The following friction options are available:

- **None**: Creates a frictionless contact. Only compressive forces are transmitted through a frictionless Contact Interface, and the surfaces will slip relative to each other whenever there is a tangential force between them.

- **Finite**: Creates a Contact with friction. The surfaces will slip relative to each other only if tangential force exceeds the friction force. The friction force is the coefficient of friction times the compressive force.

- **Infinite**: The interfacing surfaces are able to come apart in the normal direction, but they cannot slip relative to each other. For a Contact with infinite friction, Creo Simulate automatically creates slippage measures. A positive value of a slippage measure indicates that the surfaces in contact might have slid relative to each other. Therefore, the assumption of infinite friction is not accurate.

 Creo Simulate automatically creates simulation measures to calculate the contact area and the resultant force over a Contact Interface.

To create a Contact Interface, click ⬚ (Interface) to open the Interface Definition dialog box, and select **Contact** option in the Type drop-down list, as shown in Figure 7–5.

Figure 7–5

© 2017, ASCENT - Center for Technical Knowledge®

The options in the dialog box are as follows:

Section	Option	Description
References	Surface-Surface	User selects the surfaces that are in contact, or might come into contact during the analysis.
	Component-Component	Creo Simulate creates Contact Interfaces between any two surfaces that satisfy the user-defined **Separation Distance** and **Angle** criteria.
Properties	Split Surfaces	Creo Simulate splits the surfaces along the contact region boundaries.
	Generate Compatible Mesh	Creo Simulate creates geometrically coincident mesh node locations on the contact region.
Friction	None	Creates a frictionless Contact .
	Finite	Creates a Contact with finite friction.
	Infinite	Creates a Contact with infinite friction.
	Create Slippage Indicators	Creates slippage measures. Only available with the **Infinite Friction** option.
	Static Coefficient of Friction	Specify the friction coefficient at which the sliding occurs.
	Dynamic Coefficient of Friction	Specify the friction coefficient at which the sliding continues once started. Only available with the **Finite Friction** option.

Automatic Contact Detection

Creo Simulate has a tool that enables you to automatically create Contact Interfaces between parts in the assembly, based on user-specified criteria.

To start the auto detection, expand the *Interface* area in the *Refine Model* tab, as shown in Figure 7–6, and select **Detect Contacts**.

Figure 7–6

The Auto Detect Contacts dialog box opens as shown in Figure 7–7.

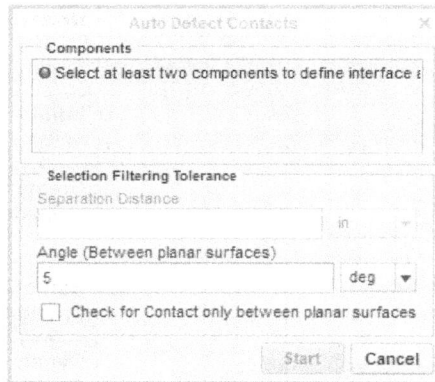

Figure 7–7

The options in the dialog box are as follows:

Option	Description
Separation Distance	Maximum distance between surface pairs on which you want to define a contact.
Angle (between planar surfaces)	Only surfaces that are at an angle less than the specified are considered.
Check for Contact only between planar surfaces	Creates contacts only between planar surfaces.

© 2017, ASCENT - Center for Technical Knowledge®

7.5 Reviewing Interfaces

Once created, all of the interfaces display under **Connections> Interfaces** in the Model Tree, as shown in Figure 7–8. You can review and delete the interfaces in the model using the Model Tree.

Figure 7–8

You can also visualize the interfaces in your model by clicking
(Review Geometry) in the *Refine Model* tab, and selecting the Connectivity options as shown in Figure 7–9.

Figure 7–9

Once you click **Apply**, the model displays in Wireframe mode, with all of the interfaces shaded and color-coded, as shown in Figure 7–10.

Figure 7–10

7.6 Setting Up Contact Analysis

Structural analysis with Contact Interfaces is a non-linear FEA analysis. A non-linear analysis is solved in small steps (controlled by the FEA solver), with the applied loads gradually incremented from no load to the full load, and with the equation system solved on every load increment. A non-linear FEA takes much longer to solve than a comparable linear analysis. Therefore, use caution when setting up an analysis with many Contact Interfaces.

The Static Analysis Definition dialog box for an analysis with Contact Interfaces is shown in Figure 7–11.

Figure 7–11

© 2017, ASCENT - Center for Technical Knowledge®

*The **Calculate large deformations** option requires the Advanced Simulation license.*

The following options must be set to run a non-linear analysis with Contact Interfaces:

1. Ensure that the **Nonlinear/Use Load Histories** and **Contacts** options are selected.
2. Activate the **Calculate large deformations** option if you anticipate a substantial sliding to occur in some contact regions.
3. In the *Constraints* and the *Loads* areas, use $f(x)$ (Function) to define the time histories for the constraints and loads in your model. The default time history is a simple ramp function with the load linearly increased from zero to the full load.
4. Set the Convergence options:
   - **Localized Mesh Refinement:** Automatically refines the mesh in the contact regions. Only available with the Single-Pass Adaptive convergence method.
   - **Check Contact Force:** Ensures convergence on contact forces.
   - **Press Fit (initial interpenetration):** Activates detection of the press fit conditions in the model (otherwise Creo Simulate ignores initial interpenetrations).
   - **Maximum initial interpenetration:** Specifies the press fit detection value. Any initial interpenetration larger than this value is ignored.
   - **Calculate detailed stresses at contact interfaces:** Enables calculation of detailed stresses in contact regions.

5. In the *Output* tab, select the **Output Steps**. This setting defines the load intervals (also called *load percentage factors*) at which Creo Simulate calculates the full results for displaying.

- **Automatic Steps within Range:** The results are only calculated for the full load.
- **User-defined Output Steps:** Enables you to define the load intervals for which the output is to be calculated, as shown in the example in Figure 7–12.

Figure 7–12

© 2017, ASCENT - Center for Technical Knowledge®

7.7 Mesh Refinement

The accuracy of the Contact analyses are affected by the mesh density in the contact areas. The element size should be smaller than the contact region.

Use the following guidelines to achieve this condition:

- Create Surface Regions to separate areas of contact from the rest of the part surface.

- Use the **AutoGEM Control, Maximum Element Size Control** option, as shown in Figure 7–13, to apply a smaller element size in the contact areas

Figure 7–13

- Use 2D models when possible. Doing so improves accuracy, eases setup, and reduces run time.

Practice 7a

Door Handle Assembly

Practice Objectives

- Create Free and Contact Interfaces.
- Set up and run a contact analysis.

In this practice, you will set up a contact analysis on a part of the door handle assembly. The assembly model is shown in Figure 7–14.

The model has been defeatured (various rounds and blends have been removed).

Figure 7–14

The area of interest is only the contact between the sleeve and barrel. The assembly that you analyze consists of a sleeve part, the barrel part, and the door slab part, as shown in Figure 7–15. The model will be solved using one possible simulation scenario.

Figure 7–15

© 2017, ASCENT - Center for Technical Knowledge®

Modeling Tasks

Task 1 - Open the model and launch Creo Simulate.

1. Open **door_handle.asm** in Creo Parametric. The assembly displays as shown in Figure 7–16.

Figure 7–16

2. Ensure that the unit system is set to **IPS**.

3. Select **Applications>Simulate** to launch Creo Simulate.

Task 2 - Apply the loads.

In this task, you will apply loads to the barrel end surface shown in Figure 7–17.

Select this surface

Figure 7–17

*To apply the load, use the **Uniform** and **Total Load** options in the Distribution area in the Force/Moment dialog box. Note that the load is applied in the Z-direction.*

1. Apply **100lbs** to the surface in the Z-direction. For the *Name*, enter **handle_load**. The model displays as shown in Figure 7–18.

Figure 7–18

Task 3 - Apply the constraints.

1. Fully constrain the door slab end surfaces, as shown in Figure 7–19.

2. For the *Name*, enter **door_const**. The model displays as shown in Figure 7–19.

Figure 7–19

3. Create a datum point in the middle of the barrel edge, as shown in Figure 7–20. Use the main assembly as the **Component for Feature**, with the barrel edge and the ASM_RIGHT datum plane as the **References** for the point.

© 2017, ASCENT - Center for Technical Knowledge®

Figure 7–20

4. Constrain the point in the X- and Y-directions to prevent the rotation and slippage of the barrel (you will use a frictionless Contact Interface in this analysis).

5. For the *Name*, enter **barrel_const**. The model displays as shown in Figure 7–21.

Figure 7–21

Task 4 - Create a Contact Interface.

In this task, you will create a Contact Interface between the sleeve and the barrel.

1. In the *Refine Model* tab, click 🔲 (Interface). The Interface Definition dialog box opens as shown in Figure 7–22.

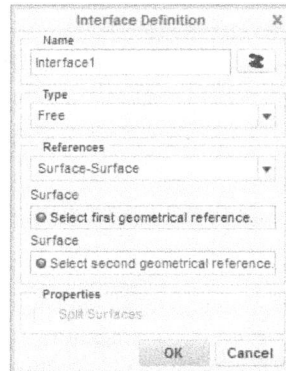

Figure 7–22

2. Expand the Type drop-down list and select **Contact**.

3. Expand the References drop-down list and select **Component-Component**.

4. Select the **SLEEVE** and **BARREL** parts as the references.

5. Select the **Split Surfaces** and **Generate Compatible Mesh** options. The Interface Definition dialog box opens as shown in Figure 7–23.

© 2017, ASCENT - Center for Technical Knowledge®

Figure 7–23

6. Accept all of the other defaults and click **OK** to finish. The model displays as shown in Figure 7–24.

Figure 7–24

Task 5 - Create a Free Interface.

The sleeve and door slab in this analysis are assumed to be only interacting through the screws. In this task, you will create a Free Interface to ensure that the sleeve is not pressing against the door slab along their surfaces during the analysis.

1. Click ▦ (Interface). The Interface Definition dialog box opens.

2. Expand the Type drop-down list and select **Free**.

3. Expand the References drop-down list and select **Component-Component**.

4. Select the **SLEEVE** and **DOOR** parts as the references and accept all of the other default options. The Interface Definition dialog box opens as shown in Figure 7–25.

Figure 7–25

5. Accept all of the other defaults and click **OK** to finish. The model displays as shown in Figure 7–26.

Figure 7–26

© 2017, ASCENT - Center for Technical Knowledge®

Task 6 - Create rigid links.

In this task, you will create Rigid Links to model the screws that attach the sleeve to the door slab.

1. In the *Connections* group, click ▣ (Rigid Link). The Rigid Link Definition dialog box opens as shown in Figure 7–27.

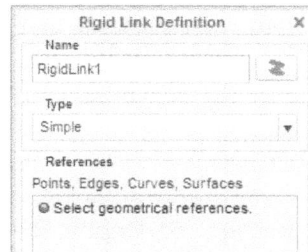

Figure 7–27

2. Select the inside cylindrical surfaces of the top hole in the sleeve and of the top hole in the door slab, as shown in Figure 7–28.

Figure 7–28

3. The Rigid Link Definition dialog box opens as shown in Figure 7–29.

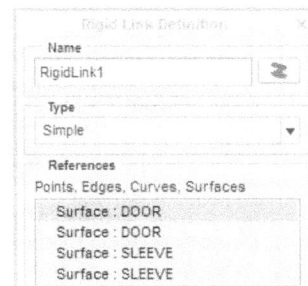

Figure 7–29

4. Click **OK** to finish. The Rigid Link displays as shown in Figure 7–30.

Figure 7–30

5. Repeat Steps 1 to 4 to create a Rigid Link for the bottom holes.

6. Use the Simulation Display box to hide the loads and constraints. The model displays as shown in Figure 7–31.

Figure 7–31

Task 7 - Review the connections.

1. In the *Refine Model* tab, in the *AutoGEM* group, click
    (Review Geometry) to open the Simulation Geometry dialog box.

© 2017, ASCENT - Center for Technical Knowledge®

2. Select the options shown in Figure 7–32.

Figure 7–32

3. Click **Apply**. The model displays as shown in Figure 7–33.

Figure 7–33

Examine the model display. Locate the Contact Interfaces and the Rigid Links. Ensure that there are no Bonded Interfaces in the model.

4. Click **Close** to finish.

Task 8 - Apply the material.

1. Assign **AL2014** to all of the assembly parts. The following values are the default material properties for Aluminum, wrought 2014-T6:
   - Poisson = 0.33
   - Young's modulus = 1.06e+07 psi

Analysis Tasks

Task 9 - Set up and run the analysis.

1. Set up a Single-Pass Adaptive convergence analysis. For the analysis name, enter **door_handle** and keep all of the other defaults. The Static Analysis Definition dialog box opens as shown in Figure 7–34.

Figure 7–34

2. Select the *Output* tab.

3. Expand the Output Steps drop-down list and select **User-defined Output Steps**.

4. For the *Number of Master Steps*, select **5**.

5. Click **User-defined Steps** and **Space Equally**. In the Static Analysis Definition dialog box, the *Output* area displays as shown in Figure 7–35.

© 2017, ASCENT - Center for Technical Knowledge®

Figure 7–35

6. Click **OK** to close the Static Analysis Definition dialog box.

7. In the Analyses and Design Studies dialog box, in the **Info** menu, select **Check Model** to check the validity of the model.

8. Run the analysis.

Results Tasks

Task 10 - Display the deformation results.

1. In the Analyses and Design Studies dialog box, click
   (Review Results). In the Result Window Definition dialog box, in the Steps list, highlight the last row as shown in Figure 7–36.

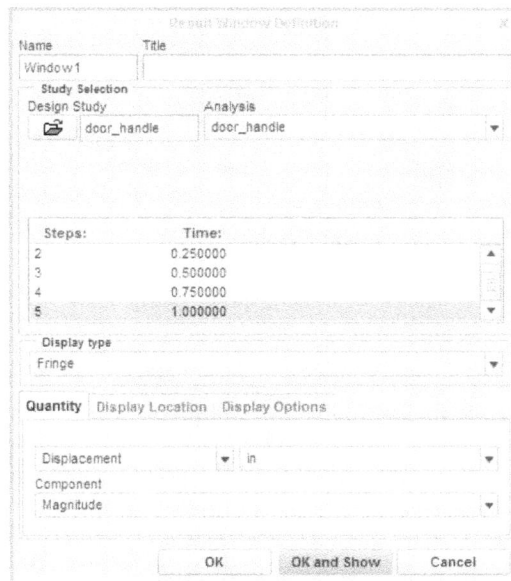

Figure 7–36

2. Select the *Display Options* tab. Select the **Deformed**, **Overlay Undeformed**, and **Animate** options, as shown in Figure 7–37.

Figure 7–37

3. Click **OK and Show** to display and animate the Displacement Magnitude result.

4. Note that the animation frames correspond to the Load Factor, from 0 (no load) to 1 (full load). Stop the animation at Step 4. The model displays as shown in Figure 7–38.

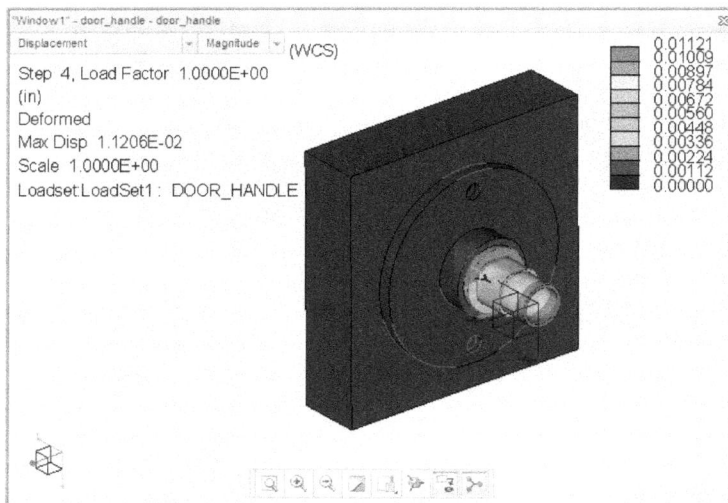

Figure 7–38

© 2017, ASCENT - Center for Technical Knowledge®

Task 11 - Display the stress results.

1. Click ✎ (Edit) to edit the result window. In the *Quantity* area, select **Stress, von Mises**.

2. Select the *Display Location* tab. Expand the drop-down list and select **Components/Layers**. Set the visibility of the **DOOR** component to **Blanked**.

3. Select the *Display Options* tab and clear the **Animate** option.

4. Click **OK and Show**. The von Mises stress plot displays as shown in Figure 7–39.

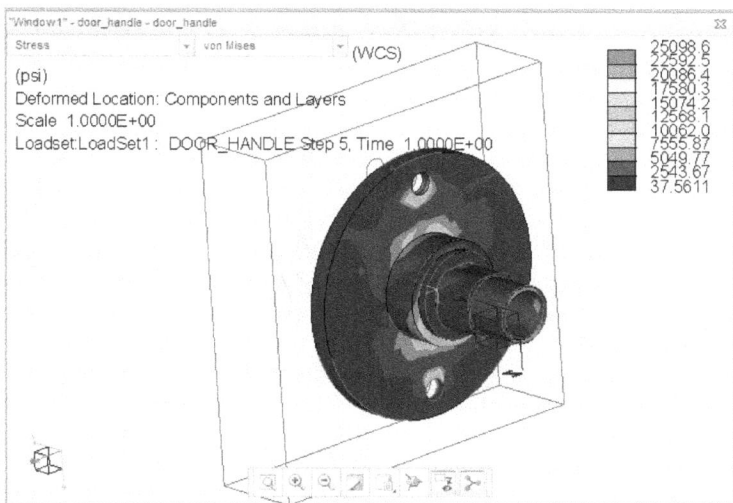

Figure 7–39

Examine the stress plot. Use the tools in the **Query** section of the *Home* tab to locate the area of maximum stress.

Task 12 - Display the contact pressure results.

1. Click ✎ (Edit) to edit the result window. In the *Steps* area, highlight the last row, and in the *Quantity* area, select **Contact Pressure**.

2. Click **OK and Show**. The Contact Pressure plot displays as shown in Figure 7–40.

Figure 7–40

3. Select ⬛ (Model Max) to locate the maximum. Note that the maximum contact pressure occurs at the back of the top of the contact region, as shown in Figure 7–41.

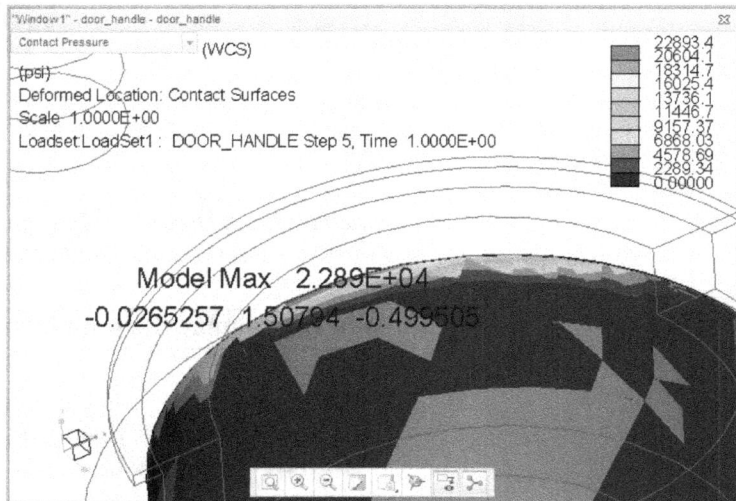

Figure 7–41

© 2017, ASCENT - Center for Technical Knowledge®

Task 13 - Display the contact pressure graph.

1. Click ✐ (Edit) to edit the result window. In the Display type
   list, select **Graph** and in the *Quantity* area, select **Measure**.
   The Result Window Definition dialog box opens as shown in
   Figure 7–42.

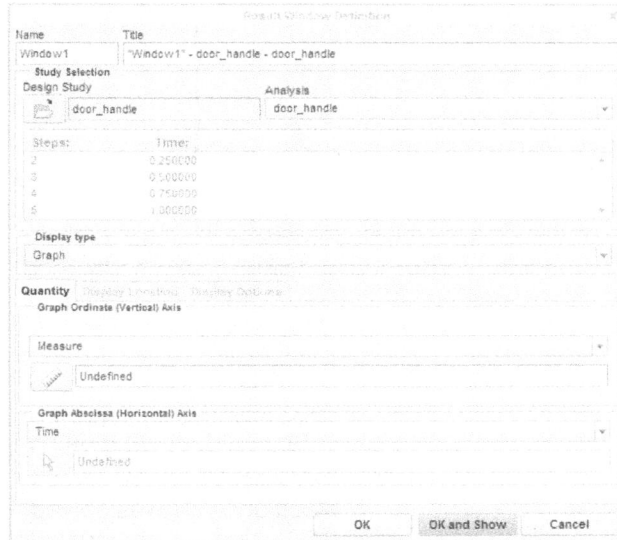

Figure 7–42

2. Click ✐ (Measure). In the list of predefined measures, select
   contact_max_pres. Click **OK** to complete.

3. Click **OK and Show**. The **contact_max_pres** graph displays as shown in Figure 7–43.

"Window1" - door_handle - door_handle

Measure   (WCS)

(psi)
Time
Scale 1.0000E+00
Loadset:LoadSet1 : DOOR_HANDLE

contact_max_pres — graph with y-axis labeled contact_max_pres from 0.00 to 25000.00 and x-axis labeled Time from 0.00 to 1.00

contact_max_pres

Figure 7–43

Note how the maximum contact pressure is increasing with the load, from no load to the full load. Although the horizontal axis in the graph displays *Time*, this is not a physical time because a static analysis was solved. Rather, it is a load factor (i.e., the 0.50 value on the horizontal axis corresponds to the 50% load applied, etc.).

4. Exit the Results and save and close the model.

© 2017, ASCENT - Center for Technical Knowledge®

Practice 7b

Pin-Jointed Assembly

Practice Objectives

- Create surface regions.
- Create Contact Interfaces.
- Refine mesh in contact regions.
- Run a contact analysis.

In this practice, you will set up a contact analysis on a pin-jointed assembly model. The assembly model is part of a hydraulic boom mechanism, as shown in Figure 7–44.

Figure 7–44

The contact analysis takes a long time and the area of interest is only the contact between the pin, boom, and pivot arm. The assembly that you will analyze consists of these parts, as shown in Figure 7–45. The model will be solved with one possible simulation scenario.

Figure 7–45

The pin is press-fit into the pivot arm holes. Therefore, the pin is fully fixed to the pivot arm. However, the boom is assembled on the pin with a small clearance, to be able to rotate around the pin when the mechanism (shown in Figure 7–44) is moving.

Modeling Tasks

Task 1 - Open the assembly.

1. Open **hydraulic.asm** in Creo Parametric. The assembly displays as shown in Figure 7–46.

Figure 7–46

All parts in the assembly must use the same system of units.

2. Ensure that the unit system is set to **mmNs**.

3. Do not launch Creo Simulate yet.

© 2017, ASCENT - Center for Technical Knowledge®

Task 2 - Create the surface regions.

In this task, you will define the surface areas that are used later to create Contact Interfaces between the pin and boom.

1. Right-click **pin_1.prt** in the Model Tree and select **Open** to open it in Creo Parametric. The pin displays as shown in Figure 7–47.

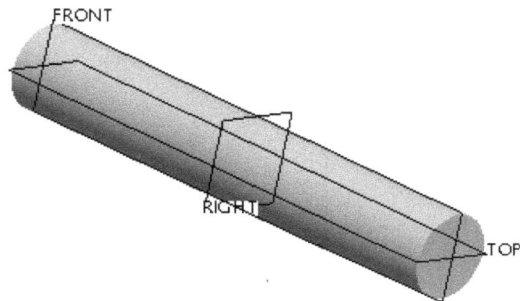

Figure 7–47

2. Switch to Creo Simulate.

3. In the *Refine Model* tab, click ▱ (Plane) and create DTM1 plane parallel to datum plane RIGHT at a distance of **80**, as shown in Figure 7–48.

The plane is created on the left side of datum plane RIGHT, using the pin orientation shown in Figure 7–48.

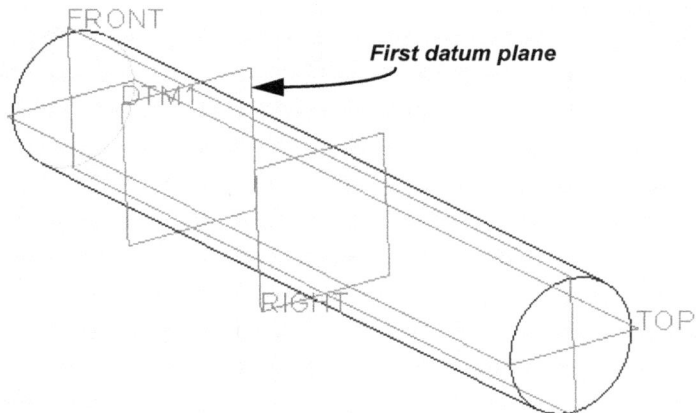

Figure 7–48

4. Create another plane (**DTM2**) on the same side of datum plane RIGHT, now at a distance of **48**, as shown in Figure 7–49.

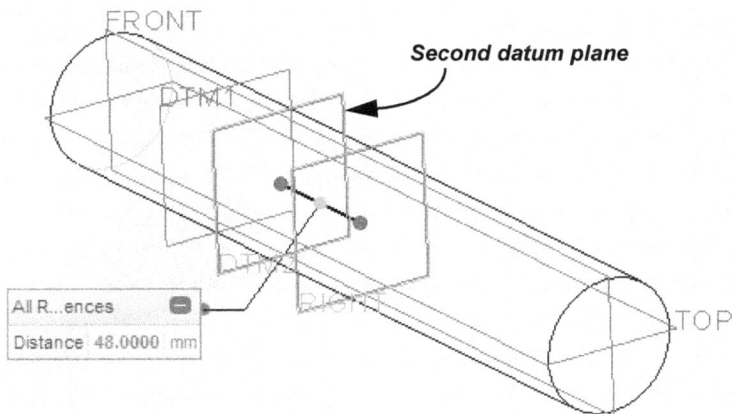

Figure 7–49

5. Create two more datum planes on the right side of datum plane RIGHT, as follows:

   • **DTM3:** 48mm offset from the RIGHT datum plane
   • **DTM4:** 80mm offset from the RIGHT datum plane

   The model displays as shown in Figure 7–50.

Figure 7–50

The datum planes you created have been placed at the ends of the boom holes, where the pin contacts the boom. The planes are symmetrical about the middle of the pin.

6. Select the DTM1 plane and click ⟍ (Intersect). The Surface Intersection dashboard opens.

© 2017, ASCENT - Center for Technical Knowledge®

7. Hold down <Ctrl> and select both halves of the cylindrical surface of the pin, as shown in Figure 7–51.

Figure 7–51

8. Click ✓ (Apply Changes) to finish. The new datum curve **Intersect_1** displays in the model, as shown in Figure 7–52.

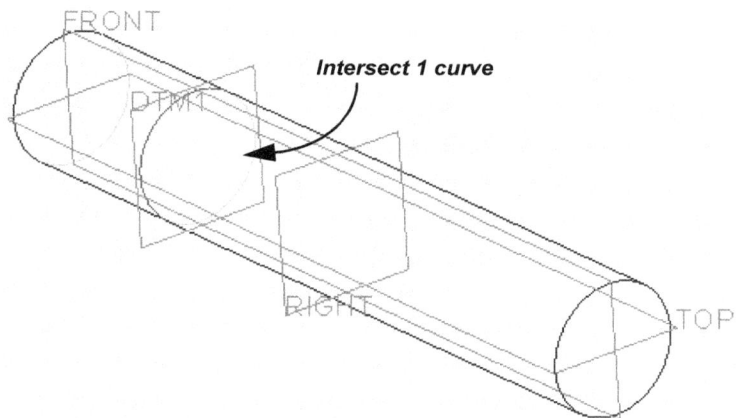

Figure 7–52

9. Repeat Steps 6 to 7 to create intersection curves between the pin surface and the planes DTM2, DTM3, and DTM4. The model displays as shown in Figure 7–53 (with the datum planes hidden).

Four intersection curves

Figure 7–53

10. In the *Refine Model* tab, click �▨ (Surface Region). The Surface Region dashboard open as shown in Figure 7–54.

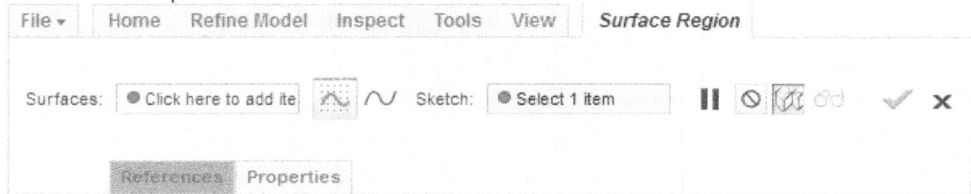

Figure 7–54

11. Select the *Surfaces* field and select both halves of the cylindrical surface of the pin, as shown in Figure 7–55.

Individual Surfaces

Figure 7–55

12. Click ∿ (Curve).

© 2017, ASCENT - Center for Technical Knowledge®

13. Select the *Chain* field and select the **Intersect_1** curve. The model displays as shown in Figure 7–56.

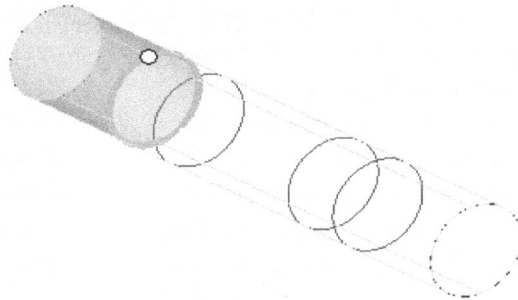

Figure 7–56

14. Click ✓ (Apply Changes) to finish.

15. Repeat Steps 10 to 14 to create surface regions using the curves **Intersect_2**, **Intersect_3**, and **Intersect_4**. The surface regions display in the Model Tree, as shown in Figure 7–57. Select the surface regions in the Model Tree and note how they highlight in the model.

Figure 7–57

Task 3 - Refine the mesh on the pin.

Refining the mesh in the contact areas improves the accuracy of the contact analysis.

1. In the *AutoGEM* group, click ⬚ (Maximum Element Size). The Maximum Element Size Control dialog box opens, as shown in Figure 7–58.

Figure 7–58

2. Select the two surface regions between the curves (these are the contact areas between the pin and the boom), as shown in Figure 7–59.

Figure 7–59

The pin diameter is 50mm.

3. In the *Element Size* field, enter **15** and click **OK** to finish.

4. Use the **Volume** option to mesh the pin. The mesh displays as shown in Figure 7–60.

© 2017, ASCENT - Center for Technical Knowledge®

Figure 7–60

Note the finer mesh that has been created on the contact areas.

5. Exit AutoGEM without saving the mesh.

6. Save and close the **pin_1** part in Creo Parametric.

Task 4 - Open the assembly.

1. Ensure that **hydraulic.asm** is open in the current window and switch to the Creo Simulate environment.

2. Expand the Model Tree and note that the Surface Regions and AutoGEM Controls created on the part level in Tasks 2 and 3 have been propagated into the assembly analysis model.

3. Use the Simulation Display dialog box to turn off display of the AutoGEM Controls.

Task 5 - Apply the material.

1. Assign **STEEL** to all of the parts in the assembly. The following values are the default material properties for HS low-alloy steel:
   - Poisson = 0.27
   - Young's modulus = 199948 MPa
   - Density = 7.82708e-9 tonne/mm^3

2. Using the Simulation Display dialog box, turn off the display of the Material Assignments.

Task 6 - Create the interfaces.

The pin is press-fit into the pivot arm holes, while the boom is assembled on the pin with a clearance.

The default Bonded Interface will apply to the mated areas between the pin and the pivot arm.

In this task, you will create Bonded Interfaces between the pivot arm and the pin, and Contact Interfaces between the pin and the boom.

1. Click ▦ (Model Setup) in the *Home* tab. Expand the Default Interfaces drop-down list and verify that **Bonded** is selected, as shown in Figure 7–61.

Figure 7–61

2. Click **OK**.

3. In the *Refine Model* tab, click ⊞ (Interface). The Interface Definition dialog box opens as shown in Figure 7–62.

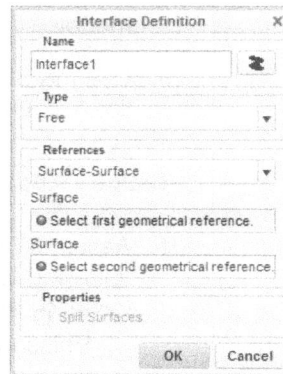

Figure 7–62

4. Expand the Type drop-down list and select **Contact**.

5. Expand the References drop-down list and select **Component-Component**.

6. Select the **PIN_1** and **BOOM_1** parts as the references.

© 2017, ASCENT - Center for Technical Knowledge®

7. Select the **Split Surfaces** and **Generate Compatible Mesh** options. The Interface Definition dialog box opens as shown in Figure 7–63.

Figure 7–63

8. Accept all of the other defaults and click **OK** to finish. The model displays as shown in Figure 7–64.

Figure 7–64

9. In the *Refine Model* tab, in the *AutoGEM* area, click
   ▣ (Review Geometry) to open the Simulation Geometry
   dialog box.

10. Select the options shown in Figure 7–65.

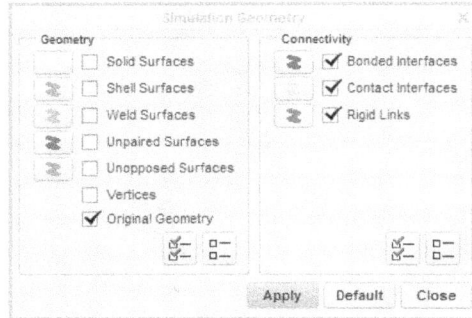

Figure 7–65

11. Click **Apply**. The model displays as shown in Figure 7–66.

Figure 7–66

Compare the interface colors (shown as shaded in
Figure 7–66) to the color scheme in the Simulation Geometry
dialog box. Ensure that the Bonded Interfaces are shown
between the pin and the pivot arm, and that the Contact
Interfaces are shown between the pin and the boom.

12. Click **Close** to finish.

13. Using the Simulation Display dialog box, turn off the
    visibilities of the Measures and of the Interfaces.

© 2017, ASCENT - Center for Technical Knowledge®

Task 7 - Apply loads.

In this task, you will apply loads to the top surface of the boom part.

1. In the *Name* field, enter **boom_load**.

*To apply the load, use the **Uniform** and **Total Load** options in the Distribution area in the Force/Moment Load dialog box.*

2. In Y-direction, apply **10,000N** to the top surface of the boom. The model displays as shown in Figure 7–67. WCS is the default coordinate system.

Figure 7–67

3. Using the Simulation Display dialog box, hide the loads.

Task 8 - Apply the constraints.

1. Fully constrain the surface of the **pivot_arm** shown in Figure 7–68. Enter **pivot_const** as the constraint name.

Ensure that the two named constraints are members of ConstraintSet1.

Constrain this surface

Figure 7–68

The model displays as shown in Figure 7–69.

Figure 7–69

This constraint is necessary to eliminate the rigid body rotation and sliding motions of the boom about the pin. The Contact Interface that you defined in Task 4 was frictionless.

2. Constrain the X- and Z-directions on the end of the surface of the boom shown in Figure 7–70. Ensure that you leave the Y-direction free. Enter **boom_const** as the constraint name.

Constrain this surface

Figure 7–70

© 2017, ASCENT - Center for Technical Knowledge®

3. Turn on the loads visibility. The model displays as shown in Figure 7–71.

Figure 7–71

Task 9 - Mesh the model.

1. Mesh the assembly using the **All with Properties** option. The mesh displays as shown in Figure 7–72.

Figure 7–72

2. Save the mesh and exit the AutoGEM dialog box.

Analysis Tasks

Task 10 - Set up and run the analysis.

1. Set up a Single-Pass Adaptive convergence analysis. Enter **hydraulic** as the analysis name and keep all of the other defaults. The Static Analysis Definition dialog box opens as shown in Figure 7–73.

Figure 7–73

*The **Contacts** option is already selected.*

2. Click **OK** to close the Static Analysis Definition dialog box.

3. In the **Info** menu, select **Check Model** to check the validity of the model.

4. Run this analysis.

© 2017, ASCENT - Center for Technical Knowledge®

Results Tasks

Task 11 - Display the deformation results.

1. Click (Review Results) in the Analyses and Design Studies dialog box. In the Result Window Definition dialog box, in the Steps list, highlight the second row as shown in Figure 7–74.

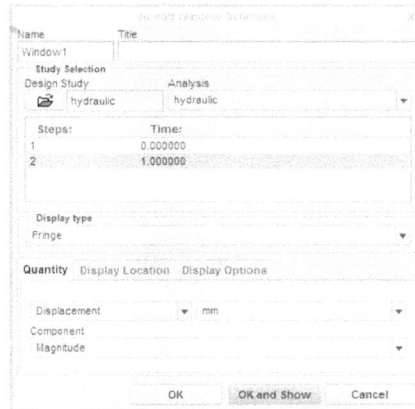

Figure 7–74

2. Select the *Display Options* tab. Select the **Deformed** and **Overlay Undeformed** options, and set the *Scaling* to **5%**, as shown in Figure 7–75.

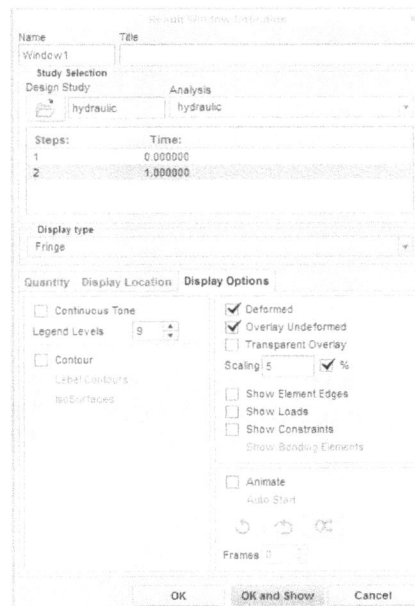

Figure 7–75

3. Click **OK and Show** to display the Displacement Magnitude result. The model displays as shown in Figure 7–76.

Figure 7–76

4. In the *View* tab, select **Saved Orientations>LEFT**. Zoom in on the bottom area. The model displays as shown in Figure 7–77.

Figure 7–77

Examine the deformation of the parts under the load.

© 2017, ASCENT - Center for Technical Knowledge®

Task 12 - Display the stress results.

1. Click ✐ (Edit) in the *Home* tab to edit the result window. In the *Steps* area, highlight the last row, and in the *Quantity* area, select **Stress, von Mises**.

2. In the *Display Options* tab, clear the **Overlay Undeformed** option.

3. Click **OK and Show**. In the *View* tab, select **Saved Orientations>DEFAULT**. The von Mises stress plot displays as shown in Figure 7–78.

Figure 7–78

4. In the Capping & Cutting Surfs section of the *View* tab, click
   (New). The Results Surface Definition dialog box opens
   as shown in Figure 7–79.

Figure 7–79

5. In the *Plane* area, select **YZ**, and for the *Depth*, enter
   -190mm as shown in Figure 7–80.

Figure 7–80

6. Click **OK**.

© 2017, ASCENT - Center for Technical Knowledge®

7. Select the **LEFT** orientation and clear ⬚ (Shaded). Zoom in on the bottom area. The model displays as shown in Figure 7–81.

Figure 7–81.

Note the well-pronounced bending stress pattern in the pin under the applied load.

Task 13 - Display the contact pressure results.

---

1. Click ✎ (Edit) to edit the result window. Highlight the last row in the Steps area. In the *Quantity* area, select **Contact Pressure**.

2. In the *Display Options* tab, select the **Overlay Undeformed** option.

3. Click **OK and Show**. The Contact Pressure plot displays as shown in Figure 7–82.

Figure 7–82

Note that the maximum contact pressure occurs at the ends of the boom bushings.

4. Exit the Results and save and close the model.

© 2017, ASCENT - Center for Technical Knowledge®

Practice 7c

Press-Fit Analysis

Practice Objectives

- Use the Solidify tool to simplify the model.
- Create Contact Interfaces with Infinite Friction.
- Set up a Static Analysis with Initial Interferences.
- Review results in the Cylindrical Coordinate System.

In this practice, you will set up a press-fit contact analysis on a shaft and a roller bearing assembly model. The area of interest is the contact between the shaft and the inner ring of the bearing. The assembly that you will analyze is shown in Figure 7–83.

Figure 7–83

The bearing ring is press-fit onto the shaft. The outer diameter (OD) of the shaft is 20mm, and the inner diameter (ID) of the ring is 19.96mm. The objective is to determine radial deformation and hoop stress in the ring due to the press-fit, without applying any other loads.

Modeling Tasks

Task 1 - Open the assembly.

1. Open **press_fit.asm** in Creo Parametric. The assembly displays as shown in Figure 7–84.

Figure 7–84

2. Do not switch to Creo Simulate yet.

Task 2 - Simplify the model.

In this task, you will simplify the model in order to reduce the analysis runtime. Since the model is symmetric, you will analyze a quarter of the assembly.

1. Right-click on **shaft.prt** in the Model Tree and select **Open** to open it in Creo Parametric. Ensure that the datum planes and coordinate system are visualized. The shaft displays as shown in Figure 7–85.

Figure 7–85

© 2017, ASCENT - Center for Technical Knowledge®

2. Select the **RIGHT** datum plane and click ⌂ (Solidify) in the *Editing* group. The *Solidify* dashboard opens as shown in Figure 7–86.

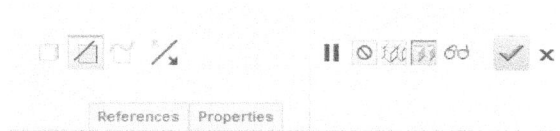

Figure 7–86

3. The Solidify tool cuts the part in half using the selected datum plane. Ensure that the tool keeps the side of the part that is in the positive X direction by changing direction of the tool operation, if necessary. The part displays as shown in Figure 7–87.

Figure 7–87

4. Click ✓ (Complete Feature).

5. Select the **FRONT** datum plane and click ⌂ (Solidify) in the *Editing* section.

6. Ensure that the tool keeps the side of the part that is in the positive Z direction, as shown in Figure 7–88.

Figure 7–88

7. Click ✓ (Complete Feature).

8. Save and close **shaft.prt**. The assembly displays as shown in Figure 7–89.

Figure 7–89

9. Open **bearing_ring.prt** and repeat Steps 2 through 8. Use the same datum planes and same directions to make the cuts. The assembly displays as shown in Figure 7–90.

Figure 7–90

Task 3 - Apply the materials.

1. Switch to Creo Simulate.

2. Assign materials as follows:
   - **SHAFT:** AL2014
     Poisson: 0.33
     Young's modulus: 73084.4 MPa
   - **BEARING_RING**: STEEL
     Poisson: 0.27
     Young's modulus: 199948 MPa

3. Using the Simulation Display dialog box, toggle off the display of the Material Assignments.

© 2017, ASCENT - Center for Technical Knowledge®

Task 4 - Create the interface.

In this task, you will create Contact Interface between the shaft and the ring.

1. In the *Refine Model* tab, click ▧ (Interface).

2. Expand the Type drop-down list and select **Contact**.

3. Expand the References drop-down list and select **Component-Component**.

4. Select the **SHAFT** and **BEARING_RING** parts as the references.

5. In the **Friction** drop-down list, select **Infinite**. The Interface Definition dialog box opens as shown in Figure 7–91.

Press fit is a fastening of two parts that is achieved by friction alone. The parts fastened by a press fit are not supposed to slip against each other, which is ensured by using the Infinite Friction option in Contact Interface.

Figure 7–91

6. Click **OK**.

7. In the *Refine Model* tab, in the *AutoGEM* area, click ▨ (Review Geometry) to open the Simulation Geometry dialog box.

8. Select the options shown in Figure 7–92.

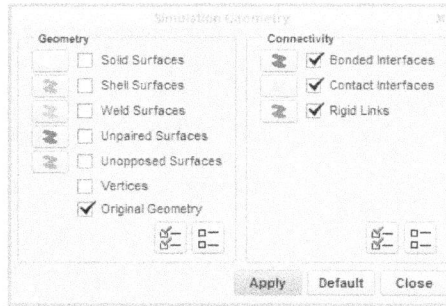

Figure 7–92

9. Click **Apply**. The model displays as shown in Figure 7–93.

Figure 7–93

Ensure that the Contact Interface is shown between the shaft and the ring.

10. Click **Close** to finish.

11. Using the Simulation Display dialog box, toggle off the display of the Measures and of the Interfaces.

Task 5 - Apply the constraints.

1. Fully constrain the back end of the **shaft** and apply two Mirror Symmetry constraints on the cutout surfaces, as shown in Figure 7–94.

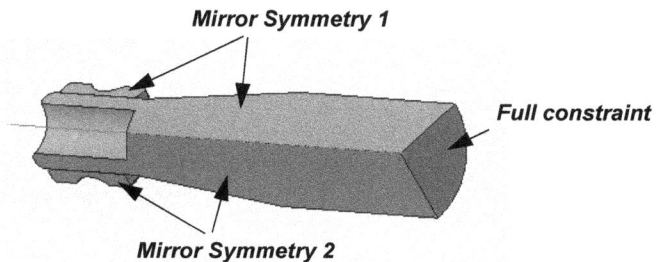

Figure 7–94

© 2017, ASCENT - Center for Technical Knowledge®

The model displays as shown in Figure 7–95.

Figure 7–95

Task 6 - Apply load.

The goal of this analysis is to determine deformations and stresses due to the press-fit alone, without any other loads. However, Creo Simulate does not permit creating a static analysis without loads. To work around this restriction, in this task you will apply a very small load to the model, which will have no effect on the analysis results.

1. Apply **0.001 N** in Y direction to the end surface of the shaft, as shown in Figure 7–96.

Load this surface

Figure 7–96

The model displays as shown in Figure 7–97.

Figure 7–97

2. Using the Simulation Display dialog box, hide constraints and loads.

Task 7 - Create cylindrical coordinate system.

The quantities of interest in this analysis are as follows:

- Radial expansion of the bearing ring, in order to later determine if the bearing balls might seize due to insufficient clearance between the inner and the outer rings.

- Hoop stresses (i.e., stresses in the direction of circumference) in the bearing ring, which are the main cause of cracking and ruptures of tube- and ring-shaped parts under radial loads.

A Cartesian (XYZ) coordinate system, such as WCS, is not suitable for obtaining the above results. In this task, you will create a Cylindrical (RTZ) coordinate system, in which R would be the radial direction on the ring, and T would be the direction around the ring's circumference.

1. In the *Refine Model* tab, click 	$\frac{y}{z}\cancel{}^x$ (Coordinate System).

2. Select the main assembly as the **Component for Feature**. The Coordinate System dialog box opens.

3. In the **Type** drop-down list, select **Cylindrical**.

4. Select references for the origin and the axes as shown in Figure 7–98.

This edge as the reference for T=90 direction

This edge as reference for Z direction

Origin at this vertex

Figure 7–98

© 2017, ASCENT - Center for Technical Knowledge®

The Coordinate System dialog box displays as shown in Figure 7-99.

Figure 7–99

5. Click **OK**. With the coordinate systems visible, the model displays as shown in Figure 7–100.

Figure 7–100

Analysis Tasks

Task 8 - Set up and run the analysis.

The OD of the shaft is 20mm, and the ID of the ring is 19.96mm. Therefore, the actual initial interpenetration is (20 - 19.96)/2 = 0.02mm. To ensure that this interpenetration is detected in Creo Simulate, you will set the value for detection to be 0.025mm.

1. Set up a static analysis as follows:
   - **Name:** press_fit
   - **Contacts:** ON
   - **Convergence method:** Single-Pass Adaptive
   - **Localized Mesh Refinement:** ON
   - **Press fit:** ON
   - **Maximum initial interpenetration:** 0.025 mm

The Static Analysis Definition dialog box displays as shown in Figure 7–101.

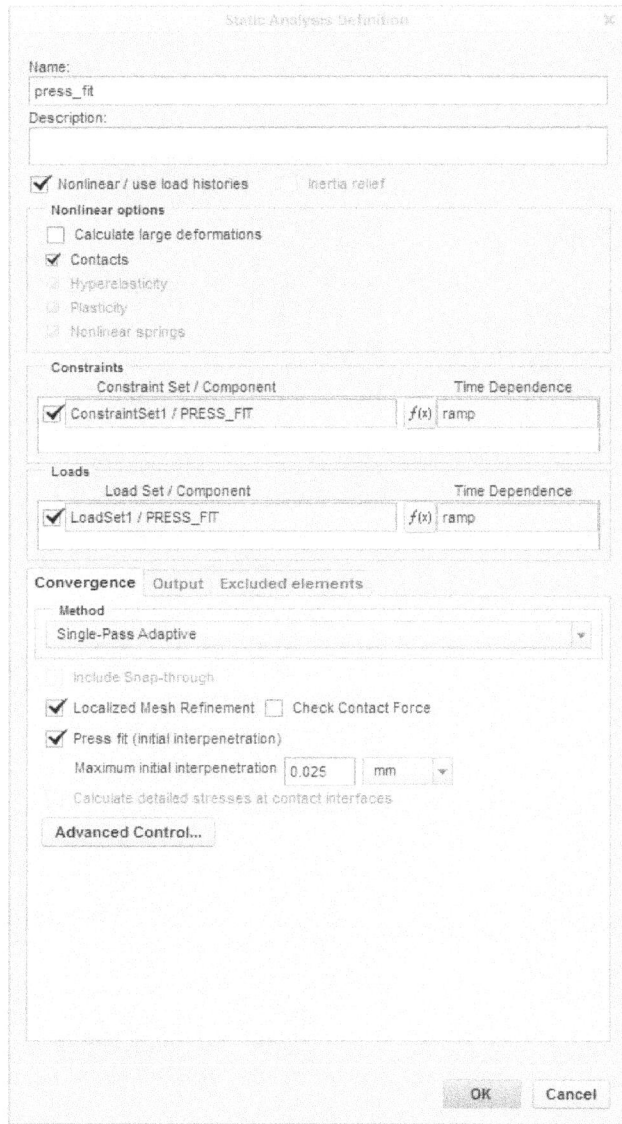

Figure 7–101

2. Click **OK** to close the Static Analysis Definition dialog box.

3. In the **Info** menu, select **Check Model** to check the validity of the model.

4. Run the analysis.

© 2017, ASCENT - Center for Technical Knowledge®

Results Tasks

Task 9 - Display the deformation results.

1. Click ![icon](Review Results) in the Analyses and Design Studies dialog box.

2. In the **Steps** column, highlight the second row, and in the Component drop-down list select **X**. The Result Window Definition dialog box displays as shown in Figure 7–102.

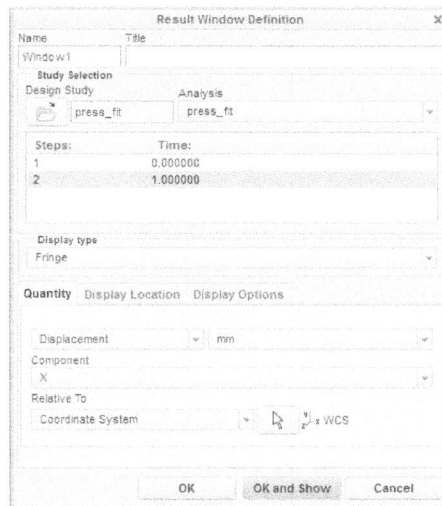

Figure 7–102

3. Click near the Coordinate System drop-down list and select **ACS0** coordinate system in the model. This is the cylindrical coordinate system that you created in Task 7.

4. In the Component drop-down list, select **R**. The Result Window Definition dialog box opens as shown in Figure 7–103.

Figure 7–103

5. Click **OK and Show**, and then select the **BACK** view. The result window opens as shown in Figure 7–104.

Figure 7–104

6. Zoom in on the bottom area of the shaft and ring, as shown in Figure 7–105.

© 2017, ASCENT - Center for Technical Knowledge®

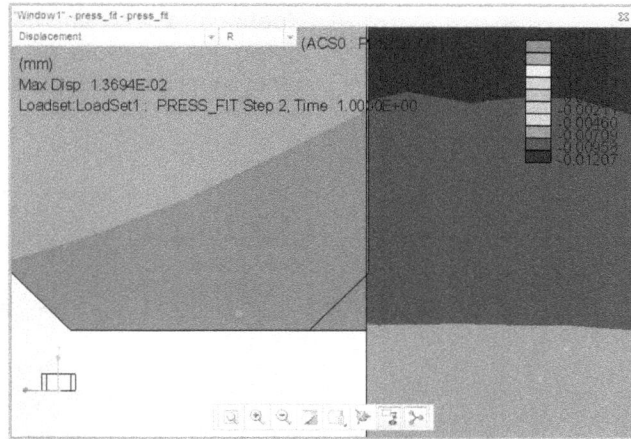

Figure 7–105

Note that there is still a visible interpenetration between the shaft and ring in this area. This is because the result is being displayed on the undeformed model (i.e. the original geometry), as before the analysis.

7. In the *Home* tab, click 🖉 (Edit).

8. In the **Display Options** tab, select **Deformed** and click **OK and Show**. The result window displays as shown in Figure 7–106.

Figure 7–106

Note that now there is no interpenetration between the parts. This is because Contact Interface strictly enforces the condition of non-interpenetration, therefore, the detected interference between the parts has been removed during the analysis.

9. Zoom out slightly and use the ⬚ (Dynamic Query) tool to determine the radial displacement at the bottom of the ball race, as shown in Figure 7–107.

Figure 7–107

The radial displacement at the bottom of the ball race is approximately 0.009 mm. Therefore, the increase in the OD of the ball race in the inner ring after the bearing assembly on the shaft is estimated to be 2x0.009 = 0.018mm, and the reduction of clearance between the inner and the outer rings to be 0.009mm.

Task 10 - Display the stress results.

1. Select the **DEFAULT** saved orientation.

2. Click ✎ (Edit) in the *Home* tab to edit the result window. In the *Steps* area, highlight the last row, and in the *Quantity* area, select **Stress, TT**.

3. In the *Display Location* tab, select **Components/Layers** and set **SHAFT.PRT** visibility to blank.

4. In the *Display Options* tab, clear the **Overlay Undeformed** option.

*T is the Theta direction in the cylindrical coordinate system, which is around the ring's circumference. **Stress TT** is the hoop stress.*

© 2017, ASCENT - Center for Technical Knowledge®

5. Click **OK and Show**. The hoop stress plot in the bearing ring displays as shown in Figure 7–108.

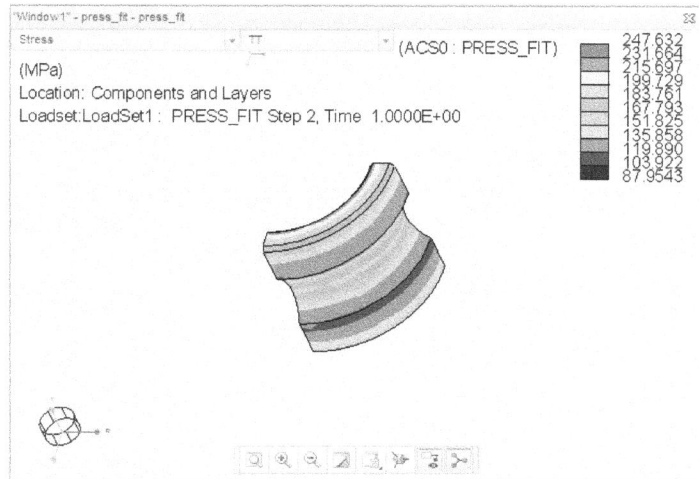

Figure 7–108

6. Using the (Model Max) tool, determine the value and the location of the maximum hoop stress, as shown in Figure 7–109.

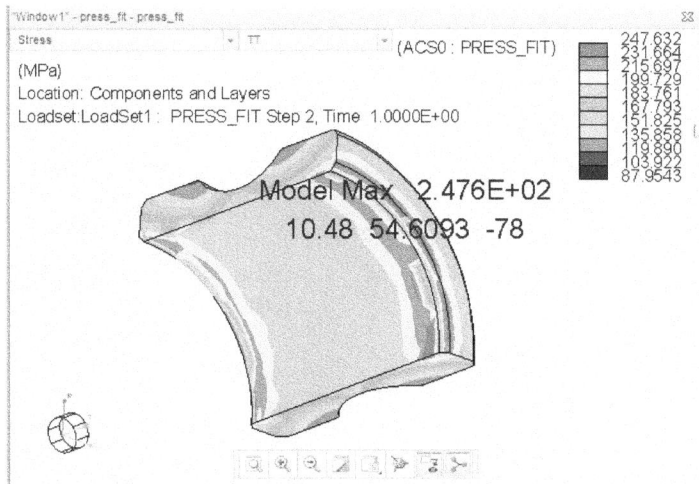

Figure 7–109

Note that the maximum hoop stress occurs on the ID of the bearing ring, and near its ends. The maximum stress is approximately 250 MPa, therefore, the grade of steel used for the ring should have a yield strength greater than 250 MPa.

7. Exit the Results and save and close the model.

Practice 7d | Contact Analysis of a Skid Shoe

Practice Objectives

- Create Contact Interfaces.
- Set up contact analysis.
- Display contact analysis results.

In this practice, you will set up and run a static contact analysis of a skid shoe pressing against a plate (shown in Figure 7–110) with minimum instruction.

Figure 7–110

Task 1 - Prepare the model for analysis.

1. Open **shoe_contact.asm** and launch Creo Simulate.

2. Apply the **AL6061** material to both parts.

3. Create a frictionless contact interface between the shoe and the plate.

© 2017, ASCENT - Center for Technical Knowledge®

4. Fully constrain the perimeter surfaces of the plate, as shown in Figure 7–111.

Constrain all four sides

Figure 7–111

5. As contact between the shoe and the plate is set up as frictionless, avoid free sliding of the shoe along the plate by constraining the back surface of the shoe in the X- and Z-directions, as shown in Figure 7–112.

Constrain this surface

Figure 7–112

6. Apply **10000lbs** bearing load in the -Y direction to the hole in the shoe, as shown in Figure 7–113.

10000lbs load in -Y direction on this hole

Figure 7–113

Task 2 - Set up and run static analysis.

1. Create and run a new static analysis with the following parameters:
   - **Analysis name:** contact_shoe
   - **Convergence method:** Single-Pass Adaptive
   - **Output Steps:** User-defined, 5 steps equally spaced.

Task 3 - Examine the analysis results.

1. Display and animate the **Displacement Magnitude** fringe plot. Use a *Scaling* factor of **100** for the deformed shape display.

   - Do the parts deform according to the applied loads and constraints?

2. Display the undeformed **von Mises Stress** plot.

   - In which area in the model are the stresses at maximum?

3. Display the **Contact Pressure** plot.

   - What is the maximum contact pressure and where does it occur?

4. Save and close the model.

© 2017, ASCENT - Center for Technical Knowledge®

Thermal Analysis

In this chapter you learn to use Thermal Analysis to measure the effect of heat transfer rates on a model.

Learning Objectives in this Chapter

- Understand the concept of heat transfer.
- Understand the Creo Simulate Thermal analysis steps and options.
- Create idealizations.
- Apply boundary conditions.
- Apply heat loads.
- Create a thermal analysis.
- Visualize the thermal analysis results.
- Import thermal results into a structural analysis.

8.1 Modes of Heat Transfer

Thermal analyses measure the effect of heat transfer rates on a model. Heat transfer is the flow of heat through a body in which there is a temperature variance. Heat transfer rates are an important part of engineering analysis in many industries. For example, heat transfer rates have a major role in the design of boilers, turbines, and combustion engines. The designer of these systems often needs to maintain high heat transfer rates while staying inside the material's limits for high temperatures. There are three modes of heat transfer: conduction, convection, and radiation.

Conduction

Conduction is the transfer of heat through a solid body or a body of stationary fluid (e.g., water or gas), in which temperature variance occurs. The conduction mode of heat transfer occurs in the atomic and molecular structures of a body. An example of conduction in a gas cylinder is shown in Figure 8–1.

Figure 8–1

The temperature difference between the top and bottom of the gas cylinder is assumed to be 10°C. The molecules of the gas on the top of the cylinder have higher energies (i.e., they vibrate more freely) because of the higher temperature. Therefore, they collide with neighboring molecules and energy is transferred to these molecules. The process continues from high energy molecules to neighboring molecules from the top of the cylinder to the bottom until equilibrium is reached.

© 2017, ASCENT - Center for Technical Knowledge®

Convection

Convection is the transfer of heat from a surface into a moving fluid (e.g., air) with a lower temperature than the surface. The heat must be conducted through material (e.g., heat exchanger) before it can be carried away by the outside air. There are two types of convection heat transfer: free and forced.

In free convection heat transfer, the moving fluid is free-flowing. For example, if a hot plate is left outside to be cooled on a day with little wind, the air in contact with the hot plate has a lower density than the air above the hot plate. This creates a circulation where warm air moves up and cooler air moves down.

In forced convection heat transfer, the moving fluid is pumped or fanned over a surface. Using the previous example, on a windy day, the primary transfer of heat is through the force of wind, while free convection still exists.

Radiation

Radiation is the emission of energy from heated surfaces in the form of electromagnetic waves. Two heated surfaces at different temperatures transfer heat to each other by radiation if there is no other means of transport (e.g., molecular vibration or air). Heat transfer by conduction or convection requires a means of transport. Radiation heat transfer works best in a vacuum.

8.2 Creo Simulate Thermal

Similar to the Structure mode, the Creo Simulate Thermal mode has three components for finite element analysis: analysis, pre-processing, and post-processing. Each component contains steps, as shown in Figure 8–2.

Figure 8–2

*Thermal mode is launched in the same way as Structure, However, instead of selecting **Structure**, you select **Thermal**.*

After you launch Thermal mode, each step in the model analysis process requires a selection of options. These options are as follows:.

Model Analysis Steps	Pro/MECHANICA Thermal Options	
Model Type	3D 2D Axisymmetric	2D Plate 2D Unit Depth
Element Type	Solid Shells Beams	Connections
Analysis Methods	Steady State Thermal	Transient Thermal
Convergence Methods	Multi-Pass Adaptive Single-Pass Adaptive	Quick Check
Design Studies	Standard Optimization	Sensitivity

© 2017, ASCENT - Center for Technical Knowledge®

Thermal Ribbon

The Thermal interface is similar to the Structure interface.

To enter the Thermal mode, click (Thermal Mode) in the Creo Simulate Ribbon. The Ribbon changes as shown in Figure 8–3. The tools in the Thermal mode Ribbon are similar to those in the Structure mode. The Loads and Boundary Conditions areas are different.

Figure 8–3

8.3 Modeling Steps

The majority of the analysis steps in the Thermal mode are same or similar to those in the Structure mode. The following steps are identical:

- Defining model type

- Applying material

- Simulation features (datums, surface regions, etc.)

- Meshing the model

- Convergence methods

- Design Studies

The steps and options that are different from their counterparts in the Structure mode, are as follows:

Interfaces

Interfaces in Creo Simulate define the treatment of mated or overlapping surfaces in an assembly model.

There are three types of Interfaces in Creo Simulate Thermal:

- **Bonded:** Models a perfect thermal bond, without any thermal resistance, between the interfacing surfaces.

- **Adiabatic:** Disables any heat transfer through the interface.

- **Thermal Resistance:** Models an imperfect thermal bond between the surfaces, where the rate of heat transfer through the interface is determined by a thermal resistance coefficient.

Idealizations

Idealizations are tools that simplify your FEA model, resulting in faster analysis. Idealizations are optional. If your model is not overly complex and solves in a reasonable time, Idealizations might not be needed.

© 2017, ASCENT - Center for Technical Knowledge®

The following types of Idealizations are available in Thermal mode, as shown in Figure 8–4:

Figure 8–4

- **Beams:** These are 1D thermal elements (also called thermal rods) in which the temperature variation only occurs in the direction of the element's axis.

- **Shells:** These are 2D thermal elements, in which the temperature variation only occurs within the element's midplane.

Applying Boundary Conditions

In thermal FEA, all of the surfaces default to perfect insulators unless you apply a heat load, specified temperature, convection condition, or radiation condition. A perfect insulator, also called adiabatic surface, means that there is no heat transfer through the surface.

Four types of Boundary Conditions are available in Thermal mode, as shown in Figure 8–5:

- Prescribed Temperature

- Convection Condition

- Radiation Condition

- Symmetry

Radiation Condition is only available with the Advanced Creo Simulate license.

Figure 8–5

Prescribed Temperature

Use the Prescribed Temperature boundary condition to enforce a specific temperature on one or more geometrical entities in your model. The specified temperature value is strictly maintained throughout the analysis.

The Prescribed Temperature dialog box is shown in Figure 8–6.

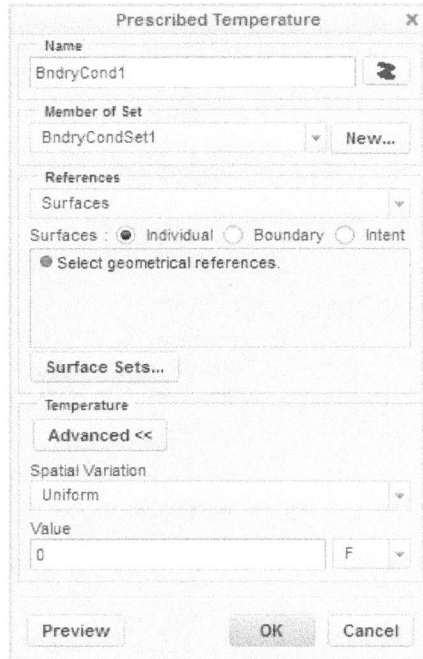

Figure 8–6

Prescribed Temperature can be applied to Surfaces, Edges/Curves, or Points. The options for the Spatial Variation are: Uniform, Function of Coordinates, and Interpolated Over Entity.

Convection Condition

Use the Convection Condition to define a convective heat exchange for one or more geometric entities in your model.

The Convection Condition dialog box is shown in Figure 8–7.

© 2017, ASCENT - Center for Technical Knowledge®

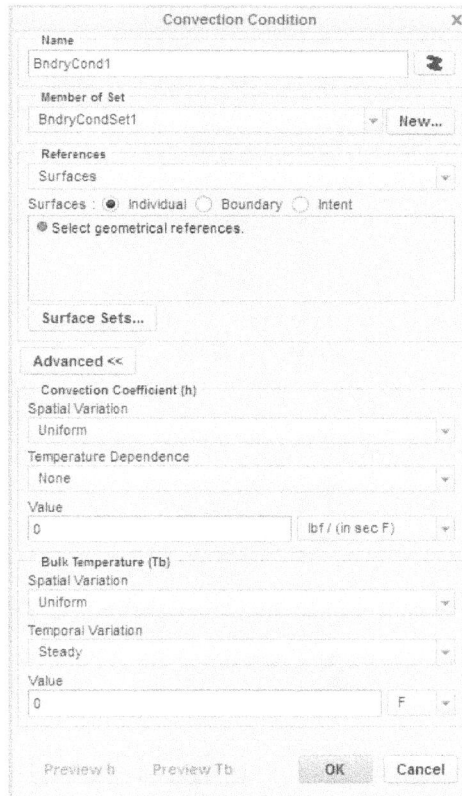

Figure 8–7

The Convection Condition can be applied to Surfaces, Edges/ Curves, or Points.

The Convection Coefficient *h* relates the amount of heat *Q* transferred between the boundary surface of area *A* at temperature *T*, and the moving fluid at Bulk Temperature T_b in the following way:

$$Q = h A (T - T_b)$$

Radiation Condition

Radiation Condition
requires an Advanced
Simulation license.

Use the Radiation Condition to define a radiative heat exchange for one or more surfaces in your model.

The Radiation Condition dialog box is shown in Figure 8–8.

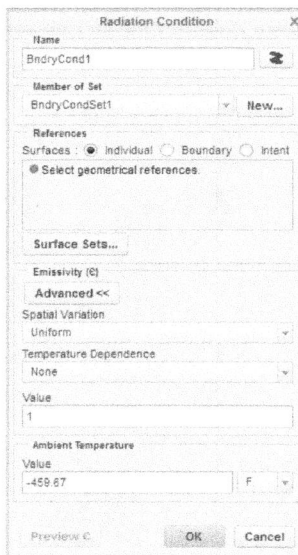

Figure 8–8

The Emissivity is the ratio of the energy radiated from a material's surface to that radiated from a blackbody (a perfect emitter) at the same surface temperature and viewing conditions. It is a dimensionless number between 0 (perfect reflector) to 1 (perfect emitter). The Ambient Temperature is the absolute temperature of the surrounding medium.

Applying Heat Loads

Heat Loads provide local heat sources or heat sinks in your model. The icon to apply Heat Loads is located in the Loads area in the Ribbon, as shown in Figure 8–9.

Figure 8–9

© 2017, ASCENT - Center for Technical Knowledge®

The Heat Load dialog box is shown in Figure 8–10.

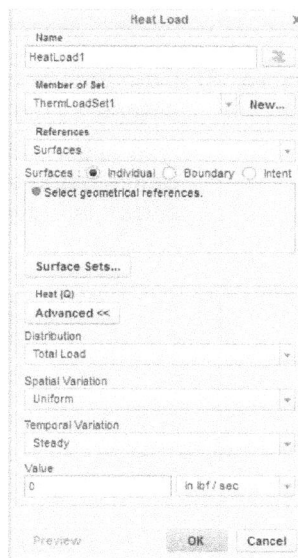

Figure 8–10

Heat Loads can be applied to Components/Volumes (to simulate internal heat generation), Surfaces, Edges/Curves, or Points.

8.4 Analysis

Analysis Types

Creo Simulate enables you to perform two types of thermal analyses on a model. You select an analysis type based on the type of simulation you want to perform. Click ⬚ (Analyses and Studies) and select the appropriate option in the **File** menu, as shown in Figure 8–11.

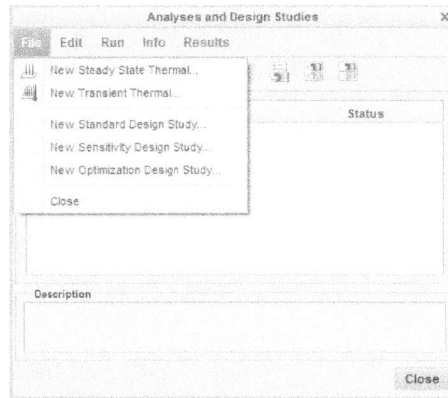

Figure 8–11

A Steady State Thermal analysis calculates the thermal response of a model to a heat load that is constant and does not vary over time. This type of analysis does not evaluate changes in temperature over time. For example, a turbine blade that is turned by steam and generates electricity would require this type of analysis because it is under constant pressure and temperature.

A Transient Thermal analysis calculates the thermal response in your model that is changing with time. The application of a heat load is not typically constant and varies over time. For example, the heat element in a toaster would require this type of analysis because it is time-dependent.

© 2017, ASCENT - Center for Technical Knowledge®

8.5 Results

Result Visualization

Thermal mode enables you to visualize many different types of results:

- Temperatures

- Temperature Gradients

- Heat Fluxes

- P-Levels

The results can be displayed as a fringe plot, as a graph along an edge, or as a curve. Fringe plots for heat fluxes can be animated for a better understanding of the heat flows.

The results are visualized and manipulated in the Creo Simulate Results environment. An overview of the icons and options in the Result Environment is shown in Figure 8–12.

Figure 8–12

8.6 Thermal Load Transfer

You can transfer the temperature field from a thermal analyses to a structural analyses and apply it as a thermal load in your structure. For example, a heat sink is shown in Figure 8–13. The temperature distribution obtained in a thermal analysis can be transferred to structure mode to determine the deformations and stresses in the heat sink as it expands.

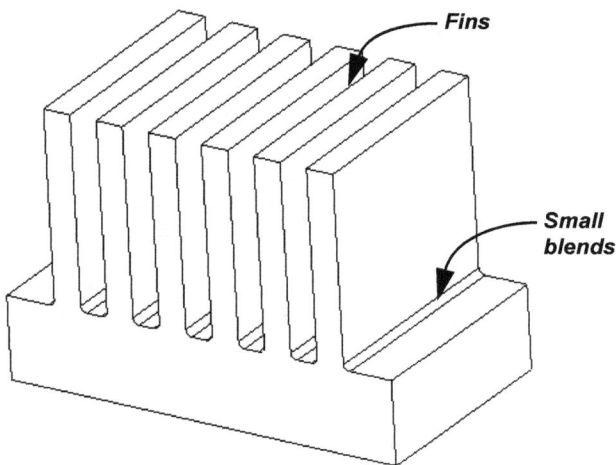

Figure 8–13

To transfer a temperature result from *Thermal* to **Structure**, expand the *Loads* area and select **MEC/T Load**, as shown in Figure 8–14.

Figure 8–14

© 2017, ASCENT - Center for Technical Knowledge®

The MEC/T Temperature Load dialog box is shown in Figure 8–15.

Figure 8–15

Practice 8a

Thermal Steady State Analysis

Practice Objectives

- Set up thermal boundary conditions.
- Set up and run a thermal analysis.
- Display the results of thermal analysis.
- Use the Load Transfer function.

In this practice, you will set up and run a thermal steady state analysis on a heat transfer device, as shown in Figure 8–16. The heat transfer device sits on a 20W CPU (heat source) and a free convection is placed on the long vertical faces of fins. The device is aluminum and has a convection coefficient of 0.01 (lbf/in F$^{\circ}$ sec). Later, you will transfer the heat load to Structure mode to run a static analysis.

Figure 8–16

© 2017, ASCENT - Center for Technical Knowledge®

Modeling Tasks

Task 1 - Open the model.

1. Open **heat_device.prt** in Creo Parametric. The part displays as shown in Figure 8–17.

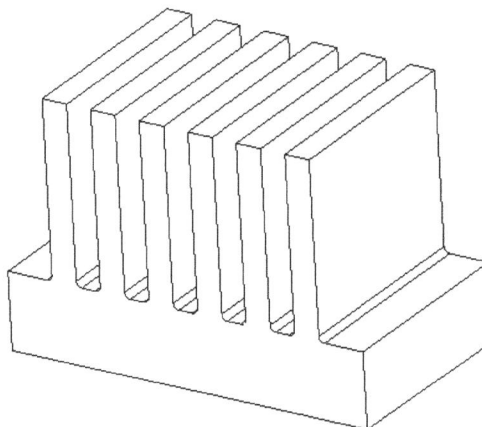

Figure 8–17

2. Ensure that the unit system is set to **IPS**.

Task 2 - Launch Creo Simulate.

1. Select **Applications>Simulate**.

2. Click (Thermal Mode) to switch to the Thermal mode.

Task 3 - Apply heat loads.

In this task, you will apply a heat load to the bottom surface of the heat device, as shown in Figure 8–18.

Bottom surface

Figure 8–18

1. Click ♨ (Heat). The Heat Load dialog box opens as shown in Figure 8–19.

Figure 8–19

2. In the *Name* field, enter **end_heat_load**. For *Member of Set*, accept the default **ThermalLoadSet1** option.

3. Select the bottom surface shown in Figure 8–18.

14.75lbf in/sec = 20Watt

4. In the *Value* field, enter **14.75**.

5. Click **Preview** to preview the applied heat load.

6. Click **OK**. The model displays as shown in Figure 8–20.

Figure 8–20

© 2017, ASCENT - Center for Technical Knowledge®

Task 4 - Apply boundary conditions.

Assume that the convection on the smaller surfaces is negligible.

In this task, you will apply boundary conditions to the long vertical faces of the fins, the top faces of the fins, and the side faces, as shown in Figure 8–21.

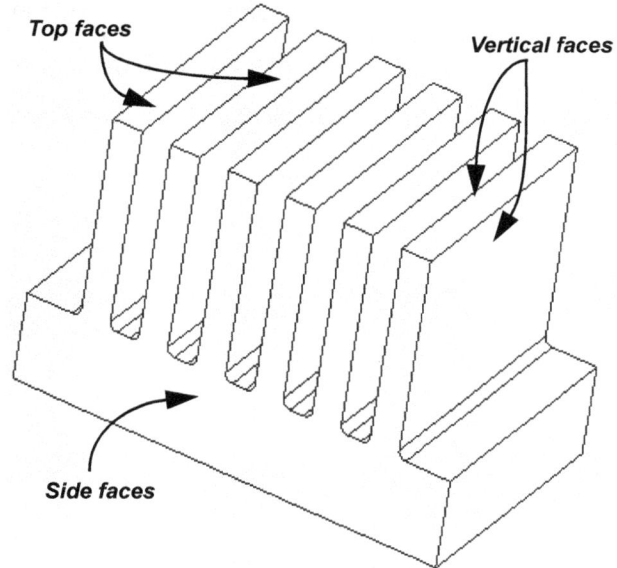

Figure 8–21

1. Click ✎ (Convection Condition). The Convection Condition dialog box opens as shown in Figure 8–22.

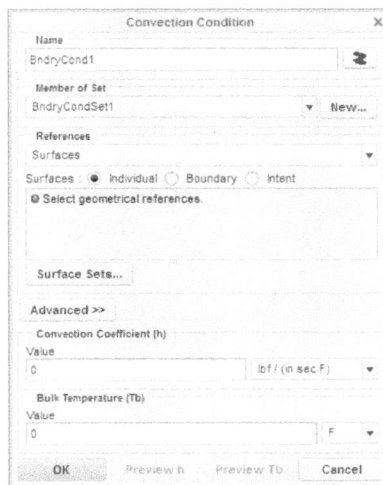

Figure 8–22

2. In the *Name* field, enter **long_face**. For *Member of Set*, accept the default **BndryCondSet1** option.

3. Select the 12 large vertical surfaces of the fins, the six top faces of the fins, and the two side faces. (Hold down <Ctrl> to multi-select.)

4. In the *Convection Coefficient* field, enter **0.01**.

5. In the *Bulk Temperature* field, enter **80**.

6. Click **OK**. The model displays as shown in Figure 8–23.

Figure 8–23

Task 5 - Apply the material.

1. Assign **AL2014** to the heat device part. The following values are the default material properties for the aluminum alloy AL2014:

   - Specific Heat capacity = 829900 in^2/(sec^2 F)
   - Thermal conductivity = 24 lbf/(sec F)
   - Density = 0.0002614 lbf sec^2/in^4
   - Poisson's Ratio = 0.33
   - Young's Modulus = 1.06e+07 psi
   - Coeff of Thermal Expansion = 1.28e-05 /F

Task 6 - Mesh the model.

1. Click ▦ (AutoGEM). The AutoGEM dialog box opens.

© 2017, ASCENT - Center for Technical Knowledge®

2. Expand the AutoGEM References drop-down list, select the **All with Properties** option, and click **Create** to mesh the model. The mesh displays as shown in Figure 8–24.

Figure 8–24

3. Close the AutoGEM dialog box and save the mesh.

Summary

In the previous tasks, you created the simulation entities needed to analyze your model. In the following tasks, you will set the analysis type and the convergence method and run the analysis.

Analysis Tasks

Task 7 - Set up and run the analysis.

In this task, you will specify the analysis type. First, the **heat_device** is analyzed using the **Quick Check** convergence option to check for errors. The importance of this option increases with the size of your model (e.g., a model with a large number of elements). The option gives you a general feel for the results and indicates that the model behaves as intended with applied boundary conditions.

1. Click (Analyses and Studies). The Analyses and Design Studies dialog box opens.

2. Select **File>New Steady State Thermal**. The Steady Thermal Analysis Definition dialog box opens as shown in Figure 8–25.

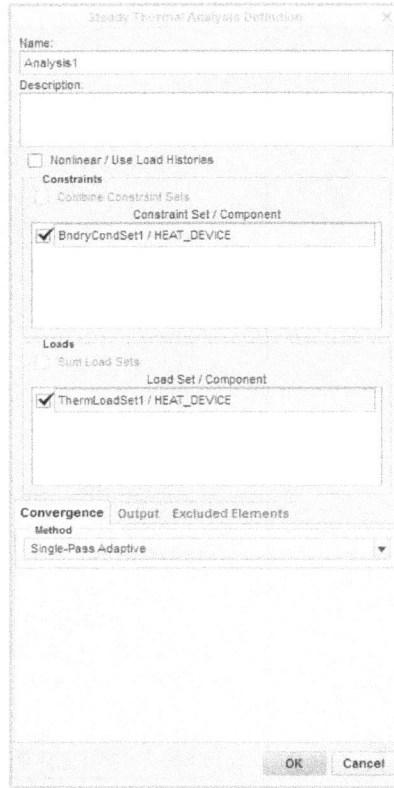

Figure 8–25

3. In the *Name* field, enter **heat_device** (heat_device is now the name of a subdirectory containing all of your results files).

4. In the *Description* field, enter **thermal analysis of a heat_device**. This step is optional, but it is helpful for identifying your analysis later.

5. For a thermal analysis, you must specify or select the boundary conditions and heat load sets. These were created in the previous steps. In this case, they are **BndryCondSet1** and **ThermalLoadSet1**. Verify that they are highlighted.

6. For the type of convergence, expand the Method drop-down list and select **Quick Check**. This option enables you to determine whether the analysis was set up correctly in your first run.

© 2017, ASCENT - Center for Technical Knowledge®

7. Click **OK** in the Steady Thermal Analysis Definition dialog box.

8. Verify that the Run Settings are correct, check the model, and run the analysis. Wait until it completes.

9. In the Analyses and Design Studies dialog box, click ▦ (Status). The Run Status dialog box opens. View the information in the window. Click **Close** when done.

Task 8 - Run the analysis using the Multi-Pass Adaptive convergence option.

---

1. With the **heat_device** analysis highlighted, select ▦ (Copy) to create a copy of the analysis. Highlight

   Copy_of_heat_device and click ✏ (Edit) to edit it. The Steady Thermal Analysis Definition dialog box for Analysis opens.

2. For the *Name*, enter **heat_device_multi_pass**.

3. Expand the Method drop-down list and select **Multi-Pass Adaptive**.

4. In the *Polynomial Order* area, expand the Maximum drop-down list and select **9**.

5. In the *Limits* area, in the *Percent Convergence* field, enter **10** percent convergence.

6. Click **OK** in the Steady Thermal Analysis Definition dialog box.

7. Start the analysis and wait until it finishes.

8. Click ▦ (Status). The Run Status dialog box opens. The following results display in the dialog box:
   - The analysis converges on pass two.
   - The flux error is 9.5% of the Max Flux, as shown in Figure 8–26.

```
RMS Flux Error Estimates:

Load Set            Flux Error      % of Max Flux
----------------    ------------    -----------------
ThermLoadSet1       1.02e+01        9.5% of  1.07e+02
```

Figure 8–26

In the Run Status dialog box, the *Measures* area is shown in Figure 8–27.

```
Measures:

         Name              Value        Convergence
   ---------------    --------------    -----------
   energy_norm:         9.831984e+02        0.0%
   max_flux_mag:        1.070105e+02        8.0%
   max_flux_x:          1.046296e+02       39.1%
   max_flux_y:          4.190372e+01      100.0%
   max_flux_z:         -1.381975e+01       34.0%
   max_grad_mag:        4.458770e+00        8.0%
   max_grad_x:         -4.359568e+00       39.1%
   max_grad_y:         -1.745988e+00      100.0%
   max_grad_z:          5.758227e-01       34.0%
   max_temperature:     2.133453e+02        0.0%
   min_temperature:     2.127237e+02        0.0%
```

Figure 8–27

Note the maximum temperature (213.3°F) and the minimum temperature (212.7°F). The quantity of interest of the analysis is the temperature. Since the temperature measures converge, you could assume that the result of this analysis is valid, despite the flux error being 9.5% of maximum flux.

The values that you obtain when you run the analysis might be different than those that have been provided. This is due to the fact that each new build of Creo Simulate produces slight variations in the creation of the mesh.

9. Close the Run Status dialog box.

Results Tasks

Task 9 - Display the temperature results.

In this task, you will create and display a temperature plot for one of the long vertical surfaces.

1. In the Analyses and Design Studies dialog box, highlight the **heat_device_multi_pass** analysis and click 🖳 (Review Results). The Result Window Definition dialog box opens as shown in Figure 8–28.

© 2017, ASCENT - Center for Technical Knowledge®

Figure 8–28

2. In the *Name* field, accept the default **Window1**.

3. In the *Title* field, enter **SURFACE_PLOT**.

4. Click **OK and Show**. The Temperature fringe plot is displayed, as shown in Figure 8–29.

Figure 8–29

Note that the maximum temperature occurs at the bottom of the heat sink, where the heat load is applied. The temperature gradually decreases to the top of the heat sink, due to convection on the fins.

5. Click ✎ (Edit). The Result Window Definition dialog box opens.

6. Select the *Display Location* tab, expand the drop-down list and select **Surfaces**.

7. Click ☜ (Select) and select the right vertical surface of the right-most fin. Click the middle mouse button when finished.

8. Click **OK and Show**. The result window displays as shown in Figure 8–30.

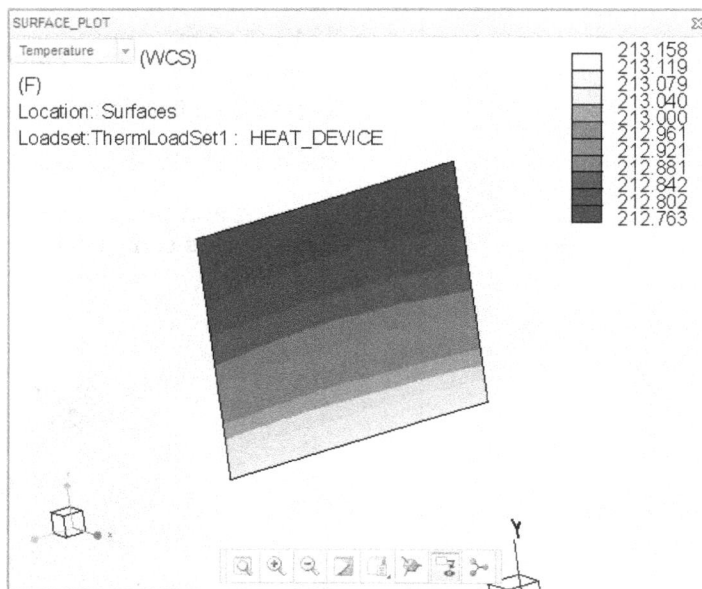

Figure 8–30

The higher the temperature gradient, the higher the heat transfer.

The temperature gradient is very small (0.4°F) and the temperature is too high throughout the surface. These results indicate that the heat device is not convecting enough heat to cool the CPU. Possible solutions include either a forced convection by means of a fan or a different heat device with more fins and a higher fin height. A sensitivity study would be useful for the second solution. Additionally, the convection coefficient could be increased by introducing surface roughness to the **heat_device** fins to enhance turbulence.

© 2017, ASCENT - Center for Technical Knowledge®

Task 10 - Display the heat flux results.

1. In the *Home* tab, click ✏ (Edit). The Result Window Definition dialog box opens.

2. In the *Quantity* tab, select **Flux Magnitude**.

3. In the *Display Location* tab, select **All**.

4. In the *Display Options* tab, select **Animate** and **Auto Start**.

5. Click **OK and Show**. Step through the animation. On Frame 5, the result plot displays as shown in Figure 8–31.

Figure 8–31

Note that the maximum heat flow occurs at the bottom of the fins. This area acts like a funnel, transferring heat from the heat source at the bottom surface to the tops of the fins.

6. Exit the Results.

7. Close the Analyses and Design Studies dialog box.

Task 11 - Transfer loads from thermal to structure.

In this task, you will transfer the temperature distribution from Thermal analysis to Structural analysis and apply the temperature distribution's thermal load in Structure mode.

1. Click ▣ (Structure Mode) to switch to the Structure mode.

2. Expand the *Loads* area and select **MEC/T Load**. The MEC/T Temperature Load dialog box opens as shown in Figure 8–32.

Figure 8–32

3. In the *Name* field, enter **transfer**.

4. For *Member of Set*, accept the default option.

5. In the *Reference Temperature* field, enter **50**.

6. Click **OK**. The model displays as shown in Figure 8–33.

MEC/T icon

Figure 8–33

© 2017, ASCENT - Center for Technical Knowledge®

Task 12 - Apply constraints.

The heat sink is bonded to the circuit board. In this task, you will apply the proper constraints.

1. Constrain the bottom surface of the heat sink in all of the translations, as shown in Figure 8–34.

Figure 8–34

Task 13 - Run the structural analysis.

1. Set up a static analysis using the **Single-Pass Adaptive** convergence option.

2. For the name of the analysis, enter **heat_structure**.

3. Run the heat_structure analysis.

Task 14 - Display the results.

In this task, you will create and display two fringe plots: one for displacement and one for von Mises stress.

1. Create the deformed fringe plot for displacement, as shown in Figure 8–35.

Figure 8–35

Note that the most deformation occurs in the fins, where material expansion due to heating is not constrained.

© 2017, ASCENT - Center for Technical Knowledge®

2. Create the fringe plot for the von Mises stress, as shown in Figure 8–36.

Figure 8–36

Note that the greatest stress occurs at the bottom of the sink, which is due to the constraint that restricts material expansion in that area.

3. Exit the Results. Save and close the model.

Practice 8b

Thermal Deformation Analysis of an Assembly

Practice Objectives

- Set up and run a thermal analysis on an assembly.
- Create an interface with thermal resistance.
- Import thermal results into structural analysis.

In this practice, you will set up and run a thermal and a structural analyses on the electronic assembly shown in Figure 8–37, with minimum instruction.

Figure 8–37

The heat source in this simulation is the Integrated Circuit (IC) part, generating 1W of heat. The heat sink is bonded to the IC. The IC is mounted, but not bonded, to the Printed Circuit Board (PCB) part. The generated heat in this design is intended to be dissipated through the means of convection by the heat sink.

Task 1 - Prepare the thermal model.

1. Open **PCB.asm** and launch Creo Simulate. Switch to Thermal Mode.

2. Apply the materials as follows:
   - **Heat sink:** AL2014
   - **IC:** EPOXY
   - **PCB:** NYLON

3. Apply the **1W** Heat Load to the IC part.

© 2017, ASCENT - Center for Technical Knowledge®

4. Apply a convection boundary condition on all vertical surfaces and on all top surfaces of the fins of the heat sink, as well as on the top surface of the PCB, as shown in Figure 8–38. Use the following convection parameters:
   - **Convection coefficient:** 0.01
   - **Bulk temperature:** 30

Figure 8–38

Since the IC is not bonded to the PCB, there is no perfect conduction of heat between the two parts.

5. Create a new Thermal Resistance interface between the bottom surface of the IC and the top surface of the PCB. Use a Heat Transfer Coefficient of **0.02**.

6. Verify the model's interfaces using the Review Geometry tool.

Task 2 - Set up and run a thermal analysis and then examine the results.

1. Create and run a new Single-Pass Adaptive steady-state thermal analysis named **pcb_thermal**.

2. Display the **Temperature** fringe plot.
   - Does the temperature field look reasonable?
   - What is the maximum temperature in the Integrated Circuit?

3. Display the **Flux Magnitude** fringe plot.
   - In which areas of the model does the most flow of heat occur?

Task 3 - Prepare the structural model.

1. Switch to Structure Mode.

2. Fully constrain the inside surfaces of all four holes in the PCB, as shown in Figure 8–39.

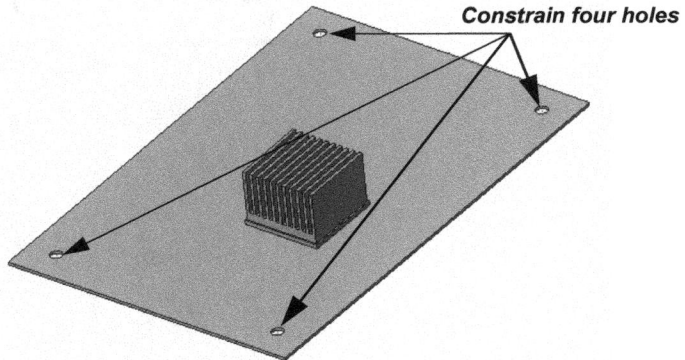

Constrain four holes

Figure 8–39

3. Apply MEC/T load from the **pcb_thermal** analysis. Use Reference Temperature **20**.

Task 4 - Set up and run a thermal analysis and then examine the results.

1. Create and run a new Single-Pass Adaptive static analysis named **pcb_struct**.

2. Display and animate the **Displacement Magnitude** deformed fringe plot.

   • Does the deformation display as expected?

3. Display the **von Mises Stress** plot.

   • Can you explain why substantial stresses occur near the mounting holes?

   • Can you think of an alternative set of supports that would decrease the out-of-plane deformation of the model as well as of the stress level?

© 2017, ASCENT - Center for Technical Knowledge®

Modal Analysis

A modal analysis in Creo Simulate helps you to determine the natural frequencies and natural modes of vibration for a model. These factors are important for models that are subjected to cyclic or vibration loads, because resonance occurs at vibrational loads that are at or close to the natural frequencies for the model. You can calculate natural frequencies and model shapes for the following types of parts: a free part (when it has six rigid body modes), a partially fixed part (when the number of rigid body modes is less than six), and a fully fixed part (when there are no rigid body modes).

Learning Objectives in this Chapter

- Understand natural vibration and natural frequency.
- Understand natural modes of vibration.
- Create a modal analysis.

9.1 Natural Frequency

All objects vibrate, when hit, struck, plucked or otherwise disturbed. When an object vibrates, it tends to do so at a specific frequency or set of frequencies. For example, it could be a guitar string or a tuning fork.

The frequency or frequencies at which an object tends to vibrate when disturbed is called the *characteristic* or *natural frequency* of the object.

If a dynamic load is applied to a model close to its natural frequency, the model exhibits a larger than normal oscillation. This phenomenon is called *resonance*. Without proper damping, the resonance can become uncontrollable and cause the model to collapse.

Natural frequencies are numbered (1st, 2nd, 3rd, etc.), with the 1st natural frequency being the lowest. The 1st natural frequency is sometimes called the *fundamental frequency* of an object.

Resonance occurs when the frequency of the forced vibrations approaches or coincides with the natural frequency of the system.

Modal analysis in Creo Simulate predicts the natural frequencies of your model so that you can determine whether or not the applied dynamic loads might cause resonance. The results of a modal analysis also help to determine whether a model requires more or less damping to prevent failure. Use a modal analysis to find the resonant frequencies for a structure under specific constraints.

© 2017, ASCENT - Center for Technical Knowledge®

9.2 Natural Modes

An object vibrating at a natural frequency creates a physical deformation, or shape, of the object. This shape is called the *natural mode* of vibration.

Using Creo Simulate, you can visualize these shapes and the frequency that is associated with them. Four mode shapes are shown in Figure 9–1. By viewing mode shapes, you can determine how a part reacts to different frequencies.

255.6Hz

868.8Hz

1026.7Hz

1440.4Hz

Figure 9–1

Note that the equation solved in Modal analysis is the equation of dynamic equilibrium (i.e., Newton's equation) with no loads included in the analysis. Therefore, the mode shapes are essentially dimensionless. When mode shapes are displayed in Creo Simulate, only some imaginary magnitudes are displayed, which are scaled to an arbitrary value.

9.3 Defining a Modal Analysis

Modal analysis parameters are defined in the Modal Analysis Definition dialog box, as shown in Figure 9–2.

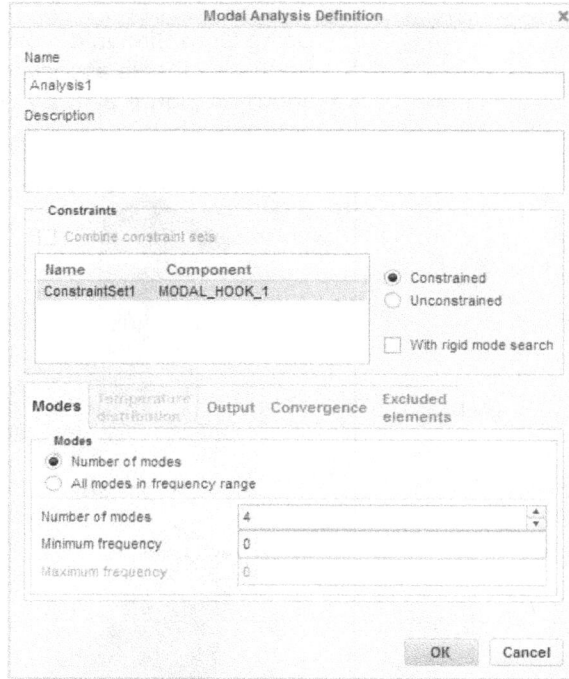

Figure 9–2

The options in the Modal Analysis dialog box are as follows:

Option		Description
Name		Enter a name for the analysis.
Description		Enter a description of the analysis (optional).
Constraints		Enables you to define the constraint set using the following options:
	Constrained	Select a constraint set, if one is available.
	Unconstrained	Solves an unconstrained or under-constrained model.
	With rigid mode search	Use when solving an unconstrained or under-constrained model, if you want to visualize the rigid body modes. Creo Simulate reports any rigid body modes that it finds.

© 2017, ASCENT - Center for Technical Knowledge®

Output		Define the output for the analysis. This tab contains the following options:
	Calculate	Select the stresses, rotations, and/or reactions to calculated quantity values.
	Plot	Enter a plotting grid density. Creo Simulate calculates and displays quantity values at the intersection of the grid lines on each element.
Convergence		Select a convergence method using the Method drop-down list in the *Convergence* tab.
Modes		Define the modes for the analysis in the *Modes* tab. This tab contains the following options:
	Number of Modes	Specifies the number of modes and frequencies for Creo Simulate to calculate.
	All Modes in Frequency Range	Requests the calculation of all modes within a frequency range in the *Min Frequency* and *Max Frequency* fields.
	Minimum Frequency	Specify the minimum frequency of a frequency range. You can only specify this if the **All Modes in Frequency Range** option is selected.
	Maximum Frequency	Specify the maximum frequency of a frequency range. You can only specify this if the **All Modes in Frequency Range** option is selected.

Practice 9a

A modal analysis enables you to find the natural frequencies and corresponding natural modes of the bracket under a specific constraint set.

Modal Analysis of a Bracket

Practice Objectives

* Set up and run a modal analysis.
* Display the results.

In this practice, you will set up and run a modal analysis on a bracket model, as shown in Figure 9–3. You will use the shell idealization to represent the thin sections of the model.

Figure 9–3

Modeling Tasks

Task 1 - Open the part.

1. Open **modal_hook_1.prt** in Creo Parametric. The part displays as shown in Figure 9–4.

Figure 9–4

2. Ensure that the unit system is set to **mmNs**.

3. Select **Applications>Simulate**. .

© 2017, ASCENT - Center for Technical Knowledge®

Task 2 - Apply the material.

The model's material properties should be as stated.

1. Assign **STEEL** to the model. The following values are the default material properties for HS-low-alloy steel (STEEL):
   - **Poisson:** 0.27
   - **Young's modulus:** 199948 N/mm2
   - **Coeff of thermal expansion:** 1.17e-5 /C
   - **Density:** 7.82708e-9 tonne/mm^3

Task 3 - Define the shell elements.

1. In the *Refine Model* tab, expand the Shell Pair drop-down list and select **Detect Shell Pairs**. The Auto Detect Shell Pairs dialog box opens as shown in Figure 9–5.

Figure 9–5

*The wall thickness in this part is 5mm. Using a Characteristic Thickness of **6mm** ensures that all thin areas in the part are detected as Shells.*

2. In the *Characteristic Thickness* field, enter **6** and click **Start**. Creo Simulate runs the automatic detection algorithm and closes the Auto Detect Shell Pairs dialog box.

3. In the *Refine Model* tab, in the *AutoGEM* area, click
   (Review Geometry) to open the Simulation Geometry
   dialog box. Accept the default options and click **Apply**. The
   model displays as shown in Figure 9–6.

Figure 9–6

Verify that the boss is displayed in gray (this is the
uncompressed area), while the thin-walled sections are
displayed in green (these are the shell pairs compressed to a
midsurface).

4. Click **Close** in the Simulation Geometry dialog box.

Task 4 - Apply the constraints.

In this task, you will apply constraints to the top and bottom
surfaces of the bracket, as shown in Figure 9–7.

*Fix these
surfaces*

Figure 9–7

© 2017, ASCENT - Center for Technical Knowledge®

1. Click 🔧 (Displacement). The Constraint dialog box opens.

2. In the *Name* field, enter **surface_fix**.

3. Constrain the surfaces shown in Figure 9–7 in all of the Translations and Rotations. The model displays as shown in Figure 9–8.

Figure 9–8

Task 5 - Mesh the model.

---

1. Mesh the model using the **All with Properties** option.

2. The model displays as shown in Figure 9–9.

The shell elements (Tri and Quad) are displayed in green and the 3D solid elements (Tetra) are displayed in blue.

Figure 9–9

3. Close the AutoGEM dialog box and save the mesh.

Summary

In the previous tasks, you created the simulation entities required to analyze your model. In the following tasks, you will specify the analysis type and convergence method and run the analysis.

Analysis Tasks

Task 6 - Run a Quick Check analysis.

In this task, the model is analyzed using the **Quick Check** convergence option, which checks for errors.

1. Click ⚒ (Analyses and Studies).

2. In the Analyses and Design Studies dialog box, select **File>New Modal**. The Modal Analysis Definition dialog box opens as shown in Figure 9–10.

The objective of a modal study is to ensure that the system does not have a resonant frequency near the operating frequency.

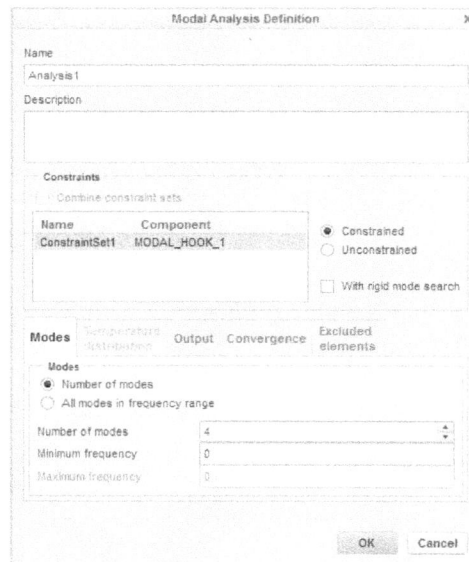

Figure 9–10

3. In the *Name* field, enter **modal_hook**.

4. (Optional) In the *Description* field, enter a description of the analysis.

5. In the *Constraints* area, accept the defaults.

6. In the *Number of Modes* field, enter **6**.

*Select the **Unconstrained** and **With rigid mode search** options when you are not sure if your model is fully constrained.*

© 2017, ASCENT - Center for Technical Knowledge®

7. Select the *Convergence* tab, expand the Method drop-down list and select **Quick Check**.

8. Click **OK** to accept the selections and close the Modal Analysis Definition dialog box.

9. Check the validity of the model and run the analysis.

10. The run should complete with the warning message "Shell compression resulted in loss of some solid material near the following geometry". Click on the lines below the warning message. Note that the warning was due to the need for Creo Simulate to adjust the length of the solid boss to the midsurfaces of the side plates.

Task 7 - Run a Multi-Pass Adaptive analysis.

In this task, the model is analyzed using the **Multi-Pass Adaptive** convergence option.

The solution converges on frequency.

1. Change the convergence method to **Multi-Pass Adaptive**. In the *Polynomial Order* field, enter **9**. In the *Limits* area, in the *Percent Convergence* field, accept the default value of **10**.

2. Run the analysis.

3. In the Analyses and Design Studies dialog box, click ▤ (Status). In the Run Status window that displays (as shown in Figure 9–11), extract the following information.

```
Number of Modes: 6

    Mode   Frequency (Hz)   Convergence
    ----   --------------   -----------
       1   2.607665e+02        3.0%
       2   9.401390e+02        7.5%
       3   1.015977e+03        8.4%
       4   1.467314e+03        3.3%
       5   1.723053e+03        3.6%
       6   1.821113e+03        3.9%
```

Figure 9–11

Note the convergence percentage for the six frequencies. The solution converges on the frequency (you set the convergence in Step 1 of this task). The convergence was obtained on pass six.

Results Tasks

Task 8 - Display the results.

In this task, you will create, animate, and display four Displacement Magnitude fringe plots for the first four modes of vibration.

1. In the Analyses and Design Studies dialog box, click
   (Review Results). The Result Window Definition dialog box opens as shown in Figure 9–12.

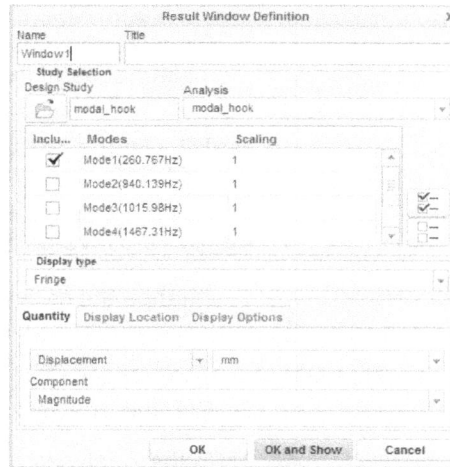

Figure 9–12

2. In the *Name* field, enter **mode1** .

3. Select the *Display Options* tab and enter the information shown in Figure 9–13.

Figure 9–13

© 2017, ASCENT - Center for Technical Knowledge®

4. Display the result plot. Step through the animation to the frame shown in Figure 9–14.

Figure 9–14

5. Create, animate, and display a Displacement Magnitude for mode 2. In the *Name* field, enter **mode2**.

6. In the *Include* column, select the second checkbox as shown in Figure 9–15, and clear the first checkbox.

Figure 9–15

7. Display the **mode_2** fringe plot. Step through the animation to the frame shown in Figure 9–16.

Figure 9–16

8. Create, animate, and display a Displacement Magnitude for mode 3. In the *Name* field, enter **mode3**.

9. In the *Include* column, select the third checkbox and clear the second checkbox.

10. Display the **mode_3** fringe plot. Step through the animation to the frame shown in Figure 9–17.

© 2017, ASCENT - Center for Technical Knowledge®

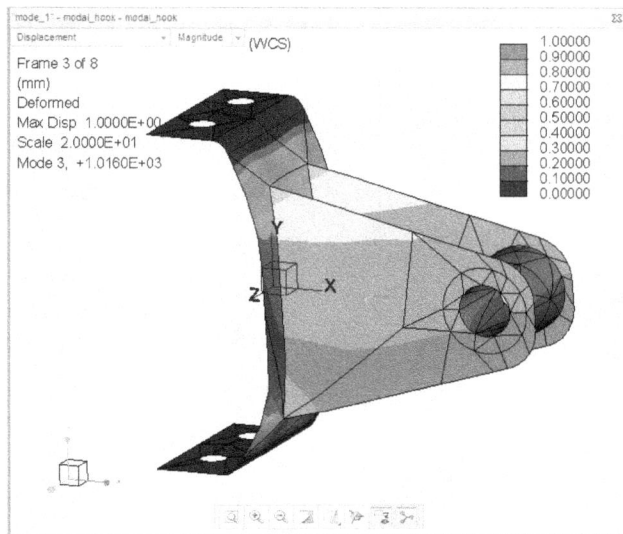

Figure 9–17

11. Create, animate, and display a Displacement Magnitude for mode 4. In the *Name* field, enter **mode4**.

12. In the *Include* column, select the fourth checkbox and clear the third checkbox.

13. Display the **mode_4** fringe plot. Step through the animation to the frame shown in Figure 9–18.

Figure 9–18

14. Exit the Results. Save and close the model.

Task 9 - (Optional) Set up and run a new analysis.

1. Delete the mesh.

2. Delete the mid-surface shells.

3. Mesh the model with only 3D solid elements.

4. Set up and run a new Multi-Pass Adaptive analysis. Enter a different name for the analysis. In the *Polynomial Order* field, enter **9**. In the *Limits* area and *Converge on* area, in the *Percent Convergence* field, accept the defaults.

5. Compare the results.

© 2017, ASCENT - Center for Technical Knowledge®

Practice 9b

Unconstrained Modal Analysis

Practice Objectives

- Set up and run an unconstrained modal analysis.
- Review the results of the unconstrained modal analysis.

In this practice, you will set up and run an unconstrained modal analysis on the frame shown in Figure 9–19, with minimum instruction.

Figure 9–19

Task 1 - Prepare the model for analysis.

1. Open **frame.asm** and launch Creo Simulate.

2. Apply the material **AL6061** to all parts.

3. Do not apply any constraints.

Task 2 - Set up and run modal analysis.

1. Create and run a new modal analysis with the following parameters:
   - **Analysis name:** modal_free
   - **Unconstrained:** ON
   - **With rigid mode search:** ON
   - **All modes in frequency range:** from **0Hz** to **500Hz**
   - **Convergence method:** Single-Pass Adaptive

Task 3 - Examine the analysis results.

1. Extract the frequency values from the Run Status window.
   - How many natural frequencies have been found in the requested range?
   - Did you notice that first six frequencies are zeros or very close to zeros?

2. Examine the deformation plots for frequencies 1 to 6.
   - Do these modes resemble rigid body motions of the model (i.e., without inducing any strain or stress)?

3. Examine the deformation plots for the other frequencies.
   - Which frequency corresponds to the twisting mode of deformation of the frame?

© 2017, ASCENT - Center for Technical Knowledge®

Welds, Springs, and Masses

Idealizations are used to simplify your model and shorten your analysis time. Three other useful idealizations are: welds, springs, and masses.

Learning Objectives in this Chapter

- Create spot weld connections.
- Create end weld connections.
- Create perimeter weld connections.
- Understand springs in Creo Simulate.
- Create springs.
- Understand mass elements in Creo Simulate.
- Create mass elements.

10.1 Weld Connections

Weld connections are analysis features that are intended to bridge gaps that occur during the midsurface compression of shell assemblies. The four types of weld connections available in Creo Simulate are: Spot Welds, End Welds, Perimeter Welds, and Weld Feature welds.

Spot Welds

Spot welds connect parts at datum point locations that you specify. An example of an assembly suitable for using spot welds is shown in Figure 10–1.

Parts spot-welded at points

Figure 10–1

A spot weld in Creo Simulate is modeled with a beam element with a round cross-section. This idealization accurately transfers forces from one part to another. However, stress values close to the spot welds might not be accurate.

The following conditions are required for successful spot welds:

• The surfaces being connected by the weld must be within 15° of being parallel to each other.

• One of the surfaces being connected must have datum points that define spot weld locations.

© 2017, ASCENT - Center for Technical Knowledge®

Use the following steps to create a spot weld:

1. In the *Connections* group, click ⬚ (Weld).
2. Expand the Type drop-down list and select **Spot Weld**.
3. Select the two surfaces that you want to connect.
4. Select the datum points where the spot welds are going to be created.
5. Enter the diameter of the weld.
6. In the Materials dialog box, select the material of the weld.

End Welds

End welds are used to connect plates that are joined at right or oblique angles, such as in T or L configurations. An example of an assembly suitable for using end welds is shown in Figure 10–2.

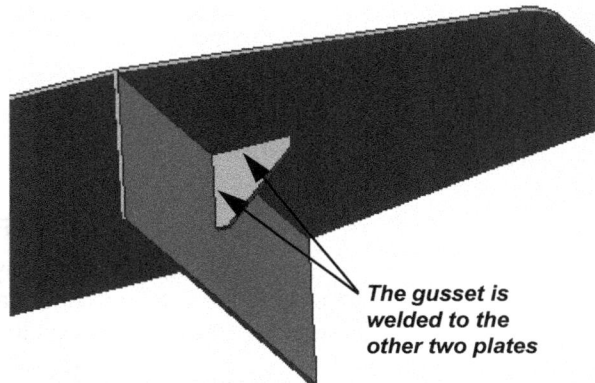

The gusset is welded to the other two plates

Figure 10–2

When an end weld is created, Creo Simulate creates shell elements to extend the mesh from one plate to join the mesh of a base plate.

Use the following steps to create an end weld:

1. In the *Connections* group, click ⬚ (Weld).
2. Expand the Type drop-down list and select **End Weld**.
3. Select the surfaces to be welded.

Perimeter Welds

Perimeter welds are used to connect plates that are parallel to one another, along the perimeter of one plate. An example of an assembly suitable for using a perimeter weld is shown in Figure 10–3.

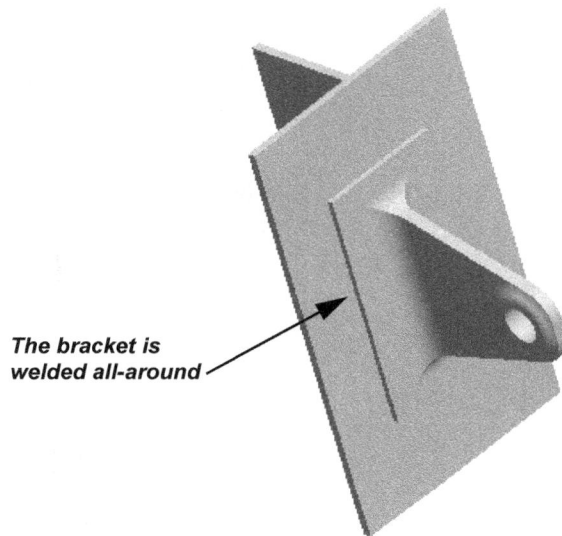

The bracket is welded all-around

Figure 10–3

Creo Simulate automatically creates a series of new surfaces to extend the edges of one plate to the surface of the other. Shell elements are created on these surfaces.

Use the following steps to create a perimeter weld:

1. In the Connections group, click (Weld).
2. Expand the Type drop-down list and select **Perimeter Weld**.
3. Select the doubler surface on which you want to place the weld.
4. Select the base surface to which to extend the weld.
5. Select the doubler surface's edges that you want to weld.
6. Enter the thickness of the shell elements that represent the perimeter weld.
7. Select a material for the weld.

© 2017, ASCENT - Center for Technical Knowledge®

Weld Features

This option permits the re-use of welds created with the Creo Parametric Welding application. The welds must meet the following criteria:

- They must be fillet or groove type welds.

- They must be surface welds.

Use the following steps to use a weld feature:

1. In the *Connections* group, click ⌐ (Weld).
2. Expand the Type drop-down list and select **Weld Feature**.
3. Select a weld feature created in Creo Parametric Welding.

10.2 Springs

Spring elements are one-dimensional idealizations that are intended to simulate the various elastic components in your model without specifying their geometrical shape.

Non-linear springs require an Advanced Creo Simulate license.

Springs in Creo Simulate can be linear (constant stiffness) or non-linear (variable stiffness). Springs can connect one point to the ground (fixed) or connect two points.

In the example shown in Figure 10–4 one spring connects two points (a point on the frame and the mass point) and a fixed to the ground spring supports the frame at the top.

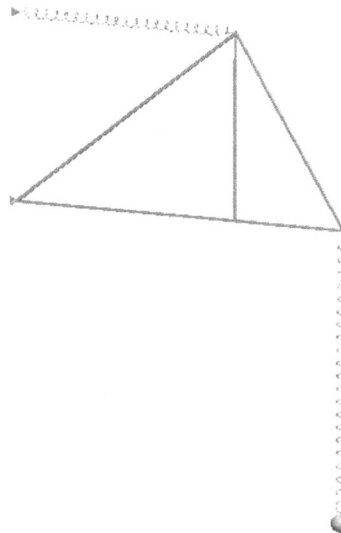

Figure 10–4

Advanced springs require an Advanced Creo Simulate license.

In Creo Simulate, you can create three types of springs: Simple, Advanced, and To Ground. Simple and Advanced springs can have any orientation, which is defined by selecting two points. To Ground springs are always parallel to a coordinate system, such as WCS.

Use the following steps to create a spring:

© 2017, ASCENT - Center for Technical Knowledge®

You cannot create zero length simple springs.

1. In the *Idealizations* group, click ≋ (Spring). The Spring Definition dialog box opens as shown in Figure 10–5.

Figure 10–5

The options in the Spring Definition dialog box are as follows:

Option	Description
Name	Enter the name of the spring or use the default name.
References	Selects geometry references. The following types of geometry references are available: **Point-Point**, **Point-Surface**, **Point-Edge**, and **Point-Point Pairs**.
Type	Selects the type of the spring. The following types of springs are available: **Simple**, **Advanced**, and **To Ground**.
Extensional Force-Deflection Variation	Selects a linear or non-linear spring: • Constant Stiffness (linear spring) • Force-Deflection Curve (non-linear spring)
Extensional Stiffness	Defines the extensional stiffness, (i.e., resistance to stretch) of your spring.
Torsional Stiffness	Defines torsional stiffness (i.e., resistance to twist) of your spring.

Stiffness

Simple springs only have two stiffness properties:

- **Extensional Stiffness:** Acting along the line connecting the two points.

- **Torsional Stiffness:** Acting about the line connecting the two points.

Advanced and To Ground springs require stiffness properties to be defined in the Spring Properties Definition dialog box, as shown in Figure 10–6.

Figure 10–6

The options in the Spring Properties Definition dialog box are as follows:

Box	Description
Set Name	Enter the name of the spring stiffness.
Description	(Optional) Enter the description of the spring stiffness.
Extensional	Enter the stiffness for the principal axes in the *Kxx*, *Kyy*, and *Kzz* fields.
Torsional	Enter the stiffness for the rotation around the principal axes in the *Txx*, *Tyy*, and *Tzz* fields.

© 2017, ASCENT - Center for Technical Knowledge®

Orientation

The spring principal axes, used to specify K_{xx}, K_{yy}, etc. stiffness directions in the Spring Properties Definition dialog box, are defined as follows:

- **To Ground spring:** The principal axes are aligned with the axes of the selected coordinate system (the default is WCS).

- **Advanced spring:** The X-principal axis is always along the line between the two points, the Y-axis direction is specified by the user (as is done for Beam elements), and the Z-axis direction is obtained as a cross-product of X-axis by the Y-axis.

10.3 Masses

You can attach a mass to a solid, shell, or beam.

Mass elements are idealizations that are intended to simulate the mass properties of various components in your model, without specifying the component's geometrical shape. For example, a mass element might be used to simulate the weight of the engine attached to the truck frame, without actually specifying the engine's geometry.

Advanced masses require an Advanced Creo Simulate license.

Masses in Creo Simulate can be **Simple** or **Advanced**. Simple masses only have translational inertia, while Advanced masses can be assigned rotational inertia (i.e., moments of inertia) as well.

Use the following steps to create a mass:

*Select **Advanced** in the Type drop-down list to create an advanced mass.*

1. In the *Idealizations* group, click ⏛ (Mass). The Mass Definition dialog box opens as shown in Figure 10–7.

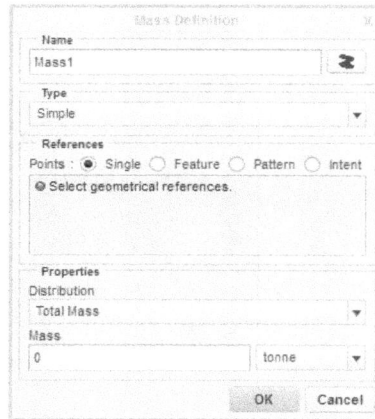

Figure 10–7

2. Enter the *Name*.
3. Expand the Type drop-down list and select **Simple** or **Advanced**.
4. Select the *References* (datum points).
5. Select the *Distribution* (**Total Mass** or **Mass Per Point**).
6. Enter the mass value.

© 2017, ASCENT - Center for Technical Knowledge®

Practice 10a | Spot Welds

Practice Objectives

- Create spot weld connections.
- Set up a spot welded FEA model analysis.
- Display the results of the analysis.

*Use the **Spot Weld** option for the small bolts, screws, and rivets in your model, and for the spot welds.*

In this practice, you will set up and run a spot welded model using the **Spot Weld** option. The assembly model is shown in Figure 10–8. The assembly model consists of four parts. You will use shell idealizations to model the parts.

Figure 10–8

Modeling Tasks

Task 1 - Open the assembly.

1. Open **spot_weld.asm** in Creo Parametric. The model displays as shown in Figure 10–9.

Figure 10–9

2. Ensure that the unit system is set to **mmNs**.

Task 2 - Launch Creo Simulate.

1. Select **Applications>Simulate** to launch Creo Simulate.

2. Click ᢓ (Simulation Display) and clear the **Display AutoGEM Controls** option to unclutter the display.

3. Click 🖹 (Model Setup). Expand the Default Interface drop-down list and select **Free** as shown in Figure 10–10.

The Free Default Interface ensures that the parts are not bonded over the mated surfaces. Rather, you will connect the parts with Spot Welds.

Figure 10–10

4. Click **OK**.

Task 3 - Define shell pairs.

1. In the *Refine Model* tab, expand 🜂 (Shell Pair) and select **Detect Shell Pairs**. The Auto Detect Shell Pairs dialog box opens as shown in Figure 10–11.

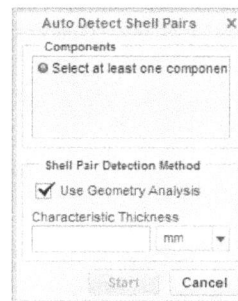

Figure 10–11

2. Select all four parts in the assembly (hold down <Ctrl> to multi-select).

© 2017, ASCENT - Center for Technical Knowledge®

*The thickness of the parts in the assembly is **5mm**. Using a Characteristic Thickness greater than 5mm ensures that all of the parts are compressed to mid-surfaces.*

3. In the *Characteristic Thickness* field, enter **8**. The Auto Detect Shell Pairs dialog box opens as shown in Figure 10–12.

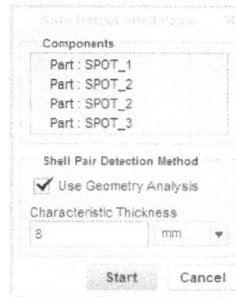

Figure 10–12

4. Click **Start**. Creo Simulate runs the automatic detection algorithm and closes the Auto Detect Shell Pairs dialog box.

5. Check the Model Tree. There should be nine shell pairs in the Idealizations section of the Model Tree on the assembly level.

6. In the *Refine Model* tab, in the *AutoGEM* area, click
   (Review Geometry) to open the Simulation Geometry dialog box.

7. Accept the default options and click **Apply**. The model displays as shown in Figure 10–13. Ensure that all of the surfaces are highlighted in green, and that no elements in the model are displayed in a different color.

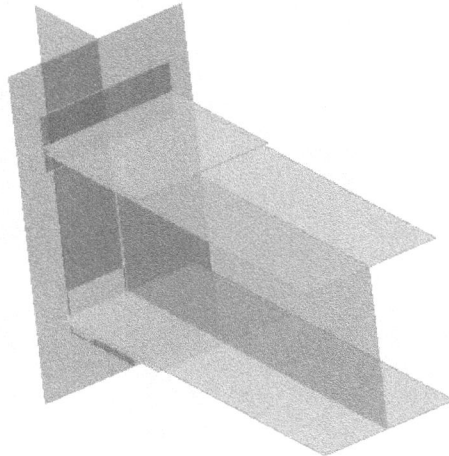

Figure 10–13

8. Click **Close** to close the Simulation Geometry dialog box.

The model's material properties should be as stated.

Task 4 - Apply the material.

1. Assign **STEEL** to the assembly parts as the material. The following values are the default material properties for HS-low-alloy steel (STEEL):
   - **Poisson:** 0.27
   - **Young's modulus:** 199948 MPa
   - **Density:** 7.82708e-9 tonne/mm3

2. Using the Simulation Display dialog box, hide the Material Assignment icons.

Task 5 - Create spot weld connections.

In this task, you will connect the plates using the **Spot Weld** option.

1. In the *Connections* group of the *Refine Model* tab, click
   ⬉ (Weld). The Weld Definition dialog box opens.

2. Expand the Type drop-down list and select **Spot Weld**.

3. Select the surfaces shown in Figure 10–14 as the *References* for the weld.

Select this surface as the first surface

Select this surface as the second surface

Figure 10–14

4. In the *Properties* area, select **Feature** option and select **PNT0**. Six points (PNT0 to PNT5) are highlighted, since they were created as one feature in Creo Parametric.

5. For the diameter, enter **10**.

© 2017, ASCENT - Center for Technical Knowledge®

6. For the weld material, select **STEEL**. The Weld Definition dialog box opens as shown in Figure 10–15.

Figure 10–15

7. Click **OK** to close the Weld Definition dialog box. **Spot Weld** icons display as shown in Figure 10–16.

8. Repeat Steps 1 to 7 for the other side as shown in Figure 10–16.

Figure 10–16

9. Repeat Steps 1 to 7 to create spot welds between the surfaces shown in Figure 10–17. Select **PNT6** when selecting the datum point feature.

Select this surface as the second surface

Select this surface as the first surface

Figure 10–17

10. Repeat Steps 1 to 7 for the other side as shown in Figure 10–18.

Other side

Figure 10–18

© 2017, ASCENT - Center for Technical Knowledge®

Task 6 - Mesh the model.

1. Click ▦ (AutoGEM) to open the AutoGEM dialog box. Accept **All with Properties** and click **Create**.

2. Close the AutoGEM Summary and Diagnostics dialog boxes when the meshing finishes. The model displays as shown in Figure 10–19.

Figure 10–19

3. Zoom in on any spot weld in the model, such as the one shown in Figure 10–20.

Figure 10–20

Note the small circular regions Creo Simulate created around each spot weld. The diameter of each region is the spot weld diameter that you entered in the Weld Definition dialog box.

4. Select the FRONT view and zoom in on the model to examine the gaps between the midsurfaces, such as those shown in Figure 10–21.

Figure 10–21

Note the beam elements (purple lines) between the parts. These are the elements that Creo Simulate automatically created to connect the midsurfaces at the spot weld points.

5. Close the AutoGEM dialog box and save the mesh.

Task 7 - Apply loads.

1. In the Z-direction, apply a load of **1000** on the edges (apply it to the edges rather than to the end surface) as shown in Figure 10–22. For the name of the load, enter **edge_load**.

© 2017, ASCENT - Center for Technical Knowledge®

Figure 10–22

Task 8 - Apply the constraints.

1. Constrain the T-beam edges (fixed all translations) as shown in Figure 10–23 (constrain the edges rather than the end surfaces). For the name of the constraint, enter **edge_constraints**.

Three edges in either end of the T-beam

Figure 10–23

Analysis Tasks

Task 9 - Set up and run an analysis.

1. Set up a Multi-Pass Adaptive static analysis. For the *Name*, enter **spot_weld**. In the *Polynomial Order* field, enter **9**. In the *Limits* area, in the *Percent Convergence* field, enter **10**.

2. Run the analysis.

3. In the Analyses and Design Studies dialog box, click 🗐 (Status) and extract the following information from the Run Status window:

- Analysis converges on pass seven.
- Stress error is 1.6% of the maximum principal stress, as shown in Figure 10–24.

```
RMS Stress Error Estimates:

Load Set            Stress Error   % of Max Prin Str
---------------     ------------   -----------------
LoadSet1            2.44e+00         1.6% of  1.49e+02

Resource Check                          (10:17:37)
   Elapsed Time     (sec):       31.77
   CPU Time         (sec):       14.77
   Memory Usage     (kb):       381435
   Wrk Dir Dsk Usage (kb):       52248

The analysis converged to within 10% on
edge displacement, element strain energy,
and global RMS stress.
```

Figure 10–24

Results Tasks

Task 10 - Display the results.

In this task, you will create and display a von Mises stress fringe plot and a deformation animation for the model to verify the applied boundary conditions.

1. Create the Displacement Magnitude animation plot. Ensure the **Deformed** and **Overlay Undeformed** options are selected.

2. Start the animation.
   - Do the applied boundary conditions behave correctly?

3. Stop the animation on Frame 5. The result plot displays as shown in Figure 10–25.

© 2017, ASCENT - Center for Technical Knowledge®

Figure 10–25

4. Create the undeformed von Mises stress fringe plot. Clear all of the **Include contributions from beams** options. Change the *Legend minimum* to **0** and *maximum* to **60**. The result plot displays as shown in Figure 10–26.

Figure 10–26

5. Locate and examine high stress areas in the model, particularly the welds and the adjacent areas. If a high stress area is located at the weld, a more detailed analysis should be performed, such as using the 3D solid model type.

6. Exit the Results. Save and close the model.

Practice 10b

Perimeter Welds

Practice Objectives

- Create Perimeter Weld connections.
- Set up a continuous welded FEA model analysis.
- Display the results.

*Use the **Perimeter Weld** option to connect parallel plates.*

In this practice, you will set up and run a continuously welded model, using the **Perimeter Weld** option. The assembly model is shown in Figure 10–27. It consists of a beam plate and a hook plate.

Figure 10–27

© 2017, ASCENT - Center for Technical Knowledge®

Modeling Tasks

Task 1 - Open the model.

1. Open **weld_1.asm** in Creo Parametric. The assembly displays as shown in Figure 10–28.

Figure 10–28

Task 2 - Launch Creo Simulate.

1. Select **Applications>Simulate** to launch Creo Simulate.

2. Click (Model Setup). Expand the Default Interface drop-down list and select **Free**, as shown in Figure 10–29.

The Free Default Interface ensures that the parts are not bonded over the mated surfaces. Rather, you will use the Perimeter Weld to connect them.

Figure 10–29

3. Click **OK**.

Task 3 - Define the shell pairs.

1. In the *Refine Model* tab, expand the Shell Pair drop-down list and select **Detect Shell Pairs**. The Auto Detect Shell Pairs dialog box opens as shown in Figure 10–30.

Figure 10–30

2. Select all of the parts in the assembly (hold down <Ctrl> to multi-select).

The thickest part in the assembly is 10mm.

3. In the *Characteristic Thickness* field, enter **10**. The Auto Detect Shell Pairs dialog box opens as shown in Figure 10–31.

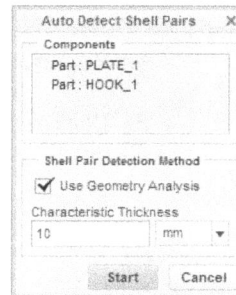

Figure 10–31

4. Click **Start**. Creo Simulate runs the automatic detection algorithm and closes the Auto Detect Shell Pairs dialog box.

5. There should be four shell pairs in the Model Tree on the assembly level.

6. In the *Refine Model* tab, in the *AutoGEM* area, click
   (Review Geometry) to open the Simulation Geometry dialog box.

© 2017, ASCENT - Center for Technical Knowledge®

7. Accept the default options and click **Apply**. The model displays as shown in Figure 10–32. Ensure that all of the surfaces are highlighted in green, and that no elements in the model are displayed in different colors.

Figure 10–32

8. Click **Close** to close the Simulation Geometry dialog box.

Task 4 - Apply the material.

The model's material properties should be as stated.

9. Assign **STEEL** as the material to the assembly parts. The following values are the default material properties for HS-low-alloy steel (STEEL):
   - Poisson = 0.27
   - Young's modulus = 199948 MPa
   - Density = 7.82708e-9 tonne/mm3

Task 5 - Create the weld connections.

*For perpendicular plates, use the **End Weld** option.*

In this task, you will connect the two plates using the **Perimeter Weld** option.

1. In the *Connections* area in the *Refine Model* tab, click
   (Weld). The Weld Definition dialog box opens.

2. Expand the Type drop-down list and select **Perimeter Weld**.

3. Select the top surfaces of **hook_1** as the doubler surface, as shown in Figure 10–33.

Figure 10–33

4. Select the **plate_1** top surface as the base surface, as shown in Figure 10–34.

Figure 10–34

5. Select the four edges of the **hook** top surface as the edges of the doubler to define the weld location, as shown in Figure 10–35. Hold down <Ctrl> to select all four edges.

© 2017, ASCENT - Center for Technical Knowledge®

Select all four edges

Figure 10–35

6. The thickness of the doubler plate is 7mm. To use the same thickness for the thickness of the weld, enter **7.00**.

7. Expand the Material drop-down list and accept the default. The Weld Definition dialog box opens as shown in Figure 10–36.

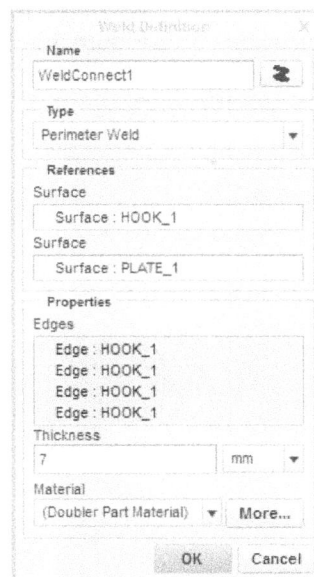

Figure 10–36

8. Click **OK** to finish. Highlight the Connections heading in the Model Tree. The **Perimeter Weld** icon displays as shown in Figure 10–37.

Figure 10–37

Task 6 - Mesh the model.

1. Click ▦ (AutoGEM) to open the AutoGEM dialog box. Accept **All with Properties** and click **Create**.

2. Close the AutoGEM Summary and Diagnostics dialog boxes when the meshing finishes. The model displays as shown in Figure 10–38.

Figure 10–38

© 2017, ASCENT - Center for Technical Knowledge®

3. Zoom in on any perimeter weld area in the model, such as shown in Figure 10–39.

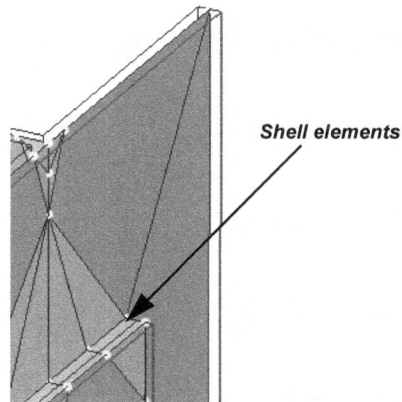

Figure 10–39

Note the shell elements that extend from the hook part edges to the base plate part. These are the elements that Creo Simulate automatically created to simulate the perimeter weld.

4. Close the AutoGEM dialog box and save the mesh.

Task 7 - Apply the loads.

1. Apply a force of **-8000** in the WCS's Y-direction to the hook's hole edge, as shown in Figure 10–40. For the name of the force, enter **hook_force**.

In the Force area in the dialog box, select the **Components** *option.*

Figure 10–40

Task 8 - Apply the constraints.

1. Constrain the edges of **plate_1** (fixed all translations), as shown in Figure 10–41.

Figure 10–41

Analysis Tasks

Task 9 - Set up and run an analysis.

1. Set up a Single-Pass Adaptive static analysis. For the name of the analysis, enter **weld_1**.

2. Run the analysis.

3. In the Analyses and Design Studies dialog box, click (Status) and extract the following information from the Run Status window:

   • The RMS Stress error is 11.6% of the maximum principal stress, as shown in Figure 10–42.

```
RMS Stress Error Estimates:

Load Set          Stress Error   % of Max Prin Str
----------------  -------------  ------------------
LoadSet1           6.69e+01       11.6% of  5.79e+02
```

Figure 10–42

© 2017, ASCENT - Center for Technical Knowledge®

Results Tasks

Task 10 - Display the results.

In this task, you will create and display a von Mises stress fringe plot and deformation animation for the model. This verifies the applied boundary conditions.

1. Create the Displacement Magnitude animation plot. Ensure that the **Deformed** and **Overlay Undeformed** options are selected.

2. Stop the animation on Frame 5. The result plot displays as shown in Figure 10–43.

Figure 10–43

3. Create the deformed von Mises stress fringe plot shown in Figure 10–44.

Figure 10–44

4. Locate and examine the high stress areas in the model, particularly the welds and the adjacent areas. If a high stress area is located at the weld, a more detailed analysis should be performed, such as using the 3D solid model type.

5. Exit the Results. Save and close the model.

© 2017, ASCENT - Center for Technical Knowledge®

Practice 10c | Springs and Masses Analysis

Practice Objectives

- Create beam elements.
- Create spring elements.
- Create mass element.
- Set up, run, and analyze an FEA model using masses and spring idealizations.
- Display the results.

In this practice, you will use spring and mass idealizations to set up and run an analysis on the model shown in Figure 10–45. The model is composed of beams and two springs. The ends of one beam and one spring are fixed, as shown in Figure 10–45. The beam joints are rigid. A mass is supported by another spring. The only load on the system is due to gravity. You will define three user-defined displacement point measures to determine the displacement of the frame at these points.

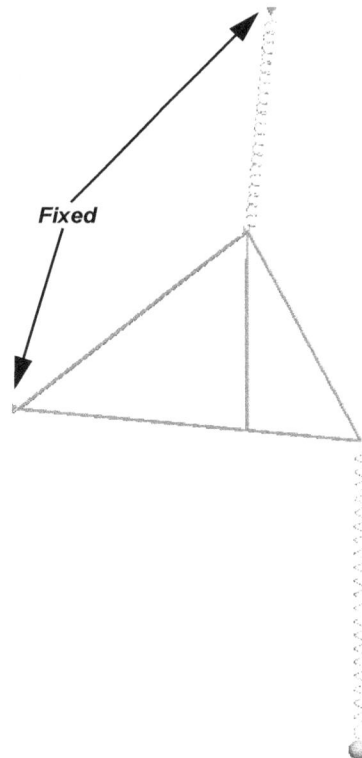

Fixed

Figure 10–45

The FEA model is shown in Figure 10–46.

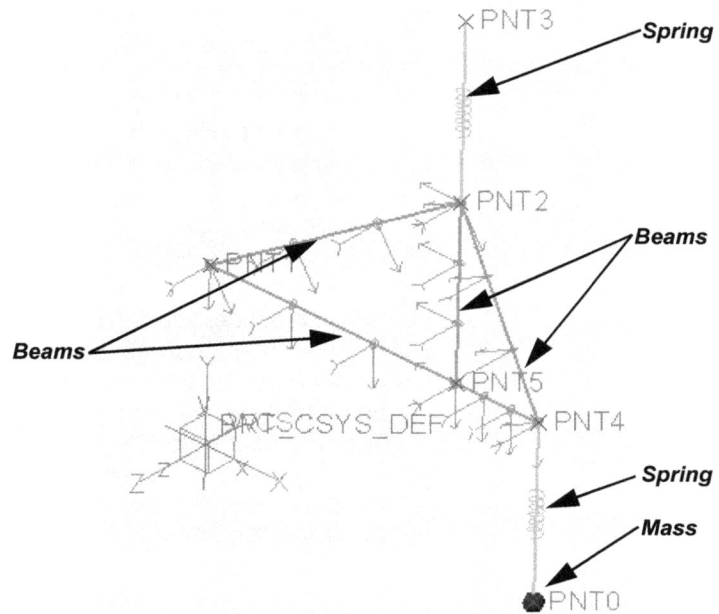

Figure 10–46

Modeling Tasks

Task 1 - Open the model.

1. Open **frame_1.prt** in Creo Parametric. The part displays as shown in Figure 10–47, with the datum planes and datum points turned on.

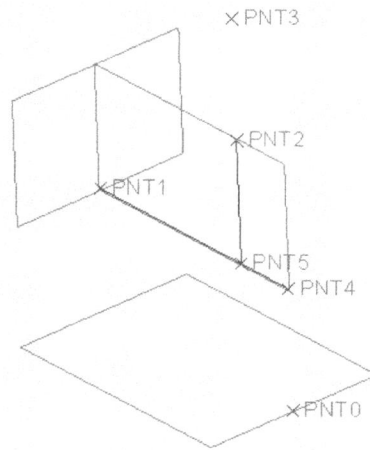

Figure 10–47

© 2017, ASCENT - Center for Technical Knowledge®

2. Ensure the unit system is set to **IPS**.

3. Select **Applications>Simulate** to launch Creo Simulate.

Task 2 - Create three beam elements on datum curves.

---

1. In the *Refine Model* tab, click ⌖ (Beam). The Beam Definition dialog box opens.

2. In the *Name* field, enter **beam_curves**.

3. Select the curves shown in Figure 10–48.

Figure 10–48

4. Assign **STEEL** as the material to the beams. The following values are the default material properties for HS-low-alloy steel (STEEL):

   - **Poisson:** 0.27
   - **Young's modulus:** 2.9e7 psi
   - **Density:** 0.0007324 lbf sec^2 /in^4

5. In the *Orientation* area, in the *X* field, enter **0**, in the *Y* field, enter **0**, and in the *Z* field, enter **1**.

6. Next to the Beam Section drop-down list, click **More**. In the Beam Sections dialog box, click **New**. The Beam Section Definition dialog box opens.

7. For the name of the section, enter **hollow_section**.

8. For the beam section, assign the **Hollow Circle**.

9. For the external radius, enter **0.5** and for the internal radius, enter **0.2**.

10. Return to the Beam Definition dialog box.

11. Click **OK** to create the beams. The model displays as shown in Figure 10–49.

Figure 10–49

Task 3 - Create two beam elements on datum points.

1. Click 📐 (Beam). The Beam Definition dialog box opens.

2. In the *Name* field, enter **beam1_2**.

3. Expand the References drop-down list and select **Point-Point**.

4. Select **PNT1** and **PNT2**.

5. For the material for the beam, select **STEEL**.

6. In the *Y Direction* area, in the *X* field, enter **0**, in the *Y* field, enter **0**, and in the *Z* field, enter **1**.

7. Accept the default **hollow_section** beam section.

8. Click **OK** to create the beam. The model displays as shown in Figure 10–50.

© 2017, ASCENT - Center for Technical Knowledge®

Figure 10–50

9. Repeat Steps 1 to 8 to create a beam element between PNT2 and PNT4. For the name of the beam, enter **beam2_4**. The model displays as shown in Figure 10–51.

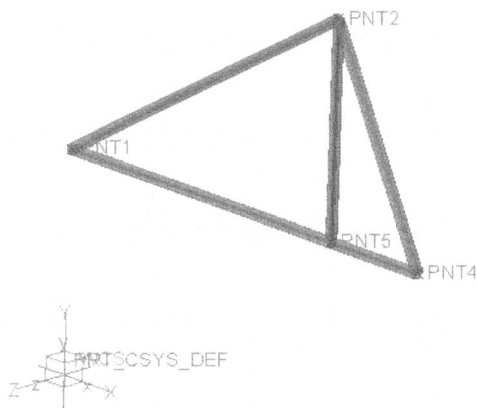

Figure 10–51

Task 4 - Create the spring elements.

In this task, you will create two spring elements: one between PNT2 and PNT3 and another between PNT0 and PNT4.

1. In the *Idealizations* group, click ≋ (Spring). The Spring Definition dialog box opens as shown in Figure 10–52.

Figure 10–52

2. In the *Name* field, enter **Spring2_3**.

3. Expand the References drop-down list and accept the default option.

4. Select **PNT2** and **PNT3**.

5. In the *Extensional Stiffness* field, enter **2500**.

6. Click **OK** in the Spring Definition dialog box. A **Spring** icon displays between PNT2 and PNT3, as shown in Figure 10–53.

© 2017, ASCENT - Center for Technical Knowledge®

Figure 10–53

7. In the *Idealizations* group, click 🖾 (Spring). The Spring Definition dialog box opens.

8. In the *Name* field, enter **Spring0_4**.

9. Expand the References drop-down list and accept the default option.

10. Select the **PNT0** and **PNT4**.

11. In the *Extensional Stiffness* field, enter **1500**.

12. Click **OK** in the Spring Definition dialog box. A **Spring** icon displays between PNT0 and PNT4, as shown in Figure 10–54.

Figure 10–54

Task 5 - Create the mass element on PNT0.

1. In the *Idealizations* area, click ⚖ (Mass). The Mass Definition dialog box opens as shown in Figure 10–55.

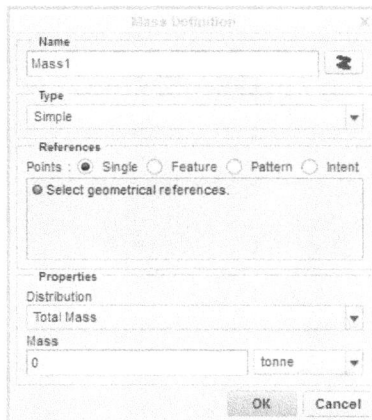

Figure 10–55

2. In the *Name* field, enter **mass_1**.

3. Select **PNT0**.

4. In the *Mass* field, enter **10**.

5. Click **OK**. The **Mass** icon displays at PNT0, as shown in Figure 10–56.

Figure 10–56

© 2017, ASCENT - Center for Technical Knowledge®

Task 6 - Apply the weight load to the model.

1. In the *Home* tab, click ⬚ (Gravity). The Gravity dialog box opens.

2. In the *Name* field, enter **gravity**.

3. For *Member of Set*, accept the default **LoadSet1** option.

1G of acceleration is **386 in/sec^2**

4. In the dialog box, in the *Acceleration* area, in the *Y* field, enter **-386**.

5. Click **OK** to finish defining the gravity load. The model displays as shown in Figure 10–57.

Figure 10–57

Task 7 - Apply the constraints.

The beams are cantilevered out from a wall.

In this task, you will apply the constraints to PNT3, PNT1, and PNT0.

1. For the name of the constraint for PNT3 and PNT1, enter **const1**. Fix all of the translation and rotations.

2. For the name of the constraint for PNT0, enter **const2**. Leave translation in the Y-direction free, and constrain all other translations and rotations. This way, the point only moves in the Y-direction. The model displays as shown in Figure 10–58.

Figure 10–58

Task 8 - Define the measures.

1. In the *Home* tab, click ⟋ (Measures). In the Measures dialog box that opens, click **New**. The Measure Definition dialog box opens, as shown in Figure 10–59.

Figure 10–59

© 2017, ASCENT - Center for Technical Knowledge®

2. Name the measure **PNT0**.

3. Select **Displacement** in the Quantity drop-down list, and then select **Y** in the Component drop-down list.

4. Select **At Point** in the Spatial Evaluation drop-down list. Click

   ▷ (Select) and then select datum point **PNT0**. The Measure Definition dialog box displays, as shown in Figure 10–60.

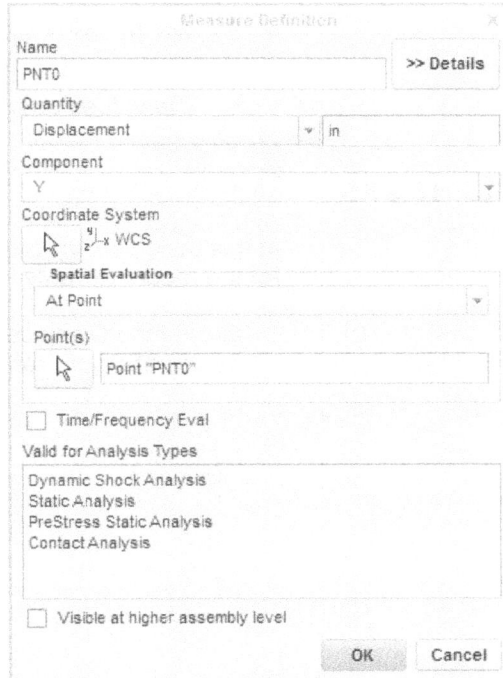

Figure 10–60

5. Click **OK** to complete the measure.

6. Repeat Steps 1 through 5 to create displacement measures in the Y-direction for datum points PNT2 and PNT4. Name the measures **PNT2** and **PNT4**.

Summary

In the previous tasks, you created the simulation entities needed to analyze your model. In the following tasks, you will set the analysis type and the convergence method and run the analysis.

Analysis Tasks

Task 9 - Set up and run an analysis.

1. Set up a Multi-Pass Adaptive static analysis. In the *Polynomial Order* field, enter **9** and in the *Limits* area, in the *Percent Convergence* field, enter **10**.

2. For the name of the analysis, enter **frame**.

3. Run the analysis.

4. Extract the following information from the Run Status window:
   - The pass number on which the analysis converged.
   - The values obtained for the user-defined measures.

Results Tasks

Task 10 - Display the results.

In this task, you will create and display a deformation animation for the model to verify the applied boundary conditions.

1. Create the Displacement Magnitude animation plot. The deformation at Frame 5 displays as shown in Figure 10–61.

Figure 10–61

2. Start the animation. Do the applied boundary conditions behave correctly?

3. Exit the Results. Save and close the model.

© 2017, ASCENT - Center for Technical Knowledge®

Practice 10d | Bracket Supported by Rubber Bushings

Practice Objectives

- Create Springs.
- Set up and run analysis.
- Display results.

In this practice, you will set up and run a static analysis of the bracket shown in Figure 10–62, with minimum instruction.

The end holes of the bracket are fixed to a rigid foundation, while the middle two holes are supported by rubber bushings in the vertical direction. The bracket is loaded in the horizontal direction at the two holes in the vertical flange.

Figure 10–62

Task 1 - Prepare the model for analysis.

1. Open **xbracket.prt** and launch Creo Simulate.
2. Apply the **AL2014** material to the part.

3. Fully constrain the inside surfaces of the two end holes, as shown in Figure 10–63.

Figure 10–63

Rubber bushings provide compliant supports to the middle holes, which is simulated with Springs.

4. For the two middle holes, create two **To Ground** springs, as shown in Figure 10–64. Use **PNT0** as the reference for the 1st spring, and **PNT1** for the 2nd spring. For both springs, use **10000 lbf/in** translational stiffness in WCS X-direction.

Figure 10–64

5. To connect PNT0 and PNT1 to the holes, create two Rigid Links, one for each hole. For each Rigid Link, select the point and the inside surface of the hole as the references, as shown in Figure 10–65.

Figure 10–65

© 2017, ASCENT - Center for Technical Knowledge®

6. Apply **1000lbs** combined load in -Y direction to the holes in the vertical flange, as shown in Figure 10–66.

1000lbs load in -Y direction on both holes

Figure 10–66

Task 2 - Set up and run static analysis.

1. Create and run a new Single-Pass Adaptive static analysis. Name it **spring_mount**.

Task 3 - Examine the analysis results.

1. Display and animate the **Displacement Magnitude** fringe plot.

   - Do the springs properly simulate compliant supports on the middle holes?

2. Display the **von Mises Stress** plot.
   - In which area in the model are the stresses at maximum?
   - Would you expect the area of maximum stress to move to a different location if rubber bushings with lower stiffness were used?

Task 4 - (Optional) Solve the analysis without compliant supports.

1. Delete Springs and Rigid Links from the model.

2. Fully constrain the two middle holes.

3. Create and run a new Single-Pass analysis. Name it **rigid_mount**.

4. Compare the results with the **spring_mount** analysis.

© 2017, ASCENT - Center for Technical Knowledge®

Chapter 11

Fasteners and Rigid Links

When analyzing mechanical assemblies, a proper simulation of the connections and various interactions between the parts is of critical importance.

Learning Objectives in this Chapter

- Understand the use of rigid links in Creo Simulate.
- Create rigid links.
- Understand fastener connections in Creo Simulate.
- Create fastener connections.

11.1 Rigid Links

A Rigid Link connects geometric entities in your model, such as surfaces, edges, or points, so they remain rigidly connected during the analysis. Rigid Links are useful for the idealization of a moving rigid structure attached to the model. The movement of the rigid structure might be part of the loading and specified by the user, or might be produced by loading on the main part of the model.

An example is shown in Figure 11–1. The heat sink/integrated circuit (HS/IC) package is bonded to the printed circuit board (PCB). The heat sink is made of aluminum, therefore, it is much stiffer than the thin PCB, which is made of plastic. The task is to determine the natural frequencies and natural modes of vibration for the assembly, using Modal analysis in Creo Simulate.

Figure 11–1

It is critical to preserve all of the masses in the system in the Modal analysis. Therefore, the mass of the HS/IC package must be included in the simulation. One option might be to model the mass by meshing the HS/IC package with solid elements and applying the material. However, a more computationally efficient approach would be to simulate the mass of the HS/IC package with a concentrated Mass located at the CoG of the package, then connecting the Mass with the PCB using a Rigid Link, as shown in Figure 11–2.

Figure 11–2

© 2017, ASCENT - Center for Technical Knowledge®

Additionally, rigid links can be used to connect two or more parts at selected surfaces.

When using rigid links, you should be aware of the following:

- The connected entities move together as one rigid body.

- The connected entities cannot deform, but the rigid body can move as a whole.

Creating Rigid Links

Use the following steps to create a rigid link:

1. In the *Refine Model* tab, click 🗐 (Rigid Link) to open the Rigid Link Definition dialog box as shown in Figure 11–3.

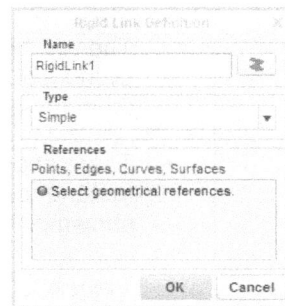

Figure 11–3

2. (Optional) Enter a name.
3. Expand the Type drop-down list and select **Simple** or **Advanced**.

    - The Advanced type enables you to control the independent degrees of freedom. Requires an Advanced Creo Simulate license.

4. Select the geometrical entities to connect (hold <Ctrl> to multi-select).

    - You can connect the surfaces or edges of your model with a free point that is not otherwise associated with the model geometry.

5. Click **OK**.

11.2 Fasteners

Fasteners in Creo Simulate simulate bolt or screw connections joining any two parts in an assembly. The connection is intended to simulate the load path within the assembly, as well as the amount of load carried by each bolt or screw. An important feature of the Fastener connection is the ability to apply the bolt preload on the connection.

Prerequisites

The model with fastener connections must meet the following conditions:

- The model must be an assembly. Any given fastener must pass through two separate components.

- The two holes participating in a fastener definition must be cylindrical and perpendicular to the part surface. The holes must have approximately the same diameter.

- There should not be any intervening geometry in the fastener's path. An example of an intervening geometry is shown in Figure 11–4.

Figure 11–4

Part Separation

In the real world, the parts connected together by a fastener are not typically bonded over the entire interface surface, yet they do not interpenetrate when a preload or external load is applied.

To ensure that the surfaces are not bonded, Creo Simulate automatically creates a Free Interface between the two parts participating in the fastener definition.

To ensure that the two parts do not interpenetrate, you can use either of the following methods:

© 2017, ASCENT - Center for Technical Knowledge®

- Define the Contact Interface between the parts (note that the Contact Interface in this case takes precedence over the automatic Free Interface). This method is the most accurate, but requires longer computation time due to the non-linear nature of the Contact Interface.

- Enable Creo Simulate to automatically use a separation spring to ensure non-penetration. This method has faster computation times, but does not permit the parts to separate, even if they would naturally do so under the applied loading.

If the automatic separation method is used, the following is done by Creo Simulate behind the scenes:

- Two annular separation areas on the contacting surfaces are automatically created, as shown in Figure 11–5. The outer diameter of the separation areas is called the *Separation Test Diameter*.

- A very stiff distributed linear spring (called the *Separation Spring*) is created between the annular areas. The stiffness of the spring ensures that the parts do not interpenetrate within the separation areas. However, since the separation spring is a linear spring, it does not let the parts separate, even if they are supposed to, under the given loading.

Part A

Part B

Separation areas

Figure 11–5

If you use the separation spring method to ensure the non-penetration of the fastened parts, it is strongly recommended that after the analysis run, you verify that all of the separation springs are in compression. If some separation springs are found to be in tension, they should be turned off, and the analysis re-run.

Fastener Preload

Creo Simulate models the fastener preload by applying enforced displacements, so the nut and bolt head areas move toward each other, which tightens the parts together. Ideally, the amount of this prescribed displacement should produce axial force in the fastener that is equal to the required preload.

The distance that the nut and bolt head areas should move toward each other to produce the required preload is a complex mechanical and mathematical problem, whose solution depends on various factors (such as model geometry, fastener geometry, material properties, etc.).

By default, Creo Simulate applies the preload value on the undeformed geometry of the fastened parts. However, when the material of the parts deforms under the bolt preload, the compressive force that the fastener applies on the parts relaxes. Therefore, in this scenario, the actual preload may be substantially lower than the value you specified.

To have the fastener apply the specified preload, you should activate the **Account for Stiffness** option in the Fastener Definition dialog box. Once you do this, Creo Simulate executes the analysis in the following steps:

1. The base analysis is run, with the preloads applied on the undeformed geometry. External loads are not applied. The resulting preloads are recorded and reported in the Run Status summary.
2. The preloads are scaled. For example, if a 100N preload was applied to a fastener and the actual preload came out as 80N, the scaling factor is 100/80 = 1.25.
3. The second and the final analysis is run, now with the scaled preloads. All the external loads are also applied.

This method results in the actual preloads being very accurate, but requiring a longer computation time as the analysis is run twice.

© 2017, ASCENT - Center for Technical Knowledge®

Creating Fasteners

Use the following steps to create a Fastener:

1. In the *Refine Model* tab, click ⚓ (Fastener) to open the Fastener Definition dialog box as shown in Figure 11–6.

Figure 11–6

2. (Optional) Enter a fastener name.
3. Select **Connecting Solids** or **Connecting Shells**.
4. Select the **Fastener Type**.
5. Selected the fastener **References.**
6. In the *Properties* area, select the required options as shown in the following table.
7. Click **OK** to complete.

Option	Description
Connecting Solids	Creates a fastener connecting two solid parts.
Connecting Shells	Creates a fastener connecting two shell parts.

Fastener Type	• **Bolt:** The first edge you select is associated with the head of the bolt, and the second edge is associated with the nut. • **Screw:** The first edge you select is associated with the head of the screw,and the second edge is associated with the other end of the screw.
References	For the **Connecting Solids** type, select the circular edges of the holes. For the **Connecting Shells** type, select either the hole edges or the datum points.
Stiffness	• **Using diameter and material:** Defines the fastener stiffness using the fastener diameter and material. By default, the fastener is assumed to have the same diameter as the hole. • **Using spring stiffness property:** Defines the fastener stiffness using a spring property.
Fastener Head and Nut Diameter	Defines the head and nut diameter for the fastener. For screws, there is no nut, so the value applies to the screw head. By default, the value is assumed to be 1.7 times the bolt diameter.
Fix Separation	Creates a separation spring to prevent interpenetration of the parts over the annular separation areas.
Separation Test Diameter	Defines the diameter of the annular separation areas. By default, the value is assumed to be twice the bolt diameter.
Frictionless Interface	If enabled, the parts are permitted to slide in a tangential direction over the separation areas.
Include Preload	Enables a preload for the fastener. Not available for the **Connecting Shells** type.
Account for Stiffness	Activates automatic scaling of the preloads as to account for the deformation of the fastened parts.
Preload Force	Defines the compressive force on the parts that results from tightening the bolt or screw.

© 2017, ASCENT - Center for Technical Knowledge®

Fastener Measures

Creo Simulate automatically creates several measures for each fastener. The fastener measures are as follows:

Measure	Description
axial_force	Axial force in a fastener.
axial_stress	Axial stress in a fastener. Calculated for the specified fastener diameter.
shear_force	Shear force for a fastener.
shear_stress	Shear stress in a fastener. Calculated for the specified fastener diameter.
bending_moment	Bending moment in a fastener.
bending_stress	Bending stress in a fastener. Calculated for the specified fastener diameter.
torsion_moment	Torsional moment in a fastener. Calculated if **Frictionless Interface** is enabled.
torsion_stress	Torsional stress in a fastener. Calculated for the specified fastener diameter.
sep_stress	Normal stress over the separation area.
intf_bend_momt	Bending moment calculated for the separation area.
intf_norm_forc	Normal force in the separation area.
intf_shr_forc	Shear force in the separation area.
intf_tors_momt	Torsional moment over the separation area.

Practice 11a

Modal Analysis of a PCB Assembly

Practice Objectives

- Create Masses.
- Create Rigid Links.
- Set up and run a Modal analysis.

In this practice, you will set up and run a Modal analysis for a PCB assembly as shown in Figure 11–7. The PCB is made of plastic, while the heat sink is made of aluminum and is much stiffer than the PCB. You will use a Mass and a Rigid Link to model the heat sink and the IC package.

Figure 11–7

Modeling Tasks

Task 1 - Open the part in Creo Parametric.

1. Open **pcb.asm** assembly in Creo Parametric. The model displays as shown in Figure 11–8.

Figure 11–8

2. Ensure that the unit system is set to **mmNs**.

© 2017, ASCENT - Center for Technical Knowledge®

Task 2 - Create a simplified representation.

The heat sink/IC package is simulated with a mass and a rigid link. In this task, you will create a simplified representation to exclude the heat sink and the IC geometry from the analysis model.

1. In the *View* tab, click 📷 (View Manager). The View Manager dialog box opens as shown in Figure 11–9.

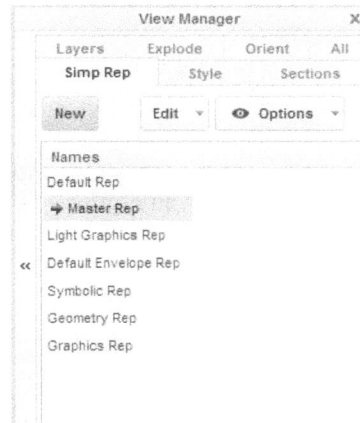

Figure 11–9

2. Click **New**. Rename the new representation as **AnslRep** and press <Enter>. The Edit:ANLSREP dialog box opens as shown in Figure 11–10.

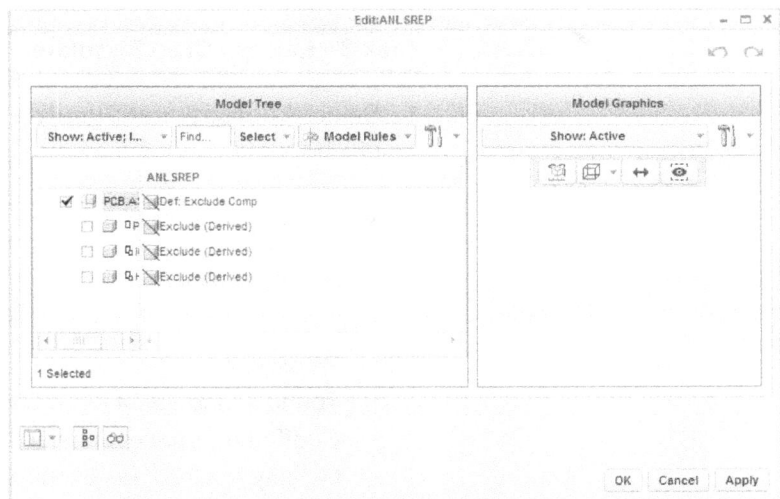

Figure 11–10

3. Set **PCB.ASM** and **PCB.PRT** to **Master Rep**, and **IC.PRT** and **HS.PRT** to **Exclude**. The Edit:ANLSREP dialog box updates as shown in Figure 11–11.

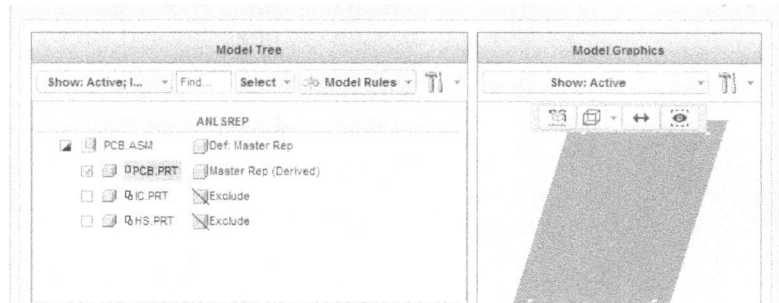

Figure 11–11

4. Click **OK** and **Close** to finish. The model displays as shown in Figure 11–12.

Figure 11–12

Task 3 - Launch Creo Simulate.

1. Select **Applications>Simulate** to launch the Creo Simulate environment.

Task 4 - Apply the material.

The model's material properties should be as stated.

1. Assign **NYLON** to the PCB part. The following values are the default material properties for NYLON:

   - Poisson = 0.4
   - Young's modulus = 4000.34 MPa
   - Coeff of thermal expansion = 7.9992e-5 /C
   - Density = 1.20014e-9 tonne/mm^3

© 2017, ASCENT - Center for Technical Knowledge®

Task 5 - Create a surface region.

In this task, you will create a surface region to model the area over which the heat sink/IC package is bonded to the PCB.

1. In the *Refine Model* tab, click ⬚ (Sketch) and create a sketch on the top surface of the PCB (in the Y-direction up) with the dimensions shown in Figure 11–13.

Figure 11–13

2. The model displays as shown in Figure 11–14.

Figure 11–14

3. In the *Refine Model* tab, click ⬚ (Surface Region).

4. In the Select a Component dialog box, select the **PCB** part and click **OK**. The Surface Region dashboard displays as shown in Figure 11–15.

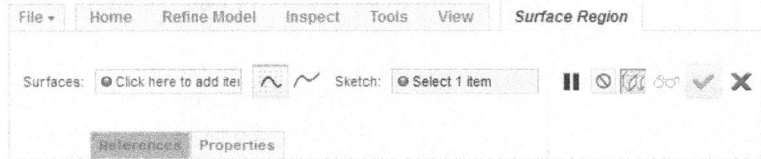

Figure 11–15

5. Activate the *Surfaces* field and select the top surface of the PCB.

6. Click ~ (Curve), activate the *Chain* field, and select the sketch. The model displays as shown in Figure 11–16.

Figure 11–16

7. Click ✓ (Apply Changes) to complete the surface region.

Task 6 - Create shell pairs.

The PCB thickness is 1mm.

1. Define the shell pairs using the **Automatic Detection** tool, with a *Characteristic Thickness* of **1**.

Task 7 - Create a datum point.

In this task, you will create an assembly datum point located at the CoG of the heat sink/IC package.

1. In the *Refine Model* tab, expand ×ˣ (Point) and select ×⁎ (Offset Coordinate System).

2. Click **OK** in the Select a Component dialog box.

© 2017, ASCENT - Center for Technical Knowledge®

*You can use **File> Prepare>Model Properties** to calculate the CoG coordinates.*

3. In the Datum Point dialog box that opens, select **ASM_DEF_CSYS** as the reference, and enter the new point coordinates as shown in Figure 11–17.

Figure 11–17

4. Click **OK** to finish.

___

Task 8 - Create a rigid link.

___

In this task, you will create a rigid link to connect the CoG of the heat sink/IC assembly with the surface region on the PCB.

1. In the *Refine Model* tab, click 🗐 (Rigid Link). The Rigid Link Definition dialog box opens as shown in Figure 11–18.

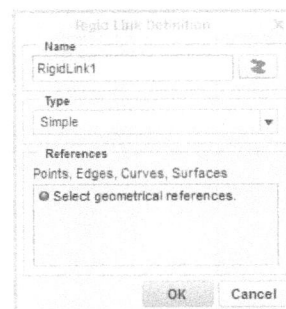

Figure 11–18

2. Select both the **APNT0** point and the surface region (hold down <Ctrl> to multi-select). Click **OK** to finish. The model displays as shown in Figure 11–19.

Figure 11–19

Task 9 - Create a mass.

1. In the *Refine Model* tab, click 🗮 (Mass). The Mass Definition dialog box opens as shown in Figure 11–20.

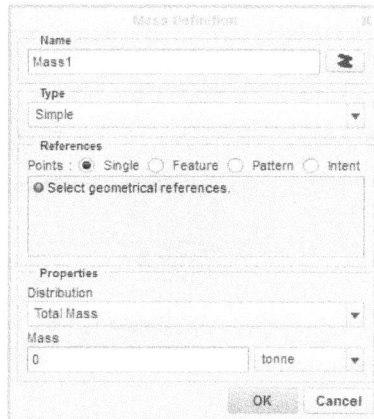

Figure 11–20

The mass of the heat sink/IC package is 130g, (i.e., 1.3e-4 tonne).

2. For the *Name*, enter **HS** and in the *Mass* field, enter **1.3e-4**. For the *Reference*, select the **APNT0** point. The Mass Definition dialog box opens as shown in Figure 11–21.

© 2017, ASCENT - Center for Technical Knowledge®

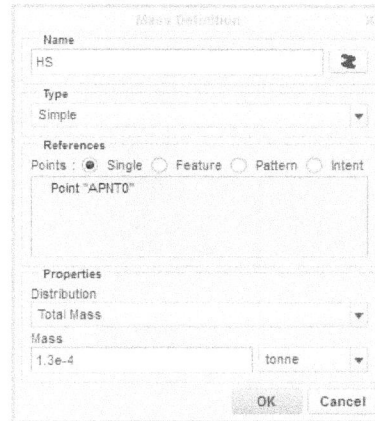

Figure 11–21

3. Click **OK**. The model opens as shown in Figure 11–22.

Figure 11–22

Task 10 - Apply constraints.

1. Constrain the edges of the four holes in all of the translations. The model displays as shown in Figure 11–23.

Figure 11–23

Analysis Tasks | **Task 11 - Set up and run a Modal analysis**

1. Click ⚒ (Analyses and Studies). In the Analyses and Design Studies dialog box, select **File>New Modal**. The Modal Analysis Definition dialog box opens as shown in Figure 11–24.

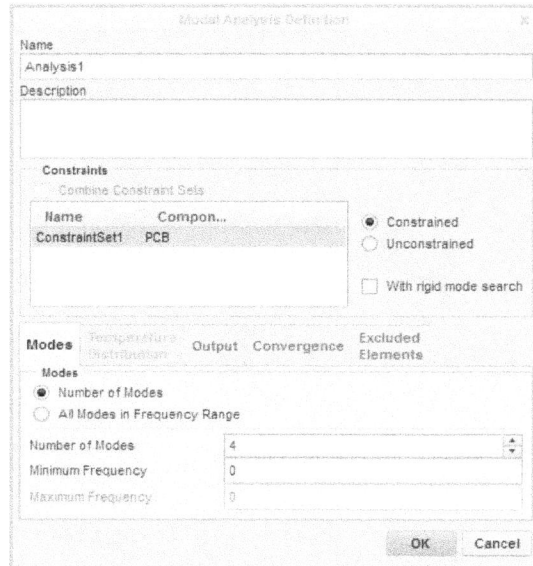

Figure 11–24

2. For the analysis name, enter **PCB**. Accept all of the other defaults and click **OK**.

3. Run the analysis.

© 2017, ASCENT - Center for Technical Knowledge®

Results Tasks

Task 12 - Display the results.

In this task, you will create and animate the Displacement Magnitude fringe plots for the calculated modes of vibration.

1. In the Analyses and Design Studies dialog box, click
   (Review Results). The Result Window Definition dialog box opens as shown in Figure 11–25.

Figure 11–25

2. In the *Name* field, enter **mode1**.

3. Select the *Display Options* tab and select the required options as shown in Figure 11–26.

Figure 11–26

4. Display and animate the result plot. Step through the animation to the Frame 3, as shown in Figure 11–27.

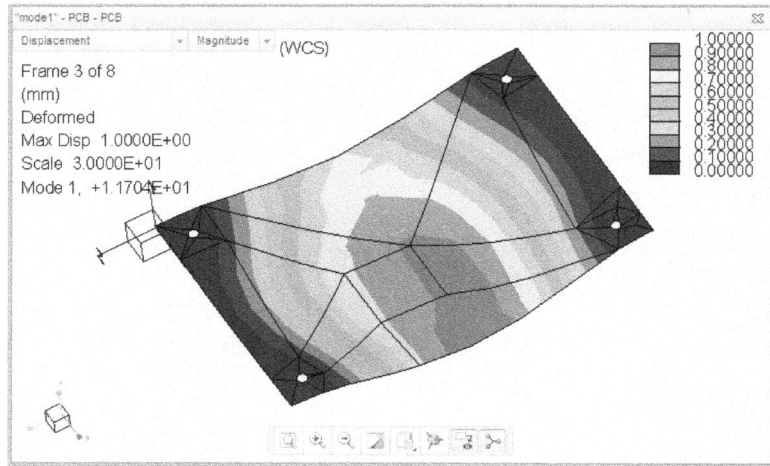

Figure 11–27

Note that the surface region area remains flat through the deformation. The area has been rendered effectively undeformable, due to the Rigid Link applied to the surface region.

5. Create, animate, and display the Displacement Magnitude plot for the mode 2. In the *Name* field, enter **mode2**.

6. In the *Include* column, select the second checkbox (as shown in Figure 11–28), and clear the first checkbox.

Figure 11–28

© 2017, ASCENT - Center for Technical Knowledge®

7. Display the **mode_2** fringe plot. Step through the animation to the Frame 3, as shown in Figure 11–29.

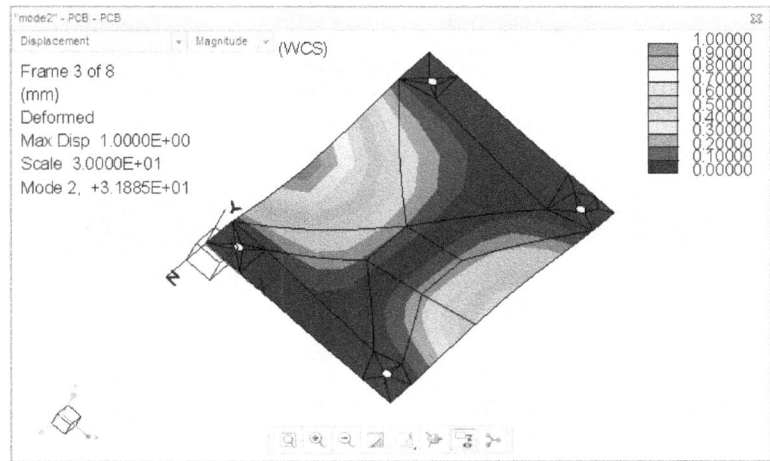

Figure 11–29

8. Create, animate, and display the Displacement Magnitude plots for Modes 3 and 4. Examine the motion of the surface region area in all of the animations.

9. Exit the Results. Save and close the model.

Practice 11b	# Static Analysis of a Mixed Solid/ Shell/Beam Model

Practice Objectives

- Use a combination of Solids, Shells, and Beams in an analysis model.
- Connect a Beam to a Solid using a rigid link.

In this practice, you will set up and run a static analysis of a bracket assembly as shown in Figure 11–30. The shaft is press-fit into the bracket.

Figure 11–30

You will use the following idealizations for the parts in the model:

- The shaft is modeled with a beam.

- The cylindrical boss, into which the shaft is press-fit, is modeled with solids.

- The bracket is modeled with shells.

You will connect the beam to the solid using a rigid link.

© 2017, ASCENT - Center for Technical Knowledge®

Modeling Tasks

Task 1 - Open the assembly.

1. Open **bracket_shaft.asm** in Creo Parametric. The unshaded model displays as shown in Figure 11–31.

Figure 11–31

2. Switch to the Simulate application.

Task 2 - Create a beam idealization.

1. Open **shaft.prt** in a new window.

2. Create two datum points as shown in Figure 11–32.

PNT0 references the shaft axis and this annular shoulder surface

PNT1 references the shaft axis and the end circular surface

Figure 11–32

3. Save and close **shaft.prt**. Return to the assembly window. The assembly model displays as shown in Figure 11–33.

Figure 11–33

4. In the *Refine Model* tab, click (Beam). The Beam Definition dialog box opens as shown in Figure 11–34.

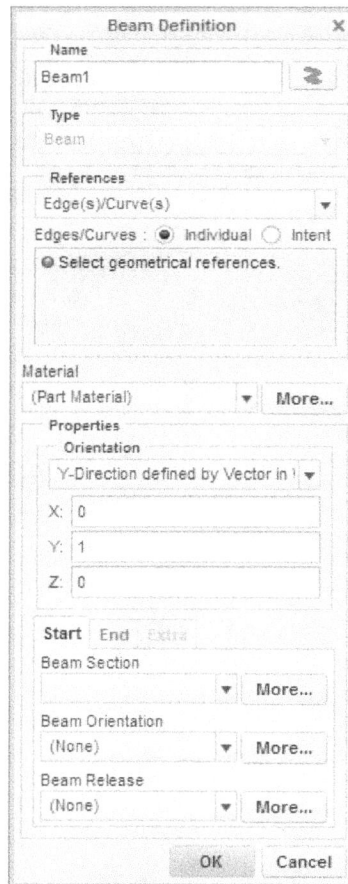

Figure 11–34

© 2017, ASCENT - Center for Technical Knowledge®

5. In the *Name* field, enter **beam_shaft**.

6. Expand the References drop-down list and select **Point-Point**.

7. Select **PNT0** and **PNT1**.

8. In the *Material* area, click **More**. The Materials dialog box opens.

9. In the *Materials in Library* area, select **STEEL**. Click ▶▶▶ (Add Material) to transfer STEEL to the *Materials in Model* area.

The model's material properties should be as stated.

10. Select ✎ (Edit) to check the material properties. The following values are the default material properties for HS-low-alloy steel (STEEL):
    - Poisson = 0.27
    - Young's modulus = 199948 MPa

11. Click **OK** in the Material Definition dialog box and in the Materials dialog box. STEEL displays in the *Material* area in the Beam Definition dialog box.

12. In the *Orientation* area, accept the default X-, Y-, and Z-values.

13. Next to the Beam Section drop-down list, click **More**. The Beam Sections dialog box opens as shown in Figure 11–35.

Figure 11–35

14. Click **New**. The Beam Section Definition dialog box opens as shown in Figure 11–36.

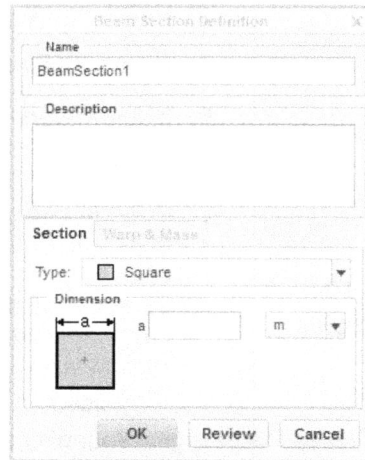

Figure 11–36

15. In the *Name* field, enter **circ_section**.

16. Expand the Type drop-down list and select **Solid Circle**. In the *R* field, enter **15**, as shown in Figure 11–37.

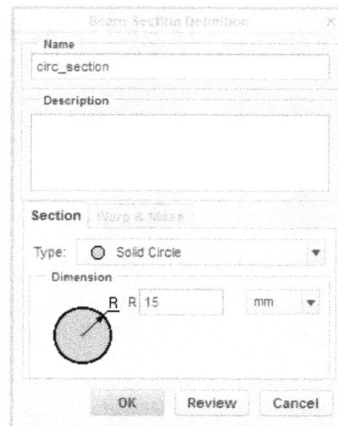

Figure 11–37

17. Click **OK** twice to close the Beam Section Definition dialog box and the Beam Sections dialog box.

© 2017, ASCENT - Center for Technical Knowledge®

18. Click **OK** to close the Beam Definition dialog box. In the wireframe mode, the model displays as shown in Figure 11–38.

Figure 11–38

Task 3 - Create shell pairs.

The bracket thickness is 5mm.

1. Use the **Detect Shell Pairs** tool with the *Characteristic Thickness* set to **5** to define the shell pairs for the bracket part.

Task 4 - Apply the material.

In this task, you will apply material to the bracket part. Applying material to the shaft part is not required for the following reasons:

- If you apply material to the shaft part, Creo Simulate will assume that the intent is to model the shaft with solid elements, and will create a solid mesh accordingly. While the intent of this simulation is to model the shaft with a beam idealization.

- The material has already been applied to the beam idealization in Task 2.

1. Assign **STEEL** to the bracket part only.

Task 5 - Mesh the model.

1. Mesh the model using the **All with Properties** option. The mesh displays as shown in Figure 11–39.

Figure 11–39

Note that the shaft has been meshed as a beam (purple line), the circular boss has been meshed with solids (blue), and the rest of the bracket has been meshed with shells (green).

2. Exit the AutoGEM dialog box without saving the mesh.

Task 6 - Create a rigid link.

In this task, you will create a rigid link to connect the end of the beam to the inside surface of the hole in the bracket.

1. In the *Refine Model* tab, click 🔳 (Rigid Link). The Rigid Link Definition dialog box opens as shown in Figure 11–40.

Note that the end of the beam idealization at PNT0 is in the middle of the hole in the boss, therefore, is not yet attached to the solid and shell elements that model the bracket.

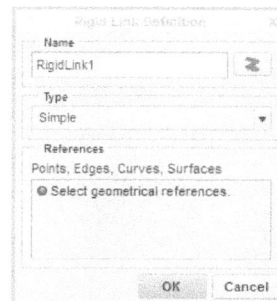

Figure 11–40

© 2017, ASCENT - Center for Technical Knowledge®

2. Select both the PNT0 point and the inside surface of the hole into which the shaft is inserted (hold down <Ctrl> to multi-select). Use the **Pick from List** option to select the surface of the hole.

3. Click **OK** to finish. The model displays as shown in Figure 11–41.

Figure 11–41

Task 7 - Apply loads and constraints.

1. Apply force 200N to the PNT1 point in negative Y-direction.

2. Constrain the edges of the four holes in the bracket part in all of the translations. Ensure that you only select edges on the outside surface of the bracket.

3. The model displays as shown in Figure 11–42.

Figure 11–42

Analysis Tasks

Task 8 - Set up and run a static analysis.

1. Set up a Multi-Pass Adaptive static analysis. For the *Name*, enter **bracket_shaft**. In the *Polynomial Order* field, enter **9** and in the *Limits* area, in the *Percent Convergence* field, enter **10**.

2. Run the analysis.

3. In the Analyses and Design Studies dialog box, click ▤ (Status) and extract the following information from the Run Status window:

   - Analysis converges on pass 9.
   - Stress error is 14.7% of the maximum principal stress, as shown in Figure 11–43.

```
RMS Stress Error Estimates:

Load Set          Stress Error   % of Max Prin Str
---------------   ------------   -----------------
LoadSet1           6.35e+00        14.7% of  4.33e+01
```

Figure 11–43

Results Tasks

Task 9 - Display the results.

In this task, you will create and display a von Mises stress fringe plot and a deformation animation for the model to verify the applied boundary conditions.

1. Create the displacement magnitude animation plot.

2. Start the animation. Verify whether the applied boundary conditions behave correctly.

© 2017, ASCENT - Center for Technical Knowledge®

3. Create an undeformed von Mises stress fringe plot. Change the *Legend minimum* to **0** and *maximum* to **40**. The result plot displays as shown in Figure 11–44.

Figure 11–44

4. Locate and examine the high stress areas in the model.

5. Exit the Results. Save and close the model.

Practice 11c | Fasteners with Preload

Practice Objectives

- Create bolted connections in solid models.
- Apply bolt preload.
- Understand how to control and adjust preload accuracy.

In this practice, you will set up and run a static analysis of the assembly shown in Figure 11–45. The two plates in the assembly are bolted together through the three holes, with a preload of 500N on each bolt.

Figure 11–45

You will use the Fastener connection to model the bolted joints. You will solve the model in two iterations:

- In the first analysis, you will only apply preloads on the bolts, without applying any other loads in the model. The objective of this analysis is to check how accurately the preloads are simulated, and to correct the amount of preload applied, if needed.

- In the second and final analysis, you will solve the model with the corrected preloads, and with all of the other loads in the model fully applied.

© 2017, ASCENT - Center for Technical Knowledge®

Modeling Tasks

Task 1 - Open the model.

1. Open **fastener_ex1.asm** in Creo Parametric. The model displays as shown in Figure 11–46.

Figure 11–46

2. Select **Applications>Simulate** to switch to the Simulate environment.

Task 2 - Apply the material.

The material properties should be as stated.

1. Assign **STEEL** to both parts. The following values are the default material properties for HS-low-alloy steel (STEEL):
   - **Poisson:** 0.27
   - Young's modulus: 199948 MPa

Task 3 - Create the fasteners.

1. In the *Refine Model* tab, click 🔩 (Fastener). The Fastener Definition dialog box opens as shown in Figure 11–47.

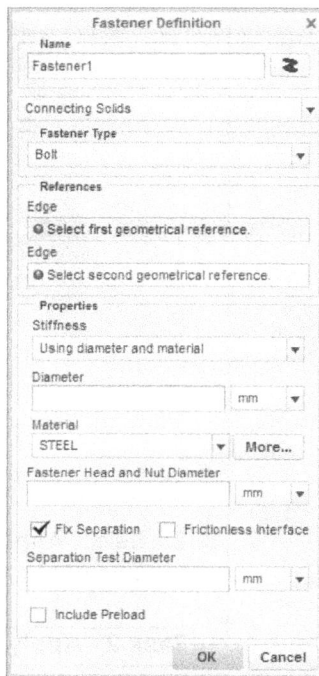

Figure 11–47

2. Select the circular edge of the top hole in the **hinge2** part as the first reference, as shown in Figure 11–48.

Figure 11–48

© 2017, ASCENT - Center for Technical Knowledge®

3. Select the circular edge of the top hole in the **plate** part as the second reference, as shown in Figure 11–49.

Select this edge

Figure 11–49

4. Select the **Include Preload** option. In the *Preload Force* field, enter **500**. The Fastener Definition dialog box opens as shown in Figure 11–50.

Figure 11–50

5. Click **OK**. A warning message box displays as shown in Figure 11–51, and the two contacting surfaces are highlighted.

Figure 11–51

Note that the message in the box informs you that the two contacting surfaces will not be bonded during the analysis, due to the application of the Fastener.

6. Click **OK** to close the message box. The model displays as shown in Figure 11–52.

Figure 11–52

7. Repeat Steps 1 to 6 to create Fasteners in the second and the third holes, as shown in Figure 11–53.

Figure 11–53

© 2017, ASCENT - Center for Technical Knowledge®

Task 4 - Apply the constraints.

1. Constrain the surface shown in Figure 11–54 in all of the translations.

Constrain this surface

Figure 11–54

Task 5 - Mesh the model.

1. Click ▦ (Mesh). In the AutoGEM dialog box that opens, select **Component Volumes** in the drop-down list, and select the **HINGE2** part.

2. Click **Create** and wait until meshing completes. Close the Diagnostics and the AutoGEM Summary boxes. The model displays as shown in Figure 11-55.

Figure 11–55

3. Click ⬚ (Simulation Display) and hide the Fasteners. Zoom in on the model and note the annular regions under the bolt heads that were created automatically for each Fastener, as shown in Figure 11–56.

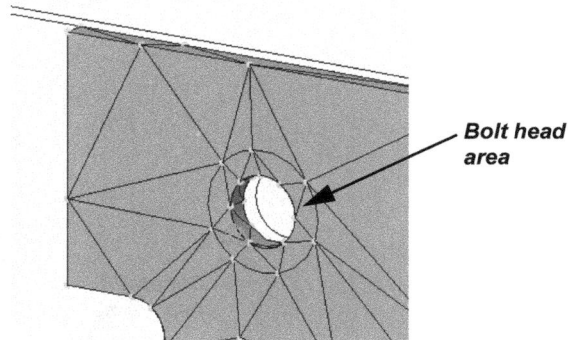

Bolt head area

Figure 11–56

4. Rotate the model. Note the annular separation areas around each fastener, as shown in Figure 11–57.

Separation area

Figure 11–57

5. In the AutoGEM dialog box, click **Delete**. In the drop-down list, select **All with Properties** and click **Create** to mesh both parts.

6. Save the mesh and close the AutoGEM dialog box.

7. Click ⬚ (Simulation Display) and unhide the Fasteners.

© 2017, ASCENT - Center for Technical Knowledge®

Analysis Tasks

Task 6 - Set up and run a static analysis.

In the preliminary analysis, you will solve the model without having any external loads applied. The objective is to test how the stiffness of the fastened parts affects the actual compressive force that a fastener applies on the model.

1. Set up a new static analysis, named **fastener1_preload**, with the options shown in Figure 11–58.

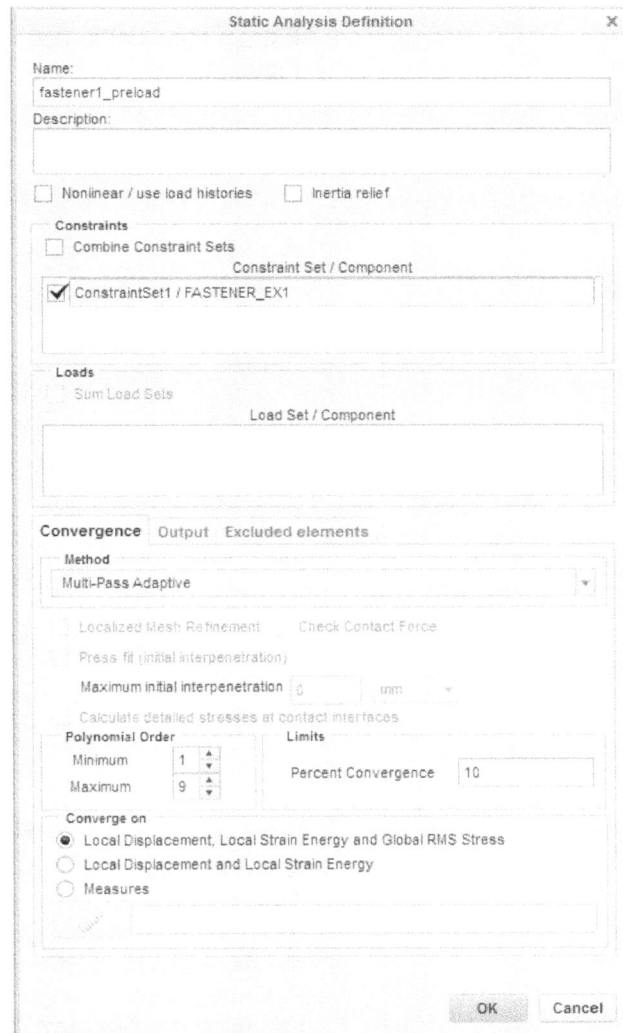

Figure 11–58

2. Run the analysis. It should converge on pass 6.

Task 7 - Check the fastener axial forces.

Since no external loads were applied in this analysis run, the force in the fasteners must be equal to the preloads that you applied in Task 3.

1. In the Analyses and Design Studies dialog box, click

    ![icon] (Status) to open the Run Status window, and scroll down to the *Measures* area.

2. Extract the axial forces in the fasteners, as shown in Figure 11–59.

Figure 11–59

Note that Creo Simulate did not get the preloads quite right. The required preloads were 500N, while the actual axial forces in the bolts are approximately 345N. This is because the **Account for Stiffness** option was not selected when the Fasteners were created in Task 3. In the next tasks, you will toggle on the **Account for Stiffness** option and re-run the analysis.

3. Close the Run Status window and the Analyses and Design Studies dialog box.

© 2017, ASCENT - Center for Technical Knowledge®

Modeling Tasks

Task 8 - Toggle on the Account for Stiffness option.

1. In the Model Tree, right-click on Fastener1 and select **Edit Definition**.

2. Select the **Account for Stiffness** checkbox, as shown in Figure 11–60.

Figure 11–60

3. Click **OK** to finish. Click **OK** in the warning message box that displays.

4. Repeat Steps 1 to 3 for the other two fasteners.

Analysis Tasks

Task 9 - Re-run the analysis.

1. Re-run the **fastener1_preload** analysis.

2. Click 📰 (Status) to open the Run Status window. Scroll down and note that the analysis began with running the Base Analysis, as shown in Figure 11-61.

```
Base Analysis to scale Fastener Preloads

    Measures:

        Name               Value        Convergence
        ----               -----        -----------
        max_beam_bending:      0.000000e+00      0.0%
        max_beam_tensile:      0.000000e+00      0.0%
        max_beam_torsion:      0.000000e+00      0.0%
        max_beam_total:        0.000000e+00      0.0%
        max_disp_mag:          2.085527e-04      2.5%
        max_disp_x:            3.431036e-05      0.5%
        max_disp_y:           -2.073626e-04      2.6%
        max_disp_z:           -2.417766e-05      0.4%
        max_prin_mag:         -3.193001e+00     14.0%
        max_rot_mag:           2.251730e-06      3.2%
        max_rot_x:             2.929513e-07      6.3%
        max_rot_y:             1.180592e-08      7.6%
        max_rot_z:            -2.235747e-06      3.2%
        max_stress_prin:       7.102858e-01      6.0%
        max_stress_vn:         2.944639e+00     17.4%
        max_stress_xx:        -1.111410e+00      0.2%
        max_stress_xy:         5.630621e-01      1.9%
        max_stress_xz:         4.038006e-01     18.6%
        max_stress_yy:        -3.183693e+00     14.3%
        max_stress_yz:        -6.111955e-01      4.1%
        max_stress_zz:        -1.078378e+00      4.7%
        min_stress_prin:      -3.193001e+00     14.0%
        strain_energy:         4.416058e-02      0.5%
        Fastener1_axial_force:    3.456047e+02      0.2%
        Fastener1_axial_stress:   4.400375e+00      0.2%
        Fastener1_bending_moment: 6.605752e-01     17.9%
        Fastener1_bending_stress: 6.728564e-03     17.9%
```

Figure 11–61

Note that the axial forces in the fasteners are exactly the same as in the first analysis run, when the **Account for Stiffness** option was off.

3. Scroll further down and note that there was also the 2nd analysis run: Analysis with Scaled Fastener Preloads, as shown in Figure 11-62.

```
Analysis with scaled Fastener Preloads and External loads

Static Analysis "fastener1_preload":

    Convergence Method: Multiple-Pass Adaptive
    Plotting Grid:      4

    Convergence Loop Log:                        (14:26:14)

    >> Pass  1 <<
        Calculating Element Equations            (14:26:14)
            Total Number of Equations:     1242
            Maximum Edge Order:               1
        Solving Equations                        (14:26:14)
        Post-Processing Solution                 (14:26:14)
        Calculating Disp and Stress Results      (14:26:14)
        Checking Convergence                     (14:26:16)
            Elements Not Converged:        1001
```

Figure 11–62

© 2017, ASCENT - Center for Technical Knowledge®

Task 10 - Check the fastener axial forces.

1. Scroll down to the *Measures* area. Note that the axial forces in the fasteners are now extremely close to the specified preload 500N, as shown in Figure 11-63.

```
strain_energy:             9.237553e-02      0.5%
Fastener1 axial force:     4.999998e+02      0.2%
Fastener1_axial_stress:    6.366195e+00      0.2%
Fastener1_bending_moment:  9.558530e-01     17.9%
Fastener1_bending_stress:  9.736239e-03     17.9%
Fastener1_intf_bend_momt:  7.507443e+00      1.0%
Fastener1_intf_norm_forc: -4.999941e+02      0.2%
Fastener1_intf_shr_forc:   4.453404e-01      7.1%
Fastener1_intf_tors_momt: -1.579677e+01      3.3%
Fastener1_sep_stress:      6.812626e-01     10.1%
Fastener1_shear_force:     5.075531e-02      9.1%
Fastener1_shear_stress:    6.462367e-04      9.1%
Fastener1_torsion_moment:  1.856835e-01     11.2%
Fastener1_torsion_stress:  9.456785e-04     11.2%
Fastener2 axial force:     4.999992e+02      0.2%
Fastener2_axial_stress:    6.366187e+00      0.2%
Fastener2_bending_moment:  1.141311e+00     23.0%
Fastener2_bending_stress:  1.162530e-02     23.0%
Fastener2_intf_bend_momt:  9.829514e+00      6.4%
Fastener2_intf_norm_forc: -5.000071e+02      0.2%
Fastener2_intf_shr_forc:   4.295910e-01      4.8%
Fastener2_intf_tors_momt: -2.543681e-01     27.8%
Fastener2_sep_stress:      7.084560e-01     20.8%
Fastener2_shear_force:     1.382126e-01      0.8%
Fastener2_shear_stress:    1.759777e-03      0.8%
Fastener2_torsion_moment: -1.367557e-02     89.1%
Fastener2_torsion_stress: -6.964913e-05     89.1%
Fastener3 axial force:     4.999996e+02      0.2%
Fastener3_axial_stress:    6.366192e+00      0.2%
Fastener3_bending_moment:  7.164811e-01      6.5%
Fastener3_bending_stress:  7.298016e-03      6.5%
Fastener3_intf_bend_momt:  7.335979e+00     10.5%
Fastener3_intf_norm_forc: -4.999974e+02      0.2%
Fastener3_intf_shr_forc:   4.182662e-01      3.6%
Fastener3_intf_tors_momt:  1.597891e+01      1.3%
Fastener3_sep_stress:      7.657714e-01     10.5%
Fastener3_shear_force:     3.471197e-02      9.7%
Fastener3_shear_stress:    4.419665e-04      9.7%
Fastener3_torsion_moment: -1.762464e-01     10.9%
Fastener3_torsion_stress: -8.976157e-04     10.9%
```

Figure 11–63

2. Close the Run Status dialog box and the Analyses and Design Studies dialog box.

Modeling Tasks

Task 11 - Apply the external loads.

1. Apply the force 100N in the Z-direction to the surface shown in Figure 11–64.

Load this surface

Figure 11–64

Analysis Tasks

Task 12 - Re-run the analysis.

1. Open the **fastener1_preload** analysis to edit it.

2. Select the **LoadSet1/FASTENER_EX1** option, as shown in Figure 11–65. This ensures that the external loads are now included in the analysis.

Figure 11–65

3. Run the analysis.

Results Tasks

Task 13 - Animate the model deformation.

1. Create the displacement magnitude animation plot.

2. Start the animation. Verify whether the applied boundary conditions behave correctly.

3. Step to Frame 5 of the animation. The result plot displays as shown in Figure 11–66.

© 2017, ASCENT - Center for Technical Knowledge®

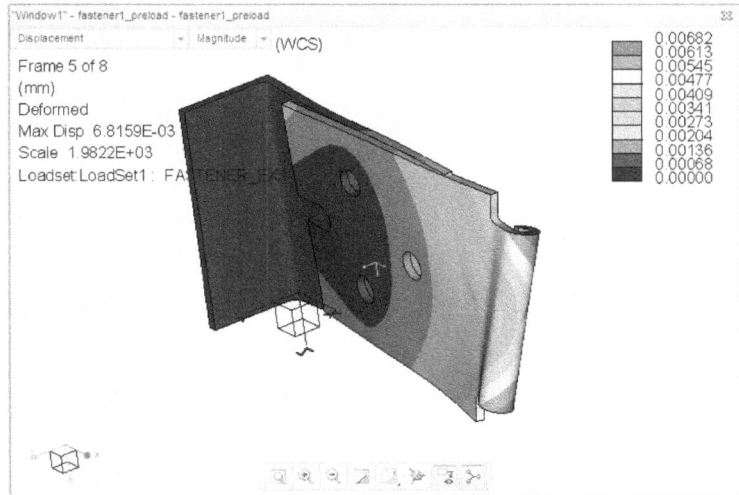

Figure 11–66

Note the interpenetration of the parts in some areas. This is a visual effect due to the deformation exaggeration via the **Scaling** factor in the *Display Options* tab of the Result Window Definition dialog box. To visually check if there actually was any interpenetration, set the **Scaling** to **1** and display the result again.

Task 14 - Display the stress plot.

1. Create a deformed von Mises stress fringe plot. The result plot displays as shown in Figure 11–67.

Figure 11–67

2. Examine the areas of maximum stress. Note the higher stresses around the bolt holes, caused by the preloads.

3. Exit the Results. Save and close the model.

Summary

In this practice, you learned how Creo Simulate works with the fastener preloads. You performed three analysis runs:

1. **Run 1:** Only bolt preloads were applied, with the **Account for Stiffness** option toggled off. You learned that applying the preload on an undeformed model, without taking into account the relaxation of the preload due to compression of the fastened parts, results in the actual forces in the bolts differing substantially from the specified preload.

2. **Run 2:** Only bolt preloads were applied, now with the **Account for Stiffness** option toggled on. You learned that taking into account the deformation of the fastened parts resulted in extremely accurate actual preloads.

3. **Run 3:** External loads applied along with the preloads, and with the **Account for Stiffness** option toggled on. This was the final analysis run that accurately simulated the preloads as well as the effects of the other loads in the model.

In practical applications with fasteners, it is not necessary to perform several analysis runs, as you did above. Instead, it is recommended to always use the **Account for Stiffness** option, apply all other loads in the model (as in Run 3 above), and let Creo Simulate do the rest of the work.

© 2017, ASCENT - Center for Technical Knowledge®

Practice 11d

Handling Surface Separation Issues When Using Fasteners

Practice Objectives

- Create fastened connections in solid models.
- Check fastener interface forces.
- Understand how to ensure the correct separation of assembly components.

In this practice, you will set up and run a static analysis of the assembly shown in Figure 11–68. The two parts are screwed together using the four holes in the flanges.

Figure 11–68

Modeling Tasks

Task 1 - Open the model.

1. Open **fastener_ex2.asm** in Creo Parametric. The unshaded model displays as shown in Figure 11–69.

Figure 11–69

2. Select **Applications>Simulate** to switch to the Simulate environment.

Task 2 - Apply the material.

The material properties should be as stated.

3. Assign **STEEL** to both parts. The following values are the default material properties for HS-low-alloy steel (STEEL):
   - Poisson = 0.27
   - Young's modulus = 199948 MPa

Task 3 - Create the fasteners.

1. In the *Refine Model* tab, click 🖇 (Fastener). The Fastener Definition dialog box opens as shown in Figure 11–70.

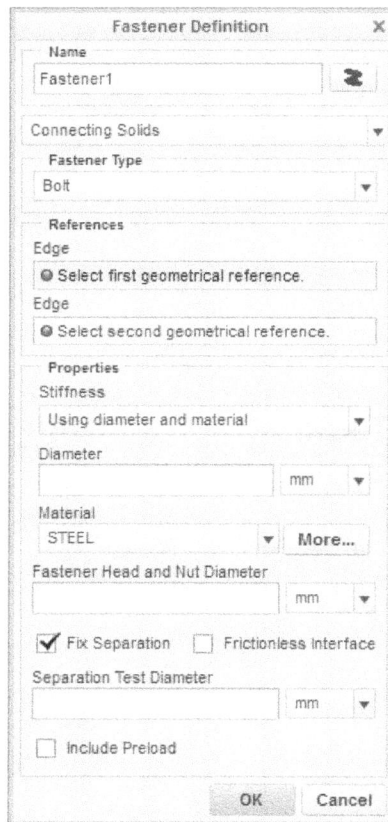

Figure 11–70

© 2017, ASCENT - Center for Technical Knowledge®

2. Select the circular edge of the top left hole in the **part2** part as the first reference, as shown in Figure 11–71.

Select this
edge

Figure 11–71

3. Select the circular edge of the top left hole in the **part1** part as the second reference, as shown in Figure 11–72.

Select
this edge

Figure 11–72

4. The Fastener Definition dialog box opens as shown in Figure 11–73.

Figure 11–73

5. Click **OK**. A warning message box displays as shown in Figure 11–74, and the two contacting surfaces are highlighted.

Figure 11–74

Note that the message in the box prompts you that the two contacting surfaces will not be bonded, due to the application of the Fastener.

© 2017, ASCENT - Center for Technical Knowledge®

6. Click **OK** to close the message box. The model displays as shown in Figure 11–75.

Figure 11–75

7. Repeat Steps 1 to 6 to create Fasteners in the remaining holes, as shown in Figure 11–76.

Figure 11–76

Task 4 - Apply the constraints.

1. Constrain the surface shown in Figure 11–77 in all of the
    translations.

**Constrain
this surface**

Figure 11–77

Task 5 - Apply the loads.

1. Apply the force **-500** in the Y-direction to the large hole, as
    shown in Figure 11–78.

Figure 11–78

© 2017, ASCENT - Center for Technical Knowledge®

Analysis Tasks

Task 6 - Set up and run a static analysis.

1. Set up a Single-Pass Adaptive static analysis, named **fastener2**.

2. Run the analysis. Wait until the Diagnostics message box displays, but do not close it yet.

Task 7 - Check the fastener separation status.

1. In the Diagnostics box, note that a warning message for all four Fasteners is displayed, prompting you that *The fix separation option for the fastener is preventing the parts from separating at locations where they should separate*, as shown in Figure 11–79. Close the Diagnostics box.

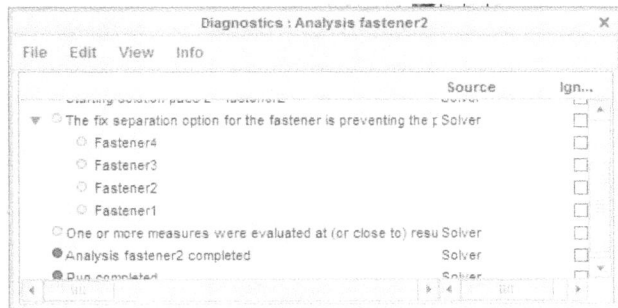

Figure 11–79

2. In the Analyses and Design Studies dialog box, click ☰ (Status) to open the Run Status window, and scroll down to the *Measures* area.

3. Extract the interface normal force (**intf_norm_forc**) measures for the fasteners, as shown in Figure 11–80.

```
strain_energy:              5.719895e-01
Fastener1_axial_force:      8.778772e+00
Fastener1_axial_stress:     4.470992e-01
Fastener1_bending_moment:   1.179204e+01
Fastener1_bending_stress:   9.609816e-01
Fastener1_intf_bend_mont:   9.457663e+02
Fastener1_intf_norm_forc:   1.172036e+02
Fastener1_intf_shr_forc:    2.145594e+01
Fastener1_intf_tors_mont:  -2.457375e+01
Fastener1_sep_stress:       7.125486e+00
Fastener1_shear_force:      4.761605e-02
Fastener1_shear_stress:     2.425065e-03
Fastener1_torsion_moment:   1.857893e-01
Fastener1_torsion_stress:   7.569738e-03
Fastener2_axial_force:      1.055817e+01
Fastener2_axial_stress:     5.377234e-01
Fastener2_bending_moment:   1.236527e+01
Fastener2_bending_stress:   1.007613e+00
Fastener2_intf_bend_mont:   8.491505e+02
Fastener2_intf_norm_forc:   1.120088e+02
Fastener2_intf_shr_forc:    2.200290e+01
Fastener2_intf_tors_mont:   2.081651e+01
Fastener2_sep_stress:       1.103926e+01
Fastener2_shear_force:      3.310653e-02
Fastener2_shear_stress:     1.686102e-03
Fastener2_torsion_moment:   1.177375e-01
Fastener2_torsion_stress:   4.797056e-03
Fastener3_axial_force:      8.299096e+00
Fastener3_axial_stress:     4.226695e-01
Fastener3_bending_moment:   1.138869e+01
Fastener3_bending_stress:   9.280336e-01
Fastener3_intf_bend_mont:   9.246866e+02
Fastener3_intf_norm_forc:   1.155038e+02
Fastener3_intf_shr_forc:    2.263905e+01
Fastener3_intf_tors_mont:   6.712481e+00
Fastener3_sep_stress:       8.398031e+00
Fastener3_shear_force:      5.465909e-02
Fastener3_shear_stress:     2.783765e-03
Fastener3_torsion_moment:  -1.064975e-01
Fastener3_torsion_stress:  -4.339098e-03
Fastener4_axial_force:      8.281038e+00
Fastener4_axial_stress:     4.217498e-01
Fastener4_bending_moment:   1.142179e+01
Fastener4_bending_stress:   9.307311e-01
Fastener4_intf_bend_mont:   9.596359e+02
Fastener4_intf_norm_forc:   1.193668e+02
Fastener4_intf_shr_forc:    2.216419e+01
Fastener4_intf_tors_mont:  -1.998357e+01
Fastener4_sep_stress:       1.127307e+01
```

Figure 11–80

Note that the interface forces for all fasteners are positive. This means that the separation springs act in tension (i.e., they incorrectly hold the parts together in that area, while the parts should actually be slightly separate).

You will later correct the separation option to enable the parts to naturally separate.

© 2017, ASCENT - Center for Technical Knowledge®

Results Tasks

Task 8 - Display the model deformation.

1. Create and display the displacement magnitude deformed plot.

2. Zoom in on the fasteners and examine the deformation, as shown in Figure 11–81. Note that the separation areas around the fasteners are unnaturally kept in contact, as predicted by the interface force signs obtained in Task 7.

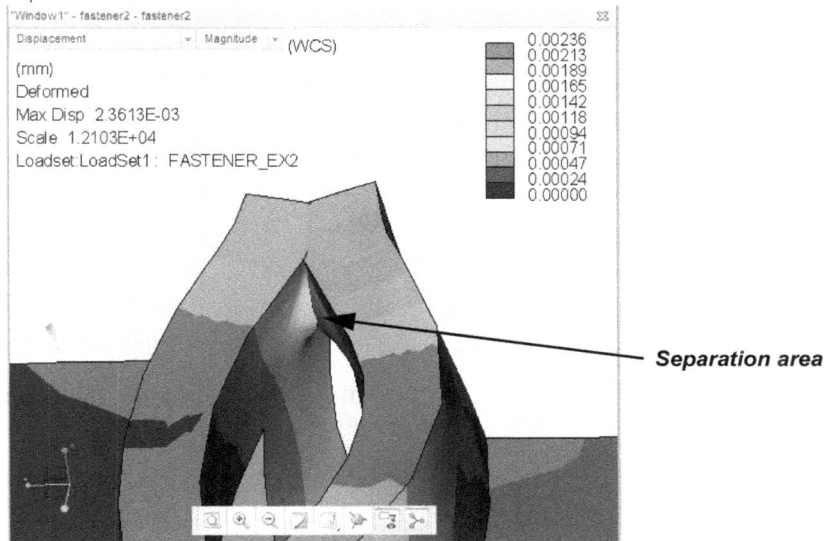

Figure 11–81

3. Exit the Results. Close the Analyses and Design Studies dialog box.

Modeling Tasks

Task 9 - Remove the separation springs.

In this task, you will remove the separation springs from the fasteners, to enable the surfaces to separate.

1. In the Model Tree, right-click on Fastener1 and select **Edit Definition**.

2. Clear the **Fix Separation** option, as shown in Figure 11–82.

Figure 11–82

3. Click **OK** to finish. Click **OK** in the warning message box that displays.

4. Repeat Steps 1 to 3 for all of the other Fasteners.

Analysis Tasks

Task 10 - Re-run the analysis.

1. Run the **fastener2** analysis again.

2. Wait until the Diagnostics message box displays. Note that it no longer displays a warning message about the fasteners.

Task 11 - Check the fastener separation status.

1. In the Analyses and Design Studies dialog box, click ▦ (Status) to open the Run Status window, and scroll down to the *Measures* area, as shown in Figure 11–83.

© 2017, ASCENT - Center for Technical Knowledge®

```
strain_energy:              1.108646e+00
Fastener1_axial_force:      1.248787e+02
Fastener1_axial_stress:     6.360020e+00
Fastener1_bending_moment:   5.428783e+01
Fastener1_bending_stress:   4.423771e+00
Fastener1_shear_force:      6.536049e-01
Fastener1_shear_stress:     3.328782e-02
Fastener1_torsion_moment:   2.054023e-01
Fastener1_torsion_stress:   8.368842e-03
Fastener2_axial_force:      1.251317e+02
Fastener2_axial_stress:     6.372904e+00
Fastener2_bending_moment:   5.492610e+01
Fastener2_bending_stress:   4.475781e+00
Fastener2_shear_force:      7.408501e-01
Fastener2_shear_stress:     3.773119e-02
Fastener2_torsion_moment:  -1.263706e-01
Fastener2_torsion_stress:  -5.148803e-03
Fastener3_axial_force:      1.251248e+02
Fastener3_axial_stress:     6.372551e+00
Fastener3_bending_moment:   5.388692e+01
Fastener3_bending_stress:   4.391101e+00
Fastener3_shear_force:      6.879691e-01
Fastener3_shear_stress:     3.503798e-02
Fastener3_torsion_moment:  -1.072663e-01
Fastener3_torsion_stress:  -4.370423e-03
Fastener4_axial_force:      1.248649e+02
Fastener4_axial_stress:     6.359315e+00
Fastener4_bending_moment:   5.443989e+01
Fastener4_bending_stress:   4.436161e+00
Fastener4_shear_force:      7.268584e-01
Fastener4_shear_stress:     3.701859e-02
Fastener4_torsion_moment:   1.625658e-01
Fastener4_torsion_stress:   6.623527e-03
```

Figure 11–83

Note that the interface measures are no longer recorded, since the separation springs have been toggled off.

2. Close the Run Status box.

Results Tasks

Task 12 - Animate the model deformation.

1. Create and animate the displacement magnitude result plot.

2. Step to Frame 5 of the animation and zoom in on the fasteners. The result plot displays as shown in Figure 11–84. Note that the parts are now slightly separate at the fasteners, which is correct.

Surfaces separate at the fasteners

Figure 11–84

Task 13 - Display the stress plot.

1. Create a deformed von Mises stress fringe plot. The result plot displays as shown in Figure 11–85.

Figure 11–85

2. Exit the Results. Save and close the model.

Practice 11e

Fasteners in Shell Models

Practice Objective

* Create fastened connections in shell models.

In this practice, you will set up and run a static analysis of the assembly shown in Figure 11–86. The two parts are bolted together at the locations indicated by three datum points.

Figure 11–86

Modeling Tasks

Task 1 - Open the model.

1. Open **fastener_ex3.asm** in Creo Parametric. The unshaded model displays as shown in Figure 11–87.

Figure 11–87

2. Select **Applications>Simulate** to switch to the Simulate environment.

Task 2 - Apply the material.

The material properties should be as stated.

1. Assign **STEEL** to both parts. The following values are the default material properties for HS-low-alloy steel (STEEL):
   - **Poisson:** 0.27
   - **Young's modulus:** 199948 MPa

Task 3 - Create shell pairs.

1. In the *Refine Model* tab, expand the **Shell Pair** section and select **Detect Shell Pairs**.

2. In the Auto Detect Shell Pairs dialog box, select both parts and enter the *Characteristic Thickness* as **3**. Ensure that the units **mm** are selected. The Auto Detect Shell Pairs dialog box displays as shown in Figure 11–88.

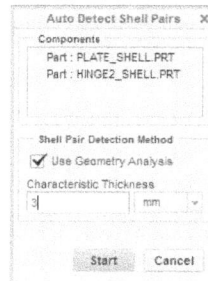

Figure 11–88

3. Click **Start** to create the shell pairs and close the dialog box.

Task 4 - Create the fasteners.

1. In the *Refine Model* tab, click 🔩 (Fastener). In the Fastener Definition dialog box that opens, select **Connecting Shells**. In the References drop-down list, select **Point-Point**. The Fastener Definition dialog box displays as shown in Figure 11–89.

© 2017, ASCENT - Center for Technical Knowledge®

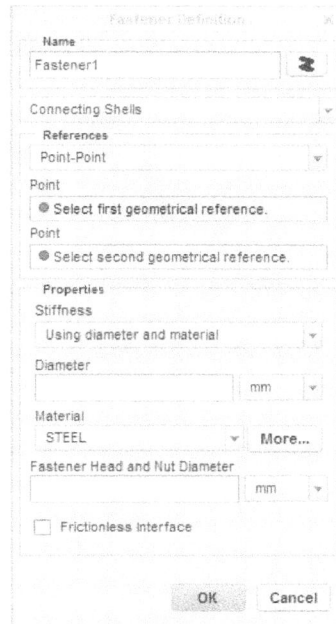

Figure 11–89

2. Select the **PNT0** and **PNT1** datum points as the references, as shown in Figure 11–90.

Select these points

Figure 11–90

3. Enter **10** as the *Diameter*, and **17** as the *Fastener Head* and nut *Diameter*. The Fastener Definition dialog box displays as shown in Figure 11–91.

Figure 11–91

4. Click **OK** to complete. Ignore the warning message that opens. The model displays as shown in Figure 11–92.

Figure 11–92

5. Repeat steps 1 through 4 for the other two pairs of points. The model displays as shown in Figure 11–93.

© 2017, ASCENT - Center for Technical Knowledge®

Figure 11–93

Task 5 - Apply loads and constraints.

1. Constrain the edge shown in Figure 11–94 for all translations and rotations.

Constrain this edge

Figure 11–94

2. Apply a **100N** force in -Z direction to the edge of the hook, as shown in Figure 11–95.

Load this edge

Figure 11–95

The model displays as shown in Figure 11–96.

Figure 11–96

Analysis Tasks

Task 6 - Set up and run a static analysis.

1. Set up a Single-Pass Adaptive static analysis, named **fastener3**.

2. Run the analysis.

Results Tasks

Task 7 - Display the model deformation.

1. Create and display the displacement magnitude deformed plot. Select **Show Element Edges** and set *Scaling* to **5%**. The result plot displays as shown in Figure 11–97.

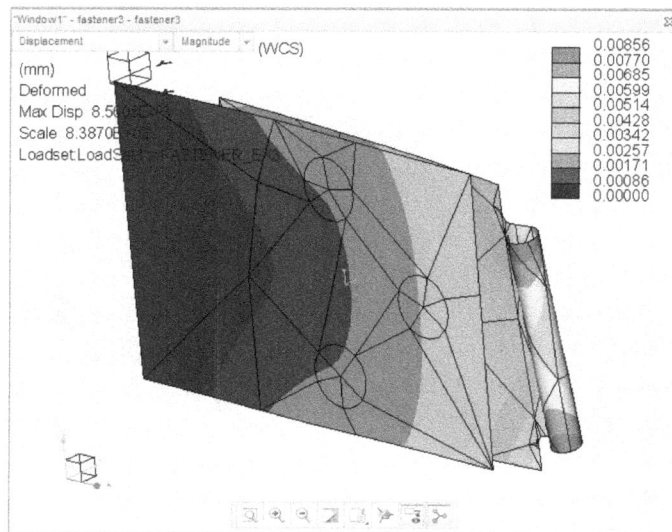

Figure 11–97

© 2017, ASCENT - Center for Technical Knowledge®

Note the circular regions Creo Simulate created around each Fastener.

2. In the drop-down lists at the top left corner of the result window, select **Stress** and **von Mises**, as shown in Figure 11–98.

Figure 11–98

The result plot displays as shown in Figure 11–99.

Figure 11–99

3. Exit the Results. Save and close the model.

© 2017, ASCENT - Center for Technical Knowledge®

Buckling Analysis

In mechanical design, a column is defined as any member that is loaded in compression. In certain cases, the maximum load a column can sustain is determined by stiffness of the column, rather than by the yield stress of its material.

Learning Objectives in this Chapter

- Understand the concepts of the buckling analysis.
- Create a buckling analysis.

12.1 Theory of Buckling

Buckling analysis predicts the magnitude of the load at which the loss of stability under compressive loads might occur. It is an important analysis for slender structures that are subject to large compressive stresses. For example, these could be structural columns or posts, bridge trusses, submarine hulls, etc.

Buckling might occur at stresses well below the yield stress. This is called *elastic buckling*. Therefore, it is important to analyze such structures for both stress and buckling.

In the example shown in Figure 12–1, a long slender column AB, of length (L) is constrained at end A and loaded with a centrally compressive load P at end B.

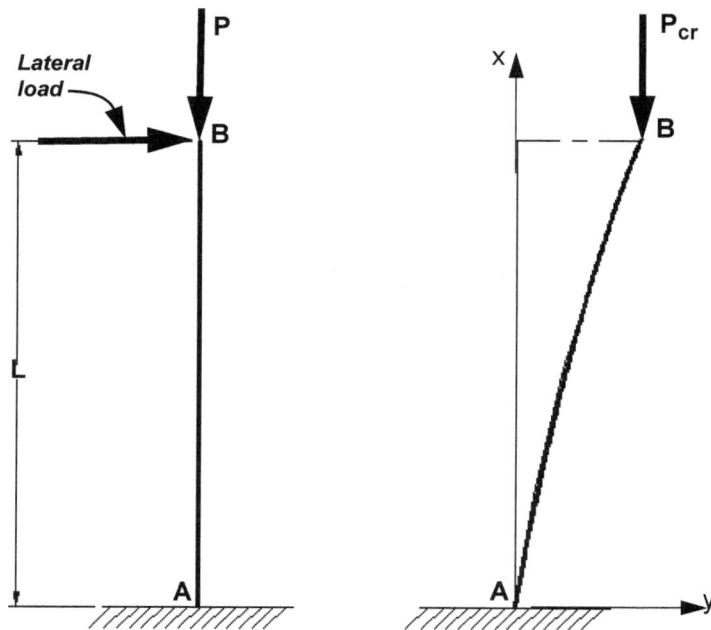

Figure 12–1

Assume that the column has the following characteristics:

* Perfectly straight

* Uniform cross-section

* Homogeneous

* Behaves elastically

© 2017, ASCENT - Center for Technical Knowledge®

When load P is small, the compressive column is laterally stable if end B is pushed slightly to one side. The column returns to its straight form as the lateral force is removed. As load P gradually increases, the straight form of the column becomes unstable and the column, if pushed to one side, remains there even if the lateral load is removed. This occurrence is called *buckling* and the value of the load at which this occurs is called the *critical load* (P_{cr}).

12.2 Creo Simulate Buckling Analysis

The buckling analysis in Creo Simulate is only available for 3D solid models.

The Creo Simulate buckling analysis is a linear or eigenvalue type of buckling analysis. The analysis predicts the critical load under which the structure is neutrally stable. The analysis solution is presented as a load factor called the *Buckling Load Factor* (BLF) and a corresponding buckling mode shape.

To produce a critical buckling load (P_{cr}), the applied load set is multiplied by the BLF:

$$P_{cr} = BLF \times P_{applied}$$

Therefore, the BLF is a safety factor for the structure against buckling. A BLF less than 1.0 indicates that the structure is predicted to buckle under the applied load.

The buckling mode shape indicates how the structure deforms at the onset of buckling. The number one mode shape is most likely to be the only one to occur. Therefore, be sure to verify your design for mode 1 as shown in Figure 12–2.

```
Number of Modes: 3

Mode     B. L. F.     Convergence
----    ------------  -----------
   1    1.106302e+01      0.0%
   2    1.695276e+01      0.0%
   3    9.939256e+01      0.4%
```

Figure 12–2

The linear buckling analysis provides a useful first order approximation of the critical buckling load for designers and generally produces results that are not conservative (the theory calculates a higher critical load than is actually observed in experiments). It also assumes that the initial loading on the model does not change the geometry. Therefore, it is recommended that you use generous safety factors.

© 2017, ASCENT - Center for Technical Knowledge®

Use the following steps to perform a buckling analysis:

1. Set up the model.
2. Assign material properties to the model.
3. Apply boundary conditions to the model (i.e., loads or constraints).
4. Create a static analysis.

   A static analysis must be defined before a buckling analysis can be created because the structure stiffness used in the buckling analysis is obtained from the static analysis. Therefore, the accuracy of the buckling analysis directly relates to the accuracy of the static analysis. You need to set a tight convergence criteria on the RMS stress, displacement, and strain energy.

5. Create a buckling analysis.
6. Run the buckling analysis.
7. Interpret the results.

To calculate the stresses and displacements on the structure at the critical buckling load, multiply the original compressive load by the smallest positive BLF, and rerun the static analysis.

Practice 12a | Buckling Analysis of a Pole

Practice Objectives

- Set up and run a Buckling analysis.
- Understand how to determine the Buckling Load Factor.
- Visualize the Buckling modes.

In this practice, you will set up and run a buckling analysis on a long slender pole, as shown in Figure 12–3. The pole has a rectangular cross-section (2 x 2) and is 13ft long.

Figure 12–3

Modeling Tasks

Task 1 - Open the part.

1. Open **buckle_pole.prt** in Creo Parametric. The part displays as shown in Figure 12–4.

Figure 12–4

2. Ensure that the unit system is set to **IPS**.

3. Select **Applications>Simulate**.

© 2017, ASCENT - Center for Technical Knowledge®

Task 2 - Apply the loads.

1. Apply a total and uniform force of **-1000** in the X-direction to the pole's hole surface, as shown in Figure 12–5.

The X-direction is relative to the WCS.

Select this surface

Figure 12–5

2. Name the load **buckle_f**. The model displays as shown in Figure 12–6.

Figure 12–6

Task 3 - Apply the constraints.

1. Fully constrain the hole on the other end of the pole (all of the translations), as shown in Figure 12–7.

Fix this surface

Figure 12–7

The constraint values are turned off.

2. Name the constraint **pole_const**. The model displays as shown in Figure 12–8.

Figure 12–8

Task 4 - Apply the material.

1. Assign **STEEL** to the **buckle_pole** part. The following values are the default material properties for HS-low-alloy steel (STEEL):

   - Poisson = 0.27
   - Young's modulus = 2.9e+07 psi
   - Density = 0.0007324 lbf sec^2/in^4

Analysis Tasks

Task 5 - Set up an analysis.

In this task, you will set up a static analysis and a buckling analysis.

1. Click (Analyses and Studies). The Analyses and Design Studies dialog box opens.

2. Select **File>New Static**. The Static Analysis Definition dialog box opens.

3. For the analysis name, enter **static_pole**. In the Static Analysis Definition dialog box, select the options shown in Figure 12–9.

© 2017, ASCENT - Center for Technical Knowledge®

Figure 12–9

4. Click **OK**. The Analyses and Design Studies dialog box opens.

5. Select **File>New Buckling**. The Buckling Analysis Definition dialog box opens as shown in Figure 12–10.

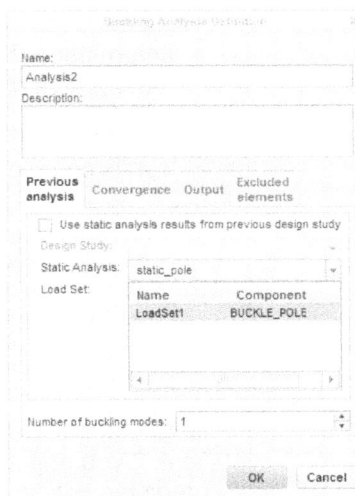

Figure 12–10

6. In the *Name* field, enter **buckle_pole**.

7. In the *Number of Buckling Modes* field, enter **3**.

8. Select the *Convergence* tab and enter the information shown in Figure 12–11.

Figure 12–11

9. Click **OK**.

10. Run the **buckle_pole** analysis.

11. In the Analyses and Design Studies dialog box, click (Status). The Run Status window displays.

12. Scroll through the Run Status window to display the analysis information. Note that the **static_pole** analysis was automatically run before the **buckle_pole** analysis.

13. Locate the BLF values in the Run Status dialog box when the run is complete, as shown in Figure 12–12.

Figure 12–12

Note that the lowest Buckling Load Factor is approximately 4. In Task 2 you applied 1000lbs compressive load. Therefore, the predicted critical load is 4x1000lbs = 4000 lbs.

© 2017, ASCENT - Center for Technical Knowledge®

Results Tasks

Task 6 - Display the buckling modes.

In this task, you will create and display three deformation animation fringe plots of the three buckling modes.

1. In the Analyses and Design Studies dialog box, click ▤ (New). The Result Window Definition dialog box opens as shown in Figure 12–13.

Figure 12–13

2. Ensure that Mode 1 is highlighted. In the Display Options tab, select **Deformed**, **Overlay Undeformed**, and **Animate**. Click **OK and Show**. The Displacement Magnitude result plot at Frame 3 displays as shown in Figure 12–14.

Figure 12–14

3. Click ✏ (Edit). Repeat Step 2 to display and animate Buckling modes 2 and 3.

Task 7 - Display the static stresses.

In this task, you will examine the stress plot for the static analysis, and determine whether the pole's material might yield before the compressive load reaches the critical buckling value.

1. In the *Home* tab, click ![icon] (New) and select the **static_pole** analysis. In the Result Window Definition dialog box, rename the window to **static_stress**. The Result Window Definition dialog box opens as shown in Figure 12–15.

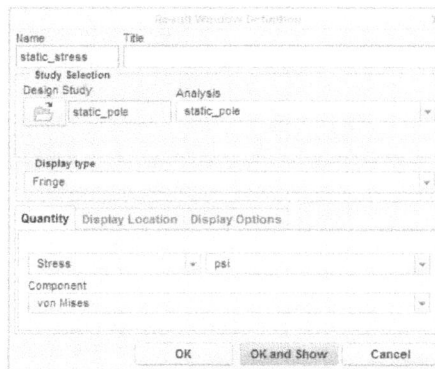

Figure 12–15

2. Click **OK and Show**. In the *View* tab, click ![icon] (Show). Clear the **Window1** line and then click **OK**. The von Mises stress plot for the static analysis opens, as shown in Figure 12-16.

Figure 12–16

© 2017, ASCENT - Center for Technical Knowledge®

3. Using the ✺ (Dynamic Query) tool, get a reading of the stress in the approximate middle of the pole, as shown in Figure 12–17.

Figure 12–17

The stress value should be approximately 250psi.

Since the static analysis was linear, the stress value at the critical buckling load can be calculated by linear interpolation. The stress at the critical load is the stress from the static analysis multiplied by the BLF: 250x4 = 1000psi = 1ksi.

According to the ASM standards, the yield stress for HS-low-alloy steels must be greater than 40ksi, which is much greater than the calculated stress value at the critical load.

Therefore, we can conclude that this pole is expected to start buckling long before the stress exceeds the material's yield point.

4. Exit the Results. Save and close the model.

| Practice 12b | Buckling Analysis of a Thin Shell |

Practice Objectives

- Set up and run a Buckling analysis.
- Determine the Buckling Load Factor.
- Determine the safety of the part against buckling and yielding.

In this practice, you will set up and run a buckling analysis on the thin cylindrical shell shown in Figure 12–18, with minimum instruction.

Figure 12–18

Task 1 - Prepare the model for analysis.

1. Open **buckle_shell.prt** and launch Creo Simulate.

To create a new material that is not in the library, copy an existing material from the library into the model, and then change the material's name and properties.

2. Apply the material:
   - **Material:** STEEL
   - **Poisson's ratio:** 0.27
   - **Young's modulus:** 199948 MPa
   - **Tensile Yield Stress:** 250 MPa

3. Use Shell Idealization:
   - **Thickness:** 1 mm

© 2017, ASCENT - Center for Technical Knowledge®

4. Constrain all translations on the bottom edge of the part, as shown in Figure 12–19.

Constrain this edge

Figure 12–19

5. Apply a **100000N** compressive load (i.e., in the -Y direction) to the top edge, as shown in Figure 12–20.

100kN load in -Y direction on this edge

Figure 12–20

Task 2 - Set up a static analysis.

1. Create a new static analysis with the following parameters:
   - **Analysis name:** static_shell
   - **Convergence method:** Multi-Pass Adaptive
   - **Maximum Polynomial Order:** 9
   - **Percent Convergence:** 10
   - **Plotting Grid:** 10

2. Do not run the static analysis.

Task 3 - Set up and run a buckling analysis.

3. Create and run a new buckling analysis with the following parameters:
   - **Analysis name:** buckle_shell
   - **Static analysis:** static_shell
   - **Number of buckling modes:** 4
   - **Convergence method:** Single-Pass Adaptive
   - **Plotting Grid:** 10

Task 4 - Examine the analysis results.

1. Display the **von Mises Stress** fringe plot for the static analysis.

   - Is the part material expected to yield under the given loading?

2. Display the buckling shapes and obtain the lowest Buckling Load Factor from the result.

   - Is the part predicted to buckle?
   - Which is expected occur at a lower load: yielding of the material, or buckling?

3. Save and close the model.

 © 2017, ASCENT - Center for Technical Knowledge®

Basics of Structural Analysis

In this appendix you will learn some basics of Structural Analysis.

Learning Objectives in this Appendix

- Understand Quantities and Units.
- Understand Newton's Laws.

A.1 Quantities and Units

Fundamental Quantities

The fundamental quantities of solid mechanics are: Length, Mass, and Time.

Derived Quantities

The derived quantities of solid mechanics are: Force, Moment, Weight, Stress, Velocity, and Acceleration.

Units

Units must be consistent to perform valid calculations. The appropriate units for common quantities of the English and Metric systems are as follows:

Quantity	English Units	Metric Units
length	Inch, in	Millimeter, mm
time	Second, s	Second, s
mass	Slug $$\left(1\,\text{slug} = \frac{1\,\text{lbf}}{386.4\,\text{in}/\text{s}^2}\right)$$	Tonne, t $(1\text{t} = 1\text{Mg} = 1\text{x}10^6\text{g})$
velocity	in/s	mm/s
acceleration	in/s^2	mm/s^2
force	Pound, lbf	Newton, N
moment	Inch-pound, in lb	Newton-millimeter, N mm
weight	Pound, lbf	Newton, N
stress	Pounds per square inch, psi	Newton per square millimeter, N/mm^2 Megapascal, Mpa $(1\text{Mpa} = 1\text{N}/\text{mm}^2)$

© 2017, ASCENT - Center for Technical Knowledge®

A.2 Newton's Laws

Newton's three laws of motion are as follows:

1. An object in motion or at rest stays in motion or at rest unless acted on by an external force.
2. For every action there is an equal and opposite reaction.
3. Force = mass * acceleration ($F = ma$).

Implications of Newton's Laws on Structural Analysis

A body remains stationary or in uniform motion in a straight line unless it is made to change that state by external forces. This is a fundamental assumption when performing a structural Linear Static analysis.

Static implies that there is no movement. It is assumed that the structure being analyzed is not free to move in any direction. Sufficient constraints must be applied to the model to remove all six rigid body degrees of freedom.

Equilibrium & Free-Body Diagrams

Free-body diagrams and equilibrium equations determine the load paths in a structure. Mathematically, this provides six equilibrium equations. The sum of the forces in each direction must equal zero and the sum of the moments in each direction must equal zero.

An example of a cantilever beam is shown in Figure A–1.

Figure A–1

Reactions to a force (F) must exist at the constraints, as shown in Figure A–2.

Figure A–2

For equilibrium to exist, the following equation must hold:

R = - F

This can be verified mathematically with the following equation:

R + F = 0

Moments

If the constraint is a hinge, the entire beam rotates because a hinge cannot react to a moment. A simple hinge would not remove the rotational rigid body degree of freedom. However, a fully fixed constraint can react to moments and you can easily calculate its magnitude.

The ability to calculate the moments acting on and within a structure is useful. Bending often accounts for a part's maximum stress. Therefore, being able to perform a quick hand calculation to validate an analysis model is helpful.

A moment is calculated at a specific location and defined by the following calculation:

FORCE x DISTANCE

An applied force (F) causes moments on a structure as it moves away from the reaction force (R). Alternatively, pure moments might be applied to the structure. Pure moments are transmitted through the system with a constant magnitude.

For static equilibrium to hold for the beam shown in Figure A–3, the sum of moments must equal zero.

© 2017, ASCENT - Center for Technical Knowledge®

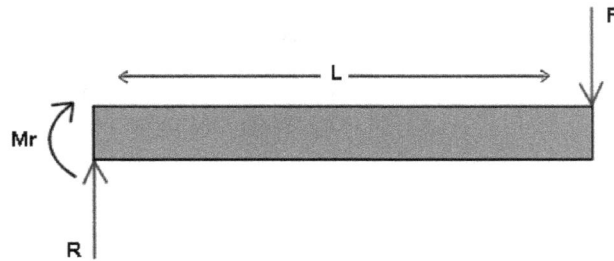

Figure A–3

If a moment is positive in the clockwise direction, the sum of the moments is as follows:

$(F \times L) + Mr = 0$

Since the net moment is being calculated at the location of the reaction force (R) the reaction force itself produces no moment. Therefore, the following equation holds:

$Mr = -(F \times L)$

Another example is shown in Figure A–4.

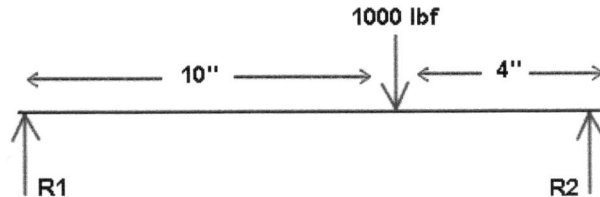

Figure A–4

This beam is supported (pinned) at both ends. Reaction forces exist when an external force is applied. For equilibrium to exist, the following equation must hold (vertical up is considered positive):

$R1 + R2 - 1000 = 0$

This single equation is not enough to determine the values of R1 and R2. An additional equation from the equilibrium of moments must be used. The following equation calculates the sum of the moments at the location of R1 (clockwise is considered positive):

$(R1 \times 0) + (1000 \times 10) - (R2 \times 14) = 0$

Using the force and moment equilibrium equations, the values for R1 and R2 are calculated as follows:

$R2 = 714.3 \text{ lbf}$

$R1 = 1000 - 714.3 = 285.7 \text{ lbf}$

In addition to determining reaction loads, engineers typically calculate the shear and moment diagrams for beams. The moment at a beam's cross-section, in conjunction with linear-elastic beam theory, is used to determine the beam bending stresses.

Shears and moments are calculated at a beam cross-section location similar to the way reaction loads were determined. Consider the beam segment on only one side of the cross-section. Imagine the location of the cross-section as a fixed constraint. The beam diagram displays as shown in Figure A–5.

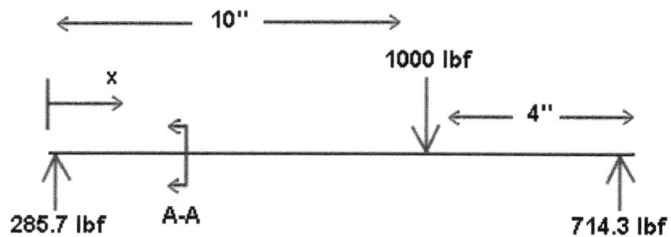

Figure A–5

The only the beam portion to the left of section A-A is shown in Figure A–6.

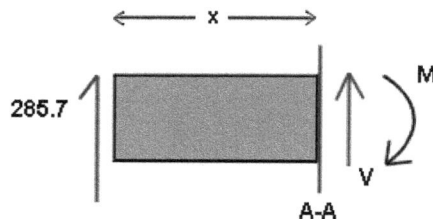

Figure A–6

The value of V is calculated using the following equation:

285.7 + V = 0

Therefore,

M = -285.7x in · lbf

The value of M is calculated using the following equation:

285.7x + M = 0

Therefore,

M = -285.7x in · lbf

© 2017, ASCENT - Center for Technical Knowledge®

If X is greater than 10in, the equations change due to the extra force. The following equations then apply:

285.7 - 1000 + V = 0

Therefore,

V = 714.3 lbf

285.7x - 1000 (x - 10) + M = 0

M = 1000 (x - 10) - 285.7x

Therefore,

M = 714.3x - 10000 in · lbf

These results can be displayed graphically by creating shear and bending moment diagrams, as shown in Figure A–7.

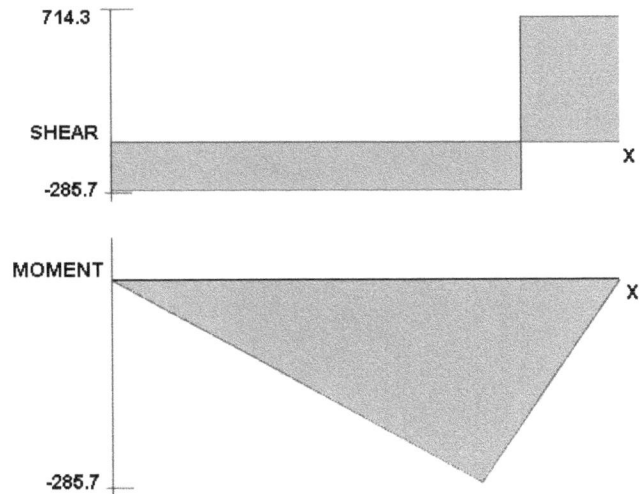

Figure A–7

Graphically, the maximum moment for this beam is directly under the applied load. The value of the moment, in conjunction with the beam bending equation, can be used to calculate the stresses in the beam.

Note that you cannot calculate reaction loads for every structure using only equilibrium. The beam diagram shown in Figure A–8 is similar to the case that you just solved. However, the ends have been fixed instead of pinned.

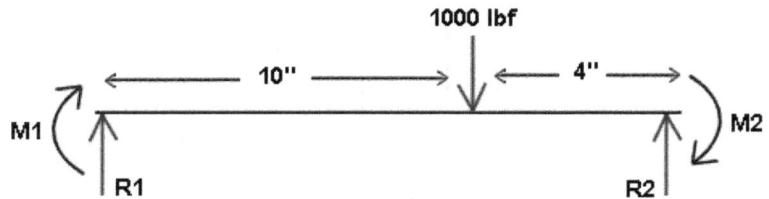

Figure A–8

Two additional unknowns now represent the moments transmitted through the ends of the beam: M1 and M2. A total of four unknowns now exist, but two equilibrium equations are available for each plane.

The following force and moment equilibrium equations (at R1) can be written:

R1 + R2 = 1000

M1 + 10(1000) - 14R2 + M2 = 0

These equations cannot be solved uniquely. Even if you try creating another moment equation at R2, the following equation results:

M1 + 14R1 - 4(1000) + M2 = 0

R1 - 1000 - R2

Therefore,

M1 + 14000 - 14R2 - 4000 + M2 = 0

M1 + 10000 - 14R2 + M2 = 0

The final equation is the same equation that you arrived at earlier. Therefore, creating another moment equation at R2 does not help. This problem is actually solvable by hand but requires additional equations that take into account the stiffness of the structure (elasticity theory). As problems become more complex, the only feasible approach often involves the use of numerical computer methods.

© 2017, ASCENT - Center for Technical Knowledge®

So far, only simple beams in a single plane have been considered. One of the most valuable uses for understanding the equilibrium equations is being able to calculate the reaction loads between different components in an assembly. This skill enables you to analyze single components from an assembly rather than attempting to model the entire structure.

Stresses

The most basic definition of stress is as follows:

$$STRESS = \frac{FORCE}{AREA}$$

Or,

$$\sigma = \frac{F}{A}$$

An example of a tensile test specimen is shown in Figure A–9.

Figure A–9

The following properties apply:

F = 1000 lbf

A = 0.1 x 0.5 = 0.05 in^2

Therefore,

σ = 1000 § 0.05

(σ = 20000) psi (20 ksi)

Once a stress has been determined, it can be used to predict the safety of the part, by comparing the stress in the part with the material's strength. A material's yield strength and ultimate strength are typically used for comparison. The yield strength is the amount of stress that a material can sustain before suffering permanent deformation, and the ultimate strength is the stress at which the material ruptures in tension.

Material properties can be displayed using a Stress-Strain diagram, as shown in Figure A–10. Strain relates to the displacements of the structure and is defined as follows:

$$STRAIN = \frac{CHANGE\ IN\ LENGTH}{LENGTH}$$

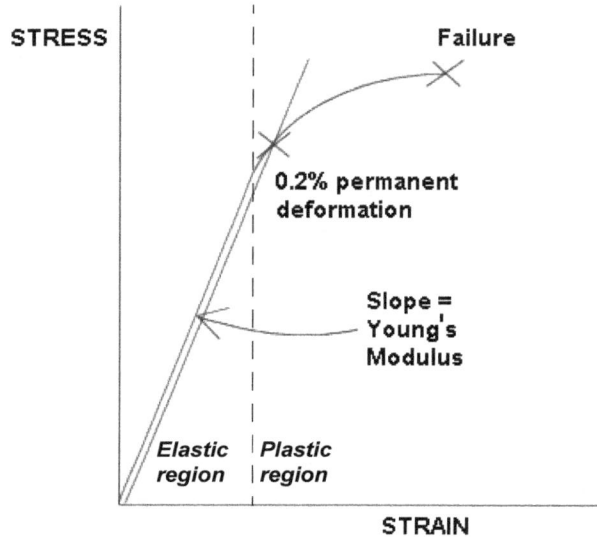

Figure A–10

Note that the initial portion of the curve is a straight line. This is called the *elastic* region. Linear static analysis assumes that the material is *only* being used in its elastic region. The slope of the curve is Young's Modulus, E. By generally accepted standards, the yield strength is determined to be the stress level at which a 0.2% permanent deformation is seen in the material. The ultimate strength is the maximum stress level that is obtained before failure.

The graph shown in Figure A–10 is an idealization. In reality, metals have an essentially linear first segment, but some materials (e.g., plastics or rubbers) do not. Although linear analysis makes the fundamental assumption of the linear material properties, it is still used frequently with plastics and other materials. To be more accurate, a non-linear analysis could be performed, but this is much more complex and costly. It is often quite acceptable to approximate a material's behavior as linear because a valuable insight into the component's behavior can still be obtained.

© 2017, ASCENT - Center for Technical Knowledge®

3D Stresses

So far, only the case of uniaxial stress has been considered. 3D has many components of stress, as shown in Figure A–11.

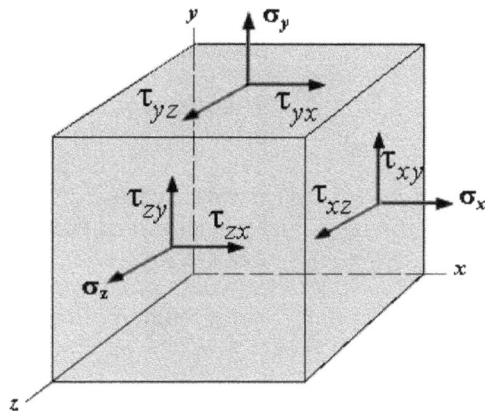

Figure A–11

σ indicates a normal stress parallel to and acting on the plane denoted by the subscript. τ indicates a shear stress acting on the plane denoted by the first subscript and parallel to the plane denoted by the second subscript.

At any point in the component, you can visualize an infinitely smaller cube. Each face of the cube can react to a tensile stress normal to its surface and shear stresses in the other two perpendicular directions. To satisfy the equilibrium of the cube, $\tau_{xy} = \tau_{yx}, \tau_{xz} = \tau_{zx}, \tau_{yz} = \tau_{zy}$.

With multiple stress components, a single value can no longer be compared against a material's yield strength. Furthermore, if the cube is reoriented (i.e., a different coordinate system is used), the stress values change. Consider the 2D example shown in Figure A–12.

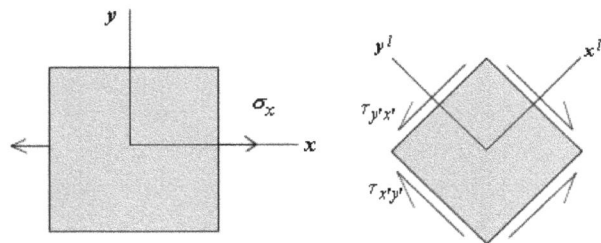

Figure A–12

Only a normal stress is shown on the left in Figure A–12. If the coordinate system is rotated, at least some of the stress in the new system must be reacted in shear. In fact, the normal stresses that must also be present to balance the vertical compression, are not shown on the right in Figure A–12.

Therefore, you cannot simply take a stress value from an arbitrary coordinate system. It is possible to find a coordinate system in which all of the stresses can be expressed as pure normal stresses through trigonometry). This is called the *Principal Coordinate System*, and the stresses expressed in that system are called the *Principal Stresses*. In 3D, three principal stresses are denoted (1, 2, and 3), which are usually arranged in a decreasing order of magnitude.

Failure Theories

Figure A–13 shows three common failure theories:

- Maximum Principal Stress theory

- Maximum Shear Stress (Tresca) theory

- von Mises Stress theory

Each theory tries to predict yielding in a general stress state.

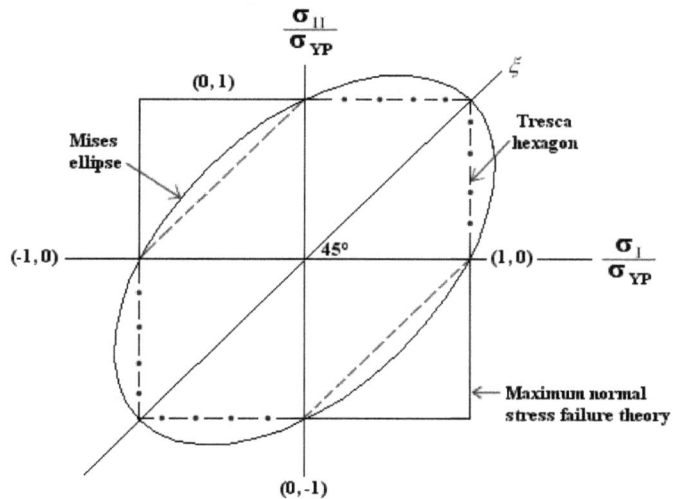

Figure A–13

© 2017, ASCENT - Center for Technical Knowledge®

The Maximum Principal Stress theory states that when the maximum principal stress exceeds the material's yield point, the material yields. The Maximum Shear Stress theory was proposed later when it was understood that yielding resulted from shearing between atoms of the solid. Finally, the von Mises Stress theory (also called *Distortion Energy* or *Effective Stress*) was determined to most closely match the experimental results for ductile isotropic materials.

In most cases, you should compare the calculated von Mises stress to the yield of the material to judge whether a component is capable of withstanding the applied loads without experiencing a permanent plastic deformation.

© 2017, ASCENT - Center for Technical Knowledge®

Appendix B

Poisson's Ratio Project

In this appendix you learn about the effect of Poisson's ratio.

Learning Objectives in this Appendix

- Apply Poisson's ratio to a model under tensile loading.

B.1 Poisson's Ratio

When a plate is subject to simple tension, the length of the plate increases in the load direction, but decreases in the dimensions that are perpendicular to the load. The ratio of the strain in the lateral direction to the axial direction is defined as *Poisson's ratio*.

Poisson's ratio is a constant for a given material within its range of elastic behavior (e.g., structural steel = 0.3 approx.).

$$i.e. \quad Poisson's\ ratio \quad = \frac{unit\ lateral\ contraction}{unit\ axial\ elongation}$$

The following example demonstrates how Poisson's ratio affects a rectangular (14x8) steel plate that is 0.2 thick, has one hole, and is under a simple tension of 20000lbs. You analyze the plate with a shell model.

You set up and run two standard design studies with different boundary conditions to indicate the Poisson's ratio effect on the analysis results.

The plate model with hole dimensions is shown in Figure B–1.

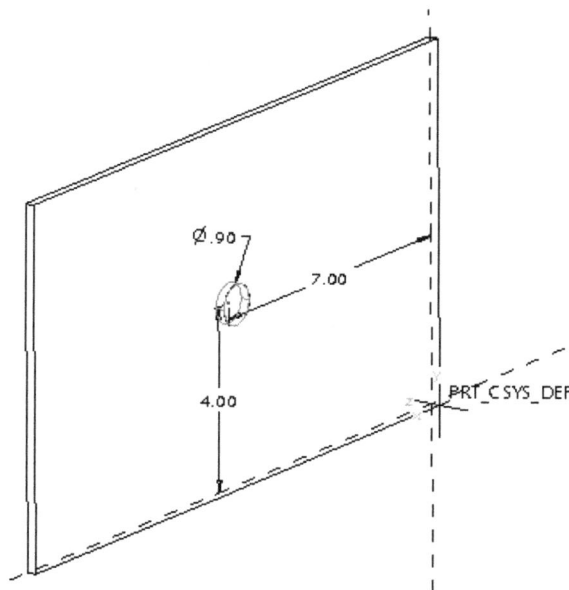

Figure B–1

© 2017, ASCENT - Center for Technical Knowledge®

Modeling Tasks

Task 1 - Open poisson_part in Creo Parametric and launch Creo Simulate.

1. Open **poisson_part.prt**. The part displays as shown in Figure B–2.

Figure B–2

2. Ensure that the unit system is set to **IPS**.

3. Launch Creo Simulate.

Task 2 - Apply the material.

The model's material properties should be as stated.

1. Assign **STEEL** to the model. The following values are the default material properties for HS-low-alloy steel (STEEL):

   - Poisson = 0.27
   - Young's modulus = 2.9e+07 psi

Task 3 - Define the shell pairs.

The plate thickness is 0.2 inches.

1. Use the **Automatic Detection** tool, with the *Characteristic Thickness* of **0.25** to define the shell pairs.

Task 4 - Apply the loads.

1. Apply a tensile load of **20000** lbs to the edge shown in Figure B–3.

The model shown in Figure B–3 is reoriented for clarity.

Figure B–3

Task 5 - Apply the constraints.

1. Constrain the edges shown in Figure B–4, using the following values:

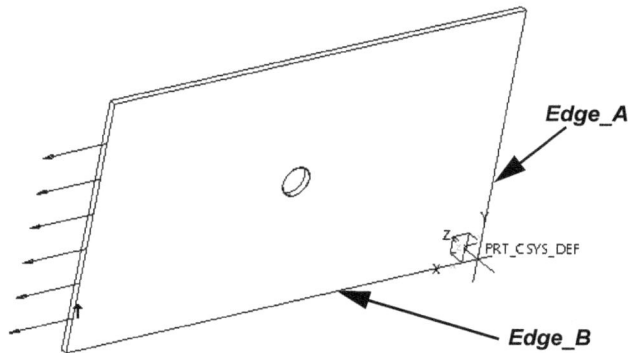

Figure B–4

Constraint Set	Edge_A	Edge_B	Description
const_1	Fixed in all translations and rotations.	Free in all translations and rotations.	The constraint set does not permit the plate to decrease in dimensions perpendicular to the applied load along edge_A. This edge is said to be over-constrained.

© 2017, ASCENT - Center for Technical Knowledge®

const_2	Fixed in X- and Z-directions. Free in Y-direction. Fixed in all rotations	Fixed in Y-direction only	The constraint set does not constrain edge_A in the Y-direction and edge_B in the X-direction. This permits the plate to decrease in dimensions perpendicular to the applied load, which causes in more realistic results.

The model displays as shown in Figure B–5.

Figure B–5

Analysis Tasks

Task 6 - Set up the analysis.

1. Set up the following:
   - A multipass analysis **Max. P order = 9** with a convergence of **1%**. Name the analysis **p_1**. Select **const_1** as the constraint set.
   - A multipass analysis **Max. P order = 9** with a convergence of **1%**. Name the analysis **p_2**. Select **const_2** as the constraint set.

Task 7 - Run the analysis.

1. Run both analyses.

2. Once the analyses have finished, open the run status and note the following details:
   - Maximum von Mises stress in the p_1 analysis = 38.20ksi (approx.)
   - Maximum von Mises stress in the p_2 analysis= 36.74ksi (approx.)

Results Tasks

Task 8 - Display the results.

3. Create and display the following:
    *   A deformed fringe color plot of the von Mises stress for analysis **p_1**, as shown in Figure B–6.
    *   A deformed fringe color plot of the von Mises stress for analysis **p_2**, as shown in Figure B–7.

The constraint set **const_1** in Figure B–6 does not permit the plate to decrease in dimensions perpendicular to the applied load. This model is said to be overconstrained. Note that the deformation of the plate is restricted and that the plate is not permitted to contract freely in the Y-direction. Therefore, the arched top and bottom edges display.

Figure B–6

The constraint set **const_2** in Figure B–7 does not constrain edge_A in the Y-direction and edge_B in the X-direction. This permits the plate dimensions to decrease in the Y-direction. Note that the deformation of the plate is uniform.

© 2017, ASCENT - Center for Technical Knowledge®

"Window1" - p_1 - p_1

Figure B–7

Task 9 - Verify the results with hand calculations.

1. Verify the following results:
   - Cross-sectional area of plate at hole = (8 - 0.9)(0.2) = 1.42 in^2
   - Stress concentration factor for hole = 2.62
   - σ_1 = max. stress at hole = (2.62)(20000)/(1.42) = 36.9ksi

   The plate is under pure tension. Therefore, the principal stresses include the following:
   - σ_1 = 36.9ksi
   - σ_2 = 0
   - σ_3 = 0
   - von Mises stress = $\{[(\sigma_1 - \sigma_2)^2 + (\sigma_2 - \sigma_3)^2 + (\sigma_3 - \sigma_1)^2]/2\}^{1/2}$ = 36.9 ksi

2. A comparison of the hand-calculated maximum von Mises value with the values obtained from the FEA analysis is as follows:

Method	vm (ksi)	Error%
Hand-calculated	36.9	0.00
Analysis [P_1]	38.20	3.5
Analysis [P_1]	36.74	0.4

Although the values are close and comparable to each other, the constraint set **const_1** has over-constrained the plate and the deformation of the plate is not uniform due to the effect of the Poisson's ratio.

© 2017, ASCENT - Center for Technical Knowledge®

Verification and Practice Examples

In this appendix you review several structural case studies.

Learning Objectives in this Appendix

- Review different case studies.

C.1 Structural Analysis

In each of the following cases, create the Creo Parametric model and use the techniques learned in the previous practices to perform the appropriate analysis. Compare the results obtained with the following theoretical values. Note that the theory values also use approximations.

Case	Description	Theory	Creo Simulate	Error %
1A	Cantilever Beam - Bending	d_{max} = .1167 in σ_{max} = 39.4 ksi		
1B	Cantilever Beam - Gravity	δ_{max} = 1.7×10^{-4} in σ_{max} = 76.54 psi		
2A	Plate w/ Hole - Tension	σ_{max} = 14.6 ksi		
2B	Plate w/ Hole - Bending	σ_{max} = 34.7 ksi		
3A	Step. Cir. Bar - Tension	σ_{max} = 2.14 ksi		
3B	Step. Cir. Bar - Bending	σ_{max} = 1.56 ksi		
3C	Step. Cir. Bar - Torsion	τ_{max} = 682.45 psi		
4A	Loaded Hole in Plate	σ_{max} = 9.98 ksi		

Case 1 - Cantilevered I-Beam

R.250
20.00
.50
3.00
.60
2.00

Figure C–1

© 2017, ASCENT - Center for Technical Knowledge®

Loadcase A

- **One end:** Immovable

- **The other end:** 5000 lbf shear (in the stiffer bending direction)

- **Material:** Steel

- Idealize the model with beam elements.

- **Young's modulus:** E = 3.0e7

- **Poisson's ratio:** n = 0.30

- **Mass density:** 7.5e-4

- **Bending moment of inertia:** $I = 3.8094$ in^4

Loadcase A Analytical Solution

$$\text{maximum deflection, } \delta_{max} = \frac{F \times L^3}{3 \times E \times I}$$

$$= \frac{5000 \times (20)^3}{3 \times (3 \times 10^7) \times 3.8094}$$

$$= \mathbf{0.1167\ in}$$

$$\text{maximum stress, } \sigma_{max} = \frac{M \times y}{I}$$

$$= \frac{5000 \times 20 \times 1.5}{3.8094}$$

$$= \mathbf{39.4\ ksi}$$

Loadcase B

- **One end:** Immovable, 1G gravity load (386.4 in/s^2)

- **Cross-sectional area:** A = 3.35365

- Idealize the model with beam elements.

Loadcase B Analytical Solution

$$w = \text{mass density} \times A \times G$$

$$= (7.5 \times 10^{-4}) \times 3.35365 \times 386.4$$

$$= \mathbf{0.9719\ lbf/in}$$

$$\text{maximum deflection, } \delta_{max} \quad = \frac{w \times L^4}{8 \times E \times I}$$

$$= \frac{0.9719 \times (20)^4}{8 \times (3 \times 10^7) \times 3.8094}$$

$$= \mathbf{1.7 \times 10^{-4} in}$$

$$M \quad = \frac{w \times L^2}{2}$$

$$= \frac{0.9719 \times (20)^2}{2}$$

$$= \mathbf{194.38 \ in \cdot lbf}$$

$$\text{maximum stress, } \sigma_{max} \quad = \frac{M \times y}{I}$$

$$= \frac{194.38 \times 1.5}{3.8094}$$

$$= \mathbf{76.54 \ psi}$$

© 2017, ASCENT - Center for Technical Knowledge®

Case 1 - Plate with a Hole

Figure C–2

Loadcase A

- **One end:** Immovable

- **The other end:** tensile load of 1000 lbf

- w=2

- d=1

Loadcase A Analytical Solution

$$\sigma_0 = \frac{1000}{(2-1) \times 0.15}$$
$$= 6667 \text{ psi}$$

$$d/w = 0.5$$

$$K_t = 2.19$$

$$\sigma_{max} = \sigma_0 \times K_t$$
$$= 6667 \times 2.19$$
$$= \textbf{14.6 ksi}$$

Loadcase B

- **One end:** Immovable

- **The other end:** Bending moment of 100 in lbf

Loadcase B Analytical Solution

$$I = \frac{(2-1) \times (0.15)^3}{12}$$
$$= 2.8125 \times 10^{-4}$$

$$\sigma_0 = \frac{100 \times 0.075}{2.8125 \times 10^{-4}}$$

$$K_t = 1.3$$

$$\sigma_{max} = \mathbf{34.7 \text{ ksi}}$$

Case 1 - Stepped Circular Bar

Figure C–3

Loadcase A

- **Large end:** Immovable

- **Small end:** 1000 lbf tension

Loadcase A Analytical Solution

$$\sigma_0 = \frac{F}{A}$$
$$= \frac{1000}{\left(\pi \times (1)^2 / 4 \right)}$$
$$= 1273 \text{ psi}$$

$$\frac{D}{d} = 1.5$$

$$\frac{r}{d} = 0.15$$

$$K_t = 1.68$$

© 2017, ASCENT - Center for Technical Knowledge®

$$\sigma_{max} = 2.14 \, \text{ksi}$$

Loadcase B

- **Large end:** Immovable
- **Small end:** 100 in×lbf bending

Loadcase B Analytical Solution

$$\sigma_0 = \frac{M \times y}{I}$$
$$= 1018.6 \, \text{psi}$$

$$K_t = 1.53$$

$$\sigma_{max} = 1.56 \, \text{ksi}$$

Loadcase C

- **Large end:** Immovable
- **Small end:** 100 in lbf torsion

Loadcase C Analytical Solution

$$\tau_0 = \frac{T \times c}{J}$$
$$= \frac{100 \times 0.5}{\left(\pi \times 1^4 / 32 \right)}$$
$$= 509.3 \, \text{psi}$$

$$K_s = 1.34$$

$$\tau_{max} = 682.45 \, \text{psi}$$

Case 1 - Loaded Plate with Hole

Figure C–4

Loadcase A

- **End farthest from hole:** Immovable

- Bearing load in hole of 500 lbf directed towards nearest end of plate.

$$
\begin{aligned}
w &= 2 \\
t &= 0.2 \\
h &= 0.70 \\
d &= 0.40
\end{aligned}
$$

Loadcase A Analytical Solution

$$
\begin{aligned}
\sigma_0 &= 500 \times (2 - 0.40) \times 0.2 \\
&= 1.56 \text{ ksi}
\end{aligned}
$$

$$
\frac{d}{w} = 0.2
$$

$$
\frac{h}{w} = 0.35
$$

$$
K_t = 6.1
$$

$$
\sigma_{max} = \mathbf{9.98 \ ksi}
$$

© 2017, ASCENT - Center for Technical Knowledge®

Practice C1

Structural Analysis Examples - Set 2

In this practice, in each of the following cases, you will create the Creo Parametric model and use the techniques learned in the previous practices to perform the appropriate analysis. For each model, define the material as steel with the following properties:

- **Young's modulus:** $E = 3.0e7$

- **Poisson's ratio:** $n = 0.30$

- **Mass density:** 7.5e-4

Case 1 - Straight Beams

Beams are usually quite easy to solve, but care must be taken when applying boundary conditions. For these straight beam examples, build a 10" long beam with 0.5"x1.0" cross-section, as shown in Figure C–5.

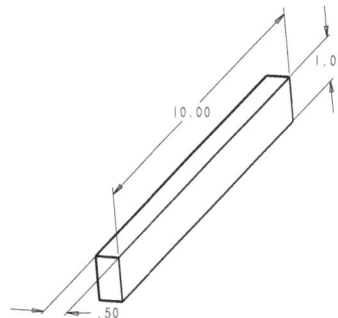

Figure C–5

Loadcase A - Fixed-Fixed Beam

1. Apply Immovable constraints to the two ends of the beam.

2. Apply a **200 lbf/in^2** uniform load as the *Load Per Unit* normal to the top of the beam. This equals a **100lbf/in** load along the beam.

3. Solve the model. Compare the results to the table in Loadcase B - All Edges Fixed – Concentrated Load, Step 5.

Loadcase B - Pinned-Pinned Beam

In this case, do not use beam elements. Mesh the model with 3D solid elements. To create a pinned connection, you must constrain a curve. Solid analyses do not have an associated moment carrying degrees of freedom. A constrained line is free to spin about the line as required for a pin joint.

1. In Creo Parametric, create a straight datum curve at each end of the beam, as shown in Figure C–6.

Figure C–6

2. Constrain the curves as **Immovable**.

3. Apply a **200 lbf/in^2** pressure. This is equivalent to the **200 lbf/in^2** uniform load (*Load Per Unit*) in Loadcase A.

4. Solve the model. Compare the results to the table in Loadcase B - All Edges Fixed – Concentrated Load, Step 5.

Case 2 - Rectangular Plate

Boundary conditions for plates must be modeled similar to those used for simply supported pinned beam-ends. For these rectangular plate examples, build the following model.

1. Build a 10in x 5in x 0.5in plate. The part displays as shown in Figure C–7.

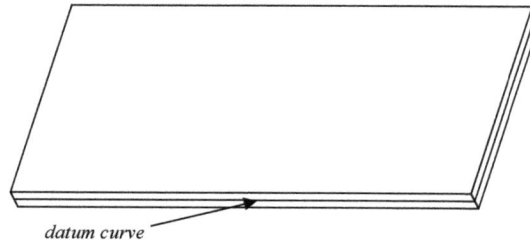

datum curve

Figure C–7

Loadcase A - All Edges pinned – Distributed Load

1. Create datum curves on the four sides.

© 2017, ASCENT - Center for Technical Knowledge®

2. Make the four curves **Immovable** to simulate simple support.

3. Apply a downward **100lbf/in^2** *Load Per Unit* normal to the top surface.

4. Solve the model. Compare the results to the table in Loadcase B - All Edges Fixed – Concentrated Load, Step 5.

Loadcase B - All Edges Fixed – Concentrated Load

1. In Creo Parametric, sketch a circular datum curve centered on the top of the plate with a radius of **0.5**.

2. Create a Surface Region using the circular datum curve.

3. Set all four side surfaces as **Immovable**.

4. Apply a *Total Force* of **10000lbf** to the small surface region (normal to surface). The loading should display as shown in Figure C–8.

Figure C–8

5. Solve the model. Compare the results to the following table.

Case	Quantity	Roark 6th Ed.	Pro/MECHANICA
1a	Max. Y Disp	-2.083e-3	
	Max. Stress	10000	
	Stress at Mid Beam	5000	
1b	Max. Y Disp	-.0104	
	Max. Stress	15000	
2a	Horz. Disp at left end neutral axis	.69	
2b	Horz. Disp at left end neutral axis	1.58	

© 2017, ASCENT - Center for Technical Knowledge®

Conversion Factors

The following table contains a list of common conversion factors.

To Convert From...	To...	Multiply By...
degree (angle)	radian (rad)	1.745329e-2
foot	meter	3.048e-1
ft-lbf	joule	1.355818
ft-lbf/sec	watt	1.355818
ft/min	m/sec	5.080e-3
ft/sec	m/sec	3.048e-1
ft/sec^2	m/sec^2	3.048e-1
horsepower	watt	7.456999e2
inch	meter	2.54e-2
kip (1000lb)	N (newton)	4.448222e3
km/h	m/sec	2.777778e-1
kW-h	joule	3.6e6
lb/ft^3	Kg/m^3	1.601846e1
lbf (pound-force)	N	4.448222
lbf-ft	N-m	1.335818
lbf-in	N-m	1.129848e-1
lbf/ft	N/m	1.459390e1

To Convert From...	To...	Multiply By...
lbf/ft^2	Pa (pascal)	4.788026e1
lbf/in	N/m	1.751268e2
lbf/in^2 (psi)	Pa	6.894757e3
litter	m^3	1e-3
mile	m	1.609344e3
ounce-force	N	2.780139e-1o
pound (lb)	Kg	4.535924e-1
slug	Kg	1.45939e1
slug-ft^2	Kg-m^2	4.214011e-2
slug/ft^3	Kg/m^3	5.153788e2
ton (2000lb)	Kg	9.071847e2
W-h	joule	3.6e3
zf-in	N-m	7.061552e-3

© 2017, ASCENT - Center for Technical Knowledge®